History of American Thought
and Culture
Paul S. Boyer, General Editor

Terry A. Cooney

The Rise of the New York Intellectuals

Partisan Review and Its Circle

The University of Wisconsin Press

Published 1986

The University of Wisconsin Press
114 North Murray Street
Madison, Wisconsin 53715

The University of Wisconsin Press, Ltd.
1 Gower Street
London WC1E 6HA, England

First printing

Printed in the United States of America

For LC CIP information see the colophon

ISBN 0-299-10710-8

for Denise

Contents

Acknowledgments

People engaged in research and writing always seem to be asking for something. Individuals and institutions that respond deserve at least public thanks.

The National Endowment for the Humanities supported my work with a Summer Stipend in 1978 and a Research Fellowship in 1980–81. The fellowship provided a block of time without which the present book would have been much delayed. The University of Puget Sound made faculty research and typing grants available at moments when they were both appropriate and necessary. These grants have allowed my indebtedness to be moral rather than financial.

For assistance both in person and from a distance, I am grateful to the archivists and librarians of the Sterling Memorial Library and the Beinecke Library, Yale University; the University of Pennsylvania Library; the Columbia University Library; the New York Public Library; the Princeton University Library; the Newberry Library; the University of Oregon Library; and the Library of Congress. Edgar M. Branch, Cleo Mitchell Paturis, Diana Trilling, and Barbara Dupee granted access to necessary materials; I owe thanks to them and to the longer list of those who granted specific permissions to quote from archival sources.

Robert D. Marcus and David Burner have given encouragement and support to this project from its inception; each long ago moved beyond the obligations of duty to generous acts of friendship. William R. Taylor and John Williams commented helpfully on the earliest writing leading toward this work. Irving Howe kindly subjected himself some years ago to a discussion of the *Partisan Review* intellectuals with me. In a spirit representing, to me, the best in academic life, David A. Hollinger welcomed the inquiries of a stranger and gave valuable summer hours to a critical reading of the manuscript in draft. Paul Boyer helped make publication of this book possible, and Cushing Strout provided valuable comments in evaluating the manuscript. The editors and staff of the University of Wisconsin Press have shown as much interest in this work, and taken as much care with it, as an author could wish.

I have benefited greatly from my day-to-day association with an energetic and supportive history faculty at the University of Puget Sound, as well as from my work with friends in other disciplines. An ongoing series of conversations with William Breitenbach, my colleague in American history, has been of particular value. Florence Phillippi has done far more than I have had any reasonable right to expect: assisting with typing the manuscript at various stages, patiently helping a novice learn the wonders of word processing, and making life flow more smoothly as only an exceptionally able departmental secretary can. June Lang and Marlene Bosanko gave conscientious service at different points in the process of typing and revising.

Teaching in an undergraduate liberal arts setting, with all its attendant involvements in student and faculty affairs, places great demands on a person's time. Research and writing are often squeezed into odd hours or weekends, and a major project consumes summers and holiday breaks insatiably. My wife, Denise Von Glahn Cooney, has developed an admirable tolerance for this work, aided, perhaps, by the fact that she takes her own discipline seriously. At the same time, she has reminded me of, and sometimes insisted upon, the importance of other responsibilities and loyalties as well, serene in a greater confidence than mine that this book would eventually be finished. Of the many things for which I owe her thanks, this is merely the most relevant; the dedication will have to cover the balance. Haynes and Evan have shared their father with his work, for the most part cheerfully, even when they would rather not.

Thanks are extended to the following for granting permission to quote from archival sources: the Yale University Library for permission to quote from the Dwight Macdonald Papers; the Special Collections division of Van Pelt Library, University of Pennsylvania, for permission to quote from The James T. Farrell Collection; the Columbia University Library for permission to quote from the F. W. Dupee Collection and the Lionel Trilling Collection; the Collection of American Literature, Beinecke Rare Book and Manuscript Library, Yale University, for permission to quote from the Delmore Schwartz Papers and the *Southern Review* Papers; the Princeton

University Library for permission to quote from the Allen Tate Papers; and the University of Oregon Library for permission to quote from the James Rorty Papers. Letters written by Leon Trotsky in the Macdonald Papers are also quoted by permission of the Houghton Library, Harvard University.

The private papers and correspondence of Dwight Macdonald are quoted with the permission of Gloria Macdonald; the correspondence of F. W. Dupee with the permission of Barbara Dupee; the letters of George L. K. Morris with the permission of Estelle F. Morris; the correspondence of Lionel Trilling with the permission of Diana Trilling; the papers and correspondence of Delmore Schwartz with the permission of Robert A. Phillips; the papers of James T. Farrell with the permission of Cleo Paturis and Edgar M. Branch; the correspondence of James Rorty with the permission of Richard Rorty; the correspondence of George Novack with the permission of George Novack; the letters of William Phillips with the permission of William Phillips; and the letters of Philip Rahv with the permission of Betty T. Rahv.

The Rise of
the New York Intellectuals

Introduction

A recent retrospective on intellectual trends describes *Partisan Review* as "certainly the most influential of American little magazines" in the period around World War II and even as "possibly the most influential little magazine ever."[1] Such a judgment conveys in perhaps too emphatic form a widely held assessment of *Partisan Review*'s significance in American intellectual life between the late 1930s and the mid-1950s. That sense of significance rests on many elements: the content of the magazine itself; its range across politics and culture; the pattern of experience represented by its history; the importance to several fields of learning of those associated with *Partisan Review*; the desire among scholars and critics to believe intellectuals mattered; and the level of attentiveness generated over many years by friends and enemies alike. This study attempts to deal with some of the patterns that justify continuing interest in the magazine without undue inflation of its historical importance.

Partisan Review provided the first and most important center for that circle of talented men and women who have come to be known as the New York Intellectuals. Defining an intellectual circle is not an exercise in precision; any list of members or affiliates must draw on informal as well as formal contacts and on evidence of shared assumptions as well as on openly expressed ideas.[2] Nevertheless, though the edges of the circle may be blurred, its existence is often plainly visible. For the period of this study, a list of those who would become "New York Intellectuals" may safely begin with the two editors of *Partisan Review* who helped guide the magazine from its founding, Philip Rahv and William Phillips. Three others who joined the editorial board in 1937 — Dwight Macdonald, F. W. Dupee, and Mary McCarthy — must surely be counted as well, though their involvement with the magazine varied greatly in intensity and duration. In the late 1930s and early 1940s, the circle

3

of support and interchange around *Partisan Review* included Lionel Trilling, Sidney Hook, Harold Rosenberg, Lionel Abel, James Burnham, Meyer Schapiro, Clement Greenberg, and Delmore Schwartz. (Greenberg and Schwartz served as editors of the magazine for a time, and at least three or four of the others were considered for, or were at some point offered, places on the editorial board.) James T. Farrell, who stood close to the magazine and its editors in the thirties, moved away in later years. In the early 1940s, Diana Trilling, Paul Goodman, and Alfred Kazin were all at work, but each stayed —or was kept—at some distance. A younger group of writers was also entering the scene. Irving Howe and Daniel Bell, Isaac Rosenfeld and Saul Bellow, all made appearances before 1945, though their major contributions and those of others their age remained largely in the future.

There is one sustained history of *Partisan Review*, James B. Gilbert's *Writers and Partisans*, a straightforward analysis that will remain a useful source of information.[3] The present account will depart from Gilbert's survey, and from other partial or unpublished studies, through its emphasis on some of the interpretive themes discussed below. What is perhaps most pertinent at the moment is to note that since *Writers and Partisans*, critical and historical work has largely been buried by an avalanche of memoirs and recollections, demanding attention for highly personalized views of the past. Some of these accounts have devoted considerable energy to settling old scores and to chalking up points against adversaries the authors have managed to outlive. Some have attempted to pursue current political lines in utterly tendentious fashion. Many have been at least as concerned with self-justification as with self-examination. And yet a number have at times achieved genuine vitality, intellectual seriousness, and a kind of insight available only to participants.[4] A historian can make use of all such sources in one way or another, though only with considerable care. The enterprise undertaken here works from the assumption that evidence from the period under study generally deserves greater weight than memory, and that the sometimes messy statements of a developing viewpoint reveal more than the neat reconstructions of hindsight.

The New York Intellectuals are perhaps most commonly associated with the period after World War II when, Richard Hofstadter has claimed, *Partisan Review* functioned "as a kind of house organ of the American intellectual community."[5] The issues that came to the fore in the postwar decade, most notably those associated with the Cold War abroad and anti-communism at home, found the New York Intellectuals ready with a set of opinions and positions that helped bring them prominence at the time and that have continued to stir controversy to the present day. So, too, they were ready to boost a new generation of American writers and to find virtues in American culture even as they maintained a sharp interest in the intellectual currents of Europe. In neither politics nor culture were the New Yorkers necessarily or even customarily united; the splits of the early 1950s have in many cases proved enduring. Yet, on the whole, the intellectuals who made up the *Partisan Review* circle entered the postwar period with a sense of shared experience, with a common loyalty to (though not always a common application of) a broad set of social and cultural values, and with a keen sensitivity to each other's ideas and opinions. Many of the questions that would trouble the postwar decade had, in fact, arisen at the end of the thirties; and many among the New York Intellectuals proved to have little patience with answers other than those they had already given. On certain fundamental issues, their minds had been set. The formative period for the New York Intellectuals fell before 1945, and it is to that period that this study will devote its attention.

A number of themes run through the interpretation provided here. Perhaps most basic is the contention that the members of the *Partisan Review* circle exhibited from a very early stage in their development an allegiance to what may be called cosmopolitan values. A detailed discussion of these values and their practical meanings belongs appropriately to the main body of the text, but a few general comments are in order. As a broad perspective, cosmopolitanism nurtured an ideal that applied to both the personal and the public, supplying at least a beam of insight on a variety of intellectual, cultural, and political questions. Cosmopolitan values demanded a resistance to particularisms of nationality, race, religion, or philosophy, and they celebrated richness, complexity, and diversity. Central to the ideal was a spirit of openness and striving—openness to variety and to change; striving for a fuller understanding of the world and for higher and more inclusive means of expression. Cosmopolitanism was by nature suspicious of dogma and quick to lash out against the narrowing of cultural possibilities. The members of the *Partisan Review* circle were by no means the only American intellectuals to embrace a cosmopolitan ideal, but especially in the period of this study they proved to be among the most vocal and effective defenders of some of its major tenets. *Par-*

tisan Review added to the general cosmopolitan perspective special concerns of its own, and the editors made of the resulting package a standard by which to judge the movements of the day. The values and assumptions thus expressed gave the magazine and its circle a more consistent outlook than has customarily been recognized.

Attention to cosmopolitan values can assist in understanding the early history of the New York Intellectuals in a number of ways. The clear majority of those who made up the *Partisan Review* circle were the children of East European Jewish immigrants or, in a few cases, had immigrated themselves as children. Their history presents as one theme a story of the entry of second-generation Jews into American intellectual life. Scholars have responded to the numerical dominance of Jews in the *Partisan Review* circle with varying strategies and interpretations. In *Writers and Partisans*, Gilbert handled this whole realm of identity and experience by ignoring it whenever possible. By contrast, the zealous literary theorist Grant Webster made it a point in *The Republic of Letters* to discuss the ethnic composition of the New York circle in order to claim that "genetically" they were "only partly or questionably Jewish" and that Jewishness did not matter in the least to their critical work. Looking to quite different issues than did Webster, the sociologist Stephen A. Longstaff took as the very center of his study of the New York Intellectuals the tension between universalism and particularism and, thus, the question of Jewish identity.[6] The argument presented here will hold that Jewishness was neither the central determinative factor for members of the *Partisan Review* circle nor something irrelevant to them. The attitude of those who were Jews toward their Jewishness can best be understood as an expression of the cosmopolitan outlook they had embraced.

The ideal of a broad and encompassing culture that lay at the heart of the cosmopolitan perspective shaped the outlook and the ambitions of the New York Intellectuals throughout their early history. Western culture as a whole provided the most general frame of reference for the *Partisan Review* circle and the widest standard of aspiration; their perspective was consciously and emphatically international. Some commentators have found in this sufficient reason to label the group "European" in its habits of mind, suggesting a certain uncomfortable distance from American culture. Such estimates fail to recognize just how heavily those around the early *Partisan Review* invested their energies and emotions in struggles over the character of *American* life and literature, and just how closely their international consciousness was tied to their national hopes.

This study will emphasize as a major theme in the development of the New York Intellectuals their persistent demand for, and their eagerness to find promise of, a rich and inclusive American culture — and especially an American literature — that could measure up to the traditions of Europe. Efforts to end the provincial status of America in the realm of art and ideas go back to the late nineteenth century at least, but the traditions that *Partisan Review* drew upon had taken specific form in the 1910s. Randolph Bourne's calls for a "Trans-National America" had given impetus to a cosmopolitan ideal that could appeal to second-generation intellectuals not only through its promise of cultural vitality and diversity, but also through its openness to the participation of new groups in the shaping of national traditions. Van Wyck Brooks's passion for a "coming-of-age" in American literature had held out the goal of a mature and sophisticated American culture equal to any in the world — a goal that could tantalize young writers who saw the emerging promise running parallel to their own careers. Within the promised culture, the writer's voice could be simultaneously American and international, just as the intellectual's identity could be at once distinct (whether Jewish or otherwise) and comprehensively human. Their particular understanding of the cosmopolitan perspective provided a link for the New York Intellectuals between private and public, between their sense of themselves and their sense of broader cultural goals and commitments.

This discussion of the *Partisan Review* circle will also argue that cosmopolitan values had a major influence on the political migration characteristic of the group, from radicalism in the thirties to Cold War liberalism by the late 1940s. For some readers, any mention of intellectuals moving away from the left during this period will conjure up images of sudden reversals, of former radicals turned virtually overnight into militant anti-Communists and aggressive critics of Marxism. There were a few, even one or two associated with the *Partisan Review* group, for whom the transformation was indeed both precipitate and extreme. Yet most associated with the magazine traveled more gradually along the road, not all of them moving at the same speed or agreeing on the route or destination. For a number in the New York circle and for *Partisan Review* itself, there was first a turning away from the Stalinist brand of communism in the name of a more genuine radicalism, and only later an uneven departure from any political position that was distinctively left. A very few maintained a radical perspective into the postwar period; a few others were never very seriously radical to begin with. Any history of the New York Intellectuals into the 1940s must recognize the diversity and the irregularity of individual experience, as it must acknowledge, in most instances, significant political change. Nevertheless, there was a cohesiveness of outlook and a continuity of underlying values among those in the *Partisan Review* circle that helped link the several phases of their experience and provide a logic for their course.

Cosmopolitan values and the literary vision with which they were closely associated quickened the radical hopes of the early *Partisan Review*; and the same values led the controlling editors of the magazine toward their break with the Communist Party. Cosmopolitanism provided a set of attitudes, references, and ideas that helped bring together the emerging New York circle in 1937 — a positive source of attraction working in harness with the negative binding force of anti-Stalinism. Later, amidst the tensions brought on by World War II, cosmopolitan values again supplied a framework for complaint and justification and a fundamental set of standards for condemnation or praise. The continuity of values within the *Partisan Review* circle made up the essential fabric, while the bright colors of political twist and distinctive turn furnished the dramatic design.

The argument that will follow rests on no single mode of historical explanation. It sees an exclusive path to understanding neither in an assumption of the autonomous development of ideas nor in a presupposition that ideas merely reflect their social and economic environments. It tries to avoid reducing the men and women around *Partisan Review* to little more than parts of themselves, although it retains a primary emphasis on their professional and not their private lives (about which one can sometimes learn far too much). The themes of this study touch upon experiences and dilemmas of considerable importance to the history of the United States in the twentieth century; yet there is an attempt to remain mindful that a more particular human story is being told as well.

In such works of American literature as *The Rise of Silas Lapham* and *The Rise of David Levinsky*, we are reminded that success as it is commonly interpreted does not come without a price. The title of this work offers a bow to that voice in our tradition.

It seeks at once to acknowledge the success of *Partisan Review* and of the New York Intellectuals and, by reference to its forebears, to suggest the continuing complexity of political, social, and intellectual choices in America.

Chapter One   Roots and Sources

New York! New York! The city is in so many ways a region unto itself. Alone in North America it stands with the great European centers in its cultural magnetism, in the richness of its modern experience, and in its capacity for excitement. Within the United States it generates beyond all other cities that mixture of attraction and repulsion Americans have felt toward their social, political, and cultural capitals. Fascination and suspicion combine in Peoria's view of New York and in New York's view of the lands beyond the Hudson. One province looks skeptically toward the other.

To brand one group of intellectuals with the name "New York" is to do more than identify the place they lived and worked; it is to call upon the resonance of the city, and to suggest that as a group they bathed in its lifestreams and augmented its currents. New York by the second decade of the twentieth century had become the center of American literary life, a breeding place for political and cultural radicalism, and the home of one of the largest Jewish communities in the world. In a study of the New York Intellectuals, each of these features commands attention.

Considering the origins of "The Jew as Modern Writer," Alfred Kazin once commented parenthetically: "without New York it would no doubt all have been different, but without New York, there would have been no immigrant epic, no America."[1] Accurate from some perspectives and absurd from others, such a statement is chiefly interesting for what it reveals about the most basic assumptions of the speaker. For many a New York Intellectual, a sense of both national and personal identity took at least part of its shape from the Jewish immigrant experience and from the particular ethos of New York. Although the influence of background has not always been readily acknowledged, the experience of growing up Jewish in New York may properly serve as the first layer in constructing an understanding of the New York Intellectuals.

10

Immigration involved an uprooting from accustomed patterns and a series of shocks for nearly all who came to America, but for few was the degree and intensity of change as great as for the Jews of Eastern Europe who flocked to the new world in the three decades before World War I. Physical, cultural, and economic changes piled on top of one another to disorient the immigrants and to reshape their community life. As Irving Howe has noted, Jews coming to America and to New York seemed to undergo a condensation of the experiences that had been played out earlier in the technologically advanced West, undergoing in a number of ways their own version of the Industrial Revolution.[2] A culture previously tied to small towns and villages was suddenly concentrated on the Lower East Side of New York into one of the most densely populated areas in the Western world. Patterns of traditional status were disrupted. Customs or ideas formerly protected by their isolation were thrown into a vat of conflicting habits and notions. Energies that had been widely dissipated now came together dramatically in the implosion of the Jewish community into New York.

In intellectual and cultural life, this concentration seemed to magnify and accelerate changes already under way among Jews. Like the Industrial Revolution, the Enlightenment had come late to Eastern Europe. Yet by the end of the nineteenth century, Western European ideas in literature and politics had reached the more urbanized Jews of Eastern Europe through the *haskalah* or "Jewish Enlightenment"; and these ideas sailed on the same ships as ancient tradition. Even without the influence of the surrounding American culture, Western ideas would have spread rapidly with the direct exposure and rapid communication that the Lower East Side made not simply possible but inescapable. The concentration of the community meant an explosion of cultural possibilities. The barriers imposed by prejudice, by social position, by religion and tradition, were largely burst asunder, releasing the mixed array of opportunities and insecurities such an eruption usually entails.

Over time, the Jews pursued the possibilities opened to them with a fervor that brought success of various kinds quite rapidly in comparison with the pattern for other groups. Jews had never been peasants, so they lacked a "peasant's fatalism and a peasant's habit of deference to superiors" that might have "curbed their desires" and slowed their assimilative mobility.[3] Jews in general avoided competing in crowded labor markets and largely escaped economic discrimination before 1910. Most important, Jewish culture held a distinctly positive attitude toward education—unlike

11

the bulk of the members of many other immigrant groups, most Jews were already literate. America offered a combination of freedom and opportunity that allowed and encouraged the passionate pursuit of learning on the Lower East Side and in Brooklyn, making education a matter of such importance that one historian has concluded: "The relationship between traditional Jewish attitudes toward learning and the existence in the United States of free public schools is perhaps the central factor in the accommodation of the East European Jewry with American culture."[4]

Although education was the pathway to eventual status and success for those who would become the New York Intellectuals, the process was hardly without pain. Learning, which parents and children prized so highly, became the locus of a series of tensions that pulled apart the generations and amplified the conflicts between traditional culture and American environment. During the day the public school expected Jewish children to speak English; at home they were more likely to hear and use Yiddish. The heavy doses of American nationalism and Protestant morality that contributed to the public educational brew created a certain disharmony with the lessons of the Hebrew schools many young Jews attended concurrently. Yet the public schools held the keys to the larger world in which second-generation Jews longed to make their mark or to achieve security, and they put tremendous pressure on the young Jew to adapt, to leave the past behind, to secure a place. The experiences of the budding intellectuals might vary with their backgrounds, their luck, and the precise years of their schooling, but over the three or more decades in which the children of the East European immigrants were growing up, the patterns remained much the same.

The series of conflicts might be marked by sharp jolts or by gradual transformations; in either case, the road led toward a step-by-step departure from traditional culture and community for the young intellectual of a certain bent. Representatives of the majority culture were more than willing to assist this process. For both Joseph Freeman, coming near the beginning of the second-generation experience, and Norman Podhoretz, coming toward the end, public school teachers took a special interest in marking the way outward and upward for their promising pupils. Each was taken into Manhattan, a symbolic journey to the "real" America; each was asked to pay homage to the alien culture of Protestant capitalism, whether exemplified in the homes of the rich or the stores and restaurants of the upper middle class; and each was enjoined to seek respectability through manners and money in this better world.[5]

Education brought bright students into contact not simply with an expanded world but increasingly, as their studies progressed, with each other and with gentiles sharing their academic interests. Small groups of friends, united by their fledgling sophistication, regarded parents and community alike with considerable discomfort. Whatever the joys of the neighborhood, immigrant behavior seemed unalterably parochial and maddeningly timid; parents were painfully limited in experience, narrow in hope, and fearful of risk. Repeatedly in recollections of youth, Jewish intellectuals have described the sense of a double existence stretching across the rift between family life and the chosen society of friends.[6]

The strain within the family, the tension between the hold of the Jewish community and the pull of the world, reflected a generational conflict not limited to the families of Jewish intellectuals, nor for that matter to Jews. The desire of the second generation to embrace a larger America and to find success beyond the ethnic community marks a classic pattern in the story of many immigrant groups. Still, with the Jews the break seemed sharper, the situation more highly charged. For a people so long contained, an atmosphere of opportunity was a chance not to be missed—by the individual, by the family, or by the people as a whole. Yet it was not the immigrant generation that could take the giant step toward success and fulfillment. The immigrants were, and saw themselves as, a "transitional generation." The charge to succeed fell upon their children. The culture of the immigrant Jewish community became a "culture utterly devoted to its sons."[7]

And it was the sons who took center stage. An air of masculine clubbiness hangs around the early years of the New York Intellectuals. Young women were sometimes present, sometimes mentioned, but seldom treated as equals. Those women who made their mark intellectually in the early years succeeded through determination, talent, and sometimes a husband's or companion's connections, not through equivalent encouragements or opportunities supported by a whole culture. The sons were the chosen ones, given love and support in many cases but also made fully aware of the expectations that came as part of the package—expectations that many found it difficult to fulfill. When in the 1940s younger and then older representatives of the New York Intellectuals began to discuss Jewish experience and their own feelings, either in essays or in fiction, the drama of the family and the question of whether they had, or should have, feelings of guilt would receive ample play.

Yet such feelings did not alter the path of the young. For some, the escape from the narrow world of parents was the central theme of their early careers, and they had no desire to change course even if they could. The Alfred Kazin of the early 1940s, if not the Kazin of later memoirs, made this clear: "I think that I have been most deeply influenced by my struggle against a merely imposed faith; and against a sentimental chauvinism. I know how easy it is for the American Jew, at least in my circumstances and of my generation, to confuse his timidity with devotion, his parochialism (or suspiciousness, grounded in the self-driven life of the Pale) with a conscious faith."[8] An "imposed faith," "sentimental chauvinism," "timidity," and "parochialism"—Kazin's list provides a reasonably good summary of what the young intellectuals sought to leave behind. But where were they heading? What attracted them in the world beyond?

For some second-generation members of many ethnic groups the goal would be rapid assimilation—becoming like the "Americans" through a wholesale adoption of the values, the aims, and the economic standards of the host society. For young Jewish intellectuals who might be inclined to embrace this alternative, there would be much to overlook in the attitudes of the dominant culture. Jewish religion and Jewish customs were more at variance with those of Protestant America than the practices of most groups; and sources of friction, both formal and random, were plentiful.[9] With the resentment of aliens and the fear of radicals (with whom Jews were often associated) rising to a crest in the immigration restriction and the assorted nativistic vulgarities of the 1920s, few bright young Jews could ignore the hostility of the larger society. Some sought respectability and security in the professions, "where they could escape stereotypic identification as businessmen, operate as individuals, and exercise fully their keen intellectual capacities."[10] Yet the more self-consciously intellectual tended to scorn this course as a complete surrender to the American middle class and its materialistic values.

What attracted a certain group of young intellectuals was a cultural promise, a literary tradition, and a pattern of social protest that together provided a basis for rejecting middle-class culture, though its sources lay embedded within that culture. Gifted members of the second generation were lured from the Jewish community by the broad Western tradition in the humanities, especially as expressed in literature; and they developed a loyalty to that tradition and to an ideal of intellectual life. For many the first moments of contact with the sweeping scope of Western literature had been times of tremendous excitement and enthusiasm, times when

14

locked doors had swung open to reveal a world unexplored. Philip Rahv recalled for a friend late in life a time when he was eight or nine, in his village in the Ukraine, when a Russian soldier gave him books by Dostoevsky and Tolstoy. Rahv's interest in literature and his serious involvement with the Russian language (as opposed to Yiddish) began at this point.[11] Such meetings between young intellectuals and Western culture have come to seem almost archetypal experiences to some. "If the young man from the provinces . . . typifies the encounter with the great world in 19th-century novels," Alfred Kazin has suggested, it is "the Jewish intellectual" who lives out that role in the twentieth century.[12]

The sense of universal significance associated with their educational commitments seemed the opposite of the narrow concern young intellectuals saw in the Jewish community. Norman Podhoretz, attending college in the forties, traveled daily from maternal proverbs to European literature on the subway. Western culture as he encountered it seemed to subsume all knowledge, including even "the best of the Jewish tradition" in its "generous and transcendent embrace." A student at Columbia College of men like Lionel Trilling, F. W. Dupee, and Richard Chase who were closely associated with the New York Intellectual community and with *Partisan Review*, Podhoretz acknowledged with his instructors that the heritage they embraced was specifically *Western*, but this appeared to be a very insignificant limitation: "To our minds, this culture we were studying at Columbia was not the creation or the possession of a particular group of people; it was a repository of the universal, existing not in space or time but rather in some transcendental realm of the spirit."[13]

Embracing Western culture, of course, did not eliminate the problem of identity for intellectual Jews. Between the striving to grasp the generous expanse of literature and the consciousness of a specific heritage, a tension existed that put its stamp on the New York Intellectuals. In general form, such a tension was hardly unique to them; Leon Wieseltier has commented that "the history of Jewish identity could be written" around the "tension between universalism and particularism." Yet however common the pressures at work, it was out of such tensions that the New York Intellectuals shaped a special identity and found, in words Wieseltier applied more generally, "their creative and critical edge."[14]

The pattern of Jewish intellectuals locating themselves in the space between—or beyond—Jewish and gentile culture was not entirely new. By the early twentieth century, the model was suffi-

ciently well established for a highly perceptive Thorstein Veblen
to find in it an explanation for the exceptional contributions of Jews
to European culture. Veblen suggested that the Jewish intellectual
achieves greatness "only at the cost of losing his secure place in
the scheme of conventions into which he has been born, and at
the cost, also, of finding no similarly secure place in that scheme
of gentile conventions into which he is thrown. . . . He becomes
a disturber of the intellectual peace, but only at the cost of becoming an intellectual wayfaring man, a wanderer in the intellectual
no-man's-land."[15] Veblen apparently influenced few sociologists on
this question, but Robert E. Park in a well-known 1928 article did
pick up on the same problem of two cultures to posit his theory
of marginality. Park saw a particular personality type emerging from
the Jew's dual cultural involvement, "a cultural hybrid." The Jew
"was a man on the margin of two cultures and two societies. . . .
the emancipated Jew was, and is, historically and typically the
marginal man, the first cosmopolite and citizen of the world."[16]

After World War II, such notions of separation from both traditional and host cultures, and of a special position on the margin
of society, became essential concepts in the New York Jewish intellectual's analysis of himself. Articles appeared with titles like
"The Lost Young Intellectual: A Marginal Man, Twice Alienated."[17]
This self-conscious public examination of one's own position, this
generalization of the young Jew's experience, was not characteristic during the thirties. Yet the patterns that emerged among the
New York Intellectuals in that period owed much to the interplay
between cultures, to the effort to establish a personal and collective identity, and to the assumption—tacit at first but later explicit
—that their experience was a central one for modern humanity.[18]

The literary preferences, the political choices, the varied careers
of the New York Intellectuals, testify to their involvement with
Western culture and its universalist ideas. What must also be acknowledged from the beginning is that the experiences of growing
up Jewish and of making a life in New York framed, shaped, and
sometimes limited their social and intellectual views. Irving Howe
has suggested that "it would be a fascinating exercise to go through
the first twenty years of *Partisan Review* to see how frequently
Jewish references, motifs, inside jokes, and even explicit themes
break past the surface of cultural cosmopolitanism and Marxist internationalism." Noting that Gilbert Seldes had marked the "dae-
monic" abandon of popular Jewish performers like Al Jolson and
Fanny Brice, who had "a fine carelessness about our superstitions

of politeness and gentility," Howe insists that "anyone old enough to remember the disdain and, still more, the anxious fear that *Partisan Review* inspired in the American academy during the 1930's and 1940's, will recognize that what Seldes said about Jolson and Brice would hold as well for Rahv and Goodman, Rosenberg and Abel, Hook and Macdonald." There was in the Jewish writer, according to Alfred Kazin, "an intensity, a closeness to many conflicting emotions, that often seemed unaccountably excessive to other peoples."[19]

Another shaping condition of the social identity of many New York Intellectuals began to be consciously acknowledged only when the attitudes and experiences of the thirties and forties had themselves become two or three decades old. Howe could then remark, "Only now do I see the extent to which our life, for all that we had decided to cut ourselves off from official society, was shaped by the fact that many of us came from immigrant Jewish families and that in New York the Jews still formed a genuine community reaching half-unseen into a dozen neighborhoods and a multitude of institutions, within the shadows of which we found protection of a kind." Even within the Stalinist ranks, "the fact of Jewishness counted in surprising ways." Radicals and intellectuals frequently insisted that they were overcoming their backgrounds and building groups based on belief beyond class and ethnicity, and sometimes they were; but to the Jewish community the reality was quite different. "What you believed, or said you believed, did not matter nearly as much as what you were, and what you were was not nearly so much a matter of choice as you might care to suppose."[20] Young Jewish intellectuals were thus free to experiment with ideas and politics while remaining, though rebels against family and tradition, under the often-unrecognized shelter of the larger New York community.

The ideas of the young writers showed the imprint of their urban environment in striking fashion. New York, with all its eager second-generation strivers knocked back by the depression, with its numerous radical parties centered always in *the* city, became the social norm behind a myriad of theories. Lionel Abel, a member of the founding generation of the New York Intellectuals, has written of himself: "I had no desire to get to Jerusalem, no expectation of living in Athens, little interest in Rome. I was eighteen. What did I know then about Paris? My whole aim was to live in New York—where I have lived practically ever since. . . . It was a city. It was The City."[21] Abel wished to emphasize his enthusiasm for New York with these words and not to denigrate other cities;

yet the implied superiority to Jerusalem, Athens, Rome, and Paris is indicative. The New York Intellectuals did not remain eighteen, and they learned a great deal about European culture. But to some degree the conviction that the ideas of Germany and France, Italy and England, Moscow and Jerusalem, had to be seen and judged from the perspective of New York never left their work.

The concentration on New York encouraged a blending of geographical assumptions with cultural judgments. Norman Podhoretz's remark that "one of the longest journeys in the world is the journey from Brooklyn to Manhattan" provided a dramatic image for the sociological journey he wished to emphasize; at the same time, it revealed the physical narrowness of the intellectuals' world, the restricted perspective of those whose Oregon Trail was the length of the Brooklyn Bridge.[22] The limitations of this bounded urban view would show up repeatedly in attempts by the New York Intellectuals to deal with rural areas and the behavior of natives beyond the Hudson. Southerners particularly played reactionary roles in the intellectuals' drama of the thirties, both in politics and in literature. Marxism, as understood by the urbanites, reinforced their distrust of agricultural folk. Rural or western political movements set their nerves on edge and seemed always threatening, regardless of changes in the intellectuals' politics. These fears were hardly irrational, since groups like the Klan and the Coughlinites did attack urban, eastern intellectuals, decry radical thought, and foster anti-Semitism. But the intellectuals reacted with incomplete and self-centered interpretations of rural movements and rural ideals, finding a tradition of anxiety and bigotry—and implicitly a potential for fascism—while ignoring the more promising possibilities and the more generous spirit of rural politics. Surely behind these attitudes lay the limited perspective of an urban province.

To suggest some of the limitations embedded within the perspective of the New York Intellectuals is in no way to deny the power of their minds, the excitement of their discourse, or the significance of their contributions to American intellectual life. Few indeed can escape the fetters of a subjective viewpoint, and perhaps most would not wish to. Out of their pasts, the New York Intellectuals brought a direct polemical style; a concern with identity and a need to establish a place for themselves; a belief in their own centrality and in that of New York City; a commitment to Western culture, to secular thought, to critical intelligence; and an eagerness to engage the world that their worst detractors could hardly find unappealing.

Side by side in New York City with the institutions and the neighborhoods young intellectuals often wished to leave behind stood a neighborhood that symbolized all the excitement and promise of the culture that attracted them. In that neighborhood lay much of what New York meant to an aspiring youth with an interest in the arts.

> One of the best things [about New York] was this: except for the museums, theatres and opera, all that was humanly essential to the city was bounded by Bleecker and Fourteenth Streets, by Second Avenue and Greenwich Street. There was no other residential section in New York. Those who lived outside this area were just pariahs—or did not even exist. . . . Wall Street might just as well have been in Illinois, and Madison Avenue was really a part of Ohio. New York City was Greenwich Village.[23]

The rest of the city might make its peace with Illinois and Ohio, with a national culture rooted in rural forms and Protestant morality, but Greenwich Village would insist on its peculiarities, on its singular restaurants and theaters, and on its mixing of people and legends from Mark Twain to Eugene O'Neill. For young intellectuals coming to maturity in the late twenties or the thirties, Greenwich Village stood as a powerful symbol of the potential for cultural rebirth; it seemed still aglow from the exploits of preceding generations.

More than any other period, the 1910s had given the Village its drawing power. Twenty-five years later Alfred Kazin wrote as if the appeal of these years were not just immediate but eternal: "Who does not know the now routine legend in which the world of 1910–1917 is Washington Square turned Arcadia, in which the barriers are always down, the magazines always promising, the workers always marching, geniuses sprouting in every Village bedroom, Isadora Duncan always dancing—that world of which John Reed was the Byronic hero, Mabel Dodge the hostess, Randolph Bourne the martyr, Van Wyck Brooks the oracle? No other generation in America ever seemed to have so radiant a youth."[24] Who, indeed, would not respond to such a romantic and shining vision of "the first great literary society in America since Concord"? The very tone in which Kazin approached the Greenwich Village of the teens, the ease with which he assumed that all of this was known, suggested the grip that the legend had on the young literary intellectuals of New York.[25]

19

In the bubbling stew that was Greenwich Village during the 1910s, the quest for literary renaissance coexisted quite comfortably with the hope of restructuring society through radical politics. The little magazines that boiled to the surface regularly, often to sink again after a moment of glory, could not help but mix culture and politics in their offerings to the rebellion. For the more important magazines of the period the blend was intentional, though none achieved the principled balance for which several had aimed. The *Masses* provided a powerful image of the intellectual romance of radicalism in John Reed—Kazin's "Byronic hero"—who dashed from strike to strike and reported memorably on revolutions in Mexico and Russia; it also contributed, through its suppression during World War I and the trials of its editors, to the radical martyrology. Yet to later literary intellectuals, the *Masses* seemed haphazard and not quite serious. In the midst of the radical thirties, Harold Rosenberg could virtually dismiss the earlier magazine with the comment that its radical principle, "both literary and social, was pure liveliness — action or appearance colorful enough to overcome dullness."[26] Enthusiasm was appealing, but it was not enough.

For a tone of high seriousness, for a leaning toward literature while maintaining contact with politics, young writers of the teens — or later — could turn to a different source. In the pages of the short-lived but highly influential *Seven Arts*, and in the writings of the group that gave it life, lay perhaps the leading expression of the cultural rebellion of the teens. This is not to say that *Seven Arts* represented a clearly defined and exclusive stance in a period noted for its lack of boundaries and its candy sampler of ideas.[27] Yet *Seven Arts*, through its aggregate of literary experimentalism, cultural nationalism, social criticism, and sense of mission, represented a singular combination of attitudes.

James Oppenheim, Waldo Frank, and Van Wyck Brooks actually ran *Seven Arts* while Randolph Bourne, Louis Untermeyer, Sherwood Anderson, and Paul Rosenfeld constituted an "inner circle" of support.[28] Brooks and Bourne, who were close friends and largely in agreement at this time, served as the intellectual leaders, expressing the dominant critical ideas. Though much of their thought accorded with the general milieu and though some of their most characteristic phrases were not exclusively their own, both contributed ideas or terms that entered the mainstream of American intellectual life through the power of their advocacy. A number of the young New York Intellectuals, through indirect influence more than direct perhaps, would begin their careers in the thirties showing clear signs that they were descendants, among others, of Brooks and Bourne.

Brooks came to *Seven Arts* at a most propitious time in his career.[29] He had capped a search for critical values and social perspective begun long before by publishing in 1915 *America's Coming-of-Age*. With a new confidence and a prophetic style, Brooks now attacked in terms that would become classic a dualism that had wrecked American life in general and American literature in particular—the split between ideal and real, theory and practice, thought and action.

> These two attitudes of mind have been phrased once for all in our vernacular as "Highbrow" and "Lowbrow." . . . What side of American life is not touched by this antithesis? What explanation of American life is more central or more illuminating? In everything one finds this frank acceptance of twin values which are not expected to have anything in common: on the one hand a quite unclouded, quite unhypocritical assumption of transcendent theory ("high ideals"); on the other a simultaneous acceptance of catchpenny realities.[30]

"Highbrow" and "Lowbrow" formed the thesis and antithesis in a dialectical pattern of which Brooks made obvious use in his analysis.[31] A proper synthesis beyond highbrow and lowbrow would bring about that mature American culture, that end to innocence, which was Brooks's passionate goal.

With *The World of H. G. Wells*, published in the same year as *America's Coming-of-Age*, Brooks disclosed that he had found in Europe a tradition that might offer solutions to the American dilemma—a tradition that linked art and society through a vision of socialism.[32] Socialism delivered a comprehensive explanation of the world, a unified viewpoint. From this perspective, Brooks could call—on the side of action—for a sweeping social criticism of capitalist industrial society to reveal, and thereby destroy, the obstacles to personal and artistic expression. At the same time he could hold up—on the side of the ideal—a vision of the organic society of the future, the society of fellowship, the society of integrated art and free personality beyond the crippling impact of commercialism and competition. The political program of socialism was really of little interest in itself; but as a framework to unify culture and politics, as a ready-made critique of the present system, as an incentive to art through its vision of the future, socialism was intellectually very useful.

21

Brooks had rejected most of the American cultural past as a series of failures. Yet recognizing, perhaps, that a national culture that did not incorporate elements of the American literary heritage would be somewhat rootless, Brooks found a scheme to make use of fragments while continuing to reject the whole. In his essay "On Creating a Usable Past," Brooks insisted that the "successful fact" was not the only thing worth looking at in literary history. The real task was "not to seek for masterpieces . . . but for tendencies," for beginnings based on the "creative impulse" that fell short of full development. By searching out such repeated starts, intellectuals could "discover, invent a usable past."[33] In the concept of a "usable past," Brooks in one sense simply codified what intellectuals had always done with cultural traditions—they had always picked and chosen elements most useful to them. Yet Brooks gave a potent and effective phrase to American literary radicals who continually faced the problem of wanting sweeping changes while sensing that a literature without traditions would be a kingdom robbed of its riches. The "usable past" was a compromise between a rigid past of inflexible dogmas and a rootless present of extreme rebellion.

If the idea of a "usable past" addressed the question of how transition from existing division to future unity might be achieved in literature, other problems involving the emergence of an integrated culture remained. In the teens, the growing diversity among the peoples of the United States could hardly be ignored. Where did the immigrants from Southern and Eastern Europe stand in relation to Brooks's vision? The question was answered partly through practice at the *Seven Arts* and more emphatically in print by Brooks's closest colleague at this time.

In a period of increasing racial and cultural prejudice, *Seven Arts* boasted a staff of mixed heritage. The pedigree Protestants Brooks and Bourne linked arms with the Jews Waldo Frank, Paul Rosenfeld, and James Oppenheim. Many German Jews had become rather comfortable and established in America—Frank and Rosenfeld were Yale graduates—but friends and enemies alike assumed that cultural differences survived. Bourne and Brooks welcomed these differences and insisted on their value.[34] Such relationships marked the emergence of an ethic of nondiscrimination among liberal intellectuals. It remained for Randolph Bourne to deliver the fundamental statement of that ethic.[35]

With his notion of "trans-nationalism," Bourne developed an attack on that narrow nativistic feeling of the teens which accepted only total assimilation to Protestant, Anglo-Saxon mores as a sign of loyalty in immigrants. An alternative to this homogenizing view lay in a recognition of the positive values rising from a mixture of cultures. Condemning the melting-pot ideal as "congenial to the ruling class," Bourne praised the "so-called 'hyphenate'" and welcomed the "cosmopolitan federation of national colonies" his presence had produced.

> America is already the world-federation in miniature, the continent where for the first time in history has been achieved that miracle of hope, the peaceful living side by side, with character substantially preserved, of the most heterogeneous peoples under the sun. . . . It is for the American of the younger generation to accept this cosmopolitanism, and carry it along with self-conscious and fruitful purpose. . . . Colonialism has grown into cosmopolitanism and his motherhood is no one nation, but all who have anything life-enhancing to offer to the spirit.

The key word for Bourne, which he repeated as frequently as this passage suggests, was "cosmopolitanism," a term that suggested the whole "enterprise of integration," promising a "new spiritual citizenship" of the world to all peoples.[36]

Bourne acknowledged his debt to Horace Kallen for setting his mind "working on the whole idea of American national ideals," and, as might be expected, Bourne's essays show Kallen's influence, particularly perhaps in the special concern with Jews.[37] John Higham has pointed to Bourne as one of those who shared Kallen's "romantic idealism," which by implication includes "Kallen's exclusive concentration on culture as the locus of group identity" and his assertion that "democracy involves not the elimination of differences but the perfection and conservation of differences."[38] Certainly Bourne shared a great optimism about the American future with Kallen, and like the whole *Seven Arts* group, Bourne saw culture as the ultimate test of the quality of group or national life; but Bourne did not share Kallen's spirit or his goals, and in the difference lay Bourne's particular importance for literary intellectuals of later years.

Kallen wanted to preserve traditional cultures, to save the past; Bourne looked to the future and saw the possibility of something distinctly new in America. Kallen sought the "perfection and conservation of differences"; Bourne valued traditional cultures for what they could contribute to a new internationalized culture available to all, yet not forced on anyone. In elaborating his ideas, Bourne rejected certain dangers of anti-nationalism. He supported no preservation of political loyalties to a homeland, and he made it clear that he was not recommending any manufactured boosting of ethnic consciousness. He found it a cause for fear that ethnic groups in America might simply preserve the old cultures they brought with them: "America runs a very real danger of becoming not the modern cosmopolitan grouping that we desire, but a queer conglomeration of the prejudices of past generations, miraculously preserved here, after they have mercifully perished at home."[39] Bourne spoke with the distaste for parochialism and rigid custom that accompanied, and perhaps inspired, the cosmopolitanism of the teens. His was no desire to perfect and conserve differences but a desire for progressive and diverse influences to break down parochialism and to "fertilize and enhance the common American life" being built by the "younger *intelligentsia* of America."[40] With its antiprovincialism, its promise of an ever richer culture, and its guarantee of social acceptance for all comers, the ideal of cosmopolitanism served equally well Protestant bluebloods rebelling against a repressive gentility and second-generation intellectuals climbing out of an immigrant milieu.

The idealism, the impatience for change, and the passion for inclusiveness inherent in this vision helped shape the critique of pragmatism developed by Brooks and Bourne. In 1915 Brooks worried aloud over "the unanimity with which during the last few years the advanced world has put all its eggs in the basket of pragmatism."[41] Pragmatism was at the same time insufficiently radical and insufficiently artistic. On the one hand, by depending too much on institutional change through the natural eruption of men's creative energies instead of through conscious destruction of old forms, pragmatism watered down socialism's economic critique of capitalism and tended to produce a quietism toward social problems and cooperative action. On the other hand, through overemphasis on the power of intelligence, pragmatism stood in danger of neglecting the ideal side of life contained in morality, philosophy, and art; it lacked an artistic sensibility. No such approach could overcome the split between highbrow and lowbrow in American literature; pragmatism was not the unified vision that could bring together politics and art.

When leading pragmatist intellectuals joined the majority in supporting America's involvement in World War I, Randolph Bourne carried Brooks's critique much further in essays made dramatic by Bourne's repudiation of his mentor, John Dewey, and by his rejection of ideas to which he had earlier been much attracted. Bourne's "Twilight of Idols" everywhere showed a concern with cultural values as opposed to specific political or institutional programs. Bourne's arguments, like those of Brooks, bound pragmatic liberalism closely to an emphasis on the mechanical and a preoccupation with means, and they deplored liberalism's insensitivity to artistic values and to a concern with ends. With such arguments, the *Seven Arts* critics established a standard line of resistance to pragmatic liberalism that would serve many intellectuals, and especially literary radicals, for decades.[42]

For all of this, Brooks and Bourne shaped their arguments in individual ways and molded their vision in terms later intellectuals could never wholly accept. More hortatory than analytical, Brooks in particular was inclined to soar toward a starry-eyed idealism and to glorify the artist as the engine of historical change. Sometimes it seemed as if America needed, in order to achieve greatness and maturity, only a single cultural hero of the type Brooks found in many European cultures: "a sour-faced American Tolstoy, an insufferable American Ibsen, an incredible American Nietzsche—just one true-blue solitary rhinoceros!"[43] There was an unchecked idealism, a too-open moralism, in Brooks and Bourne that would not correspond with the style, the social experience, or the political convictions of the New York Intellectuals. Yet, despite the differences in tone, a hint of belief in the primacy of culture and an echo of the search for an American giant would occasionally come through.

The *Partisan Review* circle would echo these predecessors in a more significant way as well. The demands of Brooks, Bourne, and the whole *Seven Arts* group for a new culture rang with a certain patriotic conviction that America was the hope of the world. This attitude has often been referred to as "cultural nationalism," but the term must be used with care. The *Seven Arts* critics certainly did not celebrate existing American traditions in the arts. Neither did they expect to create the new culture on exclusively American themes. The patriotic or nationalistic strain lay primarily in the belief that the United States offered the most promising opportunity to build the international, integrated culture of the future. While others fled to Europe or lamented American inadequacies in their chambers, Brooks and Bourne and their allies consciously worked, in David Hollinger's words, "to bring to their own national culture an intensity and scope comparable to that of European civilization."[44] The New York Intellectuals would share the goal of pro-

ducing a mature and sophisticated culture in America, able like
that of Europe to sustain both the richness of cultural tradition and
the freshness of artistic innovation.

By the time the founders of the New York group became active
in the thirties, American culture had begun to change its shape.
One of the richest periods in American literature bloomed during
the 1920s, and many of the leaders in that flowering were practitioners or disciples of literary modernism. For young American
writers, T. S. Eliot stood out as the most influential modernist,
partly because he seemed a case of local-boy-makes-good, probably
more because he combined the writing of "perfect poems," which
never "betrayed immaturity, awkwardness, provincialism, or platitude," with articulate and incisive criticism and aesthetic theory.[45]
Eliot's criticism presented a sharp contrast between the poet and
the "practical and active person"; a claim that poetry contained an
essence unto itself with few ties to the world; and an emphasis on
tradition, order, and the past—giving shape to at least one form of
the "religion of art" in the twenties.[46]

Rejecting this turn away from social concerns, Van Wyck Brooks
placed himself at the forefront of those opposing Eliot and modernism, gradually losing touch with the many capable young writers who increasingly respected the technical achievements and the
literary passion of the modernists. In the terms in which he attacked modernism and in his new insistence that content must *dic-
tate* form, Brooks demonstrated a slippage in his sense of balance;
rather than urging writers to overcome dualisms through a synthesis
of the elements in tension, he was now asserting a rigid version
of the arguments on one side.[47] In the late twenties, Brooks would
face a breakdown that left him unable to write for several years.
The Brooks who reemerged in the thirties had little to offer literary radicals.

Perhaps the best possibility for at least a continuing conversation between the modernism of Eliot and a socially conscious
criticism lay in an oft-revived little magazine, the *Dial*. The *Dial*
was reconstituted once more in 1919 in a self-conscious attempt
to follow Randolph Bourne's cultural vision. The magazine did
succeed in publishing a lively, eclectic, and impressive body of
writing; and it did encourage a cosmopolitan outlook in one sense
with its international consciousness and its stream of letters written by the likes of Pound, Mann, and Eliot from the cultural capitals of Europe. Yet in the very description of the magazine offered
by someone close to the new editors—that the *Dial* would be a

26

"*Seven Arts* without politics"—lay the key to its future. The lack of political or social interest meant that contemporary artistic currents would flow unchecked. During the 1920s the *Dial* became the leading periodical voice of modernist aestheticism in America. In the process, and despite giving the *Dial* Award to T. S. Eliot and Van Wyck Brooks in consecutive years, the magazine lost its capacity to link different artistic camps. By the time of its demise in 1929, the *Dial*, along with Eliot, had become symbolic of what the more socially conscious writers of the thirties would want to rebel against.[48]

Yet these did not exhaust the possibilities open to writers in the twenties. The effort to combine literary commitment with social concern that Brooks had represented in the teens was not inherently hostile to modernism, whatever modernism's attitude toward society. In a few writers, most notably in Edmund Wilson, a conviction that literature belonged inescapably within a social context happily coexisted with an acceptance of the modern. Born in 1895, Wilson belonged with the twenties generation: he was one year younger than e. e. cummings, one year older than F. Scott Fitzgerald. With his generation, Wilson detested the sterility of the "respectable" life and he attacked Puritanism, yet he avoided many of the extremes of the period and belonged to no clique.

Wilson embraced the serious business of being a writer and editor, as one biographer has remarked, with the air of "a young man who has put away youth as much overrated."[49] Unlike his more rambunctious contemporaries, Wilson could not for long simply throw off and ignore the literary concerns of his elders. In *Discordant Encounters*, Wilson tried to provide a balanced and accurate consideration of the ideas of the teens, something he had found lacking in the controversies of the early twenties. Although amply critical of Brooks's current posture, Wilson generously recognized the importance of his earlier contributions.[50] Brooks had, in fact, defined a number of the issues that preoccupied Wilson himself. Like Brooks, Wilson addressed himself repeatedly to the problems of culture within the American environment, and like Brooks he sought an approach that could unify the opposing forces in society. Wilson accepted the notion of a highbrow-lowbrow dualism and struggled to reconcile the need for the ideals of the refined with the need for the vitality and energy of the vulgar. He concerned himself as well with the tensions between East and West, rich and poor, Anglo-Saxon and immigrant. Wrestling with the obligations of a man of culture to his society, Wilson concluded, as Brooks had before him, that in a country desperate for a unified perspective, literary criticism was obliged to become social criticism.[51]

In the second half of the twenties, Wilson became the leading voice calling for a literature of quality that remained conscious of society. From his editorial chair at the *New Republic*, Wilson assailed commercialism, narrowness, and sloppy standards, particularly in criticism. His assaults would have been easier to dismiss had not Wilson himself come to represent the very type of the "man of letters."[52] In the 1920s Wilson encouraged both the social interests in literature linked with Brooks and the aesthetic concentration preached by Eliot, though neither in its exclusiveness; he wrote for magazines of all persuasions and edited others; he saw his own experimental plays put on by the Provincetown Players. In addition, he completed a novel, *I Thought of Daisy*, recreating in fiction the choices and problems bedeviling American culture.[53] Putting his principles to work in another sphere, Wilson published as the thirties opened his first full book of criticism, the mature and masterly *Axel's Castle*.

In this full and fair though ultimately dissenting view of the symbolist movement in literature from 1870 to 1930, Wilson provided an influential critical model that stood opposed to the Eliot-inspired formalism gathering advocates in the same period. Beginning with a commitment to context, Wilson discussed Symbolism as an artistic response to mechanistic ideas in biology and to naturalism in literature; Symbolism was closely akin to Romanticism, "a second flood of the same tide," the "second swing of the pendulum away from a mechanistic view of nature and from a social conception of man."[54] His groundwork established, Wilson proceeded to examine six major symbolist writers.

Of these, T. S. Eliot was symbolically the book's most important figure.[55] A contemporary of Wilson's and a rival for leadership in American letters, Eliot challenged Wilson, as he did later radical critics, to deal with literary and social views many found unacceptable. Wilson managed this balancing act with considerable skill, giving Eliot ample praise as poet and critic.[56] Yet Wilson had a larger aim in the book: to show the necessary involvement of the writer with his society and the desiccation of a narrow aestheticism.[57] By this measure Eliot was not so compelling a figure. Asserting his own style of contextual criticism as he wrote, Wilson emphasized that Eliot was a product of a particular society and a particular tradition that colored his work. Eliot exhibited "the peculiar conflicts of the Puritan turned artist," including "the ascetic

shrinking from sexual experience" and the "straining after a religious emotion" to take its place—"a belief that it would be a good
thing to believe, rather than a genuine belief."[58] Eliot was, in other
words, caught in the trap of American culture described by Brooks,
suffering the enfeeblements of the highbrow.

Emphasizing the necessary relationship between the cultural and
the social, and believing as had Brooks in the need for a synthesis
of the two in criticism, Wilson bluntly condemned the assumptions from which Eliot worked. Eliot's conception of poetry as "some
sort of pure and rare aesthetic essence" unrelated to "practical human uses" seemed to Wilson "absolutely unhistorical—an impossible attempt to make aesthetic values independent of all the other
values." Moreover, Eliot's recent work revealed a "reactionary point
of view." Eliot faced the past, not the present or future; he separated art from life; he was leading criticism toward narrowness and
inconsequence. However great a poet, Eliot was no model for building, vitalizing, and unifying American culture.[59]

Wilson's conclusions about Symbolism as a whole followed from
his analysis of Eliot: the movement had come to an end, for it had
reached its extreme and lacked new possibilities. Yet in this death
there was promise of new life. Wilson held forth an image of future
unity and cultural progress worthy of a Brooks or a Bourne:

> Our conceptions of objective and subjective have unquestion-
> ably been based on false dualism. . . . Classicism and Roman-
> ticism, Naturalism and Symbolism are, in reality, therefore
> false alternatives. And so we may see Naturalism and Sym-
> bolism combine to provide us with a vision of human life
> and its universe, richer, more subtle, more complex and more
> complete than any man has yet known.

New unities were possible even beyond literature; some "new and
radical simplification" might totally expel the "infinite specialization and divergence of the sciences and arts" predicted by Valery:
"And who can say that, as science and art look more and more deeply
into experience and achieve a wider and wider range, . . . they may
not arrive at a way of thinking, a technique of feeling with our perceptions, which will make art and science one?"[60]

This hope in Wilson belonged to the radical literary tradition
of *Seven Arts*, but it also had a much more immediate context. By
the writing of *Axel's Castle*, the United States had entered the depression, and writers were "becoming more and more conscious of
Russia, a country where a central social-political idealism has been

29

able to use and to inspire the artist as well as the engineer."[61] The possibilities of Marxism as a unifying philosophy would dazzle a good many literary folk in the thirties; and for some, as Wilson's remarks suggest, the power of the Marxist vision would come in part from its ability to reinforce, at least briefly, the assumptions and hopes of a critical perspective sprung from the teens.

The New York Intellectuals looked to Edmund Wilson and, consciously or unconsciously, beyond him to Brooks and Bourne for their image of the literary critic's proper scope, for a list of concerns, and for a sense of the problems inhibiting the full growth of American culture. Eliot might be, as he was for William Phillips, the source of an introduction "to the modern sensibility, especially in verse, and to the idea of a tighter, more exact, more formal approach to literature than was commonly accepted at that time." Yet Wilson was the model of breadth and style who "opened up the social and human side of literature, and set an example of a contemporary taste, roaming through the past and present, assessing new writers and relating them to our new historical experience." Wilson was the model of the "wholeness of literature."[62]

For Lionel Trilling, Wilson was the special living symbol of literary vitality and of the Greenwich Village tradition. In 1929 Trilling "signalized my solidarity with the intellectual life by taking an apartment in Greenwich Village": "to validate its present dignity, to suggest that what the Village stood for in American life was not wholly a matter of history, Edmund Wilson lived just across the way. . . . I used to take note of his evening hours at his desk." To Trilling, Wilson "seemed in his own person, and young as he was, to propose and to realize the idea of the literary life."[63]

More than any other figure of the twenties, Wilson combined a critical inheritance from the teens with the insights of the modernists. Wishing to deal with the most advanced literature of the West but unable to ignore the social environment of their age, emerging New York Intellectuals found in Wilson a demonstration that a criticism addressing both modernism and contemporary society was possible. There were other sources of standards and concerns for these young critics, some in the multiple schools of their own time, some in the deeper resources of Western literature; but no influence was more important for those with a literary bent than a critical tradition that combined culture and politics, growing out from Brooks and Bourne in the teens and, by the late twenties, exemplified most clearly in Edmund Wilson.

The city of immigrants and the city of Greenwich Village was also —and not by coincidence—the American city most friendly to radical politics. New York in the 1930s exhibited a receptiveness toward Marxism in all its varieties; and it demonstrated a particular openness to the struggle between the version of Marxism institutionalized in the Communist Party, and its several detractors and competitors. Lionel Abel once remarked that "in its excitement and depression the city picked itself up and went to Russia."

> Politically New York City then became the most interesting part of the Soviet Union. For it became the one part of that country in which the struggle between Stalin and Trotsky could be openly expressed. And was! And how! . . . No other great city followed New York. London did not, nor did Paris. And these were the "advanced" cities of the world.[64]

Abel's pride in New York's performance, and in the fact that an American city had gone beyond London and Paris, is apparent. Debates over radicalism were a form of cultural expression to Abel, as to many of the New York Intellectuals. From their engagement in the battles of the thirties came a sense of intellectual maturity and cultural experience that fed their characteristic urban pride and strengthened their growing—though restrained—sense of national self-esteem. Radicalism could gain such an apparently central place in the development of the New York Intellectuals because for a time it seemed to encompass both their social heritage as second-generation Jews and their commitment to an advanced literature.

Radical ideas had reached into many Jewish settlements in Eastern Europe, but here again New York produced a unique concentration of theories and theorists among Jews. It was not so much their numbers as the secular knowledge and the activism encouraged by their ideas that gave the radicals influence: "While the socialists, anarchists, and communists of various shades remained a minority among the immigrants, they did much to set the political tone in the new Jewish communities. They edited the Yiddish periodicals, dominated the speakers' platforms, and organized the first Jewish-dominated political action groups."[65] When the Communist Party appeared in America after World War I, Jews were prominent among its members. Nathan Glazer has commented that one "characteristic of the membership of the American Communist Party that differentiated it from almost every other Communist Party in the Western world was that a large proportion of its members were of Jewish origin."[66]

31

For young intellectuals growing up in the Jewish community, some knowledge of radicalism was hard to avoid. Perhaps a favorite uncle, or the older boy or girl across the way, or a militant worker, would introduce socialist ideas to a receptive child. Or perhaps the lessons would be learned at home from parents who had made the leap toward secularism and radicalism themselves. As the intellectually oriented youth grew older, the prominence of radicals in the media and the secular institutions of the Jewish community would be apparent. Schools and colleges provided another arena for radical activism in which a variety of sects and splinters flourished. The availability of radicalism brought many future intellectuals to its banners when they were too young to have found the way by themselves; Daniel Bell joined a socialist group at thirteen, Irving Howe at fourteen.[67] Embracing radicalism was no major decision but a natural progression for many young Jews.

The political radicalism encountered by young Jewish intellectuals was largely a European import: as it explicitly attacked the dominant social and economic forms of the United States and all capitalist countries, it implicitly dismissed the traditions of native American radicals. In part this may have been because urban Jews simply had very little contact with such traditions. Yet even when Jewish intellectuals examined native radicalism, they found rural roots, an unsophisticated ideology, and a limited concept of brotherhood—a radicalism that had never, in John Higham's words, "mounted a vigorous ideological offensive against the barriers of race and nationality."[68]

The radicalism within the larger American culture that most interested the young New York Intellectuals came to them as part of their literary and intellectual heritage. Since the late nineteenth century, literary folk had been engaged in attacking the brutish and dehumanizing aspects of American industrial society at the same time that they had been working for a more sophisticated American culture. In constructing an attack on the corruptions of commercialism in American life, Van Wyck Brooks had given fresh voice to the trend. Many writers of the twenties had loudly declared their lack of interest in political affairs; yet modernism had appealed to them in part for its aura of radicalism in culture, and nothing was more characteristic of the intellectual life of the decade than the attack on business culture by literary intellectuals. For some, the move toward Marxism in the thirties would clearly be little more than a continuation of this pattern.[69]

When the depression came, young New York writers faced the

crisis with an openness or a predisposition to radicalism, growing both from their social experience and their literary heritage. An individual's turn toward radicalism often came gradually, depending not so much on a conscious moment of decision as on the general drift of opinion.[70] Yet even when he made a commitment to Marxism, the young intellectual had not answered all of the questions facing him. What did Marxism mean to someone whose first love was literature? How did politics and culture fit together? What was it that Marxism could do for literature in particular and for American culture in general? In approaching radicalism and in beginning to consider such questions, the aspiring writer or critic might look to more than one model. The major division within the ranks of those who called themselves radicals developed between those who supported the orthodox line of the Communist Party and those who in various ways asserted their independence. For each intellectual who moved left in the thirties, this division would eventually enforce the necessity of choice.

The man who came closest to representing the orthodox Communist viewpoint in literature was almost certainly Mike Gold. Gold had dreamed of revolution and revolutionary writing since the teens, and during the rather unpolitical twenties, as Daniel Aaron has remarked, "no other writer tried more conscientiously to combat Bohemianism or expatriate indifference."[71] A founder of the *New Masses* in 1926, Gold played a large role in the magazine's early debates over the proper attitude of the radical writer toward organized politics. Against John Dos Passos and others who were calling for a radicalism of doubt without firm preconceptions and open to unexpected conclusions, Gold argued that "Moscow and revolution" should provide the guiding spirit for young writers. When the magazine's "liberals" charged that Gold's ideas presented a simplistic good-versus-evil view of the world that ignored human complexity, Gold responded that they were overly idealistic and lacked intellectual organization.[72]

In a 1928 reorganization of the *New Masses*, Gold became the dominant editor and began to mold the magazine to his own image. Gold wanted "the working men, women, and children of America to do most of the writing in the *New Masses*," to present "the raw material of the workers' art" so that if a "proletarian genius arrives, it [the magazine] will be ready for him."[73] For Gold the worker seemed always virile, masculine, and heroic, while intellectuals remained somehow effete. By demanding that American intellectuals accept such a glorification of the worker, Gold and his allies threatened a serious confrontation over standards. As Richard Pells has remarked, "ultimately, the intellectual was being asked to desert the very tools of his trade, to become a 'new man' by ceasing to think critically." Gold dismissed the artist's fears that collective thought would prove stifling to culture, arguing that the bourgeois writer's individualism led "only to little cafe cliques and minor eccentrics," whereas the great artists and thinkers "shared in the world vision of their times."[74] Few writers of quality went as far as Gold, and a number of radicals refused either to dismiss modern literature completely or to raise the worker to an exclusive literary pedestal.

Gold would continue to champion his narrow version of proletarian literature for a time. Yet he stood willing to alter his cultural stance as changes in Soviet policy directed, in the belief that literature, culture, and intellect must serve the political needs of revolutionary organization. Communism did not, in Gold's eyes, impose a rigid discipline on writers, but it did induce a "creative self-discipline." Radical writers must recognize the hard facts and drastic necessities of revolution and look beyond themselves for leadership: "A revolution is a serious hard-headed practical affair which should be managed by engineers who have a strong human gift of understanding the masses."[75] And as Gold felt he knew perfectly well, the masses longed to triumph regardless of the purity of principles. For compromise, restraint, caution, subtlety— the traits he associated with liberalism—Gold expressed little but contempt.

Another strong voice in the Communist literary camp was that of Granville Hicks, who became the literary editor of the *New Masses* when the magazine began publishing as a weekly at the beginning of 1934. Hicks's Harvard education and early career as a college English teacher stood in marked contrast to Gold's humble background and aggressively working-class behavior; and whereas Gold was "impassioned but unsystematic," Hicks was of "more disciplined, perhaps over-disciplined, intellect."[76] In his first major *New Masses* piece in February 1933, Hicks attempted to establish a code for Marxist criticism requiring that literary works deal with the class struggle, present experience with "intensity," and represent the view of the "vanguard of the proletariat." These guidelines, he believed, would provide "not only a standard by which to recognize the perfect Marxian novel, but also a method for the evaluation of all literature."[77] The idea of a "perfect" novel and the dogmatism of the standards by which he proposed to recognize it suggested Hicks's characteristic limitations.

34

The relationship of Newton Arvin to the Communist movement illustrated the complexity of position that could develop for a critic more subtle and more capable than either Hicks or Gold. Arvin showed no tendency to celebrate Gold's version of proletarianism. In 1930 he had complained: "What I do not like about the *New Masses* is the affectation of idealized proletarianism, the monotonous strumming on the hardboiled string, the hostility to ideas on other levels than one, the contempt for modulated writing and criticism, the evasion of discussion."[78] According to the later recollections of Hicks, a similar lack of infatuation with Communist cultural patterns characterized his own early attitude and that of Robert Gorham Davis (who as a thirties radical used the name Obed Brooks). Yet whatever their reservations, these intellectuals allied themselves closely to the Communist Party. Hicks and Davis largely concurred with Arvin's private judgment that Communist leaders were at the center of a "dreadful and desperate struggle . . . fighting what is really our battle for us," and that the intellectual questions that concerned them "must take their places . . . out of the thickest dust along the rim of the arena."[79]

Such an attitude toward party leadership, such a granting of primacy to social revolution over the traditional concerns of intellectuals, goes a long way toward explaining how astute and sensitive men like Arvin could—even while criticizing the crudities and simplifications of party orthodoxy—put aside their objections and remain with the Communists until the debacle of 1939. No matter how greatly they might themselves treasure intellectual values and no matter how they might separate themselves as thinking men from actual workers, writers like Hicks, Arvin, and Davis believed the intellectual to be a subordinate figure in history, whereas the Communist Party seemed a molding force. In giving up a belief in the fundamental importance of the intellectual life and of culture, they gave up much of the ground they needed to retain in order to preserve the integrity of their critical function.

On the other side of the radical divide, the forces demanding a literature and criticism free from the organizational ties of the Communist Party and free from the strictures of Soviet doctrine found a worthy champion in Edmund Wilson. To the degree that Gold embodied Party orthodoxy, Wilson gave meaning to the idea of independent radicalism. It was not that Wilson overlooked the horror of American conditions; it was not that he failed to embrace Marx in the early thirties; it was not that his hope for the future was deficient. Rather, it was Wilson's insistence on the maintenance

35

of standards, on the analytical role of the intellectual, and on the need for an *American* radicalism, that separated him from the Communists. For Wilson, politics did not override fundamental literary and intellectual values.

Wilson gained prominence in urging his liberal contemporaries to consider Marxism when, after Herbert Croly's death left the *New Republic* without a controlling editor in 1930, the magazine carried in its columns an editorial debate over the proper course for intellectuals. Wilson supported more radical ideas against George Soule's liberalism. In "An Appeal to Progressives," Wilson asserted as basic the idea that the capitalist system had broken down. Americans appeared to Wilson to be low in morale and unconvinced of the value of continuing a money-making society. Noting that liberals and progressives had been "betting on capitalism," Wilson now called for an open advocacy of socialism, hoping that "Americans would be willing now for the first time to put their idealism and their genius for organization behind a radical social experiment." Wilson even went so far as to claim that the example of Russia might well become a welcome challenge to America: "After all, the Communist project has almost all the qualities that Americans glorify— the extreme of efficiency and economy combined with the ideal of a herculean feat to be accomplished by common action in an atmosphere of enthusiastic boosting—like a Liberty Loan drive— the idea of putting over something big in five years."[80]

The terms in which Wilson praised Russia were highly significant. Wilson was not advocating that the United States copy Russia, but that Americans take inspiration from the Soviet achievement to forge their own socialist society. His essay went on to urge that American progressives "take Communism away from the Communists, and take it without ambiguities or reservations."[81] As the 1930s progressed, Wilson's distaste for the tactics of the existing Communist Party became increasingly apparent. He particularly resented the Party's "using" intellectuals, and by 1932 he was dropping caustic remarks about "the Communists' habit of manufacturing martyrs" and suggesting that intellectuals had been overly impressed with Russia.[82] These beginnings of disillusion reflected the fact that Wilson was an intellectual first, a literary man with social concerns, not a revolutionary or a politician. He not only wanted communism reworked and stamped "made in America," but he also envisioned a movement of ideas more than an upsurge of class power.

In seeking through a political ideology that unity of vision which could mend the rifts in the world of the intellectual and the writer, Wilson was much closer to Van Wyck Brooks's use of socialism as a framework for *cultural* revolution than he was to Mike Gold's use of literature and culture to glorify *social* revolution. Wilson would never allow himself to get too close to an organized party with all its entangling alliances. Yet, to others, a devotion to radical literature and a commitment to the Communist Party seemed a natural marriage in the early thirties, not a yoking of incompatible mates. If a new society was emerging and if Marxism provided a unifying vision, why could not young writers join together Wilson's critical perspective, the militance of Gold's *New Masses*, and, yes, the sophisticated literary experiments of Eliot and the modernists? The values of literature and the demands of politics could be reconciled by a proper radical perception. With such a belief many of the founding generation of New York Intellectuals began to make their way in the thirties.

Chapter Two

Partisan Review and the Appeal of Marxism

Partisan Review was born in circumstances that might have foretold to a wise observer many things about the future of the child. In some ways the infant magazine seemed a typical product of the radical enthusiasm of the early thirties, which suckled a brood of rebellious magazines in the expectation that they would mature into the leaders of a new radical community. For most of these magazines, and particularly for those thrown up by chapters of the Communist-sponsored John Reed Club, life was sometimes nasty and brutish, and nearly always short.[1] *Partisan Review* stood out because it survived, with a will to life nurtured by the advantages of its situation. As the organ of the John Reed Club in New York City, the magazine sprang up at the center of radical affairs, where it could claim more attention and more support than similar ventures elsewhere. It also began life with vision and ambition, and from very early in its history the magazine implicitly challenged the position of its seniors.

According to the most common version of *Partisan Review*'s founding, Philip Rahv and William Phillips, friends from the New York Reed Club, approached Joseph Freeman of the *New Masses* in 1933 with an idea for a new magazine. The *New Masses* had become mostly political in content, leaving little room for discussions of theoretical problems in literature and criticism or for the publication of original fiction and poetry—material that interested Rahv and Phillips. Freeman was sympathetic and helped with the organization of the new periodical, which also received the blessings of the Communist Party.[2] To raise funds for the magazine, a lecture by John Strachey, "a suave British literary Marxist," on "Literature and Dialectical Materialism" was scheduled, with Mike Gold to serve as chair. The event remained fresh years later in Phillips's recollection:

We hired a hall, sold tickets, publicized the event—all quite amateurishly, for professionalism had not yet invaded the realm of serious or radical culture. Nevertheless the lecture turned out to be a smash hit: people were begging for tickets, and trying to crash the gate. . . . We had raised the unbelievable sum of eight hundred dollars, enough to run a magazine for a year in a collapsed economy. We had no rent, no salaries, nobody to phone, and printing costs made the Depression seem like a literary utopia.[3]

In its first issue for February–March 1934, *Partisan Review* carried a long list of editors reflecting its political connections and debts. Phillips later recalled that "it was understood from the beginning that Rahv and I were the main force behind the magazine, and its chief editors."[4] Quite probably this was better "understood" by Phillips and Rahv than by some of the others. Even so, by the third issue of *Partisan Review* if not before, the two had established their individual and joint contributions as the characteristic voice of the magazine. This voice was one that soon disturbed the editors of the *New Masses*.

William Phillips, born in New York in 1907, was twenty-six when *Partisan Review* first appeared. He had come, as he later put it, "from the poor boy's land, from the Bronx and City College," but had managed to go on to a master's degree at New York University (1930) and to some graduate work at Columbia (1930–31). From 1929 to 1932 he served as an instructor in English at NYU. Although his parents were socialists, Phillips has recalled a youth devoted mainly to art: "my literary and intellectual development was rooted in the 20's, in the experience of modernism: my world was bounded on all sides by Eliot, Pound, Joyce, the Cubists, Mondrian, etc."[5] When made aware of the political left while using the *Nation* and the *New Republic* to teach expository writing, Phillips moved quickly into the John Reed Club, which he later claimed was "associated more closely with the Communist party than I realized at the time." Despite a consciousness that "its literary and intellectual level was not the highest," Phillips stayed with the club, soon becoming the secretary of the writers' group. Caught between an "awareness of the stupidities of the organization" and radical literary zeal, Phillips dreamed of a magazine to express his views and "to mobilize a group of disaffected writers looking for a similar direction."[6]

Whatever Phillips's doubts, his book reviews for the radical press before 1934 showed an application of appropriate formulae, such that the John Reed Club and *New Masses* editors might well have trusted him to edit a new periodical. In reviewing Ortega y Gasset's *The Revolt of the Masses* in 1933, for instance, Phillips repeatedly applied that most characteristic tool of communism's extreme "left" period, the theory of social fascism. Phillips spoke more than once of the "defenses of capitalism, common to fascist and social democratic theory," and assailed the "role of social fascism in Spain." At the same time, he hailed the "magnificent cultural and industrial achievements of the Soviet Union: the successful completion of the Five Year Plan, the abolition of illiteracy, the wide participation of the workers in all cultural activities, and the high level of performance in all the arts." There was little in such a review to show doubt about the Communist Party, much that was a conventional spouting of its current line.[7]

Yet Phillips held more complicated views than the Ortega piece demonstrated. In the same month in which that review appeared, Phillips published what he later called a "non-Marxist" essay in *Symposium*, arguing for the development of a "systemic authority" that could provide the basis for a more scientific criticism.[8] Although not denying Marxism its power, Phillips insisted that literature must be discussed in its own terms and related to the class struggle only through broad and general patterns—a position perhaps compatible with Marx, but hardly in line with the proletarian push of the *New Masses* in these years.[9] The William Phillips who came to the editorial board of *Partisan Review* in 1934 was much attracted to Marxism and the Communist Party, yet his first commitment had been to literature. His presence in the radical camp depended on the belief that criticism and communism could live in mutual respect.

The same thing could be said of Philip Rahv, though here the literary passion was at first partially obscured by political militance and a complex personality. At the end of Rahv's life, William Styron would call him "so secretive as to be almost unknowable," and Mary McCarthy would insist that "If no two people are alike, he was less like anybody else than anybody." There were "two persons" in Rahv, according to McCarthy: "It would be simplifying to say that one was political, masculine, and aggressive, one feminine, artistic, and dreamy, but those contrasts were part of it."[10] Some of Rahv's reticence about himself probably served to protect the softer side of his nature; some of the complexity he displayed may have been the reasonable product of a contorted and peripatetic youth. Born in Russia in 1908, Rahv moved repeatedly, had his formal education abruptly curtailed at sixteen, and ended up out of work and on his own in New York by the early 1930s. Not alone during the depression years he slept at times on park benches and stood in breadlines, but with uncommon zeal the young Rahv made use of his time in the warmth of the public library to teach himself a good deal about literature.[11]

Phillips would later comment that Rahv had "come directly to the Left without going through a modernist phase."[12] Yet that did not seem to represent Rahv's view of his own development. In responding to a magazine inquiry in 1934, Rahv described himself a few years earlier as a standard modernist waiting to be rescued by radicalism: "As so many other middle class intellectuals, though I studied Freud, Nietzche [sic], Proust, Joyce, Rimbaud, etc., I really knew and saw nothing." Rahv would later remember a time when he was so interested in literature that he paid little attention even to daily newspapers.[13] For all this, by the early 1930s Rahv was thoroughly politicized—only Marxist theory could make a hungry and jobless young man identify himself as a middle-class intellectual—and from his pen rolled the thunder of militance.

Rahv's writing through 1934 reveals at times the hyperbolic rhetoric, the extreme politicization, that one might expect from a "super-revolutionary" young radical.[14] In "An Open Letter to Young Writers" in 1932, Rahv pushed aside even the giants of modernism as "tangential to the concrete course of history" while urging the "sincere writer" to seize the "magnificent opportunity to vitalize his talent within the seething vat of world-important problems." Calling for the younger generation to release literature from "the nephitic [sic] fumes of idealist opium" as a step toward changing the world, Rahv built up to his final splenetic decree: "We must sever all ties with this lunatic civilization known as capitalism."[15] Nearly two years later, and after *Partisan Review* had begun appearing, Rahv still wrote on occasion as a passionate convert: "I have thrown off the priestly robe of hypocritical spirituality affected by bourgeois writers, in order to become an intellectual assistant of the proletariat."[16] Rahv was overly taken with his own romantic pose, and he would prove to be no one's "intellectual assistant." Yet, clearly, a militant stance and a political identification with communism were highly important to Rahv at this point.

It is all the more impressive, given such bluster, to discover the more sensitive and more literary Rahv coexisting with the propagandist. In "The Literary Class War," written for the *New Masses* in 1932, for instance, Rahv attempted to modernize the Greek idea of katharsis by adding to "Aristotelean pity and terror" the "synthesizing third factor" of "militancy, combativeness."[17] Rahv's interest in literary theory of a high order was apparent in this discussion, but even more striking was the sober effort to make use of literary tradition. A sensitivity of a different kind warmed an early review of Fitzgerald. Despite a warning to the author that was meant to be stern—"Dear Mr. Fitzgerald, you can't hide from a hurricane under a beach umbrella"—Rahv's tone was far from harsh. Mary McCarthy later noted that because the more visible Rahv seemed "an intransigent (I thought), pontificating young Marxist, . . . the tenderness of the review, despite its critical stance, startled me."[18] Rahv came to the editorial board of *Partisan Review* with a record that showed, like that of Phillips, not only a strong attraction toward the tools of Marxism and the leading role of the Communist Party, but also—and more fundamentally—a desire to build a solid theoretical structure for literary criticism, a respect for the contributions of the past, and a sensitivity to individual works.

With such interests and convictions linked especially in Rahv to an assertive spirit, one may well imagine, as Phillips has recalled, that the two were "the most dissident members of the John Reed Club."[19] Why, then, would the good proletarian editors of the *New Masses* help such prickly customers set up a magazine? The answer must lie in a recognition that the Communist cultural front, though restricted in scope, was no rigidly defined operation with a proletarian closed shop. Like other American radical movements, the Party itself was diverse and filled with argumentative sorts; the cultural side of the movement, with its politically untrustworthy literary types, was even less monolithic. The Communists, as Phillips has remarked, tried only to set the *limits* of dissent: "there was no intellectual reign of terror, at least not within the fold, so to speak. . . . On the contrary, there was a kind of cynical acceptance of disaffection and even criticism of the party by writers, so long as it was not made public or generalized into a fundamental condemnation of the Soviet regime and its satellite parties."[20] For Phillips and Rahv, this proved latitude enough in which to start a magazine and carry it on through more than two years of increasing doubt.

The question can also be reversed: why did two talented young writers want to start a magazine boasting a visible connection with the Communist movement? The longer answer to this more interesting question will occupy many pages to come. A shorter answer can point to at least one set of preconditions: "We were," Phillips has remarked, "cocky kids." The confident young editors believed they could launch a new literary movement; they believed they stood as Marxists on the pathway of promise.[21] They identified their own views with the proper interpretation of Marxism and their own critical concerns as the chief problems of literature. Such assumptions made possible the creative energy of *Partisan Review* and its circle, both in the magazine's Communist period and beyond.

The appeal of communism in the early thirties rested on its seeming ability to meet the needs of young writers on multiple levels. The depression, the push from the children of immigrants reaching maturity as the collapse came, the crisis in European politics, the logic of American literary development, and the continuing growth of a liberal intellectual stratum in American society all came together to create a unique historical situation in which Marxism, and its expression in the Communist Party, appeared in the eyes of many to contain the best answers and the only comprehensive appeal. Discussion of this appeal must necessarily tear apart and treat independently elements that operated in concert; but the unity of the appeal, its capacity to create logic out of chaos and to make the sun shine in a time of darkness, must constantly be kept in mind. To begin with what might be called the social side of the Communist allure is simply to emphasize first the atmosphere of excitement, the sense of belonging, and the promise of opportunity that characterized the radical movement during the worst years of the depression.

A fresh view of politics, membership in a movement, a taste of influence—these things are nearly always stimulants. Adherents of radical causes in the early thirties bathed in a sense of possibility and expectation; their lives were wound to a pitch of excitement by the imminence of world-shattering events in which they would have a part. In trying to explain why membership in the Communist Party seemed worth the "sacrifices and risks" he felt it involved, Granville Hicks cited the "intoxicating sense of being in the mainstream of history" and the feeling that "we were doing something."[22] Appropriately enough, Philip Rahv's revision of the idea of katharsis in 1932 promised "release through action."[23]

The excitement of action could appeal to anyone, of course, but it matched the desires of a rising second generation especially well. If the world of parents and tradition they wished to put behind them

seemed timid, narrow, and parochial, what more powerful entice-
ment could radicalism offer than the aura of heroic risk-taking ema-
nating from an international movement to raise all humankind?
Behind them in the patterns of childhood lay dullness and predict-
ability, but ahead in the embrace of the movement lay excitement
and adventure. As Irving Howe has noted, Marxism involves "a pro-
foundly *dramatic* view of human experience," with more than its
share of "inevitable conflicts, apocalyptic climaxes, ultimate moments, hours of doom, and shining tomorrows": "It was this pattern of drama which made each moment of our participation seem
so rich with historical meaning."[24]

American radicals by the early thirties could recite an erratic
history of heroic adventure and intone a dark epic of capitalist repression. Without reaching back farther than World War I, they
found ample material to fuel an indignant passion. Political censorship had undermined the Socialist Party and destroyed radical
periodicals during the war. Debs had gone to prison; alien radicals
had been deported. Bourne had died a martyr to censor-induced star-
vation (influenza was easily ignored). The government had put the
Masses editors on trial, and the Department of Justice had raided
the *Liberator* in 1922. The names of a special few—made heroes
by attacks on labor, on radicals, or on their race—became a radical
litany. To many a young writer, radicalism seemed electric.

The Marxist left reinforced its dramatic image by subsuming in
the early thirties much of the excitement and the crusading spirit
connected with the emergence of cultural modernism. If the Ar-
mory Show of 1913 had been a prewar benchmark, a more recent
set of causes moved younger writers. Mary McCarthy celebrated
the postwar battles as a "series of engagements against censorship":
"there was the battle of *Jurgen*, of *Ulysses*, the battle of evolution
at the Scopes trial in Tennessee, the battle of the school textbooks
in Chicago."[25] For many young intellectuals, such cultural engagements or their symbolic equivalents took on radical political meaning in the 1930s. "Genteel," "bourgeois," and "Humanist" spokesmen attacked "proletarian" fiction and Marxist criticism ferociously,
often with little understanding of their targets. As Alfred Kazin later
recalled, such attacks flattered young writers and "made all these
roughs out of the slums of Chicago and Brooklyn feel that they were
in the great unpopular tradition of modern literature."[26] The early
Partisan Review is full of language that confirms Kazin's view. With
zeal quite apparent, Phillips and Rahv placed themselves on the
side of the new and the vital—in the tradition of those courageous

writers and martyrs who had battled the dullness and constriction of political and cultural repression.

There was also an aura of bohemianism hovering about the radical literary venture in the thirties and a desire to sustain notions of individual self-realization—despite protestations to the contrary. Lionel Trilling later recalled that most of the intellectuals he knew in the period assumed an "irreconcilable contradiction between babies and the good life"; children were presumed to induce capitulation to the "forces of convention," and the image of parenthood was "at essential odds with that of the free and intelligent person."[27] The ideal of personal development at work in such attitudes had served (and continued to serve) middle-class Americans escaping the stuffiness of gentility, and it now suited as well the young writer casting away the conventions of an ethnic heritage. The two types shared negative attitudes toward parochialism and a positive desire for freedom and boldness. Bohemianism and radicalism intermixed in serving such desires, bringing middle-class and second-generation intellectuals together with the promise of openness, change, and excitement.

If Marxism's attraction for literary intellectuals seemed to benefit from a partial ingestion of the experimental dynamic and the rebellious energies of modernism and bohemianism in the early thirties, radical ideas also generated a vitality of their own that could not be contained by the serious nature of Marxist political theory. A potential for exuberance lurked in the very machinery of Marxist thought—a machinery that seemed to invite clever manipulation. When life broke through ideology, young intellectuals kicked up their heels and reveled in using and abusing Marxism for a bit of intellectual strutting and chicanery. Lionel Abel has recalled that

> Harold Rosenberg took the view that Marxism was two things: it was Talmud, to be sure. But it was also Cabala. And he thought that the role of literary men should be to develop the arcane, cabalistic side of the Marxist doctrine. . . . I shall never forget the evening when he proved that Helen of Troy—his argument involved both word magic and economic determinism—was really a loaf of bread! For my part, I thought a good contribution to Marxism would be the creation of a Marxist detective, who would solve crimes by calling upon dialectical materialism, even as G. K. Chesterton's Father Brown solved crimes by applying Catholic dogma.[28]

The adaptability of Marxism to such uses was no mean attraction. The New York Intellectuals would show a lasting penchant for pyrotechnics, for displays of "brilliance," and Marxism provided ample opportunity for such display whether serious or playful.

The young intellectuals who found a sense of action and adventure in Marxism had other social needs as well that excitement alone did little to fulfill. Rightly or not, they often felt as if they had cut themselves off from a familiar world. For security, for support, the young writer needed to find a new home in a new community, a place in which he or she could be accepted without challenge. In the New York of the early thirties, "people began to join parties and organizations. . . . Just to protect yourself you joined up with somebody."29

The Communist Party benefited greatly from such joining. Quick to identify literary advance as part of its program, it welcomed radical writers, as Rahv noted, "into its political home."30 The radical promise of equality and brotherhood appeared to have reached fruition on the international scene under advanced proletarian rule in the Soviet Union. In the early 1930s, for instance, the USSR managed to pose as the very type of an egalitarian society providing fair treatment for Jews. Although Jewish Party leaders and intellectuals had their private doubts about the disappearance of Russian anti-Semitism, in the early thirties it was simply assumed that the Party and radical principle would overcome all prejudices and resolve all disharmonies.31

The idea of brotherhood appealed on many levels, combining the highest idealism with the most practical of needs. If young intellectuals longed to merge with the international proletariat, they also wanted to get together with each other and have some fun. In classmates who had gone "proletarian," Alfred Kazin saw youths who "*looked* as if they had found the right answer. And they were . . . easy with girls, passing them around at dances with comradely contempt, as if being militant about everything brought immediate advantages." What appeal there could have been for the women in such "contempt" is unclear, but what greater social acceptance and security could radicalism have offered young men than to be "easy with girls"? Phillips and Rahv for their part took some pride in having developed the "best dance floor in the city." Such benefits were of no small importance in nourishing the young intellectual's sense that he had found a home.32 The writer as writer, meanwhile, was promised a "harmonious functioning within his class," a "solidarity with his readers," and an "intimate relationship between reader and writer" through identification with a proletarian audience.[33] Both socially and intellectually, the artist or critic of humble background and radical sympathies would be accepted; he would belong.

To enter a world of excitement and heroism, and to be welcomed there as an equal, gave the young writer reason enough, perhaps, to ally himself or herself with a radical organization. Yet the Marxist parties could offer second-generation intellectuals another social plum quite as dear to them—opportunity. Emerging into the world with high ambitions, and made impatient in some cases by long years of preparation and sacrifice, talented youths from immigrant neighborhoods often found their drive for status and success thwarted by the depression. In the plentiful clubs, newspapers, and magazines of the radical movement, young writers found chances for leadership, publication, and even fame that seemed far more open to them than the literary channels of the dominant culture.

As Phillips and Rahv discussed the choices confronting the young writer during the early stages of their own radicalism, it was obvious that political idealism shared attention in their respective outlooks with the consideration of literary opportunities. The militantly proletarian Rahv, addressing those of his own generation in 1932, knew how to identify with and to exploit the radical promise of advantage, even as he urged an essentially political choice: "We, the young writers, . . . who are intent on a literary career, whose works are beginning to appear here and there in the magazines, are now faced with a key decision that will undoubtedly determine the entire course of our literary existence. Shall we take on the coloration of the bourgeois environment, mutilating ourselves, prostituting our creativeness . . . , or are we going to unfurl the banner of revolt . . . by identifying ourselves with the class-conscious proletariat?"[34] There was a consciousness of insecurity here as beginning writers faced a decision that would "determine the entire course" of their literary futures. The political choice was also a career choice, and Rahv seemed to urge radicalism in part out of the belief that to choose the bourgeois path would lead to a dead end, while revolt might end in glory.

In a 1934 discussion of radicalism's appeal for writers, Phillips argued that the generation of the twenties had risen in a time of expansion, "when artists could satisfy their desire to flaunt society and yet reap the material benefits which a prosperous middle class could offer." Though officially scornful of such compromises and bourgeois comforts, Phillips sounded almost envious of those ear-

lier writers and their prosperity. Discussing the turn toward radicalism, he emphasized necessity over moral passion:

> the gravity of the economic crisis has levelled most of us
> (and our families) to a meager, near-starvation existence.
> Opportunities for cashing-in are gone, and we have no illu-
> sions about their return. The kind of reputation which used
> to bring jobs as editors, lecturers, and readers in publishing
> houses, holds no lure for us, because those jobs have been
> whittled down to a few sinecures for stand-patters and tight-
> rope walkers. The bourgeoisie does not want us, and we
> could not accept the double-dealing which these jobs
> require.[35]

Stuck in poverty, looking for work, believing that "opportunities
for cashing-in" were gone never to return (a note of regret here?),
young writers were obviously vulnerable to the promises and the
possibilities of radical politics. The claim of moral superiority to
"double-dealing" comes in Phillips's remarks almost as a petulant
afterthought—a response to the bitter conclusion that aspiring intellectuals were neither wanted nor needed by the dominant culture.

In absorbing the second-generation intellectual's resentment of
poverty and closed opportunities, radicalism may well have performed an ironic service for the capitalist society it opposed. The
Communist Party provided a sense of possibility for a group of extremely capable and articulate people who might otherwise have
vented their frustrations in quite different ways. Lacking the kind
of outlet that the Party made available, the political style of the
thirties could have become far more crabbed and acidulous. As it
was, the Communist Party and other radical groups contained
within themselves a good deal of the pushing and shoving and the
sourness that accompanied the scramble for status and jobs among
young intellectuals on the left.

Within a year of *Partisan Review*'s founding, the editors discovered that even moderate success could easily evoke suspicion from
the established and jealousy from those surpassed. In December
1934 Granville Hicks questioned the need for "scores and scores"
of radical magazines and demanded primary support for the *New
Masses* as "the principle organ of the revolutionary cultural movement." Hicks argued that "no work should appear in other revolutionary magazines that could be effectively used in the *New
Masses.*" *Partisan Review* had sinned, in Hicks's eyes, by refusing
to accept a limited and subservient role. Rather than print mainly

contributions from the New York Reed Club, *Partisan Review* had sought the best material available and published many "well-established writers" of the left. Moreover, it had reviewed many of the same books as the *New Masses*. Not at all happy with such competition, Hicks suggested that *Partisan Review* limit itself to "long, theoretical critical essays"—an injunction that may be roughly translated as get thee to a hermitage.[36]

Hicks's efforts to clip the wings of *Partisan Review* and other less vigorous magazines contained forebodings of eventual break-up and disaster for the radical literary movement. The attempt to exert a central discipline and to solidify the authority of the *New Masses* assumed in practice what some literary leaders had proclaimed in their puffed-up speeches—a cohesive group of radical writers. No such group existed. Moreover, Hicks tried to swim backwards in his assault on *Partisan Review*. The magazine had appeared in part because of the *New Masses'* failure to deal adequately with literature. Far from handing on the best pieces to someone else and taking a back seat, Rahv and Phillips expected from the first to assume leadership on literary issues and to publish pace-setting fiction and poetry. Hicks was asking Rahv and Phillips to abandon both their personal and their intellectual ambitions, something they were not about to do. Hicks's remarks implied as well a narrowing of opportunities for young writers; fewer magazines meant fewer chances for publication. Fred R. Miller, editor of *Blast*, replied vigorously to this threat with an attack on both the *New Masses* and *Partisan Review* for neglecting the writing of unemployed radical workers.[37] *Partisan Review* thus stood accused, on one side, of being too ambitious and, on the other side, of thwarting the ambitions of others. The question of opportunity was a touchy one within the radical camp.[38]

Interest in success and sensitivity to opportunities did not mean that career concerns dominated the lives of young writers. As the New Deal moved American government leftward and the Popular Front strategy carried communism rightward, the political gap between radicalism and liberalism narrowed, and a variety of jobs opened up for the well-educated.[39] Yet the fledgling New York Intellectuals resisted in the thirties the obvious attractions of expanding bureaucracies and secure public jobs. They wanted success, but a success achieved through the exercise of mind and one consistent with their principles. No master plan for getting ahead served to guide them through the succession of difficult moral and political choices of the thirties; at each moment ambition had to find expression as only one part of the complex of motivations that drove them.[40]

Organized radicalism, then, held considerable social attraction for young intellectuals. To those frustrated by circumstances, and to those trying to shake the neighborhood dust of parochialism and timidity from their feet, Marxist politics offered excitement, action, and a sense of importance. To the aspiring writer, the radical movement promised acceptance, belonging, opportunity—a home and a career. Yet for all its genuine luster, the social appeal of communism took its greatest power from the fact that it operated together, in moving young writers leftward, with the even stronger pull of Marxism in the realm of ideas. No appeal was more important to the editors of *Partisan Review* than the appeal to their minds and values.

Edmund Wilson's exhilaration at the collapse of the "Big Business era," his sense of freedom and power as "the bankers, for a change, were taking a beating," typified the reaction of many cultural intellectuals to the massive depression of the 1930s. Like Wilson, they claimed to have felt cramped and cheapened by the attitudes of the 1920s, which all "involved compromises with the salesman and the broker."[41] The economic earthquake seemed to open the door to a new society more conscious of artistic values. Such optimism rested on the assumption that the old system had failed irrevocably, a conclusion that proved to be at best premature.

Yet in the depths of depression, it was easy to believe that a major historical change was under way, that capitalism would of necessity give way to a new form of economic organization. Moreover, because of the spreading assumption that literature must reflect major shifts in economic structure, many believed that previously established literary modes had met their demise along with the capitalist economy and that something new must appear. Among those systems of belief vying to carry out a social reconstruction and to provide the framework for a new literature, there seemed to be only two real possibilities: Phillips identified them in 1934 as the "alternative forces—Communism and Fascism."[42] No writer could avoid making the choice between these forces, Phillips and Rahv believed; and neutrality was impossible.

The Russian example made a strong case for communism. *Partisan Review*'s opening editorial underscored the stark contrast between "the economic and political crisis of capitalism" and "the successful building of socialism in the Soviet Union."[43] Typically for a young radical, Rahv welcomed as accomplished fact "the successful completion of the Five-Year plan, and the growth of Communist influence at home and the world over," and he dismissed as "old wives' tales" the "favorite atrocity stories of the capitalist press about forced labor and the execution of thousands of peasants in the USSR."[44] The Soviet Union sustained the promise that ideology could become reality, fueling the belief that socialist revolution was everywhere in the West just around the historical corner.

Though the political, economic, and humanitarian sides of the radical promise had their attractions, it was this sense of an imminent historical leap that carried the greatest appeal for writers as writers. By applying Marxist ideas in a rather formulaic fashion, many could argue that because a great bourgeois literature had been concomitant with the rise of the bourgeoisie, a great proletarian literature would necessarily accompany the triumph of the working class. To the editors of the early *Partisan Review*, the expectation that a cultural revolution would accompany the political one was an article of faith and a major cause of their attachment to communism. "During the period of social ascent," Rahv explained, "a class is able to produce powerful works of art that are mainly materialist in conception; during its decline its spiritual production likewise deteriorates." Bourgeois artists and writers were thus capable only of "barren experimentation and superficial cleverness," not of great art.[45] The new outlook of Marxism and the anticipation of proletarian ascent, by contrast, offered the writer a central role in the creation of the greatest literature in history.

The mood of expectation supported by the promise of a cultural flowering was not without its qualifying limits. The radical movement, and particularly the Communist Party, could attract and retain some writers only so long as it seemed to leave room for literature to develop in its own way. A firm conviction that the creative intellectual must maintain the right to choose stood behind the assertion in *Partisan Review*'s first editorial that the magazine would "resist every attempt to cripple our literature by narrow-minded, sectarian theories and practices." Phillips and Rahv gave substance to this claim by suggesting a model for radical discourse that allowed much room for give and take: "and we welcome readers and writers alike to use our columns for stating their reactions to our policy and to the contents of each issue. Only in the course of such collective discussion and reciprocal influence can a revolutionary literature reach maturity."[46] Phillips and Rahv started out in the way they intended to go, insisting that literature could thrive

51

only through intellectual ferment and with plenty of room for debate.

Neither *Partisan Review* nor its primary editors always sounded so open to diverse opinion; on this matter as on most others, contradictory inferences may be drawn from the published essays or from the party struggles of the early thirties in which Phillips and Rahv were involved.[47] Yet the generally strong insistence on the writer's freedom that runs through the early *Partisan Review* sends a cautionary message to those who study the period: although many aspects of the Communist appeal for writers may be discussed in general terms, different groups of writers interpreted the promises and the requirements of Party affiliation quite differently. By seeing what they wished to see in Marxism and the Communist Party, writers like Phillips and Rahv constructed for themselves a radical perspective that would conform to their fundamental values and goals. When the Party's version of Marxism contradicted these personal or group interpretations, it was not literary conviction but political loyalty that suffered.

The particular perspective fashioned by Phillips and Rahv had its full share of vagaries and inconsistencies, and its true lines were often obscured by a glaze of political fervency. A careful reading of the early *Partisan Review* makes clear, however, the fundamental importance of the intellectual commitments the editors brought with them on the journey left in shaping their conceptions of radical purpose. First, they defined the problems and the goals of literature in a way that revealed a heavy debt to the American critical tradition flowing especially from the early work of Van Wyck Brooks. Second, at so basic a level that direct articulation seemed unnecessary, they assumed the superiority of a set of values that may best be summed up using one of Randolph Bourne's favorite terms, "cosmopolitanism." Third, and closely related to both of the previous two, they understood history as a complicated, continuous, and open-ended process demanding that intellectuals give as much serious attention to the merits of the past—particularly the literary past—as to its demerits. There would prove to be ample cause for friction between these ideas and the doctrines of the Communist left; yet the early *Partisan Review* exuded hope. The editors came to Marxism believing not that it must be reconciled with their conceptions, values, and beliefs, but that it embodied them. This perception added indispensable weight to the intellectual appeal of Marxism for *Partisan Review*.

Van Wyck Brooks had diagnosed the inability of American culture to produce a mature literature as the consequence of an enduring division in American life that could be mended only through the medium of a great healing and unifying movement. Despite the need to cast off some of Brooks's ideas, the dialectical pattern used by Brooks, as well as the homage paid to socialism as explanation and as goal, made the basic lines of his analysis compatible with a radical viewpoint in later periods. Phillips and Rahv did not set out consciously to follow Brooks in *Partisan Review*; but their preoccupation with the various divisions in American culture as well as in the radical movement itself, and their early obsession with the idea of synthesis as the key to a higher literature, demonstrated their debt to a tradition of analysis in which Brooks was the dominant figure. If this can be accepted, then it is no longer a surprise to come upon Rahv announcing matter-of-factly in an early issue of *Partisan Review*: "Bourgeois literature is by no means homogeneous. The central cleavage one notes in it is the cleavage between commercial and intellectual art."[48] Rahv and Phillips would normally avoid the terms "highbrow" and "lowbrow," but "intellectual" and "commercial" or other substitutes would serve just as well to mark their debt.

Since the goal was synthesis, the obvious task facing the writer in the early thirties was the unification of art. The depression created an opportunity even greater than that of the teens from a Marxist perspective, for as Rahv noted, "it is only in times of intense class struggle that this dualism in negative modern art is sundered and broken."[49] Amidst the ruins a mature American literature could finally arise, and the radical movement was to serve as midwife. Marxism had made tipsy even the sober Edmund Wilson; no wonder that such a heady potion could move writers at the beginning of their careers to near drunkenness. The task of the writer, as Phillips and Rahv saw it, was to use Marxism to create the synthesis necessary for an advanced and unified literature. From such a cultural perspective, Marxism was not exclusively or even primarily a guide to political action, but beyond all else a philosophical framework within which a longstanding literary dream might be fulfilled.[50]

To absorb literary modernism into a new radical art, the Marxian synthesis would have much to overcome. Attempts to define "modernism" have emphasized attitudes hostile to the very idea of a unified, shared understanding of the world. "'Modernism' has come to denote," one student has commented in an effort at summary, "a family of artistic and intellectual movements that have been

radically experimental, spiritually turbulent and militant, icono-
clastic to the point of nihilism, apocalyptic in their hopes and fan-
tasies, savagely destructive to one another and often to themselves
as well—yet capable of recurrent self-renewal."[51] Stephen Spender
has distinguished between the "modern" and the "contemporary,"
presenting the modern as the opposite of the "rationalist, sociological, political and responsible." Reinforcing Spender's point, Irving Howe has noted in much of modernist literature "a bitter impatience with the whole apparatus of cognition and the limiting
assumption of rationality."[52]

The rejection of politics and the flouting of rationality would
hardly seem to sit comfortably with an advocacy of Marxism or
with support for an organized party. Modernism's dependence on
a coterie of informed and sympathetic followers has little obvious
relation to a concern for the whole society or for the masses. And,
in fact, modernism was bluntly rejected by many radicals, either
for these reasons or because, like some around the *New Masses*,
they rejected all bourgeois literature. Yet for the early *Partisan Review*, modernism was something to be seriously reckoned with.
Phillips and Rahv valued the literary achievements of modernism;
they recognized that the modern movement was emphatically international and that it had advanced the integration of American
and European writers; and they found in modern literature devastating attacks on middle-class industrial society. Of course modernism was bourgeois and inadequate to present needs; this seemed
only to support a conclusion that the situation was ripe for a new
movement. Modernism's creative energies could flow forward into
the new radical literature while its anti-social and anti-rational traits
were left behind. This would be the glory of the promised synthesis, that it would incorporate the positive elements of all previous
traditions.

The acceptance of Marxism as a systematizing intellectual framework, rather than as a source of precise explanations or directives,
became evident in the very terminology with which *Partisan Review* referred to Marxism. By alluding constantly to the Marxist
"philosophy," Phillips and Rahv kept the attention of their readers
directed toward radical ideas at the level of theory. Arguing that there
need be "no contradiction between philosophy and experience," Phillips and Rahv nevertheless made it clear that "such a contradiction
is inevitable if the philosophy is false"; and all philosophies except
Marxism were false.[53] Because no other philosophy could bring together without contradiction the artist's specific experience and a

broad understanding of the world, Marxism provided the *only* pathway to a unified and mature American literature. Marxism was the philosophy of the present, of that golden moment when the "movement of history has again made possible the much desired integration of the poet's conception with the leading ideas of his time."[54]

In the early *Partisan Review*, the editors tried energetically to apply their faith in the possibility of a radical synthesis to specific critical problems. Setting out to discuss the relation of form and content in literature (one of the many dualisms that needed to be brought to an end in the new understanding of art), Phillips insisted that his analysis depended upon the "unified outlook and sensibility which the Marxian philosophy provides." The answer to the problem was to treat form and content "*as two aspects of a unified vision*": form and content must be brought together in a synthesis developed within the artist's sensibility. The pervasive problem of dualism had been created by "idealist estheticians"; it would be solved through a synthesis built upon the general philosophical perspective of Marxism.[55]

In the first flush of Marxian enthusiasm, the need to achieve synthesis seemed to Phillips and Rahv a small barrier to literary or personal progress. At times *Partisan Review* described a radical literature on the edge of breakthrough; at times the editors proclaimed that the threshold had already been crossed. When carried away by his own zeal or lured into confusing his observations with his hopes, Rahv could assert that the "new class novels" and even the "new literary magazines" were "signs of a promise fulfilled," demonstrating "the fusion of theory and practice in American revolutionary literature." That Rahv could use the simple existence of magazines like *Partisan Review* to help "prove" the achievement of synthesis suggested both his capacity for wishful thinking and the intensity of his desire to see a vital new culture emerge.[56]

Phillips made a parallel attempt to treat his hopes as reality by implying that radical criticism had already achieved a unified outlook and near-scientific authority. Declaring that the liberal critic whom he targeted "begs the entire question of determining which are the most important forces of tradition and which the genuine forces of revolt," Phillips claimed bluntly: "a Marxist is no longer in the dark about this. In fact, he proceeds to estimate the correct balance of this stress and strain in specific forms of proletarian literature in successive stages of its progress."[57] This image of the literary critic performing a few simple calculations to produce artistic judgments showed the most extreme side of Phillips's long-

ing for systematic criticism, and it belied all the balance and caution of his considered position.

Phillips and Rahv, for all their occasional lapses into overblown
claims, normally treated the creation of literature and the practice
of criticism as difficult and demanding tasks requiring great skill
and sensitivity. They knew, and repeatedly said in various ways,
that the effort to bring system to the discussion of literature (much
less to its creation) must observe some inherent limits. For all their
attraction to the methods and the authority of science, they recognized the fact that (as one historian has put it) "science differed
from literature, which, while often containing insights that seemed
to apply to the entire human species, was nevertheless shot through
with cultural particularity."[58] From Phillips's pre-*Partisan* "Categories for Criticism" through such later articles as the jointly written "Private Experience and Public Philosophy" in 1936, Phillips
and Rahv took as a major problem the working out of a proper relationship between the broader generalizations of Marxism (the "Public Philosophy" of the second title) and the idiosyncratic aspects
of individual experience embodied in specific works of art. It was
never assumed that the general philosophy could explain everything
or turn common writers into major artists.

In speaking to their fellow radicals in early 1935, the editors of
Partisan Review lectured that individual creative ability was as
necessary to radical literature as a correct political outlook:

> The degree of individual talent, . . . is an irreducible factor in
> judgment. All that ideology does is to help light up areas of
> experience, but it does not grant you the eyes with which
> you see. *It is the most advantageous interaction of talent
> and ideology, which permits the development of a great
> literature.*[59]

The same emphasis on the importance of the individual artist working with freedom to express his uniqueness appeared in various
other forms until Phillips and Rahv began to strain their capacity
to produce new metaphors. By 1936 they were asserting that "no
matter what color it runs to, centrally heated rhetoric stifles the
spirit"; only the poet who tempered his symbols "in the fires of his
own imagination" could produce "that intensity and truth which
is poetry."[60] The artist's sensibility, the understanding and insight
of each writer, must be the arena in which synthesis occurred, or
the whole enterprise of radical literature would fall short of its
promise.

The early *Partisan Review* looked to Marxism believing that it could provide systematic philosophical underpinnings for rapid advances in literature and criticism while at the same time leaving ample room for the singular qualities of art. For Phillips and Rahv, Marxism promised both synthesis and freedom in literature, and they looked to the Communist Party to encourage what were for them the principles of Marxism. When they found themselves opposing other radical critics and later the Party itself on basic cultural issues, the editors of *Partisan Review* struck out with a sense of righteousness and betrayal, sure that it was others and not themselves who had abandoned or perverted the essential spirit of radicalism.[61]

In addition to its promise of important philosophical services, Marxism appealed to the editors of *Partisan Review* because it seemed to encourage and embody a set of values to which Phillips and Rahv gave their almost unquestioning allegiance. Cosmopolitan values in general form had enjoyed rising support among left-of-center intellectuals since the early years of the century. A cosmopolitan perspective stood opposed to parochialism, whether regional, national, or ethnic. Emphasis fell on a broad and inclusive understanding of experience, with individual and cultural differences valuable for what they could bring to the larger outlook. No individual or group heritage was to be scorned or excluded; neither was it to be narrowly celebrated. A particular heritage might be a source of enrichment, but it must not be a cause of limitation. The effort to maintain a balance between blending and distinctiveness gave cosmopolitanism a good deal of its character; yet at first, because it assumed a background of closeminded prejudice and stale tradition, its emphasis fell chiefly on moving away from particularism and toward a richer integration and breadth. Phillips and Rahv were buried to their necks in the assumptions of the cosmopolitan perspective and accepted its patterns as the natural shape of their own thought.[62]

In the early 1930s Marxism appeared to serve cosmopolitan purposes with its offer of a unifying movement and a unifying outlook that could overcome bias, fragmentation, and inadequacy. Both the welcoming of all comers to the radical cause and the promise of a synthesis respectful of diversity contributed to this image. And in the quest for a mature American literature, Marxism's aura of internationalism held special appeal. Since the teens and the friendship of Brooks and Bourne, there had been ties for some American writers between cosmopolitan values and the problem of literary adequacy. To become more cosmopolitan was to move American writing closer to European standards. Almost paradoxically, therefore, writers could pursue *national* cultural ambitions by making American literature more *international*. Behind *Partisan Review*'s enthusiasm for the growth of revolutionary art lay the conviction that the emergence of a higher and more vibrant culture, equal to or surpassing any in Europe, could occur right here in America. The special qualities of American writing would produce an enriching variant of world radical culture that was, in accordance with the cosmopolitan pattern, both unique and part of the whole. Phillips and Rahv's eagerness that "revolutionary literature reach maturity" could thus indicate at once their radical enthusiasm and their fidelity to the familiar American goal of cultural equality with Europe.

If Marxism seemed compatible with a broad cosmopolitan perspective, it also encouraged more specific attitudes and assumptions that, for the editors of *Partisan Review*, were inseparable from the body of cosmopolitan values. Openly hostile to religion, Marxism was emphatically secular in the worldview it proclaimed. This was all to the good as far as Phillips and Rahv were concerned. Especially for young Jews with an experience of both immigrant forms and the conventions of the dominant society, active religious belief appeared inescapably restrictive. Moreover, secularism was associated with the whole growth of rational and critical thought since the Enlightenment, which constituted a fundamental presupposition of cosmopolitanism in *Partisan Review*. The tradition of reason held a powerful intellectual attraction for Phillips and Rahv, with the appeal shading over once again into social concerns. Marxism's claims to be scientific thus involved more than the promise of system. As David Hollinger has noted, "Science sought truth of a sort that would command assent from persons of any national, religious, or ethnic background; it was concerned with propositions that were in no way culture-bound."[63] Marxism, conceived of as the highest expression of secular and scientific reason, presented itself as a champion of cosmopolitan values.

In the first half of the twentieth century, cosmopolitanism served the intellectuals who embraced it as a general ideal that helped them distinguish their notions of appropriate cultural values from the ideas of those more attached to established customs and single traditions. Because cosmopolitanism as an ideal spelled out no specific program and created no detailed agenda, its adherents were free to give allegiance to the more precise design of any politics friendly to their broad perspective, as Marxism seemed to be. They were also free to offer their own fuller definitions of what an acceptable set of cosmopolitan values should properly entail. In their own filling in of the basic ideal, Phillips and Rahv made it apparent from very early in the history of *Partisan Review* that they believed movement toward a higher level of culture meant movement toward greater sophistication. For *Partisan Review*, certain firmly held biases about what was sophisticated and what was not became an integral part of the magazine's cosmopolitan outlook.

Cities ranked as vastly more sophisticated than the countryside. Ideas or trends identified as urban in *Partisan Review* nearly always turned out to be positive; those branded as rural generally ranged along a negative scale from merely backward to highly dangerous. Part of this prejudice the editors may well have absorbed from the literary ethos of the twenties that reveled in its superiority to Main Street and the world of hicks and yokels. More may have come from the narrow urban experience of most of those associated with the magazine and their sense of a nativist countryside hostile to their ideas and their kind—factors that made the emphasis on urban superiority a matter of both self-congratulation and self-defense. Signs of a city-based sophistication included a sensitivity to the formal qualities of art, a recognition of complexity and difficulty, and, always, seriousness about ideas.

If urban intellectuality deserved approbation, its opposites were presumably worthy of scorn. *Partisan Review* and its editors often summed up a lack of intellectual sophistication with such terms as "popular" or "commercial," in which they managed to blend inherited literary attitudes with a hint of the radical critique of capitalist society. The popular and the rural were presumed to be linked in many cases, and either might suggest the narrow nativistic side of American culture against which cosmopolitanism commonly defined itself. Phillips and Rahv conjoined all of these meanings in their disparaging use of "populist," making that label the antithesis of cosmopolitan values.

Partisan Review, then, without direct discussion or formal definition, constructed an outlook that may be briefly described in two opposing lists of values and traits. The magazine and its editors looked with special favor on ideas and attitudes that could be classified as secular, scientific, rational, urban, international in spirit, intellectually sophisticated, and broadly inclusive. They generally dismissed or condemned patterns of belief and interpretation that struck them as religious, mythic, rural, narrowly national, popular, simplistic, or restrictive. Throughout the 1930s in *Partisan Review*, editors and major contributors looked to these opposing worlds of value to find common ground for analysis and a language of praise and blame. Cosmopolitan and anti-cosmopolitan values were not only positive and negative respectively, but also — especially when radical ideology shaped the discussion — progressive and regressive, advanced and backward.

Marxism both gave direction to the quest for synthesis and helped sustain the notion that cosmopolitan values were on an upward march; yet in neither case did Phillips and Rahv's hopes for the future take their essential shape from Marxist assumptions. Rather, the two editors chose to emphasize in their interpretation of Marxism ideas that supported goals and attitudes already largely in place. The same conclusion might apply to their notions of historical process. Firm conceptions of the significance of the past and its relation to positive change stood at the core of the cosmopolitan perspective developed in *Partisan Review*, and they patently shaped what Phillips and Rahv meant when they spoke of Marxism.

The editors understood radical ideas to require of writers and critics not an abrupt dismissal of the past (as some Communist writers suggested), but a deeper appreciation of literary tradition. Phillips and Rahv identified themselves with "the thin line of revolutionary writers who are trying to assimilate the whole past." Whatever other reasons conscientious Marxists might have to study history, the two young critics clearly expected benefits from the effort that were specifically literary. Phillips argued, for example, that an "entirely adequate prospect in history can be had only from an exhaustive retrospect." The "exhaustive" study of the literary past promised, in this case, a deeper understanding of the present and the future. At another point, the editors jointly issued the admonition that "unless we are acutely aware of the body of literature as a whole, no standards of merit are possible."[64] Believing that the influence of radicalism must make literature more sophisticated, not less so, Phillips and Rahv worried a good deal about standards on the left and regularly looked to literary tradition for guidance on matters of artistic quality. The past contained a richness that serious writers simply could not afford to ignore.

The attempt to be both militantly radical and sensitive to the heritage of tradition created understandable intellectual tensions for Phillips and Rahv, especially during 1934. In an early essay they identified one of the problems facing radical literature as "the differentiation between class-alien and usable elements in the literature of the past." The very terms "class-alien" and "usable" suggested the balancing act the editors were trying to perform: "class-alien" was a purely political concept that emphasized *exclusion* of all ideas or materials not judged appropriate by *political* standards; "usable," implying the notion of a "usable past" made popular by Brooks, urged an *inclusion* in the writer's world of traditional elements selected on the basis of *literary* standards. The spirit of the two terms was quite opposed, and it soon became clear with which Phillips and Rahv were most in sympathy. The editors sought to make the idea of usability mean a serious and sincere grappling with literary tradition, not a wholesale rejection of its major works accompanied by graverobbing extractions of isolated fragments.[65] The past as a source of standards, and the past as a repository of lessons in writing, became familiar themes in the early criticism of Phillips and Rahv.

For *Partisan Review* at its best, the traditions of literature had affinities not with the short-term strategies of radical politics but with the broad humanistic vision of Marxism to which its editors were most strongly drawn. Respecting the past meant retaining "the cultural acquisitions of humanity as a *background of values*."[66] Art was part of what made life worth living, and the traditions of art helped sustain cultural and social progress. Phillips and Rahv spoke with great regard, almost with reverence, about "the function of art in making life significant by giving form, meaning, and continuity to human experience": "Individual life would remain hopelessly pragmatic and isolated from its historic context were it not for the continuous transmission of human values, hopes and motives — in short, the mind of mankind. If the fund of human experience were not socialized by such instruments as art, the intelligence and rational behavior of man would remain a constant potential."[67] As Phillips and Rahv saw it, attempts to divorce radical literature from the past denied the very idea of synthesis, and blanket attacks on the heritage of culture threatened a loss of sophistication that could only undermine artistic advance.

Change was a matter of continuous process for Phillips and Rahv, and Marxism appealed to them in part because they believed in the early thirties that the notion of evolutionary change found its highest embodiment in the philosophy of dialectical materialism. Radical ideas could have a dramatic impact on literature, according to *Partisan Review*, because Marxism showed the way to significant change without a sharp disruption of literary tradition. Time and time again, the editors tried to identify radicalism with notions of process and continuity. Rahv announced that one novel proved "the validity of the Marxian principle of cultural continuity" because the author had "not made the mistake of discarding the literary heritage." Phillips asserted that "the art of a new class introduces decisive slants into a *continuum* of sensibility." The editors together declared in 1936 that progress toward an integrated radical art had come through the work of those who understood that theirs was a "revolt within the tradition of poetry rather than against it." Phillips and Rahv would not let go of their conviction that change must grow out of the past and must attempt no highhanded denials of it.[68]

The emphasis on continuity in *Partisan Review* was not intended to provide justifications for opposing radical change, but to promote the right kind of radical development, particularly in culture. When Phillips and Rahv warned that without artistic continuity with the past mankind's "intelligence and rational behavior" would remain fixed at a "constant potential," they held up the serious threat—and to them it was nothing less than that—of cultural sterility and intellectual stagnation. A correct understanding of the Marxist philosophy and literary tradition would produce an "everfresh balance" between the writer's unique qualities and his general social outlook. The thrust of their whole conception of change was that although there could be no sudden leaps, there must be ongoing development, perpetual rebirth, ever-present opportunity. Marxism properly understood sustained both continuity and dynamism. Vulgar Marxism, like any body of fixed ideas, limited development and stunted growth, producing only stasis and "the tedium of endless repetition." The conviction that change must be continuous and open-ended reflected another side of the spirit of cosmopolitanism that shaped the entire perspective of *Partisan Review*.[69]

The appeal of Marxism for Phillips, Rahv, and the early *Partisan Review* depended, then, on at least three fundamental beliefs about its promise and meaning: the belief that Marxism could provide a unifying philosophy to end the longstanding divisions in American culture; the belief that Marxism embodied and would advance cosmopolitan values; and the belief that Marxism supported respect for the past within an appreciation of constant change. These ideas helped define a positive position for *Partisan Review*; they also helped to separate that position from some of the passions and principles that constituted the meaning of Marxism for others. It has frequently been suggested, for example, that radicalism provided some of its adherents with a substitute for religious faith or that communism became a vehicle for "messianic" or "utopian" visions.[70] However appropriate such images might be to describe the longings of some radicals, they have little to do with the perspective developed in *Partisan Review*. The version of cosmopolitanism embraced by Phillips, Rahv, and others who would join them later was openly skeptical of religious feeling; their notions of history and process allowed room neither for the sudden leap to glory implied by "messianic" ideas nor for the perfect and static goal integral to the yearning for utopia. They were radicals of another stripe.

The division between those who longed for utopian or millennial bliss through Marxism, and those like Phillips and Rahv who assumed continuing conflict and change, was sometimes sharp. At such moments the fundamentally different assumptions that led intellectuals to Marxism, and the deeply opposed interpretations of its import, came out from under the obscuring cover of the "radical movement." One such clarifying confrontation of ideas came in the fourth issue of *Partisan Review*. In an "alleged conversation" with Joseph Wood Krutch, Sergei Eisenstein had reportedly remarked that in the classless society "with perfection reigning and no unsatisfied desires left, art, being essentially a compensation, will wither away." Rahv reacted angrily to Eisenstein's remark, declaring that "this idea of the classless desert of art is at loggerheads with the basic principles of Marxism," and he went on to a more sweeping statement of his position:

> It is absurd to speak of "perfection" in characterizing the classless society. Change the Marxist recognizes as the sole absolute, and in the classless society there will be new contradictions and new struggles—with this difference, however: these new contradictions and struggles will develop on an incomparably higher level. For it is then, with the extinction of the fight for individual existence, that man will for the first time in history actually enter into his human estate.[71]

Rahv had issued a strong rejection of the very possibility of stasis or perfection in society. The revolution ushering in a classless society was not the ultimate goal. Politics and ideology were means—means to remove the obstacles to culture found in "the fight for individual existence"—not ends. When Phillips and Rahv commented elsewhere that "today Marxism is [the] most advanced ideology," they left ample room for the notion that tomorrow another choice might be necessary.[72] *Partisan Review*'s characteristic perspective contained its full complement of literary idealism, but it did not invest radicalism with religious emotion or nurture messianic and utopian dreams.

The critical bias against religion, perfectionism, and fixed doctrine in *Partisan Review* owed a good deal to the philosophical tradition of American pragmatism. In the middle 1930s, one man stood above all others in offering intellectuals a version of radical thought with a distinct pragmatic tinge — Sidney Hook. A scholar of Marx and a graduate student of John Dewey, Hook felt that he could merge the philosophies of both into a system that would answer the needs of the present without injustice to either. In addition to a flood of shorter pieces, he published two books on Marxism that gave full and creative expression to his ideas: *Towards the Understanding of Karl Marx* (1933) and *From Hegel to Marx* (1936).

Hook's interpretation made Marxism very much an open-ended rather than a deterministic philosophy. According to Hook, Marxism took into account all of the social and historical factors impinging on human conduct, and it assumed that an individual's perceptions and behavior were influenced by his class origins and his social environment. It nevertheless left ample room for human choice and human action to change the future, and it saw that future as indeterminate and difficult. Unity in Marx's thought was to be found "not in his specific conclusions but in his method of analysis." It was thus conveniently possible "to dissociate the Marxian method from any specific set of conclusions, or any particular political tactic advocated in its name." Hook's version of a Marxist approach to change held that after the revolution, struggles would persist "on a more elevated plane" as mankind dealt "not with the problem of social existence, but with the deeper problems of personal development."[73]

Phillips and Rahv certainly knew of Hook's work — Phillips was in a class of Hook's on Marxism in 1933 — and if their own views were not strongly influenced by Hook, then there was a remarkable coincidence of interpretation.[74] The ideas of Marx, of Dewey, and of Hook became something of a blend, and the editors of *Partisan Review* seem to have read all three and incorporated parts of each into their own notions of radical thought. Yet Hook's position and the inheritance of social thought he represented were not wholly satisfactory to Phillips and Rahv. Some hesitancy about his ideas might have arisen in the early thirties simply because the two editors were drawn toward the Communist apparatus just at the time when Hook was becoming increasingly hostile to the

Party. The more serious and more lasting reservations, however, were rooted in the side of the editors' heritage that suggested that there were limitations in the whole naturalistic and pragmatic tradition.

Cultural radicals going back to the teens had shared some of the assumptions supporting pragmatism and its offshoots. Nevertheless, Van Wyck Brooks with his animadversions on the dominance of pragmatism and Bourne in his impassioned wartime essays had developed an argument that pragmatic theory, first, emphasized technique and method at the expense of clear purposes and goals and, second, lacked sensitivity to the spirit and the needs of art. Sidney Hook, in merging Deweyan process with radical ends, tried to present a philosophy in which Marxism overcame the seeming neutrality of pragmatic method by achieving a combination of method with direction.[75] In addressing one standard complaint of cultural radicals, Hook's ideas may have helped Phillips and Rahv believe that rational analytic procedures could be married to a revolutionary cause. Yet the charge of insensitivity to art and culture remained.

An emphasis on the exercise of intelligence such as that found in Dewey, Bourne had charged in 1917, represented only half of what was needed. The properly integrated perspective contained "intelligence suffused by feeling, and feeling given fibre and outline by intelligence."[76] Pragmatism had come to seem too dry, too closed, too mechanical—prepared to categorize, to adjust, and to tame life but not to make full room for its diversity, its artistic vitality, and its uniqueness. Such a critical stance toward pragmatic social theory shaped Phillips's and Rahv's reactions to the ideas of Dewey and Hook. In considering the relation of form to content, for example, Phillips rejected both Dewey's and Hook's analyses of the question because they remained trapped by categories that could not comprehend the spirit of a living art.[77] Even in later years, when Hook had become a close political ally of *Partisan Review*, there would remain significant differences between Hook and most of the literary intellectuals around the magazine over just how far pragmatic philosophical method could extend into the realm of culture.

Phillips and Rahv combined in their own ideas, and gave to the early *Partisan Review*, a commitment running in two directions. This double commitment, woven into the basic fabric of the editors' radical cosmopolitan perspective, made the intellectual stance of the magazine distinctive. *Partisan Review* demanded both the regularizing and predictive authority of system and science in intellectual life, and the openness, looseness, and freedom to accommodate the variety, spontaneity, and uniqueness of literary creation. The editors might place most of their weight on one foot in a particular essay in order to counterbalance what they saw as excess in the views of others, but their dual commitment never remained hidden for long. The Marxism that Phillips and Rahv embraced was a Marxism that promised both system and freedom, intellectual power and an absence of restrictions on ideas. And once having found and shaped a perspective that would sustain their literary dreams, the editors of *Partisan Review* were loath either to give it up or to accept any competing view of what Marxism ought to mean. The notions of cultural advance within a framework of cosmopolitan values that informed the early *Partisan Review* did not add up to a fully developed literary-philosophical position. But they did give the magazine substance and bite, and they did help it resist, through a certain independence of analysis and judgment, some of the more extreme postures of the period.

Chapter Three | Cosmopolitanism and the Threat of Reaction

When read at a distance of several decades, the literary disputes of the thirties seem marked by a sharpness and bitterness out of proportion to the surface issues at stake. Sincere concern over specific interpretations of literature or even the prickly vanities of critical reputation go only part of the way toward explaining the tone of these debates or their deeply rooted presumption of sweeping relevance. Writing *On Native Grounds* while memories of these battles were still fresh, Alfred Kazin tried earnestly to explain the mood of the period. For the critics of the thirties, he wrote, the crisis in criticism was "really a crisis in the whole moral order of civilization, a crisis in which critics, seeking and applying new standards, illuminating the necessary social forces, helping to create a brilliant new literature, would play a leading role." Criticism became a "philosophical front where the great central forces seeking to rebuild the world were locked together in battle," and critics stood convinced that they were "helping to save the whole domain of culture."

If Kazin's explanation said little about the actual impact of criticism, it said much about the way critics saw themselves. Phillips and Rahv often took on just such a mantle as Kazin described. Yet Kazin saw in the critics of the thirties much more than a belief that their ideas might be vital, structuring, or even conclusive. He saw in the critical temperament of the decade a dark and threatening side — critics characterized by "quarreling factionalism" and "narrowness." The conservative Formalists emerged in Kazin's picture "as a race of conscientious fanatics, working in fragmentary elucidations, stifling in their narrow zeal," while the "typical Marxist . . . persistently subordinated esthetic values to a rigid social doctrine." Although there might seem to be little in common between the Formalists and the Marxists, "the search for an absolute that each represented brought them together in spirit."[1]

67

On both political and literary grounds, Kazin's view was too simplistic, too insistent on the polarity of the thirties. Such an explanation of the immediate past reflected a desire to leave it behind as quickly as possible. Kazin went so far as to label the criticism of the thirties "a totalitarianism in an age of totalitarianisms," suggesting in this rather strained use of a still-new term less a desire to analyze than a desire to condemn. No such uncomplicated tale of extremism can encompass the contending currents of the thirties, and it certainly cannot describe with any insight the early history of *Partisan Review*. Yet it was the *Partisan Review* intellectuals themselves who helped provide the explanations and the images of the thirties that, in the hands of others, tended to mask or bury the magazine's values and its history. One of the major props of Kazin's picture of criticism was the linkage between left and right asserted in the claim of absolutism and implied in the charge of "totalitarianism." *Partisan Review* had participated actively in creating and justifying that linkage in the minds of intellectuals. Indeed, the notion of "totalitarianism" embodied the central conclusion of the magazine's circle about the Communist Party and the Soviet state under Stalin.

The process by which *Partisan Review* moved toward this conclusion made up a vital part of the magazine's history in the thirties. At the level of public commitments and surface loyalties, it would seem by 1937 that the editors of *Partisan Review* had sharply reversed themselves. Deeper currents told a different story. From the beginning in 1934, the values that formed the lineaments of *Partisan Review*'s cosmopolitan perspective shaped the positions of Phillips and Rahv and brought them into increasing conflict with the sanctioned cultural programs of the Communist Party. On questions of intellectual standards and cultural values, the record of *Partisan Review* in the thirties is not primarily one of sharp change but one of fundamental continuity.

Making its debut in the midst of the moral and political storm and stress of the early thirties, *Partisan Review* shared fully in the sense of significance and expectation surrounding literature and criticism. Convinced that a great literature was struggling to be born, Phillips and Rahv anticipated that *Partisan Review* would lead in settling the necessary questions to speed it on its way. They expected to matter, and for a time their confidence in the radical movement was a reflection of their confidence in their own ideas. Within the first two issues of *Partisan Review*, the two editors began to present a rather broad scheme for understanding the emergence of radical literature and to assert their own values as essential. Perhaps Phillips's early essay "Three Generations" can serve to illustrate the ways in which the parts of the editors' perspective meshed in a single interpretive vision, and the ways in which cosmopolitan values molded their critical and polemical stance.[2]

Phillips's essay laid down emphatic claims about the nature and direction of contemporary literary development. The three generations under discussion—American writers representing respectively the teens, the twenties, and the thirties—formed a dialectical pattern for Phillips within which the first two groups provided the necessary opposing tendencies and the youngest, the "proletarian generation," offered the "synthesis." The pattern assumed a strong forward movement from the bourgeois past to the radical present, and it drew primary attention to the generation that would fuse divergent trends and raise literature to new levels. The imminent synthesis, in this view, was powerful testimony to the beneficial effects of a Marxist philosophy in culture.

At the same time, another pattern was at work: Phillips made the recent history of American literature a condensed version of the history of French literature described by Edmund Wilson in *Axel's Castle*. There was an important difference, however. French literature, which had long been recognized as the most advanced, was running out of gas; American literature, starting late, had rushed along its parallel course while accelerating. Several decades behind the French in the teens, American writers had caught up to them in the twenties and now, through the development of radical literature, were about to surge beyond the exhaustion of symbolism and the decline of the bourgeoisie to claim preeminence. The dream of a mature American literature marched hand in hand with the vision of radical synthesis in the structure of "Three Generations." The triumph of American culture and the triumph of radical culture would occur together. Indeed, for the early *Partisan Review* they were identical.

Phillips's specific descriptions of the American literary generations provided evidence of the values informing the editors' notions of cultural progress. Phillips chose his words carefully to reveal the contrast between the two earlier generations and the pattern of advance toward the present. The generation shaped before World War I—Phillips mentioned Dreiser, Anderson, Lewis, Robinson, and Sandburg—exhibited "a firm setting in American soil, and a social interest." Not technically or intellectually advanced, writers of this period were "generally free of sophistication and verve, almost to the point of provincialism"; they remained unaware of the "'autonomous,' speculative capacities of the mind." To provide a label, the style of the teens was naturalism, "the nearest thing to the Zola period in France that America had produced." This was a "sociological" generation, rooted in the bare facts of a rural America and trailing far behind European literary developments.

The "lost" generation of the twenties repudiated the outlook of the teens, according to Phillips, just as their "French forerunners, the Symbolists, Cubists, Dadaists, and Surrealists," had repudiated Zola's naturalism. Rejecting the obsession with social facts, they took as their prototype "Paul Valery, to whom writing was a form of speculative research." Writers experimented with the "linguistic methods of Joyce," with the "extreme 'detached' techniques of Dadaism and Surrealism," and with the possibilities of other traditions. It was clear that this generation produced a more sophisticated American literature, for Americans were now operating on the same level as contemporary French writers. Phillips declared in summary that "the period turned out to be one of transition, one of infiltration of new currents, one of cosmopolitanization." Criticism at the same time became "more urbane, more subtle."

Both earlier generations were labeled "extreme" in some way; and the contrast between an immersion in social facts and head-in-the-clouds "speculative research" simply restated the familiar opposition of lowbrow and highbrow. Yet it was quite apparent in Phillips's choice of terms that—despite the interest of good Marxists in the sociological approach—he favored the generation of the twenties. Progressing along its upward path toward maturity, American writing had climbed from a "firm setting in American soil" to a "more urbane, more subtle" height; it had moved in the direction of city forms and away from rural values. On intellectual grounds the contrast between the more provincial and the more cosmopolitan generations was clear. Whereas writers of the teens were "free of sophistication" and unaware of the "'autonomous,' speculative capacities of the mind," the generation of the twenties reveled in speculation and experimentation and assimilated "many significant ideas of the period." Phillips was arguing that literature must be open, sophisticated, and complex. He was also suggesting that literature took on such traits as it became increasingly the product of an urban sensibility.

The process of "cosmopolitanization," as Phillips described it, implied even more, suggesting a change in the social as well as the intellectual environment. The movement from near provincialism toward intellectual openness and radical synthesis signified the arrival not just of new ideas but of new men. Phillips and Rahv cherished, and cultivated, this possibility. Believing that the circumstances of the early thirties gave promise of lifting up the most significant body of writers in history, the editors of *Partisan Review* worked to identify that promise with the younger men and women of their own generation. Phillips's notion of "cosmopolitanization" leading toward synthesis quietly erected an intellectual turret gun that could swing either right or left to bring potential rivals under withering fire.

To the right were most of the writers of the past, who naturally fell short of the rising generation because they lacked the most advantageous political-philosophical structure for their work. Phillips could readily acknowledge in his analysis that the modernist writers and critics of the twenties had made important strides. Yet, though they might worthily strive for a more objective and scientific criticism, their efforts were doomed to failure, since "for the most part (with the exception of some of the recent work of those who have accepted Marxism), their premises are false." Phillips hastened to add, however, that their admirable aims would not be lost, for the new generation felt fully equipped "to effect these aims in our criticism."

If modernists, crippled by the lack of Marxism, proved inadequate in one direction, older radical writers who had bypassed the modernist experience fell short in the other. A start toward "revolutionary literature" had indeed been made by "a few confident pioneers" like Joseph Freeman, Michael Gold, and Joshua Kunitz. But now "a new generation of revolutionary writers" was rising. Which generation should take the lead? The older writers, it seemed, had missed the modernist boat: "the strain and the exigencies of pioneering kept them from assimilating the literary spirit of the twenties." For the younger writers, on the other hand, it could be safely said that "the spirit of the twenties is part of our heritage."

Phillips and Rahv claimed for their own generation the benefits of both youth and maturity. Writers of their age group had grown up at just the right pace to absorb ideas from the teens, to experience modernism, and to adopt Marxism as the depression struck; yet they retained the youthful vigor and ambition that could provide fresh insight and energy to propel radical literature ahead. The "proletarian generation" had the advantage of not having "to make any *transition* to a revolutionary outlook"; younger writers bene-

71

fited from the "added perspective" time had given them, which was enabling them "to assimilate many currents which the revolutionary pioneers in the intensity of their struggle had to ignore." Phillips and Rahv, in effect, dismissed the older radicals with a pat on the back for past services.

The patterns of the dialectic and of the highbrow-lowbrow understanding of American culture, when tied to the values of cosmopolitanism and the assumption of progress, delivered to relatively inexperienced critics a basis for confident judgments of past generations and contemporary rivals alike. Both patterns allowed Phillips and Rahv to see themselves as holding a balanced, well-integrated position in the center of a dynamic stream, while their predecessors or opponents inevitably adopted "extreme" opinions that would confine them ultimately to some historical eddy. Because only movement toward a proper synthesis could be truly progressive, those who overemphasized one-sided commitments could potentially be judged counter-progressive. And because urban, secular, intellectual, and cosmopolitan values were so intertwined with the notion of literary advance, any hint of rural, religious, anti-intellectual, or parochial values might well raise an alarm against cultural, social, and political reaction.

The critical instrument fashioned by Phillips and Rahv was strong and flexible, but it was also itself vulnerable to distortions and to dogmatic usage. Especially in the early years of Marxian enthusiasm, cultural targets were sometimes chosen on political as well as on literary grounds, and there was a great temptation to let the fire fly in accordance with the passions and prophecies of the moment. Such a tendency was evident even within "Three Generations." Believing that writers must move toward either communism or fascism, Phillips found it all too easy to assume a direct connection between literary talent and correct political choice. By logical extension, lesser talents would tend to make the wrong political choice, so those not choosing communism must be the less gifted writers: "It seems almost natural that Allen Tate, for example, whose poetry and criticism is so turgid, should have receded into the reactionary hybrid of Harvard humanism and Southern feudalism." Nothing could do more to undermine Phillips's and Rahv's theoretical emphasis on balanced and sophisticated criticism than such a simplistic approach. The two editors had to struggle constantly against the tendency toward quick and facile judgments of those who differed from them. And it was a struggle they often lost. Yet though they failed in these early years to achieve the level of critical sophistication to which they aspired, Phillips and Rahv had staked out a cultural position that gave them both orientation and identity.

Armed with a magazine and a framework of ideas, Phillips and Rahv stood ready to resist whatever threatened the development of a radical synthesis. At *Partisan Review*'s birth, this seemed to require frequent comment on the inadequacies of bourgeois art when compared with the emerging richness of revolutionary civilization. Such discussions of non-Marxist writers provided a proving ground where Phillips and Rahv could elaborate their critical perspective, apply their standards, and develop their language of reproach.

The most pervasive weakness of literature over the previous century had been philosophical. From "Gustave Flaubert to E. E. Cummings," Rahv declared, the "middle class literature of despair" had attacked the philistinism of modern life without seeing its sources in the "predatory social order" of capitalism. Without the clarifying framework of Marxist materialism, without adequate contact with social ideas, the insurgence of modern writers had remained "locked in the cage of philosophic idealism."[3] Formalism, a critical approach associated mainly with southerners that would lead into the "new criticism" of the 1940s, demonstrated the imbalance engendered by idealism in its tendency to "beat a forced retreat from meaning" and to concentrate on "the single dimension of technique." Such criticism was "constantly evading the responsibilities of a unified approach."[4] The mention of "responsibilities" contained a hint of moral judgment and a strong claim to a higher seriousness on the part of radical critics like Phillips and Rahv. The quest for a "unified approach" had always been something of a crusade.

At the level of general analysis, it was rather easy to dismiss bourgeois writers as lacking an adequate philosophy. Specific discussions required a more elaborate argument to make room, first, for a defense of what Phillips and Rahv found to be positive in the literature of the past and, second, for the individual qualities of particular writers and works. The editors were forced in these discussions to identify more clearly what they approved and what they rejected; and this meant a more specific revelation of the values on which their general claims about intellectual adequacy and literary progress rested. The articulation — and over time the evolution — of the editors' stance unfolded in part through their attempts to deal with the critical problems presented by T. S. Eliot.

An acknowledged influence on Phillips and Rahv themselves and

73

on their whole generation, Eliot quite obviously qualified as a major modernist figure and as a writer of exceptional talent; yet he had turned right, not left, at the end of the twenties. The problem facing Phillips and Rahv, given their assumptions, was to preserve the importance of Eliot as a critical and poetic influence, while explaining away and condemning his present conservatism. Rahv made his first attempt to accomplish this feat in an early essay that rated Eliot "one of the most significant voices of the age." Eliot's first book, *Poems*, exhibited the "intense dynamism of profound revolt" as the poet struggled "to tear off the mask of piety and virtue from the smug bourgeoisie of New England." There was "no compromise, no cowardice." The work was "vital with genuine social substance" and "a positive step" toward a new worldview through "repudiation of the old."

But then came the fall. Eliot lost his courage and sounded a retreat. The poet sought escape from bourgeois decadence in religion, retreating as he did so to a historical stage that had preceded the rise of the bourgeoisie—feudalism. The values of "Anglo-Catholicism in religion, royalism in politics, and classicism in literature," Rahv declared, were "utterly irrelevant" to a twentieth century in which it was "as possible to be a religious poet as . . . to be a feudal knight." Eliot had plunged precipitously into reaction: "The ancestral complex, the calvinistic past, and the false evasions of the classic bourgeois had all re-asserted themselves," and Eliot was "left to creep . . . back to Beacon Street via the new-humanist local."[5]

There are several things worth noting about Rahv's analysis. First, it assumed a firm link between politics and literature. When Eliot was a rebel, he was a rebel in both spheres; when he retreated, it was on all fronts. Second, Rahv's positive and negative terms ranged across the cultural, political, and social realms. He associated Eliot at various points with a New England regional tradition, with Beacon Street, with the "calvinistic past," and with "puritan" gentility —all of which formed an interconnected representation of an American cultural establishment evoking social resentments as well as literary hostility. Opposite this imagery Rahv placed the positive forces of "plebian" rebellion and the "age of science." Third, the pattern that Rahv's analysis suggested became a bulwark of *Partisan Review*'s early position: major figures in the modernist movement had made important contributions in the twenties that must not be overlooked, but they had lost their power through a failure of will and an inability to grasp the proper philosophical perspective. Such a pattern meshed nicely both with the claim that twenties modernism provided an essential experience that older radicals had missed and with the argument that this highest of recent cultural achievements must now be transcended by a younger generation.

The values and assumptions behind Rahv's analysis soon provided support for extending the condemnation of Eliot's present position. Given the belief that all writers must move toward either fascism or communism, the logic of what conservative attitudes might indicate seemed clear. In only the second number of *Partisan Review*, Phillips followed this logic to its conclusion in a bitter attack on Eliot provoked by Eliot's remark that "reasons of race and religion combine to make any large number of free-thinking Jews undesirable." Phillips's anger at Eliot steamed forth: "the evolution of his views toward the right, the implicit reactionary politics throughout his writing, and his latest medley of feudal and Catholic themes in *After Strange Gods* leave no doubt as to his position. Only the blind would hesitate to call Eliot a fascist." Phillips ticked off the counts against Eliot that had sent him into the depths: Eliot's recent pronouncements demonstrated "an ever more ecstatic espousal of the church, the state, an aristocracy of intellect, racial purity—in short, of most of the forces and myths which foster fascism." And Eliot had subscribed to "the feudal agrarianism and regional patriotism championed by the contributors to *I'll Take My Stand*."[6]

Taken together, Rahv's and Phillips's attacks on the Eliot of the thirties incorporated into one image of reaction the dangers and failings of religion, feudalism, regionalism, upper-class cultural castes, resistance to scientific thought, "authoritarianism," nationalism ("the state"), ruralism, and racism. The spectrum of negative judgments in these attacks depended directly on the positive values from which the editors worked—the values they believed essential to progress toward a radical cosmopolitan synthesis. From their perspective, the modernists for all their contributions, and the Formalist critics for all their technical knowledge, were one-sided extremists of a distinctly highbrow type who, in the radical context of the thirties, were socially, intellectually, and politically regressive.

This, at least, was the conclusion that in all its harshness made sense to Phillips and Rahv during the first year of *Partisan Review*'s existence. The most pressing task appeared to be correcting the excesses of aestheticism by instilling literature with a respect for social ideas and by encouraging the unifying outlook of a radical philosophy. Even within the ranks of those who had declared their sympathy for radicalism, the lingering influence of aestheticism remained a problem. The trouble with pseudo-radical writers of the "right-wing tendency," Phillips and Rahv complained, was that their work differed "but slightly from that of liberal bourgeois writers." Their "semi-revolutionary approach" led not to a new literature but to a warmed-over version of modernism.[7] The right wing stretched across a broad front, including, with varying degrees of culpability, most who placed too narrow an emphasis on the techniques and methods of literature, and all who fell short of Phillips's and Rahv's own confidence in radical ideas.

Yet even in *Partisan Review*'s earliest days, at the height of the magazine's enthusiasm for the Communist Party and revolutionary militance, there was another side to the editors' criticism of existing literary modes. Synthesis could not be achieved by reversing the one-sided emphasis of aestheticism and rushing to the opposite extreme—a preoccupation with social concerns and immediate politics at the expense of artistic quality. This was the position of the "leftists" who were leading proletarian literature astray.

As soon as Phillips and Rahv had their feet firmly planted at *Partisan Review*, they began to address systematically distortions within the radical movement. Announcing in their first joint editorial that Marxian criticism had not faced squarely the problem of "diverse tendencies" in radical literature, Phillips and Rahv gave notice that they intended to cause trouble by mocking the "illusion" that "revolutionary writers constitute one happy family." Within a few paragraphs they had launched what was to remain one of their most sweeping assaults on the failings of "leftism" in proletarian literature:

> Its zeal to steep literature overnight in the political program of Communism results in the attempt to force the reader's responses through a barrage of sloganized and inorganic writing. "Leftism," by tacking on political perspectives to awkward literary forms, drains literature of its more specific qualities. . . . It assumes a direct line between economic base and ideology, and in this way distorts and vulgarizes the complexity of human nature, the motives of action and their expression in thought and feeling. In theory the "leftist" subscribes to the Marxian thesis of the continuity of culture, but in practice he makes a mockery of it by combating all endeavors to use the heritage of the past. In criticism the "leftist" substitutes gush on the one hand, and invective on the

other, for analysis; and it is not difficult to see that to some of these critics Marxism is not a science but a sentiment.[8]

The central argument in this multifaceted attack was the charge that politics — represented in this negative context by the "political program of Communism," *not* by Marxism — was distorting culture and draining literature of "its more specific qualities." Involvement with the catchpenny realities of the business of politics seemed to have the corrupting effect on art that was typical of the lowbrow.

If the "rightists" had been led astray by their adherence to the wrong philosophy, the "leftists" proved that even with an apparent devotion to the correct philosophy, false interpretation could have the most serious consequences for cultural understanding. The vulgar belief of "mechanical materialism" that the economic base directly determined ideology stood behind "leftism"; rather than helping to solve the problem of dualism, it created in the writer a new dualism "between his artistic consciousness and his beliefs."[9] A proper perspective would achieve synthesis through a grappling with "the dialectical interaction between consciousness and environment," between highbrow intellect and lowbrow realities. Confident that the position of *Partisan Review* was the correct one, Rahv spoke elsewhere as if there could be no debate about the relation of radical ideas to literature: "Marxism fights the vulgarization of literature by its 'leftist' hangers-on; it will not and cannot support the desire of a group of primitives to hypostasize their lack of talent and to repudiate the cultural heritage."[10] The charge of primitivism, like that of no talent, was meant to sting.

Quite obviously, Phillips and Rahv did not associate "leftism" with the promise of the rising proletarian generation. When the editors of *Partisan Review* spoke of a desirable proletarian literature, they had in mind writing that would represent their own vision of radical synthesis. The struggle to distinguish between the proper proletarian course and the errant path of "leftism" was one motive behind the balancing act performed in "Three Generations," where Phillips assailed the "leftists" for repudiating the modernist heritage altogether and for simply returning to "the tradition of primitive, 'popular' writing."[11] Those who rejected the intellectual advances of the twenties, according to Phillips and Rahv, were doubly damned as extremists and provincials. Whereas the cosmopolitanized critics of the twenties might at least strive "for objectivity (as opposed to gush)," the "leftists" substituted "gush on the one hand, and invective on the other, for analysis," throwing overboard the methods of critical intelligence by preferring sentiment to science.[12]

The tendency to use "quantitative standards" in the chase after popularity introduced all the degradations of commercialism, parochial simplicity, and anti-intellectualism associated with the lowbrow tradition. A genuine radical literature must look to different standards. The new poetic methods of the twenties that "leftists" scorned were "not mere eccentricities, but the result of the assimilation of urban environments in poetry, reflecting the entire modern sensibility." Coming to grips with urban complexity and sophistication marked a progressive achievement that radical writers must build upon, not deny. The traditional dualism in American culture, which "leftism" threatened to prolong, cried out for the healing power of a synthesis based on cosmopolitan values.[13]

The recognition of what proletarian literature had thus far been, and the vision of what it might be, formed poles of frustration and enthusiasm in the editors' attitude toward radical culture. Rahv exhibited both feelings in one of his many pronouncements calling for a richer and less restrictive approach to radical writing:

> Our poets cannot return to the vapid sublimities of Victorian
> verse, or to the homespun doggerel of the sectarian past.
> Neither is it necessary to encase Marx's titanic brain in a
> steel helmet. The variety and complexity—yes, exactly that—
> of our philosophy and of our experience, to be recreated,
> must command a poetry both various and complex.[14]

The images created in radical art must not be one-sided and simplistic but unified and whole: "political content should not be isolated from the rest of experience but must be merged into the creation of complete personalities"; and the artist must comprehend "human experience in all its multiplicity." Those who failed to understand this were guilty of an "excessive rationalism" and "a vulgar utilitarian attitude to writing."[15] Variety, complexity, multiplicity—such terms laid down a demand for openness and diversity in radical literature, qualities that Phillips and Rahv found sadly lacking in the writing most vigorously encouraged by the Communist Party. The editors of *Partisan Review* were not yet ready in the first issues of the magazine to proclaim that the most prominent leaders of proletarian literature, the editors of the *New Masses*, were "leftists" and thus subject to all their strictures; but that was clearly what they were suggesting.

The challenge to "leftism" burst forth from the same wellspring of positive values that had poured its critical streams on Eliot. Although certain elements, like the question of religion, did not carry over at this point, both campaigns were rooted in the same analysis of the dualism in American culture, in the same assumptions about the desirability of synthesis, and in the same body of cosmopolitan values and attitudes. But if this was the case, why did the attack on "leftism" not flow to its logical conclusion? Like Eliot and the Formalists, the "leftists" were one-sided, narrow, and extreme; for different reasons, each group stood accused of restricting free-thinking intellectuals and stultifying literature; both impeded the forward movement of culture; both obstructed the further progress of cosmopolitanization. For their sins, Eliot and the Formalists were declared reactionary, even fascist. What about the "leftists"? Were they not reactionary by the same standard?

In 1934 such a conclusion could not be allowed. And there is no sign that Phillips and Rahv ever considered this possibility. Because the correct radical position on literature was still in the making, because the direction of Communist cultural development was about to be changed through the leadership of *Partisan Review*, because the "leftists" were at least radical allies in a world still firmly bourgeois, Phillips and Rahv had no cause to develop an explicit parallel between left and right extremes. Yet the potential was there. As tensions grew between *Partisan Review* on the one hand, and the *New Masses* and Communist policy on the other, that potential moved closer to being tapped.

Phillips's and Rahv's optimism that they could change the direction of proletarian literature was seemingly rewarded within a few months of *Partisan Review*'s founding. "From its first issue," Walter Rideout has remarked, "*Partisan Review* had become the base of operations for one side in a literary civil war." The *Partisan* side in this war, insisting on the importance of high artistic standards for radical literature, had gained enough ground against "leftism" to claim a major victory at the national meeting of the John Reed Clubs in September 1934. According to the report published in *Partisan Review*, "members of the writers' commission . . . directed a collective attack against writing which consists of unconvincing, sloganized tracts disguised as poetry and fiction." The report left no doubt as to who should claim the credit for this surge of right thinking; the discussion "indicated that *Partisan Review* was exerting a wide influence among the young writers." Phillips and Rahv each gave a speech to the conference delegates, and Phillips became a member of the National Committee of the Reed Clubs. The young editors seemed to have ample reason to be pleased with their first months of work.[16]

Yet the same report contained hints that perhaps *Partisan Review*'s self-congratulation was a bit hollow. The notation that Alexander Trachtenberg "brought the greetings of the Communist Party to the conference" suggested that the young writers were not entirely on their own. Trachtenberg did join in "denouncing the sectarianism of the cultural movement," and his proposal "that the National Committee of the John Reed Clubs take the initiative in organizing a National Writers' Congress" gave no reason for suspicion. But in fact the decision had already been made in Party councils to disband the John Reed Clubs. International Communist policy was beginning to shift toward the preoccupation with opposing fascism that would lead to Popular Front cooperation with liberals.[17]

Partisan Review happily publicized the Writers' Congress for which Trachtenberg had called. At the same time, the editors put in a plug for the Reed Clubs as one of the "richest sources" of radical literary experience and eagerly offered *Partisan Review* as a forum for "thorough discussion" of the issues to be addressed. Such comments hinted that perhaps the editors had begun to wonder about the implications of the congress idea for their magazine and for the younger radical generation.[18] By February of 1935, the New York Reed Club had been closed down. The Communist Party had informed only those club members who were also Party members of this move, and Party leaders apparently intended to dump permanently those "writers" who had not published.[19] Although Rahv and Phillips (who was not a Party member) may have had their doubts about the high-handedness of this, they were probably sympathetic to the idea of encouraging only "real" writers.

In any case, *Partisan Review*, still announcing that it was published by the John Reed Club of New York, carried through on its plan to devote the April–May issue to discussions in preparation for the Writers' Congress, with Phillips and Rahv contributing the centerpiece on criticism. Although Phillips and Rahv did not use the term "leftism" in their essay, they complained of the failures of earlier Marxist criticism in language that made it clear that the magazine's literary stance had not been abandoned. Newton Arvin declared himself largely in agreement with Phillips and Rahv, and even Granville Hicks conceded a good deal to their position. But for all his concessions, Hicks still tried to claim a radical superior-

80

ity through a counterattack on "uncomradely sniping and back-biting," "little cliques," and "meaningless decalogs" loftily presented. The struggle for leadership was far from over.[20]

The direction in which Communist policy would move was becoming clear in a general way, but the more specific implications of the shift toward cooperation with bourgeois liberals emerged gradually amidst a good deal of confusion. That the Communist Party would in fact control the Writers' Congress, no one questioned; but the highest cultural authorities the Party could boast were grappling in 1935 with a whole spectrum of new issues as they struggled to come to terms with the coming shift.[21] The First American Writers' Congress finally convened in New York on April 26, 1935. The tone of the Congress promised a new Communist respect for literature. In the only public session, Party chief Earl Browder declared that the Communists wanted writers only to be good writers —politically conscious, but free to pursue their art.[22] Yet the results of the assembly created difficulties for the editors, some immediate, some over a longer term, that kept Phillips and Rahv ill at ease.

The League of American Writers brought to birth by the Writers' Congress meant a broader Communist appeal to middle-class intellectuals. Whether that was good or bad depended on the issue at hand and the perspective of the viewer. Phillips and Rahv had insisted that bourgeois literature belonged within the literary *heritage* of the radical writer, but they had also argued vigorously that radical literature must *supersede* its predecessors. Through the League of American Writers, and in line with the Popular Front policy officially introduced at the Seventh Congress of the Communist International (July–August 1935), radical writers were asked to cooperate with many of the political and literary tendencies they had been attacking for years. Ultimately, the new policy implied that "the *specific* Marxist viewpoint must largely disappear." The Congress sent the "proletarian" novel into rapid decline, and within a year the whole notion of "proletarian" culture was becoming something of an embarrassment.[23] For young writers whose aspirations and idealisms were tied up in the hope for a great radical literature, this was not necessarily good news.[24]

The editors of *Partisan Review* occasionally suggested irritation over the Communist abandonment of young writers and of a distinct radicalism.[25] Yet in 1935 Phillips and Rahv remained strongly attached to the Communist movement, whatever the reservations they may have felt. The fact that Rahv was asked to join the Finance

Committee of the new League shortly after the Writers' Congress seemed a good sign. So did the ability of the magazine to go on. The editors announced that *Partisan Review* was now a "revolutionary literary magazine" without organizational affiliation, "edited by a group of young Communist writers" whose purpose would be "to print the best revolutionary literature and Marxist criticism in this country and abroad." And, indeed, *Partisan Review* seemed briefly to do well in its effort to diversify and prosper.[26]

Behind this front, however, the editors were in a period of doubt, and their literary campaigns stood in abeyance. After the summer of 1935, neither Phillips nor Rahv made a contribution to the magazine for a run of three issues. While the editors were trying to make sense of the new situation and to establish *Partisan Review* on an independent basis, the Communist Party was attempting to treat the magazine as a pawn of its policies, considering both an attempt to kill off *Partisan Review* and the possibility of making it an official organ of the League of American Writers.[27] What emerged in early 1936 instead of a magazine serving the League was a combination of *Partisan Review* and Jack Conroy's *Anvil*. Through all of this, Phillips and Rahv had not lost editorial control nor changed their views.[28]

The first issue of *Partisan Review and Anvil* was a hybrid reflecting the mixture of old and new currents in radical – and literary – politics. The magazine reprinted a speech by Waldo Frank delivering the standard People's Front message that opposing fascism was the highest duty of the intellectual. Carl Van Doren's short piece – full of writers "reaching to the American subsoil"– betokened the whole panoply of nationalistic appeals that would rapidly accumulate to form a major Popular Front campaign. (Later in 1936 Earl Browder would run for President with the slogan "Communism Is Twentieth-Century Americanism.") At the same time, other articles pointed toward old battles and continuing tensions within the literary movement. Most significantly, James T. Farrell's "Theatre Chronicle" gave clear notice that the new *Partisan Review and Anvil* would not judge literature by simple political standards or endorse every work of the radical stalwarts. Although he indicated his respect for earlier scripts by Clifford Odets, Farrell blasted a new Odets play, *Paradise Lost*, as "a burlesque" full of "dull speeches and swaggering platitudes." Farrell marveled that the play could be "so consistently, so ferociously bad." Such remarks did not go unnoticed.[29]

Farrell had been a thorn in the side of the *New Masses* crowd for some years.[30] His attack on Odets's most recent play brought Mike Gold rushing to battle, eager to put Farrell in his place. But Gold did not see Farrell alone as the problem; this kind of trouble, from Gold's viewpoint, had been characteristic of *Partisan Review* and of Phillips and Rahv. Under the pretense of reviewing the newly merged *Partisan Review and Anvil*, Gold launched an attack not just on Farrell, and not just on the immediate cause for provocation, but on Phillips and Rahv, their magazine past and present, and the whole body of opposition to "leftism." Gold thus took quarrels old and new into a public forum and forced a choosing of sides.

Phillips and Rahv, in Gold's view, were guilty of a "terrible mandarism" [*sic*]; they carried "their Marxian scholarship as though it were a heavy cross"; moreover, they used "a scholastic jargon as barbarous as the terminology that for so long infected most Marxian journalism in this country, a foreign language no American could understand without a year or two of post-graduate study." Intellectuality, for Gold, had always been a curse, but the angle of his attack had changed. Now the appeal was not to the worker's level of understanding but to that of the "American"—a shift in terms for Gold, but not a shift in meaning. To Farrell's remarks on Odets, Gold directed the second half of his offensive. Farrell had made a "sour attack" motivated by "prejudice," and he lacked "the objectivity, fairness and generosity—let us also add, common sense—to be a critic." Such an assault left no options for Gold's targets but retaliation or abject surrender, and it soon brought an end to the uneasy truce over "leftism."[31]

The campaign of late spring and summer revolved around the publication of Farrell's *A Note on Literary Criticism*, a book that proved to be the most substantial consideration of Marxist aesthetics by an American Marxist written during the thirties.[32] Launching his own barrage against "leftism," Farrell combined the arguments of Phillips and Rahv, the complaints of other writers, and his own perceptions in a sustained assault on the leading lights of the *New Masses*: they had confused literature with propaganda; they had failed to understand the importance of the literary heritage; they had ridden roughshod over the qualities of uniqueness in individual writers and individual works; and they had introduced political standards into their criticism that produced vulgar, oversimplified, and irrelevant judgments. The leftists were themselves divided by Farrell into "two noticeable streams" that "usually meet in the same rut." On one side was the tendency represented by Michael Gold, the "school of revolutionary sentimentalism"; on the other stood a "mechanically deterministic 'Marxism,'" practiced especially by Granville Hicks.[33]

The applause for Farrell's book in *Partisan Review and Anvil* came from Alan Calmer, a member of the editorial board, a former national leader of the Reed Clubs, and a writer close to Phillips and Rahv in his views. The defiantly titled "Down with 'Leftism'" heaped praise on Farrell's work and predicted an outraged reaction from those who had been taken to task. Farrell won plaudits for his ability to "handle intellectual concepts"; the "leftists," by contrast, were described as suffering from "easy formulas," a "lack of ideas," "oversimplified beliefs," and "a narrow, anti-esthetic attitude." Calmer thus emphasized once again the contrast between an intelligent, complex, sophisticated understanding of literature (embodied in *Partisan Review*) and a crude "leftist" anti-intellectualism. Due to their lack of "thought-out principles," according to Calmer, "leftist" critics had "swung from one extreme of their position to the other"—from "literary praise of the most mediocre writers who eulogize the revolutionary workingclass" to "political approval of the most 'successful' authors whose sympathies are remote from the workingclass movement." There was "no longer any excuse" for "leftism," Calmer declared, and its continuation would "stunt the growth of proletarian literature."[34]

Beyond giving support to Farrell, Calmer's essay accomplished four things. First, it reaffirmed under new circumstances that the *Partisan Review* critics would continue to oppose vigorously the "political evaluation of literature" favored by the *New Masses* and apparently by the Communist Party. Second, it made clear that Calmer (and beyond him Phillips, Rahv, and Farrell) did not view Popular Front encomiums for bourgeois writers as evidence of some new phenomenon in criticism; on the contrary, such gush merely proved the persistence of "leftism." "Left" critics had "swung from one extreme of their position to the other," but it was the same position. Third, Calmer's essay revealed a lingering appeal to the possibilities of "proletarian literature." This did not mean the formulaic strike novels encouraged by Gold but the hoped-for radical literature that could raise American culture to sophistication and greatness. Fourth, with its anticipation of strong reactions to Farrell's book, Calmer's essay demonstrated that the editors of *Partisan Review and Anvil* knew full well what they were doing in siding with Farrell and in continuing their battle against "leftism." There was to be no backing away from a quarrel with the *New Masses*, and perhaps the Party.

The appearance of Calmer's essay brought the expected tempest. Farrell transcribed with a certain sardonic glee Phillips's report of a *New Masses* party at which people "frothed at the mouth" and "ranted" about Farrell and about Phillips and Rahv. On the next day Phillips and Rahv both came to see Farrell and delivered more reports. Having knowingly kicked a hornet's nest, they were measuring the reaction and charting the prospects for being stung.[35] Both Isidor Schneider and Granville Hicks made attempts to answer Farrell (and, implicitly, Phillips, Rahv, and Calmer). Despite efforts to dismiss and belittle his position, neither of the replies proved very effective. As Farrell pointed out in a rebuttal, his critics had granted much of his case against "leftism." The only real question that remained was whether the sins of the past were continuing in the present, and on this matter the sides held irreconcilable views.[36]

A few observers at the time and a number of scholars since have suggested that the battle against "leftism" was pointless by 1936 and that the struggle to gain for literature the freedom to develop on its own had been won with the shift to the Popular Front.[37] In fact, from the perspective of *Partisan Review*, the issues in 1936 were largely continuous with those of 1934, Popular Front or no. The *New Masses* and *Partisan Review and Anvil* went at one another not simply over the old issues of "leftism" and not simply over the new issues raised by Popular Front literary tactics, but over both at once; to the participants in the struggle, the fundamental differences between them remained much the same.

Part of the friction was undoubtedly generated by conflicts between personalities, by petty vanities on both sides, and by the jousting between an established older leadership and ambitious newcomers. Yet, even though such factors provided one source of tensions and, indeed, one level of continuity, the basic division between the *Partisan Review* critics and the *New Masses* rested firmly on intellectual and literary grounds. Given their hope that radical writing would lead the way toward a mature American literature, Phillips and Rahv could no more accept a celebration of mediocre bourgeois novels because of their authors' political leanings than they could join in glorifying mediocre strike novels. The flare-up of 1936 was no mindless reenactment of an obsolete quarrel but part of a continuing debate over the values and purposes of radical culture. The complex of values that Phillips and Rahv had applied in their criticism during 1934 would now serve as a basis from which to evaluate the Popular Front strategy in literature; and those values would play a central justifying role as Phillips and Rahv began to move away from the Communist Party.

The process of weighing Popular Front trends entered a new phase with a symposium in the third number of *Partisan Review and Anvil*, "What Is Americanism?" Reflecting the concerns that troubled the editors themselves, the symposium questions raised difficult and touchy issues involving the relationship of American to European culture, the relevancy of native radical movements to Marxism, and the significance of "the American spirit" for revolutionary literature. Phillips and Rahv did not answer the questions themselves, nor did they have a spokesman for their position waiting in the wings, but anyone familiar with the perspective established in *Partisan Review* over the previous two years might have detected in their questions an implicit critique of the Popular Front drift toward a folkish Americanism.[38]

Several responses published in the symposium claimed, as Phillips and Rahv might have expected, that there was indeed a common bond between Marxism and the American tradition. Some of these answers could only have increased the editors' suspicions about the new Popular Front nationalism. Newton Arvin, for example, praised radical writers as the best representatives of American life, and he wished only that more of them would become personally and emotionally involved with "our Yankee culture." Contemporary writers need not have "radical or national memories" that were "natively American," he conceded, but they must reject the "seedy cosmopolitanism" of the modernist twenties. Arvin thought it commendable that "leftwing writers" had produced "some of the most intensively localized and 'nativized' books of the last two or three years."[39] Such a response seemed almost to go out of its way to rouse submerged fears of nativist prejudice, to celebrate a Protestant Anglo-Saxon tradition, and to insult the broadening and experimental tendencies of modernism. If Arvin represented the policies of the Popular Front, the editors could only see in those policies a call for the surrender of their literary vision, their critical intelligence, their cultural ambitions, and their social identities.

Other responses to the symposium questions raised very different concerns. William Troy, for example, questioned whether radicalism really had anything of value to offer the writer. It was difficult, Troy announced, "for the artist who cares anything for his role to achieve a really logical bridge between dogmatic Marxism and literature."[40] Phillips and Rahv could not evade the need to reply to such skepticism. Their answer pointed once more at the "leftists" and their Popular Front heirs. If critics like Troy doubted the possibility of a logical tie between Marxism and literature, it was because they were looking (as Troy's language attested) at "dogmatic Marxism" and the formulas of politicized criticism, not at the powerful yet supple generalizing philosophy to which Phillips and Rahv gave their allegiance.

Rahv made effective use of this explanation in reviewing Stephen Spender's *The Destructive Element*. With a proper radical synthesis his implicit model, Rahv argued at some length that Spender's treatment of current writing placed too much emphasis on the consciousness of the individual artist and too little on the philosophy of Marxism. Yet if this was the case, there were reasons for the lack of proper balance, according to Rahv: "much of Spender's shrinking from the ultimate meaning of Marxism arises from the false interpretations of it transmitted by various popularizers and vulgarizers, who insist on equating their *very own* village culture with dialectics." If Spender associated Marxism with "strident simplifications" and "dictatorial precepts" in art, it was because he had "merely taken the 'leftists' at their word." The terms of reproach in Rahv's swipe at "leftists" indicated a gradually hardening attitude toward the "false interpretations" of Marxism that seemed to dominate Communist literary policy; and the values of cosmopolitanism were at the core of the expanding condemnation. Rahv's outburst against "leftism" paved the way for rather generous praise of Spender's "analysis of specific writers," including Joyce, James, Lawrence, Eliot, and Yeats — modernists who for all their faults represented a tradition sharply opposed to that of "village culture."[41]

The conclusion only suggested by Phillips in 1934 was beginning to approach full and logical expression. The "leftists" were to be understood within the familiar pattern of analysis that saw American literature perennially stunted by its fondness for one-sided extremes. It was this pattern that Alan Calmer invoked when he noted that "leftism" had produced "a type of sterility as harmful in its own way as the arid results of pure aestheticism."[42] *Partisan Review* was now explicitly comparing the two extremes as obstacles to the emergence of a mature American literature. "Left" was being equated with "right" as a way of condemning the left. Even as this connection between extremes was growing stronger, however, the editors struggled to preserve their belief that the positive literary values they saw in modernism were, as Rahv's comments on Spender had implied, superior to the vulgarizations of "leftism." And this soon brought adjustments within their own intellectual assumptions.

The troubling fact that many modernist writers and pro-modernist critics were unabashedly conservative in their political views demanded some degree of censure from a radical magazine, and *Partisan Review* continued to oblige with condemnations of "reactionary" social values from a cosmopolitan perspective.[43] Yet when Philip Rahv came to assess Eliot's *Murder in the Cathedral*, there was a new twist to his argument on the literature associated with such values. Through at least their essay on "Criticism" for the Writers' Congress in 1935, Phillips and Rahv had insisted that when Eliot entered his "Anglo-catholic phase, his ideology set up a wall between his poetic talent and its realization."[44] In Rahv's new estimation of June 1936, this convenient pattern of rejection, with its assumption of a sure harmony between literary quality and political enlightenment, came apart at its most important seam.

Murder in the Cathedral was not to be scorned, for "Eliot spoke his message of darkness in the unmistakable accents of a major poem": "The critics had decided that Eliot's godliness had done for him, and here he was flying in the face of their stigmas." Some critics on the left had "declared the play to be fascist, and hence, by implication, beyond the pale of analysis and interpretation." This was "ludicrous." Rahv did not deny that Eliot was still the "fugleman of literary reaction"; on the contrary, he wholeheartedly agreed that "of late Eliot has been steering close to fascism." What Rahv would not allow was the easy transformation of this political judgment into a literary judgment. Seemingly oblivious of his own earlier conviction that Eliot was "done for," Rahv almost jeered at the "left critics" in their discomfiture. The Marxist philosophy and the radical experience must have a literature that could express their "variety and complexity," Rahv insisted. Eliot's verse was "various and complex"; it had "an historic sense, both of language and of events"; it was "precise, contemporary, sustained by a sensibility able to transform thought and feeling into each other and combine them in simultaneous expression." In short, as the use of several key words revealed, Eliot now seemed to Rahv a living model of major poetic achievement.[45]

Rahv had dissolved the idea of a *necessary* connection between radical ideas and significant contemporary writing. This partial separation of politics and literature gave the editors of *Partisan Review* room to find positive value in current non-Marxist writing as they had always found worth in the bourgeois literature of the past. The separation also served immediate polemical purposes and signified that a condemnation of the cultural politics of "leftism" was now as important to Rahv as condemnation of the political right. Rahv had not retreated either from his view of Eliot as a re-actionary or from the general perception of highbrow aestheticism as one-sided and inadequate. Rather, he had tried to focus attention on the qualities that, from *Partisan Review*'s perspective, made for great works of art, whatever the writer's politics or the normal limits of his literary outlook. Eliot had escaped intellectual and historical backwardness through a "dislocation of the poet's intention" that made him share in the meanings of the present as a "contemporary." Once again Rahv had worked out, in trying to deal with Eliot, a pattern that could be more broadly applied. Especially after 1937, the editors and contributors to *Partisan Review* would find in the great literature of the nineteenth and twentieth centuries a striving toward synthesis, often against the writer's intention, that made such works a fitting object for the magazine's praise.

The new assessment of Eliot marked an important turning for Phillips and Rahv. They had looked to the Communist Party to provide broad support for the cultural advance they envisioned. The Party had been expected to lead in the education of the proletariat toward the support of a complex and cosmopolitan radical culture. With this hope in decline, Phillips and Rahv began openly to turn their literary attention toward those who had created a cultural tradition and supported the development of modernism—the intellectuals and the highbrows. This was not an abandonment of the proletarianism of the *New Masses*, which they had never endorsed; it was the beginning of a departure from their own unrealized version of proletarianism.

Growing doubts about the policies and attitudes of the Communists came to a head for Phillips and Rahv in the winter of 1936–37. During their months of teetering on the fence, Phillips and Rahv in a joint essay, "Literature in a Political Decade," tried to assess what had happened to contemporary writing and to affirm once again their own point of view.[46] They continued to show a fascination with the logic and the appeal of Marxism. Yet the cocky political pronouncements of 1934 were largely absent when Phillips and Rahv recounted once more the failings of their customary literary targets. And with their rather superficial language of Communist militance stripped away, the emphasis fell even more heavily than before on a condemnation rooted in the values of cosmopolitanism and shaped by a preoccupation with the weaknesses of native literary traditions.

Regionalism in the early thirties, the editors announced rather condescendingly, had "continued to attract those provincial talents that resented the intellectual rapacity of New York." (Defensiveness and parochialism sulked in the hinterlands; confidence and intelligence glowed from the metropolis.) In the South, that most benighted of provinces to the radical New York mind, regionalism "laid claim to a political program of its own" that combined "religion, small property, and a vague neo-classicism," three historically backward forces. The critical attack directed toward the right was familiar.

Although the charges of narrowness and backwardness applied in different ways, the dissection of the cultural programs nourished by the Communist Party similarly drew upon notions of cosmopolitan advance. The ideas of Hicks and Gold—Phillips and Rahv would now name names—were "more in the sectarian tradition of Upton Sinclair than in the great tradition of Karl Marx." Here as elsewhere, Sinclair represented not only political narrowness but the one-sided, almost provincial, "sociological" fiction of the teens. Radical writing had the potential to "transform the literary consciousness of America"; but the "leftists" reinforced the "basic failure" in American writing, and the average proletarian novel remained "imprisoned within a pragmatic mold." By tying Communist literary efforts to a continuing burden of national parochialism, Phillips and Rahv could associate sophistication, cosmopolitanism, and cultural progress directly with their emerging opposition to the Party. And because the Party had presumably sacrificed the integrity of radical ideas to take up the Popular Front alliance with liberals, Phillips and Rahv could continue to believe that their own position represented genuine Marxism as well. Thus, they argued, the failure of revolutionary literature under Communist leadership could not be attributed to the "Marxist elements" in the radical brew but "to the pragmatic patterns and lack of consciousness that dominate the national heritage."

Indeed, Phillips and Rahv complained, "the very forces that the Left set out to combat were reinstated by the vulgarizers of Marxism." Unable to escape the lowbrow tradition that was dominant in American culture, "leftism" had encouraged its continuation. "Intellectual tendencies" were "smashed or distorted" by "such traditional forces . . . as pragmatism, populism, regionalism, and the false materialism of the literary shopkeepers." Even many writers nurtured by the twenties had not escaped the gravitational pull of this provincial tradition: "their modernism was no more than a cultural veneer glossing the old village furniture." In a summation that spoke volumes about their values and their frustrations, Phillips

90

and Rahv declared that behind all these American methods lay an "anti-intellectual bias, which constantly draws literature below urban levels into the sheer 'idiocy of the village.'"

If anything, Phillips and Rahv felt more strongly the failings of the radical movement in criticism, the field with which they identified most personally. Here, their belief in progressive change based on cosmopolitan values operated openly as an ethical standard. Criticism, they declared, was "almost a pure product of the city," and it was a "primary function" of the intellect. Unfortunately, criticism could also be produced by people whose values and judgments corrupted critical writing. The Popular Front liaison with Americanism led down just such a path, and the complete failure of that misguided marriage had become apparent in the cultural crimes of a leading Popular Front critic: "Recently a prominent liberal, Malcolm Cowley, disposed of several important theoretical problems on the ground that they were nothing more than the inventions of 'big-city' intellectuals. Such an attitude speaks for the longing to retreat to the quietism of rustic life, and is no less degraded for being masked in the easy charms of sincerity." This was not radicalism but conservatism. This was "retreat." And perhaps because the Popular Front still claimed to be progressive or even radical, its underlying quietism was "degraded," its whole existence a lie, its cultural stance a moral abomination.

In their dissatisfaction with Communist literary policy, Phillips and Rahv had increasingly applied to the critics of the *New Masses* and their Popular Front allies a kind of condemnation earlier directed primarily against the poetry and criticism of the right. A striking transformation had occurred in their attitudes toward the cultural implications of the Communist organization. It was not so much that the two editors had changed their values or their larger perspective—these, in fact, remained remarkably stable. It was rather that they had lost their faith that the Communist Party cared much about literature in its own right; they had lost their confidence that the radical movement dominated by the Party would encourage the maturation of American literature; and they had lost their conviction that two young critics with a magazine could shape or affect the Communist literary program. Communist policy now stood condemned as anti-urban, anti-intellectual, anti-cosmopolitan; it was static, narrowly utilitarian, dictatorial, and degraded. The Communists and the liberals of the Popular Front were, in short, a backward and retrograde force in American culture.

Phillips and Rahv had walked to the brink of the direct charge that would have completed the logical development of their position — the claim that Communists were in fact reactionary and not fundamentally different from fascists. The argument they had made firmly linked Communist "radicalism" with right-wing reaction; the two extremes of left and right had come together through their opposition to enlightened cultural values. When in December 1937 the first editorial of a reorganized *Partisan Review* described the Communist movement as "totalitarian," it did no more than express in a single word the conclusion Phillips and Rahv had reached after more than three years of active radical criticism. The charge that the Communists preached a new religion and the direct accusation that the Party was in fact reactionary—these, too, would come.[47] But first Phillips's and Rahv's political disenchantment with the Party and the Soviet Union would have to catch up with their cultural alienation.

Before turning to the story of Phillips's and Rahv's actual break from the Communist Party, it is important to note the positive literary vision that continued to glow even within the generally negative analysis of "Literature in a Political Decade." The central theme of Phillips's and Rahv's appeal in 1937 was a call for greater "consciousness," a higher intellectual awareness. If the Communists were determined to celebrate the popular and the lowbrow, Phillips and Rahv would place ever greater stress on intellect as a necessary balancing force. There must be confrontation through intelligence with contemporary "moral and intellectual contradictions," not escape from them into "idealizations of the promised land." American writers under Communist leadership were simply persisting in a "futile attempt to create a literature in one country—futile because inevitably a contradiction arises between the international consciousness of intellectual life and the provincial smugness of the literature itself."

"Literature in one country" could only be taken as a slap at Stalin's slogan "socialism in one country," and, indeed, the phrase provided as strong a political reference as Phillips and Rahv were yet ready to make. That a full rejection of Popular Front policy was intended, however, became amply clear from the solution Phillips and Rahv proposed: the "Europeanization of American literature"—a program antipodal to Newton Arvin's celebration of "Yankee culture." This call for "Europeanization," which has proven to be a summons quite easily misread, must be kept in its proper context. It did not announce any dramatic new perspective for Phillips and

Rahv. "Europeanization" simply updated the "cosmopolitanization" blessed by Phillips in 1934.

Yet if the call for "Europeanization" should hardly have surprised those who had followed the criticism of Phillips and Rahv, it nevertheless reflected a shift in their level of confidence. In 1934 Phillips had been able to assume that a degree of "cosmopolitanization" had already occurred in the modernist twenties and that the process would continue. This was the direction of historical advance in American writing, and the young editors of *Partisan Review* had fully believed that the radical movement would join and augment the progressive stream. The emphasis on "Europeanization" in 1937 demonstrated that Phillips and Rahv were by this point convinced that "leftism" and Popular Front Americanism had so undermined the advance of literature that even the gains of modernism could no longer be assumed. Eager to rush toward a higher future, the editors found themselves boats against the current, borne back ceaselessly to defend principles they had once taken for granted. The call for "Europeanization" represented an effort by Phillips and Rahv to salvage their hopes for a mature American culture.

For Phillips and Rahv, Europe was the antidote to Gopher Prairie and its like. But the goal was not to imitate Europe and thus to remain its province. The goal in 1937, as in 1915, was to bring a new sophistication to *American* literature, to broaden the national culture by making it more international and more cosmopolitan without discarding its particular qualities. Phillips and Rahv's model for the relationship of the United States to international culture ran clearly parallel to Bourne's design for the relation of diverse ethnic groupings to the larger American culture. The new outlook must produce a literature cosmopolitan in its ideas but national in its specific content: "In the same way as Thomas Mann's work is deeply rooted in the German soil, even while his complete ethos generalizes the intellectual experience of Europe, so the American novelist, rising to a high level of consciousness, would carry the particulars of American life into the main stream of world culture."

Were the young critics discouraged by their experience thus far? At the end of "Literature in a Political Decade" came a paragraph that suggested, at the very least, a brave front to the contrary. Never so lyrical in their criticism as Brooks, nor quite so fond of old seeds sprouting and new ages dawning, Phillips and Rahv still managed to find a rich potential for renaissance in American culture. American life, Phillips and Rahv announced, was "the most modern, variegated, and plastic in the bourgeois world"; the "material pre-requisites of Socialism" had matured, and the bases for "profound cultural readjustments" were in place. The "potency" of the American situation awaited only the "consciousness of the artist." Release from "bondage to the pragmatic past" required only courage and will—the artist "must dare claim his true inheritance." This was the vision of cultural radicalism: the intellectual and the artist, heroic and determined, would lead a revolution in culture to usher in a new American age, and the particular features of national experience would nurture a literature to surpass the best efforts of an aging Europe.

If the literary program and the critical framework advanced by Phillips and Rahv in the thirties carried on an American tradition of cultural radicalism, it also served more personal needs. The positive complex of values that lay behind Phillips's and Rahv's criticism summarized the life they had led and the choices they had made. Their program rejoiced in the ethnic mix, the urban confidence, and the perpetual flux of New York. It reflected, and helped to sustain, the efforts of young intellectuals to define for themselves a cultural position dependent neither on the Jewish community nor on traditions steeped in nativism. The negative counterparts to their values most often represented the worlds Phillips and Rahv wished to leave behind. Religion and "feudalism" characterized not only the values of formalist critics but the traditional culture of Jewish orthodoxy. Parochialism and a village mentality were traits not only of lowbrow American culture but also of the first-generation immigrant community. Timidity might be attributed to real parents who feared the larger world or to intellectual fathers like Eliot who backed away from the conflicts of modernity. Outsiders by choice or necessity to the dominant cultures of community and nation, Phillips and Rahv invested their futures in the dramatic expansion and substantial elaboration of a cosmopolitan position that as yet gave rise to cultural streams of limited force. Idealism, ambition, and identity were bound together in a quest for the kind of culture that could provide an intellectual and social home. If the essays of the young New York Intellectuals were often humorless and argumentative, if insecurities were wrapped in bravado, if passion was with difficulty restrained, perhaps it was because there seemed at every point to be so very much at stake.

Chapter Four | The Break

The journey away from the Communist Party during 1936 and 1937 was full of backtracking and indecision for Phillips and Rahv. At times, they would seem to the watchful eye of the more impetuous James T. Farrell timid and irresolute; at times, opportunistic and weak-principled. Phillips's own recollections describe the period as one of doubt, insecurity, and drift. To a degree, their experience was one common to many of those intellectuals who at one time or another broke away from the Party.[1] Yet whatever its common elements, the story of Phillips and Rahv carries a special significance, for it is also the story of *Partisan Review*, a magazine of uncommon importance.

William Phillips suggested thirty years after the fact that left-wing intellectuals faced a rankling dilemma in the thirties: on the one hand, "we felt that the Communist party was a bad influence, organizationally and ideologically"; on the other hand, "it seemed to us the only party capable of doing anything, the only party capable of providing some kind of central force around which to organize." The contradiction Phillips suggested had been evident in the concerns expressed by Hicks and Arvin in the early thirties and was apparent as well at the Writers' Congress of 1935. The loyalty of writers to the Communist Party, even at this moment of great public unity and optimism, seemed to have little to do with their writing and much to do with the special political role of the Communist movement.[2] Within this context, Phillips's and Rahv's reluctance to break with the Party in 1936, despite their advanced disaffection on literary grounds, made sense.

Breaking away entailed not only political shock but also a series of more personal dislocations. Leaving the Party, Phillips recalled, was "not easy for anyone, and for some it was traumatic." As Joseph Freeman would later explain, "the cumulative revolutionary tradition is not only one of liberty and equality, but of *fraternity.* . . .

95

To leave is to be damned by your former comrades and friends — and your own conscience." Such pressures came to bear on the editors of *Partisan Review* in 1936–37. Phillips described the feeling as one opposite to that sense of comradeship, unity, and energy that accompanied identification with the Party:

> when one broke away . . . , one had a terrible sense of loneliness and paralysis. It was very hard to do anything. None of us was so sure of himself that he could just go out and act simply and directly. There was a period of about a year or two of drifting.[3]

Questions of opportunity were also involved. If association with the Communist Party opened up certain chances for publication and prominence to the young writer, breaking away closed down those possibilities. Especially in New York, Party control seemed to stretch powerfully into the magazines and publishing houses on the left, with the reality of influence expanded into a myth of dominance through Communist legend and threat. Phillips and Rahv had reached out for prominence through their magazine and were loath to lose the special opportunities that *Partisan Review* gave them. Yet a break with the Party endangered those tenuous channels of support that had kept the magazine going, even after it became officially independent in 1935. Renegades lived with the fear that opportunity would be choked off, ambition stymied.

The challenge facing Phillips and Rahv as they grew increasingly distant from the Communists was to create a political, intellectual, and social world apart. Already estranged from Jewish tradition and alien to American nativism, they now faced the prospect of cutting themselves off from the politics that had provided an intermediate home. Neither the severance of Communist ties nor the construction of a new group identity would come easily to them.

After the issue of June 1936, *Partisan Review* moved into a summer hiatus. Phillips and Rahv had put themselves in a difficult position. They remained politically and practically under the Communist umbrella: the editors had received Party-related support to keep *Partisan Review* afloat, and they continued to negotiate with the League of American Writers over the possibilities of organizational sponsorship. At the same time, Phillips and Rahv had launched a new offensive against "leftism" and its practitioners; they had identified themselves and their magazine with the sweeping strictures of Farrell's *Note on Literary Criticism*; and they had begun to challenge the shiny new strategy of the Popular Front in literature. During the summer, this already unstable combination of rampant cultural disaffection and presumptive political unity was brought under further stress by two explosions on the international scene. By calling into question for Phillips and Rahv the political integrity of the Communist Party and the Soviet Union, each began to cut away at the only links that still held the young critics.

The first explosion came in Spain. The Spanish Civil War infused life into the rather feeble League of American Writers and gave a new sense of vitality and purpose to the Popular Front. Here was a clear anti-fascist cause on which liberals and radicals could unite. Yet if this was the broader impact on the left, the immediate observations and conclusions of Phillips and Rahv led in quite a different direction. Farrell recorded a conversation with the two editors in mid-August in which all lamented the slow responses of Popular Front governments to the situation in Spain and complained that the Soviet Union under Stalin had "ditched the proletariat of one country after the other."[4] Such remarks suggested growing doubt about the relation between radical principle and Soviet policy that later intervention in Spain could not fully erase.

The second explosion came within the Soviet Union itself with the unfolding of the Moscow Trials and the allegations of a Trotsky-led conspiracy against Stalin's regime. Phillips and Rahv were clearly troubled by the trials, though they resisted at first any direct condemnation. According to Farrell, the two were arguing in late August that if the accused were innocent, they were poor bolsheviks for not having made a political speech in court; if they were guilty, they deserved condemnation. Rahv, Farrell noted after another conversation, was practicing "suspended judgment" and leaning toward the notion that "there must have been a conspiracy."[5]

Attitudes toward the Communist Party, the Popular Front, and the trials soon became tied up with the question of whether *Partisan Review* would continue publication. The longstanding question of whether the magazine might serve the League of American Writers in some official capacity had come up again. Already in May, the League had loaned *Partisan Review* one hundred dollars, and the magazine was in desperate need of continued financial transfusions. In September, when Rahv joined the League's executive committee, the parties got down to serious bargaining. Phillips and Rahv announced privately that they were going to "set conditions," but the League negotiators had their own demands, which required services by the magazine to the League and the appointment of two new members to *Partisan Review*'s staff. Phillips and Rahv told Farrell that League representatives were "vague about the immediate possibilities of money"—perhaps what *Partisan Review* needed most—while promising organizational support that the editors might well have feared. Phillips and Rahv brought to Farrell on the same day a copy of what proved to be the final issue of the first *Partisan Review* (October 1936). The pretense of a serious merger with *Anvil* had been dropped, and only Phillips, Rahv, and Calmer were listed as editors.[6]

In early October, at a party given to explore the possibilities of raising money for *Partisan Review*, Farrell purposely brought up the Moscow Trials in front of people from the *New Masses* camp and announced his "firm belief that it was a frameup of Trotsky." When Phillips and Rahv did not get in touch with him for several days after the party, Farrell began to suspect that the Communists had "put some heat on them." Farrell then heard a story from Felix Morrow, told to Morrow by Lionel Abel, that Rahv and Phillips some time before had been "called up on the carpet by the party, asked about their views, about whether or not they intended bringing over Partisan Review to the Trotskyites and the Socialist Party etc, and that they had to make what amounted to confessions of faith."[7]

Meanwhile, at the very time Farrell was wondering if his opposition to the Communists had scared Phillips and Rahv away, the editors were considering once again at least a temporary arrangement with the League of American Writers. Their hopes for *Partisan Review* led in two directions: they wanted quality and independence, but they also wanted to survive and find support. Political considerations produced a similar split. Radicalism must be a matter of principle, but radical principle seemed crippled without embodiment in a movement. Though they rejected the proposals to put *Partisan Review* in the service of the League, preferring suspension of the magazine to loss of independence, Phillips and Rahv had not yet decided which way to turn.[8]

Two months later, at the end of December 1936, Phillips and Rahv came to see Farrell and declared themselves "through with the Stalinist movement." According to Phillips and Rahv, the movement was "completely dead and demoralized," with "scarcely any one working or producing anything." Their disaffection took the concrete form of proposing to hold a meeting at Farrell's to discuss the prospects of renewing *Partisan Review* under Socialist auspices if that party would offer freedom and support. A week later, they were backtracking again. Phillips reported that Malcolm Cowley had attacked him and Rahv at an executive meeting of the League, claiming they were cynical and disaffected; but whether this had anything to do with the editors' second thoughts about leaving the Communists for Socialist support was unclear.[9]

By this time Farrell found Phillips bursting with a "whole string of arguments against the Trotsky movement, Trotskyists, etc," which Farrell rejected as "rationalizations": "It is merely that they—he and perhaps Rahv—are doing their damndest to find reasons for not breaking with the Communist Party and the official movement." Phillips "kept talking about the lack of an independent organ" and openly worried that he might be left with "no place to write" if he moved toward the Trotskyists. Clearly the questions of opportunity and influence were serious ones for the young editor. Moreover, with their experience confined to New York, where the Party was strongest, Phillips and Rahv seemed to believe in the vast power the Communists often claimed for themselves and to fear the Party's retribution, to Farrell's obvious dismay: "The pervasive fear of the CP which seems to be so apparent amongst certain NY intellectuals works in their minds, and constantly twists their views about. . . . Indecisiveness is going to paralysize [sic] them if this state of mind persists." Phillips and Rahv were indeed caught in the field between opposing camps with their will to act seized by "paralysis," as Phillips himself would admit thirty years later.[10]

By mid-January Phillips and Rahv were again exploring the possibility of Socialist Party support for *Partisan Review*. One meeting held at Farrell's led to an appointment with Norman Thomas. On the day arranged, Phillips and Rahv grew hesitant once more and called Farrell to ask if they might skip the meeting, claiming they now feared political control by the Socialists. Later, as Farrell put it, "the cat came out of the bag." Phillips and Rahv had been sounding out other possibilities for their magazine, and "finally, as a feeler, William asked me would I write for Partisan Review if it continued without breaking with the Stalinist movement." Farrell found the editors' conduct in the whole matter "a little bit contemptible" for its "pusilanimity [sic]." Phillips and Rahv were "nice boys" who might be too indecisive and hesitant ever to make a mark.[11]

Nothing happened to change Farrell's opinion over the next two months as the issue posed by the Moscow Trials began to boil. By this point, the trials had become a topic of obsessive discussion, and Farrell wrote ominously that bitterness over the trials was running very deep: "There is now a line of blood drawn between the supporters of Stalin and those of Trotsky, and that line of blood appears like an impassable river." Earl Browder had just said at an anti-Trotskyist meeting, according to Farrell, that Trotskyists handing out leaflets at Communist meetings should be "exterminated." In the midst of this "very bitter business," Phillips and Rahv still delayed taking sides for a time. Toward the end of February, the two were once again approaching Farrell to discuss the chances for an independent magazine and offering at the same time the hypothesis that those who confessed in Moscow were "half-Stalinists, and half Trotskyists." They impressed Farrell on this occasion "as being two intellectuals on the type of those we read of in the nineteenth century Russians, endlessly talking and spinning theories, and the like."[12]

The waverings of Phillips and Rahv had now been prolonged for more than half a year since the first discussion with Farrell of taking *Partisan Review* out of the Communist camp. By March of 1937, however, the climate created by the debate over the Moscow Trials was quickly making any half-hearted or unclear allegiance impossible. Though Phillips and Rahv could not quite make up their minds either to affirm their support for the Party or to break with it, the Communists were increasingly ready to conclude that the always troublesome editors were political enemies. Their decision was being made for them. In late March Phillips and Rahv reported to Farrell that they were "fairly rapidly being read out of the movement."[13] By this time, the prospects of a break may well have seemed less intimidating to Phillips and Rahv than they had a few months before. The drifting editors had begun to make new connections and to discover new possibilities of anchor against the harsh winds of Party displeasure.

Perhaps most important to the course Phillips and Rahv would ultimately take were a set of new people whom the two editors began to meet in the midst of their disorientation. Frederick W. Dupee had become the literary editor of the *New Masses* toward the end of 1936, and as such he might have seemed an unlikely ally for Phillips and Rahv. Yet Dupee was neither a member of the Communist Old Guard nor a narrow political enthusiast. Raised in Chicago, he had come East after two false starts elsewhere to attend his father's college, Yale, where he became by his own testimony a "convinced literary man." The vague search for "order and orthodoxy" that Dupee saw in his college enthusiasms led, in his own mind, to an infatuation with the "orthodoxy" of Communist politics in the mid-thirties. Yet Dupee was never terribly attracted by

American proletarianism. Even after coming to the *New Masses* he remained, as William Phillips and Granville Hicks could later agree, "not very political."[14]

A certain sympathy grew up between Dupee and the troubled young editors of the defunct *Partisan Review*, who continued to write occasional book reviews for the *New Masses* into early 1937. Dupee soon introduced Phillips and Rahv to a friend of his, Dwight Macdonald. Also from a well-established family, Macdonald had attended Phillips Exeter and then Yale, where he met Dupee and shared his cultural enthusiasms. In 1929 Macdonald joined the new Luce publication, *Fortune*, as a writer and editor, remaining there some seven years. He would later seem almost apologetic about not having become a radical more quickly, explaining that "I came late to the revolutionary movement . . . partly because I went to Yale instead of, for example, 'City College.'"[15]

Whatever his political sympathies to begin with, Macdonald belonged to that group of *Fortune* writers "whose job compelled them to find out what really went on behind the façade of American capitalism." By late 1936 Macdonald was moving rapidly toward the left; Dupee wrote to him in October to say how glad he was that Macdonald had decided to vote for Earl Browder. At about this point as well, Macdonald apparently read Marx for the first time and began his passionate affair with radical theory.[16] A day-long argument with Phillips and Rahv a few months later shifted the course of Macdonald's development (according to Phillips's later account) away from cooperation with the Communist Party and toward a decision to help revive *Partisan Review*.[17]

There was a similarity in the concerns of the several parties now coming into contact. In the early spring of 1937, Dupee was going through his own version of the process that had led Phillips and Rahv away from the Communists. At one point Dupee wrote to Macdonald of his "fast-growing doubt of whether it is possible for an intellectual to play party politics (the Party being what it is at present)—and remain an intellectual." Such doubts made Dupee increasingly uncomfortable in his position at the *New Masses*, which he had thought of "resigning several times during the last two weeks." Dupee's "doubts and differences" were "so many and so unorganized," and he was "so exhausted with thinking about them," that he avoided trying to list them all. Clearly he was torn between his notions of intellectual and critical integrity and his sense of the Communist Party's organizational significance, just as Phillips and Rahv had been torn. And, like them, he faced a choice in his role as an editor between accepting the compromises dictated by politics in order to retain any involvement or influence at all, and asserting his independence and his principles at the probable cost of his current radical identity and his job.[18]

Macdonald's intellectual testing took place outside the confines of the left, but it too raised the questions of integrity and compromise. The writers on *Fortune* more sympathetic to radical views had won some victories, but by 1937 Macdonald had concluded that these victories merely enabled *Fortune* "to establish a credit for editorial independence which may be drawn against later to justify some piece of right-wing propagandizing."[19] The distorting influence, for Macdonald, was the political and economic power of capitalism, and it took the same form in his complaints as the Communist Party did for Dupee, Phillips, and Rahv. Each had some dream of an "independent" magazine, politically left but unhampered by compromises with organizational strategies or commercial motives. Discovering their shared feelings in early 1937 brought some measure of comfort and hope for all concerned.

While Phillips, Rahv, Dupee, and Macdonald followed their varying paths, the war within the left set off by the Moscow Trials proceeded apace. The brunt of the Stalinists' wrath in 1936 and 1937 was directed against the American Committee for the Defense of Leon Trotsky, a body whose strength was made possible by the merger of the Trotskyists with the Socialist Party in June of 1936. Liberal and intellectual sympathizers of the Socialists joined an alliance to find asylum for Trotsky when he was forced out of Norway and then to gain a hearing for him in his Mexican sanctuary. The attitude of the Communist Party toward the Defense Committee was one of uncompromising hostility, and the pressures brought to bear by the Party inadvertently set another future *Partisan Review* editor on the course toward open opposition.[20]

Mary McCarthy was, by all accounts including her own, not very seriously interested in the finer points of radical politics. Assuming that the Communists represented the only radical possibility and attracted by their mystique, she was never closer to identifying herself with the Party than in 1936. Yet she spent that summer in the West and—as every intellectual New Yorker would have been eager to predict—fell out of touch with the news. McCarthy reentered radical social circles in the fall, knowing nothing of the Moscow Trials or the issues they had generated. At a party in November, McCarthy found herself being asked by James T. Farrell, in the midst of a group of people, to declare whether she thought

Trotsky was "entitled to a hearing" and to the "right of asylum"; McCarthy answered affirmatively, assuming that she was merely assenting to obvious democratic procedure. Four days later she found herself listed on the letterhead of the American Committee for the Defense of Leon Trotsky and, feeling that her name had been misappropriated, planned to deny her membership. Before she could do so, however, the phone began to ring as people who were barely acquaintances called, often very late, to advise her to leave the committee. With some committee members this tactic was successful, but McCarthy was driven by the pressure against her to determined resistance. Only after becoming committed did she begin to find out what the charges were all about, learning to her delight and "astonishment" that the trials appeared to be a "monstrous frameup" and that she was on the side of virtue.[21]

The spring of 1937 was a time of rapid developments in the Stalin-Trotsky face-off. The Defense Committee was busily organizing in March a "Commission of Inquiry into the Charges Against Leon Trotsky in the Moscow Trials" to go to Mexico and allow Trotsky to answer the accusations made against him. The most important appointment to the commission was that of seventy-eight-year-old John Dewey, "America's outstanding liberal," as chair. The Communist Party attempted to obstruct the commission in every way it could imagine; some eighty-eight prominent writers and liberal intellectuals signed an open letter opposing its work. Such tactics produced the kind of negative result with Dewey that they had with Mary McCarthy. Sidney Hook later recalled that "Dewey made up his mind irrevocably [to go to Mexico] only after he became aware of the efforts and far-flung stratagems of the Communist party to *prevent* him from going." The hearings held in Coyoacan, Mexico, in mid-April 1937 were probably as important for their symbolism as for the "not guilty" verdict on Trotsky that would eventually be announced in December. Conscientious dissenters *within the left* had successfully brought off an investigation of high political consequence in the face of concerted opposition from Popular Front liberals and the Communist Party.[22]

The movement to provide Trotsky with an asylum and a hearing was of no small consequence for those who would come together on the second *Partisan Review*. The Trotsky campaign brought together people of varying persuasions and created new channels of communication on the anti-Stalinist left. It was through the meetings organized by the Defense Committee that McCarthy came to know the "PR boys" (meaning Phillips and Rahv); and Macdonald made a monetary contribution to the work of the Dewey Commission and tried to assist its fundraising. Increasingly, through open choice or the coercions of the political climate, members of this embryonic group were coming to identify with each other and with a radical opposition to Stalinism.[23]

The nature of this opposition can easily be misunderstood, as it was to some extent by the Stalinists when they labeled opponents indiscriminately as Trotskyists. Among Phillips, Rahv, Macdonald, Dupee, and McCarthy, there stood not one who was fully prepared in early 1937 to oppose the Communist Party on broad political grounds or to champion the ideas of Trotsky. In April Dupee remarked to Macdonald in a letter on the trials: "I don't know anything about Trotzky. I must read him!" Macdonald had himself begun to read the basic radical texts only recently. McCarthy, trying to make herself an expert on the trials, read for the first time "a little in the Marxist canon." Even Phillips, though he had clearly studied at least some works of Marx before, reported from his vacation spot in the summer of 1937 that he was then busy reading Trotsky, Marx, and other radical texts. Such people were hardly ready to wage a campaign as the ideological partisans of Trotsky.[24]

Macdonald spent "several long evenings" with Rahv and Phillips in April, and by the beginning of May plans for the revival of *Partisan Review* were definitely afloat. Nothing about them, according to Macdonald's explanation to a friend, suggested advocacy of a Trotskyist position or direct political confrontation with the Communist Party: "Our idea is to make it a non-political Marxist journal of literary criticism and general cultural interest. . . . This sheet will have no affiliations and will print no polemics or articles on immediate political and tactical problems."[25] The planning was made possible by yet another Yale friend of Macdonald and Dupee, the painter George L. K. Morris, who had the means to finance *Partisan Review* and who himself cared relatively little about politics. Here was the magazine's first "angel," the very thing for which Phillips and Rahv had longed. The bedraggled spirits of the two editors must have soared at the prospects opened anew by Morris's purse.

By the end of May 1937, a group had clearly come into being that was ready to oppose the Popular Front and the Communist Party on cultural grounds. The call had gone out for a Second American Writers' Congress to be held in early June. On May 27 Rahv, Phillips, McCarthy, Farrell, and a few others met to "formulate plans for an opposition" at the Congress, with the understanding that Macdonald was also a part of their group. According to Farrell's report, there was little clear idea of how to proceed. Rahv and Phillips at first wanted the protest to be "non-political" and planned "merely to call for a proposal on a Marxist position in literature." Phillips would later recall that the Congress dissidents were "really pushed or propelled by Mary McCarthy and Dwight Macdonald," who "felt it was immoral not to express our opposition to the way the meeting was run."[26] Just before the Congress, Dupee came to a parting of the ways with the *New Masses*.[27] The editorial board of the planned *Partisan Review* could thus be completed, with Dupee joining Phillips, Rahv, Macdonald, McCarthy, and Morris. This group, with the deletion of Morris and the addition of Eleanor Clark, chose to invade the session on criticism at the Second Congress, over which Granville Hicks was presiding. At the center of their attack, Hicks later recalled was "the fact that the Communist party was dominating the Second Writers' Congress. It was the truth."[28]

Reporting on the Congress to Farrell shortly after it had occurred, Rahv and McCarthy mentioned that they had been attacked or resisted by Robert Cantwell, Newton Arvin, and Granville Hicks. Yet Rahv and McCarthy gave the impression that the gathering as a whole was "dead and deadly," with the papers that were read "utterly dull." This was not a report from people who felt they had crossed the Rubicon. The next day Rahv announced that Dupee had been expelled from the Communist Party as a result of what Farrell called "the meagre opposition there was at the Congress." Both Rahv and Farrell thought the Party was grossly overreacting to a minor incident.[29] Whether because they had been disaffected for so long and endured so many disagreements, or because in the crush of events and positions and stances they had simply lost track of what might cause a conclusive break, Phillips and Rahv seem not to have realized that the protest at the Writers' Congress would mark their final passage into opposition in the eyes of the Party.

What Granville Hicks remembered after thirty years was that with their action at the Writers' Congress, Phillips and Rahv "suddenly denounced Stalinism and transformed [*Partisan Review*] into an independent journal."[30] If the image of sudden change is not literally correct, it accurately reflects a certain perception of the events of June 1937 and pays rather dramatic homage to their cultural significance. The dissension at the Writers' Congress was not simply an internal affair, a squabble within the ranks of the kind radical parties generated in prolific number. The Congress was intended to be a carefully staged event, winning publicity for the

Popular Front and bringing liberals together with radicals in a festival of anti-fascist unity. The oppositionist band to which Phillips and Rahv belonged disturbed the smooth unfolding of the script. The troublesome presence of the *Partisan Review* group delivered a challenge to the Party's plans for cultural dominance on the left comparable to the Dewey Commission's check in the political realm.

If in June of 1937 the Popular Front seemed a great grazing beast and the *Partisan Review* group but a gadfly, a beginning had been made. With the aid of new friends and associates who provided certain assurances of social support and professional opportunity, Phillips and Rahv had finally cut themselves adrift from the Party and committed themselves to bringing out a magazine once more. The task that remained for Macdonald, McCarthy, Dupee, and the two veterans of *Partisan Review* was the considerable one of rallying the non-Stalinist troops behind their venture and of giving life to the idea of independent radicalism in print. To this task, the five prospective editors turned their talents and energies in the summer of 1937.

The editors of the new *Partisan Review*, Phillips has recalled, made up "a remarkably aggressive and varied board," a "jaunty, raucous, quarrelsome group, always disagreeing about something."[31] If the disagreements contributed to a high level of intellectual excitement around the magazine, the "varied" nature of the board helped put into practice the cosmopolitan values that the editors shared. The atmosphere on the left was not necessarily friendly toward a cosmopolitan approach in matters of ethnicity. Early expressions of Popular Front thinking had sometimes seemed to identify Americanism with assimilationism; later formulations celebrated particularist feeling. Nathan Glazer has noted that by 1938 "'sectarian' was used to refer not to the tendency for a group to emphasize its national culture, but quite the contrary, to the tendency of Communists of immigrant background to *refuse* to emphasize it!"[32] *Partisan Review* was interested neither in assimilation nor in particularism, but in cosmopolitan balance and openness to choice. The editorial board that came together in 1937 exemplified this idea as a pattern for group relations.[33]

Phillips and Rahv themselves came from one of the newer immigrant groups, the East European Jews, whose progeny were just beginning to affect American intellectual life in substantial ways. They were the founders, the veterans, the political sophisticates, who had built up a range of connections and experiences that would be part of their contribution to the magazine. The trio from Yale — Macdonald, Dupee, and Morris — with their upper-middle-class families of established respectability and their Ivy League connections, supplied *Partisan Review* with ties to the traditional cultured stratum of American society. Their presence gave firmer anchor, as Phillips and Rahv surely felt, to the magazine's desire for cosmopolitan integration and to its notions of maturation in American culture.

Mary McCarthy brought yet another element to the editorial board. Born in Seattle in 1912, then orphaned when she was six, McCarthy was shipped between two sets of relatives as a child, being given a strict Catholic education on the one side and the freedom to lose that same Catholic faith on the other. Graduating from Vassar in 1933, she entered the New York literary world with reviews and essays for the *New Republic* and the *Nation*. McCarthy came from quite a different background than the Chicago working-class haunts of James T. Farrell, but she and Farrell and a very few others gave *Partisan Review* delegates from the scattered intellectual offspring of the Catholic American Irish. This, too, added to the cosmopolitan social vision a more immediate credibility.[34]

By the end of June 1937, preparations for the revival of *Partisan Review* were moving into a more active stage. Nancy Macdonald (married to Dwight) had been selected as the business manager for the magazine. Morris sent her his first contribution — a check for three hundred dollars — at the end of the month.[35] When Phillips, Macdonald, and Dupee left New York for vacations during the summer, correspondence filled with the magazine's business flew about the countryside. The editors had become a group with a clear purpose, if not always a clearly stated rationale, and they seemed to thrive on their sense of comradeship and alliance-building.

Many of the magazine's strongest allies were radicals of varying stripe who had soured on Stalin and the Communist Party earlier than Phillips and Rahv.[36] One group had come together in the late 1920s under the leadership of Elliot Cohen, the managing editor of the *Menorah Journal*, to undertake a "nonreligious sociological attempt to understand the role of Jews in modern society."[37] Some members of this group would have no particular relation to *Partisan Review* a decade hence. Some, like Herbert Solow and Felix Morrow, would be minor contributors or useful acquaintances. One, Lionel Trilling, would become the most influential literary critic among the New York Intellectuals, publishing regularly in *Partisan Review*.

From 1929 to 1932 the Menorah group edged toward the Communist Party and its various offshoots. (Cohen gave up his editorship in 1932 and would drift about until he surfaced again as the first editor of *Commentary* in the 1940s.) The particular vehicle that attracted the group was the National Committee for the Defense of Political Prisoners (NCDPP), associated with the Communists' International Labor Defense. Yet the group was never very dependent on the Party, precisely because the Menorah writers already belonged to a circle "with a sense of purpose, identity, confidence, and its own leaders." In May 1933 several members of the Menorah group resigned from the NCDPP, including Cohen, Solow, Trilling, a friend of the group named George Novack, his wife, Elinor Rice, and her close friend Diana Rubin (who would become Diana Trilling). In early 1934 many from the same circle expressed public opposition to the Party when they signed a letter of protest against Communist tactics in breaking up a Socialist rally at Madison Square Garden. Some members of the group, like Solow and Novack, moved into Trotskyism; others remained on the left without clear organizational ties.[38] Trilling, one of the least political of the group, would later say of himself that "only for a very short time, and then quite presumptuously, did I think of myself as a Marxist." Yet after reading an account of the group that seemed to downplay their political seriousness, Trilling insisted that "the group was nothing if not political in the particular mode of radical politics at the time."[39] Not all members of the group were deeply engaged in radicalism, but they were politically well-informed and made up a significant cluster of opposition to Stalin by the mid-1930s.

In their resistance to the Communist Party and its tactics, the Menorah group had fallen into loose alliance by 1934 with another body of radical dissidents whose scholarly seriousness about Marx was beyond question. The most obvious tie among most in this second cluster was their involvement with the independent socialist Conference for Progressive Labor Action, which became in 1934 the American Workers Party (AWP), led by A. J. Muste. The Musteites included Sidney Hook, James Burnham, V. F. Calverton, James Rorty, and to some degree Edmund Wilson. Hook was now head of the philosophy department at NYU. Burnham, a colleague of Hook's at NYU, had earlier edited the magazine *Symposium*. Calverton was the editor of the *Modern Monthly*, and Rorty had been

a founding editor of the *New Masses*, though he had left that
magazine when it had become more rigidly Communist.

The AWP existed independently for only a few months. The
Trotskyists, finally convinced that their separation from the Communist Party was permanent, had begun to look for allies in the
United States and abroad. The model for this strategy became the
1934 entry of French Trotskyists into Leon Blum's Socialist Party,
the so-called French turn. The American equivalent led in its first
stage to negotiations between the Trotskyists and the AWP that produced in December 1934 a formal fusion of the two into the Workers Party. Although the majority of AWP members joined the new
party, and Burnham became one of the chief editors of the monthly
New International, some, including Hook, who had helped bring
the merger about, took no active role in the organization. Nevertheless, the fusion of the AWP and the Trotskyists brought together
in a loose circle of sympathy the *Menorah Journal* group, the Musteites, the original American Trotskyists, and various intellectuals
influenced by Trotsky, including Meyer Schapiro, Lionel Abel, and
Louis Hacker.[40] By the fall of 1935, with the new organization less
than a year old, the Trotskyists began to prepare for a second phase
of the "French turn" strategy—union with Norman Thomas's Socialist Party. In June of 1936 the Workers Party officially dissolved,
with most of its members joining the Socialists.[41]

By no means were all the intellectuals who were former Musteites, former *Menorah Journal* writers, or convinced Trotskyists
firmly united under the Socialist umbrella in 1936 and 1937. Although some were loyal to party or doctrine, others made independence of party a point of pride; sharp differences over theory and
practice limited positive cooperation.[42] Yet all remained sensitive
to radical issues and linked by their opposition to the Communist
Party. The Moscow Trials brought the anti-Stalinist intellectuals
into a common front: on the issues growing out of the trials, Trotskyists and Socialists worked in harmony; Musteites and Menorah
writers joined together once again; veterans of anti-Stalinism merged
their efforts with those of newer arrivals to that cause. The network thus created was of considerable comfort to those just ven-
turing forth on the path of opposition.

When the editors of *Partisan Review* began to seek contributions
and to build up their base of support in mid-1937, they turned logically to some of the leading intellectual opponents of the Communist Party. Open to suggestions about both people to approach
and topics to consider, the editors quickly followed up on their own

contacts and on those they could make through friends. Philip Rahv wrote to Macdonald in July, for instance, that he had "invited Schapiro, at the suggestion of Abel, to write an essay on the esthetics of John Dewey or to present us with some ideas for work he might like to do for us." Rahv later reviewed some of Abel's own proposals for articles, and asserted with evident enthusiasm, "I am all for Abel, for I think he is among the best minds we have to draw upon for contributions."[43] James Burnham at first sought a clear commitment from *Partisan Review* to Trotskyist views. Nevertheless, by early September Dupee was able to report that Burnham had given the magazine his cooperation if not his whole-hearted enthusiasm. Sidney Hook threw up no doctrinal barriers to involvement with *Partisan Review* and by late July had promised an essay on Kenneth Burke's most recent work. Such contributors indicated that the magazine was acceptable to, and receptive toward, a number of radical viewpoints; and though the editors might complain in private about someone's politics—as Phillips did about Hook's—they were sensible enough to welcome support for the magazine from various directions.[44]

With their plans for *Partisan Review* emphasizing literary and cultural discussion more than political analysis, the editors were also busy in mid-1937 seeking commitments from writers and critics of talent or reputation. In the literary sphere, they felt pressure to build a respectable alternative to the Popular Front. For the early issues of the new *Partisan Review*, the editors reached beyond the immediate context of New York radicalism to acquire contributions from Arthur Mizener at Yale and from Henry Levin and F. O. Matthiessen at Harvard. They called on the critical talents of William Troy and won a review from the gifted R. P. Blackmur. But the critic the editors most wanted to publish in their magazine was Edmund Wilson.

Macdonald took on the task of winning over Wilson while the other editors followed his progress eagerly and nervously. In early July Dupee wrote of his disappointment "that Wilson failed to burn up the wires with enthusiasm," but told Macdonald, "I trust you to bring him around, if anyone can." Rahv offered Macdonald tactical advice, and Phillips wrote to Farrell requesting his assistance in the wooing. By early August Rahv had heard good news from Macdonald and was optimistic: "The contact you have made with Wilson is really important; once we get him to contribute regularly we have set the pace for others of his calibre." Here, indeed, was the major point of the pursuit. Shortly afterward, Wilson seems to have backed away, earning a brisk letter from Macdonald. Dupee found Wilson's behavior a "pretty dirty trick, and his casualness annoying." Yet by mid-September the fences had been mended, and Dupee was free to fidget over whether Wilson would make the first issue's deadline. The whole nervous history of the chase suggested just how important Wilson was to the editors, and how reluctant they were to think ill of him. A considerable sense of relief and triumph must have prevailed when a Wilson essay arrived in timely fashion.[45]

The literary hopes of *Partisan Review* included the publication of poetry and fiction as well as criticism. Although James T. Farrell was a political friend and a novelist of considerable prestige in the thirties, his relationship with the new magazine developed only with difficulty. The editors had their doubts about his more recent fiction but could not afford to alienate or ignore him. Part of Farrell's new novel appeared in *Partisan*'s first issue of 1937.[46] John Dos Passos, long a respected but nettlesome author in the eyes of the Communist Party, responded to a solicitation from Rahv with barbs directed at Popular Front Americanism and a story that he claimed to have dug up from his desk drawer.[47] Wallace Stevens provided a poem for the first issue, and William Carlos Williams, before his participation became embroiled in political controversy, offered a verse that the editors decided not to use.

In some cases the approach to writers was a matter of recruiting old friends. Mary McCarthy had been one of four talented women writers who had together created a "rebel literary magazine" as undergraduates at Vassar, the others being Elizabeth Bishop, Eleanor Clark, and Muriel Rukeyser. After lunch with McCarthy, Rukeyser agreed to give *Partisan Review* a poem (though it never appeared); the others proved stalwart contributors in the first year of the new magazine.[48] Macdonald, in turn, was able to call upon James Agee, whom he had known at *Fortune*, who contributed poems and later a story to *Partisan Review*. Yet the most valuable piece of creative writing that the editors acquired in 1937 was almost certainly the story by Delmore Schwartz, "In Dreams Begin Responsibilities." A student of James Burnham, Sidney Hook, and Meyer Schapiro, Schwartz had already won Phillips's attention with a verse play in the *New Caravan* collection. When he submitted his story to *Partisan Review* in August of 1937, the editors "had the sense to recognize it as a masterpiece," as Macdonald later put it, and soon Schwartz was a regular part of *Partisan Review*'s social circle.[49]

The editors of *Partisan Review* had in fact done very well for themselves. Before the new magazine ever appeared, they had won contributions or promises of support from established writers and from relative newcomers, from fervent Trotskyists and from political independents, from academics and from free-lance intellectuals, and from a considerable variety of literary critics. Around the nucleus of the editorial board had gathered an array of associates who would provide regular sustenance to the magazine. Beyond them were more distant friends and contributors who would deliver occasional aid. Especially from the inner group that began to take on a collective identity from its involvement with *Partisan Review*, the editors needed all the social, intellectual, and political support they could get in 1937, for the Communist Party with its Popular Front allies was an imposing foe and one that willingly brooked no opposition on the left.

Given *Partisan Review*'s long-term success, it is all too easy to downplay or to forget how fragile the magazine's existence seemed in 1937, even—or perhaps especially—to its own editors. Because the circle of supporters that the magazine attracted proved talented, productive, and influential, it requires a conscious effort to remember that in 1937 most of them had published relatively little and were far from confident of their own success. Because *Partisan Review* in hindsight seems to have established itself quickly and forcefully, the hesitation and the fence-straddling of Phillips and Rahv in 1936 and early 1937 appear to reflect an excessive timidity, quite out of line with the intellectual courage and principled opposition often claimed by the anti-Stalinists. Yet on several levels the editors were indeed required to show their fortitude; and within the context of Party attack, the *Partisan* leaders earned their badge of courage.

When battle raged, Philip Rahv was frequently near the heart of the conflict. In March of 1937, not yet separated from the Communist Party, Rahv engaged in a skirmish in the *New Masses* that ended in a direct claim that the Popular Front position was "nothing but 'infantile leftism' turned upside down."[50] Soon closed off from the *New Masses*, he was able to continue publishing regularly through a series of reviews in the *Nation*. Rahv more than once chose to contrast the writer's proper regard for workmanship, moral values, and integrity with surrender to the corruptions of expediency and politics.[51] Such themes were obviously intended as a rebuke to Communist critical practices. In August Rahv managed to work into a review a positive reference to André Gide's recent critique of the Soviet Union. Later, he dismissed one set of Popular Front stories as the product of a "conveyor-belt" and tied the novels of two Party sympathizers to the formulas of Hollywood and the literary pabulum of melodrama.[52]

Rahv's *Nation* reviews provided a preview of the threat that a revived *Partisan Review* held for the *New Masses* and the Communist Party. The anti-Stalinists were a small minority on the left, as Party spokesmen delighted in pointing out, but a very troublesome minority. They insisted on being vocal in their dissent; they possessed individually and collectively a great deal of intelligence and polemical ability; and now they seemed prepared to get behind a magazine that would provide them with a regular forum. With tactics justified by their presumably noble ends, the critics and functionaries of the Party moved to deny the legitimacy of *Partisan Review* and the honesty of its editors, and to shut off every channel of support the Party's tentacles could reach.

The open Communist attack began with an item in the *New Masses* headed "Falsely Labeled Goods" that attempted to cast the integrity of *Partisan Review* into doubt before the magazine had appeared. In an effort to warn away Popular Front followers, the *New Masses* predicted Trotskyist sympathies for the new magazine though avoiding any specifics. An eagerness to besmirch *Partisan's* editors even led the *New Masses* to claim the magazine had been "stolen."[53] This remark transformed the *New Masses* attack from a burden into an opportunity for *Partisan Review*, as Dupee quickly saw: "the N.M. editorial was a blunder, in the sense that they lied about the ownership of the magazine—a simple fact which can easily be verified. We think we should push our advantage in this as far as possible."[54]

The letter that Phillips and Rahv soon addressed to the *New Masses* said much about how the two veterans of *Partisan Review* were coming to see their own history. They reviewed the changes in control over *Partisan Review* that had occurred between 1934 and 1936, with ownership and management at last falling completely to Phillips, Rahv, and Alan Calmer. "From whom, then, was the name of the magazine stolen?" the editors asked. "Surely not from ourselves?" For Phillips and Rahv, the early history of *Partisan Review* had already come to be defined not in terms of cooperation with the Communist Party, but in terms of incessant conflict with the *New Masses*: "every informed writer and reader knows that the *New Masses* and the *Partisan Review* were constantly at loggerheads on the problems of revolutionary literature. . . . The *New*

Masses . . . has always been part and parcel of the very tendency which the *Partisan Review* was fighting." Phillips and Rahv even claimed that *"Partisan Review* was started against the opposition of the *New Masses,"* and they minimized the attitudes they had earlier shared with Communist critics. The editors of the *New Masses* in responding emphasized the agreement of the past and the sharpness of the present break: "the writers in the *Partisan Review* and the writers in the *New Masses* agreed on those fundamental political principles which the present Trotskyite editors of the *Partisan Review* attack."

Behind the two views of the past were two sets of quite different assumptions. And in the differences lay the source for two versions of *Partisan Review*'s history, each with roots in reality though dramatically unlike the other. Phillips and Rahv assumed that the primary issues were cultural; with this in mind, the past was a record of conflict between two magazines "at loggerheads on the problems of revolutionary literature." The *New Masses* editors, by contrast, assumed that political questions came first; from their point of view, literary disputes were distinctly secondary to the more important agreement on "fundamental political principles." The difference in basic assumptions ran through the entire 1937 exchange between editorial boards, with the charges and counter-charges generally flying past one another rather than meeting on a common issue.[55]

Some of the attacks launched against *Partisan Review* came in the *Daily Worker*, the general tenor of which may be judged from the title of the first blast by Mike Gold: "A Literary Snake Sheds His Skin for Trotsky." Granville Hicks picked up the more serious campaign in the *New Masses* with an essay that tried both to discredit Phillips and Rahv and to defend the Communist literary record. In his most preacherly tone, Hicks declared that "Communism is good news" and that "the sectarians are not those who affirm the truth of Communism but those who quibble, and bicker, and nag, and deny." Responding specifically to "Literature in a Political Decade," Hicks combined a sneering personal attack on Phillips's and Rahv's critical competence with an attempt to dismiss their ideas as a "mixture of platitude and pedantry . . . not so much false as unimportant." He did not pause to explain why he was devoting so much energy to the refutation of platitudinous and unimportant ideas.[56]

The resources of the Communist Party were not limited to verbal blasts. The Party's ability to dominate the social lives of its members was also brought into play against those connected with the reviving magazine. According to the account set down by Farrell, William Phillips's wife, Edna, was expelled from her Party section after being offered the chance to remain in the Party if she left her husband. She did not recover easily from this wrenching experience, which grew out of her indirect involvement with the *Partisan Review* board. Farrell recorded several weeks after her expulsion that "Edna still seems to feel and miss the Party"; she had not yet "completely readjusted her life."[57]

If expulsions were sometimes an emotional jolt for those cast out, they were also a warning to those who remained with the Party. Writers in particular were vulnerable not only to the threat of social ostracism but also to the fear of losing their access to publication. This threat was at least implicit when Party sympathizers were asked to stay clear of *Partisan Review*. Dupee reported to Macdonald in September that Josephine Herbst had already been *"asked to boycott us,"* and Dupee concluded "that the same kind of campaign of personal appeal and pressure will be organized against us that was used with members of the Trotsky Committee." To face such a prospect without flinching took considerable nerve in 1937.[58]

Given both the actual and the assumed power of the Communist Party, the editors of *Partisan Review* could not help but be genuinely concerned over their future. In early November, with the first issue of the revived magazine coming out in a week, Farrell noted that Phillips and Rahv seemed to be "a little bit worried and frightened because the Stalinists attacked them so viciously." And the campaign was not over. The *New Masses* chose this time to announce a literary supplement once a month, with Farrell commenting: "This is obviously a move to counter any influence which *Partisan Review* might win." When the first new *Partisan Review* made its appearance, Rahv reported that "The Stalinists are trying to prevent some newsstands from selling it, and . . . in a few buildings, they have succeeded." The extent of the Communists' efforts disclosed the degree to which the very existence of *Partisan Review* exerted pressure on the Popular Front.[59]

In the first issue of its new literary supplement, the *New Masses* offered its readers two long articles by prominent Party critics and familiar foes of *Partisan Review*, Granville Hicks and Mike Gold. As Dupee had predicted, their complaints followed a pattern developed in the Communist campaign against the Trotsky Defense Committee. A year before, Gold had attacked "a little group of Phi

Beta Kappa Trotskyites," including Sidney Hook, James T. Farrell, and the "New York coffee-pot intellectuals," as people infected with a "simple inability to accept the internal discipline of any organization." When he returned to the assault in 1937, Gold opined that intellectuals were "peculiarly susceptible to Trotskyism, a nay-saying trend," and that those affected took their energy from the "simple malice of the Joycean intellectual, hating life." Gold remembered "the same people only a decade ago" as "eunuchs" seeking potency, needing sex, and desperately making the "ivory tower . . . into a bedroom." To affirm his own working-class virility, Gold declared loudly, "I want to spit whenever I think of it." If such tactics were intended to entertain and solidify the more militant supporters of the *New Masses* — and a good deal of the political rhetoric on all sides in the thirties seems to have served such purposes — perhaps Gold succeeded. But as usual, the sneering and smearing obscured his substantive point.[60]

Hicks mounted his assault on opponents of the Popular Front from a different direction, but he too followed precedent. In 1936 an early attack on the Trotsky Defense Committee had singled out for criticism two editors of the *Nation*. Hicks sought to apply pressure again in "A *Nation* Divided," an analysis that gave a clean bill of health to articles and editorials that praised the Soviet Union while bringing under close and hostile scrutiny those book reviews that had dared to criticize Stalin, the Communist Party, or the writing of Popular Front sympathizers. Hicks went through a long list of "reviewers opposed to the Communist Party" who had appeared under the literary editorship of Joseph Wood Krutch, including Anita Brenner from the *Menorah* group, James Rorty, Edmund Wilson, Philip Rahv, Sidney Hook, James Burnham, and James T. Farrell. With Krutch gone, Margaret Marshall had taken over the book review section in 1937, and Hicks found her worse because she dared to publish the "little group of individuals" who had disturbed the Second American Writers' Congress. Rahv was singled out for special opprobrium as a "turncoat" suffering from "general incompetence as a literary critic." Hicks asked quite directly for pressure against the *Nation* to exclude *Partisan Review* writers.[61]

The inaugural issue of the *New Masses* "Literary Supplement" had given eight of its first eleven pages to attacks on the *Partisan Review* editors, their associates, and the arguments of their camp. Hicks and Gold were not interested in matching wits with their opponents on matters of literary judgment or Marxist theory; they were interrested in discrediting and isolating *Partisan Review* and its supporters. The fact that all of this furor arose over a magazine able to place only some six hundred copies of its first issue on the newsstands reflected an environmental fact of major importance to the decade's radicalism: most of the intellectual debate on the left took place in New York City, and even in a rather small part of New York City. Contending factions were not scattered across the country; they shared the urban terrain. Political allegiances were not distant abstractions; they were an inescapable part of daily life. Factional enemies literally rubbed elbows in New York, for radical ideas were the province of New York and New York was in part a radical province.

Mary McCarthy, upon rereading her *Partisan Review* pieces from the period, was led back into vivid recollection of the physical setting of the magazine's offices: "This whole region [Union Square] was Communist territory; 'they' were everywhere — in the streets, in the cafeterias; nearly every derelict building contained at least one of their front-groups or schools or publications. Later, when the magazine moved to the old Bible House on Astor Place, *The New Masses* had offices on the same floor, and meeting 'them' in the elevator, riding down in silence, enduring their cold scrutiny, was a prospect often joked about but dreaded." McCarthy also remembered a sense "of being surrounded physically, of running a gamut."[62] It was within this environment that Phillips, Rahv, Macdonald, Dupee, and McCarthy made their decisions to oppose the Communist Party; and it was here that they earned their claims to personal and intellectual courage.

On the eve of *Partisan Review*'s rebirth, Dupee described for Macdonald the activities of a week in the magazine's new office:

> People pouring in. Independents and semi-independents demanding to be assured that we are not Trotskyites. Trotskyites demanding assurances that we are not Stalinists or 'Centrists.' Fears rising in us that all the political notoriety may frighten away [independent critics] such as Troy, Blackmur, Zabel etc, on whom we're absolutely dependent. Interviews: Wednesday with the 'Clarityites' Zam and Tyler; yesterday with [Trotskyist leader James Patrick] Cannon.[63]

Dupee's account was a catalogue of the pressures being brought to bear on the magazine from non-Communist sources. Combined with the actions of the Party, such pressures made those within the editorial circle all too acutely aware of their own, and of each other's, weaknesses. Phillips, Rahv, and Dupee were veterans of radical politics and of literary criticism—able to be trusted not to embarrass the magazine or to blunder through innocence. The same could not be said of the other three. McCarthy has recalled, for instance, that the other editors were "afraid that I was going to do something, in real life or in print, that would 'disgrace *Partisan Review.*'" George Morris, in turn, was "so 'confused' politically that one day he went into the Workers' Bookshop (Stalinist) and asked for a copy of Trotsky's *The Revolution Betrayed.*" Macdonald was rapidly acquiring a knowledge of radical theory but at first suffered from doubts about his ability to apply that theory and worried that the cultural level of *Partisan Review* would be too highbrow for him.[64]

As he tried to bring the first issue together, Dupee reported with frustration that Phillips had not even begun his piece: "I've had it out with him to the point where the nerves of us both are in shreds." Phillips seemed "constitutionally unable to do anything until the last minute; argument only produces a tidal wave of rationalizations." Rahv, "though infinitely more efficient around the office," caused similar concerns with his delays in preparing an editorial for *Partisan Review.* Macdonald had suggested that Dupee take on a more formal role as the "core" of the magazine staff, but Dupee wisely backed away from this possibility: "William's laziness plus Phil's sometimes insane panics and vacillations plus the temperamental flaws of the rest of us merely constitute a human situation which will have to work itself out. And unless it works itself out without the special intervention of any one individual, which in the long run would amount to Martyrdom, then it can't be said to have worked itself out successfully." If this seemed to offer less than encouraging prospects for a magazine not yet begun, Dupee was quick to turn away from the contemplation of personal blemishes, as if the simple recitation of his concerns had produced an immediate therapeutic effect:

These problems, personal and political, are all real enough, but that doesn't mean that we can[']t solve them. In fact when one succeeds in detaching oneself for a moment from the anxiety which they breed, one is really tremendously stimulated by it all. What an opportunity! Scarcely any group in the world is in our position to accomplish something. And I'm convinced that we have enough talent among us to really cope with the opportunity. The grasp, penetration and articulateness of P. and R. [Phillips and Rahv] are sometimes amazing.

Doubts and depressions were bearable in 1937 because they could occasionally be swept aside by a tide of exalted hopes.[65]

For Dupee, Phillips, and Rahv, who had once been inspired by the Communist promise, the rebirth of *Partisan Review* brought with it a rejuvenation of purpose and vision. To their minds the Party had distorted the meaning of radical literature and destroyed the excitement and possibility the movement had once possessed. With the new *Partisan Review*—independent in outlook and support—the editors embraced an opportunity to regain their sense of mission, to recapture the feelings of movement and excitement, to revivify the cause of radical literature. A telling barometer was Phillips's and Rahv's analysis of the literary situation—a kind of evaluation that nearly always said as much about their own mood as about the state of American writing. The language of 1937 echoed the formulations of 1934: "Signs of a new turn are now appearing; notes of rebellion are heard on all sides, and as the work of the younger writers is straining to break through the creative formulas of the thirties, the urge to revaluate the immediate past can no longer be denied."[66] Once again the culture was at a turning point, youthful rebels promised new fertility, and literature stood poised to spring toward higher levels. And, once again, *Partisan Review* would seek to be the agent of that advance.

Chapter Five | The Politics of Anti-Stalinism

With controversy already assured, the opening statement of the new *Partisan Review* for December 1937 did its best to spell out the magazine's position on several fronts. In its new form, the editors declared, *Partisan Review* would be at once radical in tendency and "unequivocally independent." The magazine would remain "aware of its responsibility to the revolutionary movement in general," though specifically disclaiming "obligation to any of its organized political expressions." The statement might have stopped there, but it did not. Even as the editors maintained that their "underscoring" of the magazine's independence was not based "primarily on our differences with any one group," their statement belied that claim through its preoccupation with the Communist Party. "Party literary critics," the editors charged, rode herd over radical writing with the "zeal of vigilantes." The Communists had encouraged an intrusion of political factionalism into culture, distorting literature through irrelevant considerations and producing a "ruinous bitterness among writers." The Communists were clearly a central concern for *Partisan Review*.

Yet the editors could say with some justice that their concern for literary freedom did not owe its origin to current differences with the Party. Their statement asserted a fundamental continuity: "Formerly associated with the Communist Party, *Partisan Review* strove from the first against its drive to equate the interests of literature with those of factional politics." The magazine's reappearance on an independent basis rested on the conviction "that the totalitarian trend is inherent in that movement and that it can no longer be combatted from within." The editors recognized, in other words, that *Partisan Review* had once been inside the Communist movement and was now outside, but they argued that this shift occurred as part of a consistent drive to protect the interests of radical literature. The implication, in fact, was that the Party

120

had changed, that repression within Communist ranks had grown greater, that the stable principles of *Partisan Review* had come under increasing attack from the enforcers of a mutable dogma.

In summing up their intentions for the revived magazine, the editors stressed the freedom of opinion and the diversity of literary viewpoint an independent stance would allow. *Partisan Review* would demand no "conformity to a given social ideology or to a prescribed attitude or technique." For the editors, such a position was entirely consistent with a radicalism that would support critical thinking and the free flow of ideas: "Marxism in culture, we think, is first of all an instrument of analysis and evaluation; and if, in the last instance, it prevails over other disciplines, it does so through the medium of democratic controversy." The new *Partisan Review* would seek to provide such a medium—an aim that implied more openness, more questioning, more room for doubt than had existed earlier.[1]

The positions announced in the editorial statement were significant ones, but exactly what did they mean? In 1937 such pronouncements remained generalizations that had yet to be tested and given specific content in practice. For *Partisan Review*, the whole notion of an independent radicalism awaited definition. Behind a tone of assurance, the editors struggled with a host of uncertainties and worked out from day to day the meaning of their principles and values.

The new *Partisan Review* intended from the first to create a radical opposition to Communist and Popular Front influence in American culture. Guided by their own charges against the Communists, the editors might have anticipated that opposition on cultural grounds would seem to the Party little different from opposition on political grounds. They might have known from their own experience that they would be roundly condemned as opponents of the Soviet Union and allies of fascism, whatever their protestations to the contrary. Yet they began their work hoping to escape the logic of their situation, hoping to forestall a full-fledged Communist campaign against them by declaring *Partisan Review* a "Literary Monthly" and by restraining, in some cases, their own political instincts.[2] Within its first half-year, *Partisan Review* would move by jagged steps to an explicit anti-Stalinism based on political as well as cultural criticisms of the Party, but such a position was a matter of evolution rather than a constant policy present at the creation.

Perhaps uncertainty over the magazine's proper political stance was most visible in the editors' early discussion of whether to print the work of André Gide. In early 1937 Gide had published *Return from the U.S.S.R.*, a report that found much to criticize in Russian society. Transformed from ally to enemy in the eyes of the Communists, Gide had been harshly attacked by Party sympathizers; in response Gide prepared another book, *Second Thoughts on the U.S.S.R.*, to answer his critics. The idea that this might offer a special opportunity for *Partisan Review* first came from Rahv. Pointing out to Macdonald in late July of 1937 that Gide's second book had just appeared in French, Rahv suggested that both the publishers and the liberal magazines would probably ignore the new work, having "had enough" already: "Why can't we take the initiative and publish in our first number a series of extracts from the book[?]." Rahv was "excited" over the prospect of publishing Gide and over the nature of the book's attack on Communist attitudes toward literature; and for a time this enthusiasm banished all hesitation.[3]

By early September permission had been obtained from Gide to excerpt his book. Yet reservations soon began to appear. Dupee expressed doubts to Macdonald about using Gide and brought up the question of retaining valued contributors in the face of Communist pressures: "The Troys etc. can be counted on to go along with us, and even put up with a lot of nuisance from the Stalinists, providing that we can prove to them that we are *really* non-political. Yet the Gide piece, though written by a literary man, is purely political." Dupee's concerns defined the editors' dilemma in 1937. They wanted to speak out against Stalinism, and they admired Gide's powerful critique; yet they also wanted to publish a cultural magazine free of factional limitations ("non-political" in Dupee's revealing phrase), and they feared a loss of literary support should they give too much attention to politics.[4]

Rahv had also changed his mind. Although Macdonald and perhaps McCarthy wanted to go ahead with the material, the majority of the board decided against publishing the Gide piece in the first issue. A letter from Rahv to Gide in late November made it clear that Communist hostility and the fear of losing contributors had influenced the editors' decision not to publish. The decision seemed to be permanent. Then, just ten days after having told James T. Farrell that the piece had been "definitely rejected," Phillips announced that the Gide material would appear in the magazine's second issue. The January 1938 *Partisan Review* published excerpts from *Second Thoughts on the U.S.S.R.*, and a letter went out from the editors to Gide explaining that they now felt the piece should appear in spite of its possible effects.[5] What had happened in that ten days? The most likely cause of the shift in editorial opinion would seem to be the appearance of the December 7, 1937, literary supplement to the *New Masses* containing the lengthy attacks on *Partisan Review* and its supporters by Mike Gold and Granville Hicks. If Party critics were going to do their worst in any case, the doubting editors may well have reconsidered where the gain would lie in not printing Gide.

The Party's tendency to attack wildly and to heap vituperation on its opponents probably accounted for the addition of a short polemical section called "Ripostes" to the first few issues of the new *Partisan Review*. The "Ripostes" of December 1937 charged that the Communist press, without ever having seen the new *Partisan Review*, had attacked it "savagely, and at times hysterically" and on an "entirely political" basis. The reply noted especially the misquotation of one of Rahv's unpublished WPA manuscripts that "the Party's OGPU somehow laid hands on." Rahv had written, in a sentence *Partisan Review* felt was "accurate to the point of being positively banal," that "the literary Left-wing movement is particularly native to New York, for its underlying philosophy, Marxism, is a product of European thought." The *Daily Worker*, quoting this sentence without the word "literary," assailed Rahv for taking the "counter-revolutionary line" of trying "to smear Communism as 'foreign'" and condemned "Rahv's services to the fascists." *Partisan Review*'s response was sharp: "According to this line of reasoning, the real friend of fascism was Marx himself who, not foreseeing that Communism would become Twentieth Century Americanism, was gauche enough not to be born in a Kentucky log cabin." This was a direct mockery of the Popular Front strategy, enlivened by the editors' ready contempt for rural and nativistic patriotism, and it illustrated once again the tendency of the Party's repressive campaign to drive the editors toward a more openly political stance. Yet though such a response was clearly steeped in political differences, the editors could fairly say that their retort was primarily a defense of their cultural viewpoint. The magazine had not yet taken up a fully developed anti-Stalinist position that would allow direct political criticism of the Soviet Union or the Communist Party.[6]

Within the editors' notions of cultural criticism, however, much was possible. The book reviews alone in the first issue were sufficiently hostile to the Communists and their sympathizers to make the editors' distinction between cultural and political critique —

and the whole debate over publishing Gide—seem rather hollow from a distance. Lionel Trilling gave the lash to Robert Briffault's *Europa in Limbo*, turning the positive critical appraisals of his work into an emblem of Communist literary inadequacy. "If there is one thing the dialectic of history teaches," Trilling lectured, "it is an attitude on cultural matters . . . [that] is difficult and complex." The attitude of Briffault and his allies was simple, and dangerous because "indiscriminate, irresponsible and ignorant of the humanity it seeks to control." Trilling posed no direct political challenge, but his cultural criticism attacked on such a broad front that few could mistake his animosity toward Communist policies in general.[7]

Trilling at least left something to the imagination. No similar discretion restrained the political temper of Sidney Hook, who reviewed Kenneth Burke's *Attitudes Toward History* for the first issue of the new *Partisan Review*. Hook had little to gain by mincing words, and from first to last he indicted Burke for an absence of what might be called intellectual professionalism. Philosophical and practical objections to Burke's arguments led to the assertion that Burke had functioned as a "propagandist" while neglecting his duties as a "craftsman." Burke demanded "ideological homogeneity," Hook charged; relativism for him became "only a relativity of *phrasing* for the one true line," which was a "party-line." Hook managed to bring in references to the touchiest kinds of political issues, suggesting that Burke had swallowed Stalinist distortions of the past as well as the accusations made during the Moscow Trials. Burke's true function, Hook acidly remarked, consisted in being "an apologist, not after the fact, but *before* the fact, of the latest piece of Stalinist brutality."[8]

Hook's political vehemence could not have been unexpected. Yet even after this inflammatory piece by a prominent opponent of the Communist Party had appeared in *Partisan Review*, the editors still hesitated to let the magazine seem too openly political. For three weeks after the first issue appeared, the editorial board remained reluctant to print their excerpts from Gide.[9] At least some of the editors, in making their distinctions, were trying to observe a very fine line indeed. They had begun the new *Partisan Review* by seeking to promote their anti-Stalinism while avoiding its consequences, and that they could not do.

The decision to print Gide made the second issue of *Partisan Review* more openly political than the first. In the excerpts chosen, Gide condemned the Soviet Union unequivocally and closed with an outburst that could have become a theme song for many of the anti-Stalinist intellectuals: "The U.S.S.R. is not what we hoped it would be, what it gave promise of being, what it still tries to appear to be; it has betrayed our hopes."[10] *Partisan Review* published at the same time a response to Hook from Kenneth Burke and Hook's reply to it, providing from the beginning that sense of vibrant exchange and direct conflict between ideas that would give *Partisan Review* its reputation for intellectual excitement in the late thirties. Burke managed to show by quoting a long passage from his book that Hook had concentrated on a small section of it and exaggerated the directness of its implications for politics. Yet Burke's effort to counterattack mainly gave Hook a chance to exhibit his polemical skills in a slashing response that again gave vent to a long list of complaints against the Stalinists.[11]

The editors, meanwhile, were able to make hay out of a blatant *New Masses* attempt to stifle *Partisan Review*. The second "Ripostes" section devoted itself primarily to the successful effort by the Communists to keep William Carlos Williams from publishing in the new magazine. Williams had in fact submitted two poems for consideration at the editors' request, and they had announced that his work would appear in *Partisan Review*. But after these were returned to him along with a request to see more, the *New Masses* accused *Partisan Review* of having falsely announced Williams as a contributor, quoting the poet to the effect that *Partisan Review* had none of his contributions and would receive none. On inquiry, Williams explained that he had chosen to continue his contributions to the *New Masses* and to ignore the new magazine when he "found the *New Masses* violently opposed to you on political grounds, so much so that they refused to print me if I remained a contributor to *Partisan Review*." Here was the kind of pressure on writers that the editors had both feared and expected from the Communists, and they made the best of the situation by publicizing the incident.[12]

If the editors had once imagined that caution might gain them credit with the Communist Party, the *New Masses* had by now dashed that idea. If the editors had once thought it necessary to curb political comment to retain the support of largely non-political critics, that reason, too, had lost its power as the magazine established a foothold and demonstrated its serious intellectual intent. The path seemed open toward a stronger political stance. Whether, or in what way, *Partisan Review* might travel down that path was not yet clear. The editors argued that radicalism stood in support of their positive literary goals; yet they had to admit privately, at least, that the program on which they had launched *Partisan Review* was "hard to formulate."[13]

A major obstacle to any clearly defined posture was their own experience with the Communist Party and their determination to keep *Partisan Review* free from any formal political ties. A skittishness about organized parties and radical doctrine was perhaps most apparent in the editors' relations with the Trotskyists and with Leon Trotsky himself. Enormously impressed by Trotsky and wishing in some way to win his favor, the editors of *Partisan Review* nevertheless kept him at arm's length and demonstrated that they were entirely sincere and acutely sensitive about the magazine's independence.

Trotsky's appeal, for the *Partisan Review* intellectuals, operated on a number of levels. To begin with, Trotsky was quite simply the most visible and the most significant symbol of radical opposition to Stalin; and the Moscow Trials had made him a rallying point for the non-Communist left. A theorist of considerable power and scope, Trotsky provided a ready-made critique of Stalinism cast in Marxist terms. Bitter about the damage done by Stalinism to their own hopes, the *Partisan Review* intellectuals welcomed the negative analytical bite of Trotsky's work. Yet Trotsky's critique of Stalinism also appealed because it did not go too far. Followers of Trotsky could maintain their faith in radical thought, the socialist promise, and the original potential of the Russian Revolution. Indisputably a man of powerful intellect, Trotsky had also been a man of affairs, and the organizer of military victory for the revolution. Trotsky exemplified the combination of theory and action, culture and politics, that so many intellectuals had longed for but that so few were able to achieve. Now he seemed almost alone to represent the true socialist vision of Bolshevism, to hold out for intellectuals the possibility that their Marxism was sound and their belief in the revolution justified, since the corruptions of the vision could all be laid at the doorstep of Stalin.

Even with all this, more was necessary. The chief source of the *Partisan Review* editors' professed dissatisfaction with the Communist Party lay in its attitudes toward literature; it seems unlikely that Trotsky's ideas could have attracted them for long were not his cultural conceptions taken to be vastly superior to those of the Party. In fact, Trotsky upheld several principles that meshed very well with the editors' own inclinations in 1937. More than a decade before, Trotsky had attacked the concept of a narrowly "proletarian" culture in *Literature and Revolution,* insisting that once the revolution had been won and a new culture had begun to emerge, the proletariat would no longer exist as a class. Trotsky insisted that culture developed through the "historic succession" of generations; and because the standards of true culture were always high, intellectuals for the present must lead in artistic contributions and in guarding standards and traditions.[14]

Members of the editorial board would later remember Trotsky's significance in different ways, but each emphasized ideas or traits with which the new *Partisan Review* could identify. Phillips would later recall that it was Trotsky "who came out for [the] principle of radical continuity." Rahv looked back on Trotsky as the "great outsider," an image suggesting a special appeal to those seeking sustenance for opposition and dissent. And McCarthy found in Trotsky a man "who possessed those intellectual traits of wit, lucidity and indignation which I regarded, and still regard, as a touchstone." It is difficult to imagine any one becoming, or remaining, a partisan of Stalin on such a basis.[15]

For a variety of reasons, therefore, ranging from the political and the theoretical to the literary and the personal, the editors of *Partisan Review* were sympathetic to Trotsky as they worked to organize the magazine on a new basis in the summer of 1937. Given their respect for him and their search for significant contributors, it was perhaps a natural step for the editors to invite Trotsky to write for them. Dwight Macdonald made the approach. *Partisan Review,* Macdonald explained in a letter to Trotsky, would be an "independent Marxist journal" with an emphasis on "literature, philosophy, culture in general, rather than on economics or politics." Macdonald went on to offer a series of suggestions for contributions, with his tone suggesting high confidence that Trotsky would cooperate and that he would accept the primacy of cultural topics in the magazine. Yet, as Trotsky quickly sensed, the letter reflected uncertainty. Approaching Leon Trotsky in the midst of the Moscow Trials and asking him, in effect, to avoid "economics or politics" indicated a divided purpose. It is not even clear whether the editors would have published his contribution in their first issue had he offered one—for the publication of Trotsky's writing on any subject would surely have been more inflammatory politically than excerpts from Gide.[16]

Trotsky on his part proved to be rather more rigid and demanding in practice than the editors seem to have expected. Responding to Macdonald, he declared that he would be "very happy to collaborate in a genuine Marxist magazine pitilessly directed against the ideological poisons" of Stalinism. Whether *Partisan Review* was such a magazine remained an open question for Trotsky. Moreover, the immediate mention of collaboration implied a relationship quite beyond what the editors had in mind; at the end of the letter, Trotsky raised the question of "systematic rather than episodic collaboration." Trotsky would have preferred to have *Partisan Review* accept his guidance and control, and he assumed for himself from the first the role of both teacher and judge. In making it clear that he expected a "programmatic declaration" from *Partisan Review* and that he would like to see it "before its publication if possible," Trotsky demanded in effect that the magazine pass a political litmus test.[17]

The editors of *Partisan Review* had no intention of placing themselves at Trotsky's disposal whatever their respect for him. They were serious about maintaining their political independence, even as they longed to make an impact. Rahv declared Trotsky's letter "ridiculous" and endorsed Edmund Wilson's advice that *Partisan Review* should stay away from the Stalin-Trotsky controversy. At the same time, Rahv suggested that the magazine could not "avoid taking a hand in it," and he remained "eager" to gain Trotsky as a contributor. One of the editors would later remark that *Partisan Review's* interest in independence came "from our head" and perhaps "from an instinct of self-preservation," while "in our hearts we felt . . . that political interest, nay commitment, was an essential part of the equipment of the Compleat Thinker."[18]

Macdonald tried to explain *Partisan Review's* policy in a second letter to Trotsky accompanied by a brief program for the magazine. *Partisan Review* would not take "any specific position on questions of Marxist strategy," nor would it take part in "*immediate* political controversies"; the magazine would remain, by Macdonald's lights, "ideological in character, rather than political." All the editors were in their own political lives opposed to Stalin, believers in a Leninist program, and eager for a new radical party to replace the Comintern, according to Macdonald; but as editors they could not "impose such ideas on the literary contents" of their magazine. Macdonald was thus asking in the name of *Partisan Review* that Trotsky and others separate discussions of Marxist theory from questions of radical practice, and that they allow a distinction between the intellectual as writer and the intellectual as political citizen.[19]

Such attempts to stake out a territory for free debate apart from practical and immediate concerns were not new.[20] Yet the argument had seldom impressed champions of political commitment, and the editors themselves found it difficult to make their distinctions work in 1937. Macdonald's own letter pointed to a mingling of literary and political considerations that undercut the separation of spheres he had described. The distinctions were likewise muddied by the claim that though charges of Trotskyism were "inaccurate," the editors were "by no means ashamed or frightened by the connections they establish between your ideas and our magazine." And what was Trotsky to make of a renewed request for contributions on cultural and literary questions, with Macdonald acknowledging that "of course, your approach to cultural problems fully involves your entire political position"? Where were the lines to be drawn?

Trotsky's second response in early September 1937 made a particular point of the "special blow against 'political dogmatism'" in the brief statement of *Partisan Review*'s position Macdonald had sent him. Trotsky insisted that the "average philistine" understood "political dogmatism" to mean any "definite political program, even every serious political thinking" [*sic*]. The Stalinists were characterized by "political servilism" and had no dogma at all; hence, the *Partisan Review* formula of opposing dogmatism was "not correct." Both the tone of Trotsky's letter and his indication that he would wait awhile before deciding "if and how far we can go along" created frustration among the editors, especially as Trotsky remained for them a compelling figure.[21]

Trotsky's relations with *Partisan Review* were not helped by his association with the political stratagems and the shrill language of the Trotskyist organization in the United States. The followers of Trotsky were by the summer of 1937 ready to complete the "French turn" by separating themselves from the Socialist Party, taking many members of the Young People's Socialist League with them.[22] The editors of *Partisan Review* watched the whole process with interest and with some anxiety that the tendency toward a politicized approach to cultural matters might exist among Trotskyists as well as Stalinists. This fear seemed only to be confirmed by the reception the first issue of *Partisan Review* received in the *Socialist Appeal*, the Trotskyists' major publication in this period.

The *Appeal* accused *Partisan Review* of proposing "to remain independent, i.e. neutral and indifferent," toward revolutionary politics, and of being "culpable of ignoring, and thus denying in practice," the close bond between literary and political concerns. The editors carefully chose these charges to repeat. With a hint that such logic was ridiculous, they remarked, "So the *Appeal*, by equat-

ing independence with indifference, lands us in pure estheticism."
On this ground, the editors could erect their defenses: the Trotskyists were saying such things merely because *Partisan Review* had
not endorsed their movement (the very charges thus became proof
to *Partisan's* readers that the magazine was truly independent).
Moreover, they suggested, the claim that *Partisan Review* was riding the pendulum toward aestheticism suggested a misrepresentation of both the editors' expressed attitudes and the contents of the
first issue.[23] A stronger answer to the Trotskyists' "over-zealous
simplifications" and "ultimate demands" came in a letter written
to the *Appeal* by John Wheelwright and published in *Partisan Review*. Although a Trotskyist himself, Wheelwright charged in stern
language that the Trotskyists as a party were behaving like the Stalinists in attacking *Partisan Review*. In the process, he saved the
editors from any need to make such a comparison on their own.[24]

The attitudes displayed in the *Socialist Appeal* tended to make
Partisan Review more hesitant about any closer ties with the Trotskyists. Yet the editors had left the position of Trotsky himself conspicuously free from condemnation, and they remained hopeful of
some contribution from the exile. A letter arriving from Mexico
at about this time brought the harshest criticism yet from Trotsky,
who nevertheless managed, like the editors, to leave the door open
for future cooperation. Speaking "very frankly," Trotsky announced
his "general impression that the editors of *Partisan Review* are
capable, educated, and intelligent people but *they have nothing to
say*." *Partisan Review* could protect its cultural interests only by
fighting for a definite political program, and Trotsky's argument
implied that his program was available. In language that was meant
to sting, Trotsky accused *Partisan Review* of wishing in the main
"to demonstrate its respectability" and went on to charge the editors with seeking to create a "small cultural monastery." Aware of
the harsh bite of his statements, Trotsky suggested that if the editors found his tone too sharp, it would only prove that they wished
to publish a "peaceful 'little' magazine"—a remark that turned a
familiar characterization of literary periodicals into a scornful epi-
thet. If, on the other hand, they did not find his tone a "hindrance"
(that is, Trotsky implied, if they were political grown-ups), the exchange could continue.[25]

Philip Rahv rose to Trotsky's challenge. Replying with a letter
more extensive, more detailed, and more serious than any of Macdonald's had been, Rahv seemed to step in as a political veteran
and to speak as a senior partner on the *Partisan Review* board. Much

could be conceded. Rahv was prepared to admit insecurity and uncertainty in the early issues of the magazine. But he was also prepared to react vigorously to Trotsky's critique and to challenge the exile's behavior. Rahv's letter, reflecting the combination of insecurity and bold assurance that shaped the new *Partisan Review*, spoke more frankly than any program published in the magazine itself.

It was the larger world, the "objective situation," that Rahv blamed in part for the magazine's vagueness of purpose. *Partisan Review* was "the first anti-Stalinist left literary journal in the world"; at the same time, it was "encumbered with a Stalinist past" and "subject to the tremendous pressure of the American environment towards disorientation and compromise." Given this context, Rahv insisted, it was "inevitable" that the new *Partisan Review* should "grope for direction, feel its way towards possible allies, incline to deal somewhat gingerly and experimentally with issues that ideally require a bold and positive approach, and lastly—that . . . it should in some respects have leaned over backward to appear sane, balanced, and (alas!) respectable." Rahv's admission of *Partisan Review's* early tentativeness almost went too far. The magazine did want to be "balanced" and intellectually "respectable"; and Rahv's "alas," if honestly meant, was simply one more reflection of a mind divided.[26] As his letter to Trotsky went on, Rahv turned as much to attack as to defend.

Although Trotsky was a strategist and a theoretician of major stature, Rahv did not shrink from calling his judgments and his perspective into question. Rejecting the personal rebuke directed at the editors, Rahv suggested that Trotsky was so wrapped up in his ideological positions that he was not seeing clearly the realities of the moment. For Rahv, those realities were most pressing. Chief among them was the impact of Stalinism on radical intellectuals, to which Trotsky had shown little sensitivity. Recent experience demanded that radical ideas should be examined anew, that intellectuals should take stock, and this could not be done from doctrinaire positions aping the rigidities of Stalinism.

The editors had asked Trotsky to participate in a symposium they were planning, to be entitled "What Is Alive and What Is Dead in Marxism?" To Trotsky, both the proposed symposium and the assumptions behind it were suspect. He complained that the editors approached Marxism as if they were "beginning history from a clean page." Many of the writers whose participation they sought could not be "entrusted with deciding whether Marxism is a living force." Trotsky "categorically" refused to participate.[27] Rahv's response was as frank as Trotsky's scolding. To Rahv, a symposium presupposed "a tolerance of several points of view," or there was no rationale for its publication. Trotsky's was a purist attitude that ignored reality: "Unfortunately, to many people the defeat of the working classes in Russia and Western Europe together with the moral abyss revealed by the Moscow trials, are tantamount to a *theoretical* refutation of the basic principles of Marxism. Surely, this melancholy fact will not be abolished by the refusal of Marxists to take it into account." The editors of *Partisan Review* continued to believe in the "basic principles," Rahv asserted; but "in order to convince others," believers could not approach them with doctrinal lectures and threats of excommunication.

The editors of *Partisan Review* clearly had their differences with Trotsky and shared some of the doubts associated with "skeptical and agnostic tendencies." Yet there was a common ground. In anti-Stalinism the two parties could find a basis for cooperation. By expressing bitterness toward the Communist Party and the Soviet Union more openly, *Partisan Review* could take a stronger political stance. Growing disaffection and doubt, when directed toward Stalinism, could be taken to represent growing political commitment. Given this situation in which negative critique could be seen as positive statement, Rahv was able to concede *Partisan Review*'s political uncertainty and yet claim radical achievement, to reject Trotsky's demands and yet promise a magazine that would please him more. The key was anti-Stalinism.

According to Rahv, *Partisan Review* stood at a turning point. The task of giving the magazine "firm direction," of "filling the notions of independence and freedom with an aggressive radical content," remained ahead. The editors planned "to re-orient the magazine, to stiffen its ideological spine," with a long editorial statement in the April issue (the fifth) "that no one will be able to dismiss on the ground of its being abstract or gently negative. We intend to call things by their right names." Rahv could promise, and deliver, a more open political commitment because the editors had clearly been moving toward a more direct engagement with Stalinism in any case. The trend owed something to the exchanges with Trotsky, to Communist attacks, and to the magazine's dependence on contributors whose quarrels with the Party were open and sharp. Yet there were even more fundamental forces at work.

The complex of cultural values that underlay many of the editors' opinions in both literature and politics worked to deepen continually their antipathy toward the Communists and their sympathizers. Judgments based on such values had earlier led toward *Partisan Review*'s break with the Party, and they now shaped the nature and extent of the magazine's opposition to it. When the statement promised to Trotsky appeared, it was an essay by Rahv alone attacking the Moscow Trials. This seemed, for a time, to have the desired effect of improving relations with Trotsky. Yet what it delivered was not a positive commitment to his cause but an impassioned, agonized cry against Stalinism that was very much in *Partisan Review*'s own terms—established by the values of cosmopolitanism.

As the new *Partisan Review* got under way, the urban-cosmopolitan aggregation of values was much in evidence. A sharing of biases and assumptions provided a significant basis for agreement and cooperation between the members of the new editorial board and their close intellectual allies. The private correspondence of the editors in July 1937, for instance, seemed almost self-consciously to emphasize such ties. With one person and then another going out from New York on vacation, the letters "home" carried reports on the hinterlands that seemed to double as expressions of loyalty. Dupee wrote from a spot near Chicago: "People out here really are appalingly [sic] *crude, dull, ignorant*, and complacent." Phillips reported from Vermont that all around him he saw the "idiocy of the village"; he claimed to be gaining a sense of the farmer's "oxcart indifference"; and he plaintively begged for news on the grounds that he was "losing that sense of event and situation which comes from talking to people in New York." From Manhattan, meanwhile, Rahv complained to a vacationing Macdonald that the city was practically deserted, leaving few chances for the "intellectual fraternization" it normally offered. The country was isolation, narrowness, and ignorance; the city was information, sophistication, intellectuality.[28]

The first issues of the new *Partisan Review* saw editors and contributors bring the country-city dichotomy into the discussion of a wide variety of ideas both American and European. Trotsky had argued, according to Phillips, that "the Revolution ushered in a more conscious and more direct struggle between the values of the city and those of the country." The tendency Trotsky had regarded as "the most revolutionary literary movement" was the one that represented "the most extreme, bohemian—urban—reaction to the old society."[29] Macdonald described an older tradition of humor in America based "on the small town culture of the hinterland" and declared that it was allied politically with "the populists." When World War I "destroyed the populist position in humor as in politics," a "sophisticated" humor moved in as "the provinces steadily lost ground to the intelligentsia of the big cities." McCarthy inquired into Maxwell Anderson's commercial success, and found this "native middle-westerner" to be "a genuine *naif*, a rustic," with a mind "like a musty, middle-western law-office of thirty years ago"; Anderson had "no system of intellectual values," at least none that an urban critic could respect.[30]

The defense of *Partisan Review*'s cultural vision became a crusade in the magazine's book review section. Reflecting both firm conviction and considerable nervousness, reviewers repeatedly condemned values antagonistic to cosmopolitanism as fertile soil for fascism. James Burnham declared Thurman Arnold "against science, for myths and the religion of the blood," while explaining in a footnote that Arnold's ideas were not fascist but merely "material for exploitation" by fascists. Meyer Schapiro mocked Frank Lloyd Wright's view that "a primitive state of democratic individualism in the Eden of the small towns and the farms was perverted by the cities." The "reactionary character" of Wright's vision became apparent, according to Schapiro, in the attitudes of the man he had chosen as co-author: Baker Brownell shared "the Nazi enthusiasm and vagueness about the folk . . . which he opposes to the landless immigrants with their 'unnatural' and un-American urban interests." The connection between rural values and a discriminatory nativism, between anti-urban sentiments and political reaction, seemed obvious to Schapiro. The same body of assumptions provided the basis for an even more fully developed attack on Thomas Hart Benton's "Populist Realism." It would be "premature," Schapiro remarked, to call Benton a fascist; but intelligent people should note his "appeal to the national sentiment" and be set on guard by "his conceited anti-intellectualism . . . , his hatred of the foreign, his emphasis on the strong and the masculine, his uncritical and unhistorical elevation of the folk, his antagonism to the cities, his ignorant and violent remarks on radicalism"—in short, by Benton's antagonism toward the whole cosmopolitan perspective.[31]

If fascism provided the clearest standard of intellectual retrogression and depravity, it was Stalinism that had brought the magazine's new circle together. Frequently, essays in *Partisan Review* played upon the shared values of the group in assailing the Communist Party and its Popular Front sympathizers as culturally backward, anti-intellectual, and narrowly dogmatic. The Stalinists contradicted all that was positive, and Phillips condemned them with a range of epithets that made little sense except in the context of his larger frame of values. Communist critics in the early thirties had simply been "mouthing many of the populist platitudes of Upton Sinclair," Phillips declared. Their criticism was merely the "pseudonym of orthodoxy"; and orthodoxy was for "tender-minded writers" the "passport to Utopia"—an escape from difficulty, from the turmoil of change, and from the rigors of open-ended scientific thought. Sidney Hook drew on similar assumptions in attacking Kenneth Burke's "ambivalent attitude towards science," in which Hook found an approach "strikingly similar to that of contemporary neo-Thomism." Combined with Hook's charge that Burke sought "ideological homogeneity," the comparison unveiled a bleak anti-cosmopolitan fusion of religion, authoritarianism, and resistance to critical thought.[32]

The intellectual and cultural values that had guided Phillips, Hook, and others also informed Rahv's reprobation of the Stalinists for their sins against literature. In an article assaying the writers' congresses held under Communist sponsorship in 1935 and 1937, Rahv enumerated the failings of the Popular Front strategy in literature from *Partisan Review*'s perspective. The Party was guilty of "throwing overboard the whole theory of scientific socialism," presumably giving up its claims to rational and analytical thinking in the process of abandoning genuine Marxism. What had replaced revolutionary principle, according to Rahv, were "the stars and stripes of New Deal Marxism"—non-radical, aggressively nationalistic policies. Such a stance placed literature at the mercy of popular standards and commercialism, for "the gates of the dialectic had been thrown wide open to any successful money writer." The Popular Front was actually "defending the status quo": "In literature this can only mean the artificial revival of values that have been historically transcended and a thousand times deflated." Stalinist attitudes were to Rahv's mind mystifying, mechanical, anti-scientific, nationalistic, commercial, historically backward, static, and authoritarian. They stood opposed to *Partisan Review*'s conscious viewpoint on every count.

The writers associated with *Partisan Review* increasingly saw the positive values that made up their cosmopolitan outlook as essential to the preservation of critical thinking—as a perspective outside which the intellectual could not fulfill his obligations. The differences between *Partisan Review* and the Stalinists were not simply matters of differing opinion, of critical judgment, or of political theory in Rahv's eyes; at bottom they were matters of profound ethical significance. The Communist Party had been afflicted with "moral degeneration"—*moral degeneration*! The Stalinists stood "not only . . . between the writer and Marxism but between him and the most elementary kind of integrity." To be an intellectual in the modern world implied certain fixed attitudes and values for Rahv: "The tradition of individual judgment, of skepticism, of scientific verification is inherent in the very terms and conditions of knowledge." Stalinism represented not skepticism but "blind faith and accommodation," not a "critical, revolutionary consciousness in art" but the attitudes of a "bureaucratic, authoritarian regime." Rahv insisted that there could be only one choice for those who aspired to the life of the mind: "It is impossible for the intellectual to make the moral and political compromises that Stalinism demands of him without betraying himself."[33]

Even with this, however, on at least some points Rahv's assault against Stalinism remained limited. Rahv was not yet ready to draw explicit comparisons between Stalinism and fascism. Neither was he prepared to indict Stalinism under a stronger political label than the editors had used before—"reformism." In the statement he had promised Trotsky, which appeared two months later, Rahv freed himself and *Partisan Review* from both these constraints. Here, with the values of cosmopolitanism on open display, *Partisan Review*'s anti-Stalinism came to full flower.

"Trials of the Mind" established a benchmark in the development of Rahv's ideas and in the evolution of *Partisan Review*. Reflecting a culmination of sorts in the discussions with Trotsky, it marked a conscious decision to speak out more openly on political questions. Though the Moscow Trials provided the immediate subject, Rahv in fact delivered a judgment on the entire history of the Communist movement under Stalin. The essay constituted a summing up of his disappointments with radicalism, both by intent and through the barely disguised feelings of anger, pain, and fear that gave the piece its timbre. Only at this point did Rahv's rage toward the Communist Party reach full expression in *Partisan Review*; only at this point was his break complete.

Radicalism had once meant militant hope and confidence. From its very first lines, "Trials of the Mind" suggested just how much had changed: "Our days are ceasing to be. We are beginning to live from hour to hour, awaiting the change of headlines. . . . We dread the Apocalypse." There was no affirmative vision here, no sense of understanding or control. The newspapers shouted the brutalities of Hitler, and in Moscow the "firstborn of October" were being massacred by the State: "What an inexhaustible repertoire of shame and catastrophe!" Intellectuals had once embraced the belief that Marxism supplied "a marriage of science and humanism": "But now, amidst all these ferocious surprises, who has the strength to reaffirm his beliefs, to transcend the feeling that he had been duped?"

Yet Rahv did not believe that the intellectual must be crippled by doubt. His anguish was genuine, but he had not lost entirely his sense of positive values, and he knew where to direct his wrath. If the radical vision had been brought low, the Communist Party and Stalin bore the burden of responsibility. The Moscow Trials served for Rahv as both actual and symbolic event; early in the essay he elaborated the message his title proclaimed—that beyond any immediate political questions, the fate of intellect in the modern world was at stake. "We too, all of us, are in the prisoner's dock. These are trials of the mind and of the human spirit." In these wider trials, Rahv was prepared to speak as both prosecutor and judge. The crucial historical events of the period constituted "supreme tests of character, of political integrity, of moral fortitude . . . it is by subjecting the behavior of the intellectuals to these supreme tests that we can best judge not only their politics, but their morality,—in fact their culture itself." That many of his contemporaries had failed these tests, that in their own trials they would be found guilty, was evident in Rahv's bitter reference to their "moral collapse."

The notion that the Moscow Trials and their larger context demanded a moral choice indicated that Rahv's talk of doubt applied mainly to radical doctrine—to the fate of Marxism "in its Russian captivity"—and not to fundamental values.[34] As readers of *Partisan Review* might have learned to expect, the confrontion pitted the whole modern complex of secular, scientific, forward-looking values against the retrograde forces that were their negative counterparts. Trotsky and Stalin themselves carried the standards for the forces of light and darkness. Trotsky stood as the symbol of the October Revolution and the original promise of communism. Stalin was the crude and cunning master of "the State and the Party." As Phillips and Rahv had earlier argued, the Bolsheviks were to them "the most consistent Russian Westernizers." Nearly thirty years later Rahv would still be making the point that "Trotsky—at times in spite of himself—stands for the Western and libertarian and internationalist trend in the communist movement." Stalin, by contrast,

137

withdrew into nationalism, authoritarianism, and "oriental despotism." As Alfred Kazin described the trials, "The victim was usually a revolutionary intellectual of the old type, a 'westerner' who had lived abroad, often a Jew, brought down by the sly and venomous Georgian who . . . had killed the theorists, the intellectuals, who still embodied the *elan* of the Russian Revolution." The cosmopolitan European intellectual stood opposed to the "Georgian" Stalin with his rural parochialism and "Asiatic backwardness." When Rahv suggested that "peasant guile" was no substitute for internationalism, he called upon a long string of intellectual biases.[35]

Phillips, Rahv, and others had hinted earlier at the presence of a religious mentality in Stalinism, but the charge of religiosity, so strongly associated for *Partisan Review* with intellectual conservatism and political reaction, had not been made explicit. Now, in his effort to read the Stalinists out of contemporary intellectual life, Rahv hesitated before no accusation that might reveal their backwardness. Despite the trials, many believers in the Soviet promise "still cling to their faith," Rahv noted; and every attempt to explain the supposed crimes exhausted "the resources of the rational." The trials could in fact be understood only in terms of religion and magic: "Hence it is not really political criminals who are being tried, but sinners, evildoers, perhaps sorcerers." The manipulation of religious feeling to bolster the State, and the merging of people and government through ritual persecution of national enemies, signaled the homogenizing and narrowing influence of reaction.

And reaction was precisely what Rahv intended to decry. The old Bolsheviks with their Western, cosmopolitan, and scientific values had created a positive view of revolution; the trials as rites of primitive religion and nationalism presented "the problem of revolution negatively, as counter-revolution." So, too, with Marxism; the reactionary nature of Stalinism proclaimed itself through the perversion of values basic to radical thought. Marxism distinguished itself from all other doctrines, according to Rahv, through its "particular use of history" as "both its science and its rhetoric." History implied an openness to change, the complexity of shifting contexts, the bonds of continuity. Stalinism opposed all of this. The Moscow Trials falsified "plain facts," perverted the "historic orientation" of the Russian Revolution's leaders, and plotted to "assassinate the history of Leninism." From Rahv's point of view, Stalinism was the antithesis of true Marxism.

At the dawn of *Partisan Review* in 1934, William Phillips had condemned T. S. Eliot for his allegiance to "feudal" ideas and his espousal of religion and the state—attitudes that Phillips associated with fascism. In 1938 Rahv condemned the Moscow Trials and Stalinism for promoting much the same set of values, with primitive rites substituting for feudalism as the emblem of backwardness. *Partisan Review*'s framework of values had changed very little, but the Communist Party and the Soviet Union had gradually moved, in the estimation of the magazine, from powerful agencies of progress to nefarious embodiments of those negative tendencies once associated primarily with fascism. Rahv's analysis now pushed past all political hesitation by leveling the charge of counterrevolution and by explicitly tying together "the drastic solutions of the crisis which fascism and communism offer to society." A process begun long before had finally reached completion. Rahv brought to fulfillment in "Trials of the Mind" the equation of fascism and Stalinism through the medium of a cosmopolitan perspective.

In linking fascism and Stalinism as reactionary forces, Rahv placed *Partisan Review* behind the argument that most infuriated the Communist Party and its Popular Front sympathizers. The whole idea of a people's front against fascism depended upon the belief that the Communists were the leaders of world opposition to Hitler. Rahv's attack challenged the basic political assumptions of international Communist strategy and made it clear that *Partisan Review* had moved toward more active anti-Stalinist agitation. Such a discordant note, especially when raised in the name of a purer Marxism and a more sophisticated literature, visibly irked those proclaiming a united cultural front as the only progressive position. In the spring of 1938, the League of American Writers filed suit against Rahv, trying to collect the one hundred dollars that had been loaned to the old *Partisan Review* before its break with the Party. Phillips and Alan Calmer should have been equally liable for any debt, but according to Macdonald the League was "more interested in persecuting Rahv than in getting cash."[36]

A public response to *Partisan Review*'s anti-Stalinist declarations came from Malcolm Cowley in the pages of the *New Republic*. Cowley hollowly suggested that "political differences could have been overlooked" if *Partisan Review* had stuck to its original intention to stay away from party politics; but the tone of Cowley's complaint made it clear that what irritated him was not so much the quantity of the magazine's political commentary as its direction. *Partisan Review*'s political writing, he grumbled, was "all of the same type—attacks on the Soviet Union, on literature and art in the Soviet Union, on politics in the Soviet Union, on American friends of the Soviet Union, a grand anti-Russian campaign under the infra-red banner of the [Trotskyist] Fourth International."[37] The editors of *Partisan Review* argued in reply that opposing the influence of the Communist Party was not the same thing as following the party line of the Trotskyists. Accusing Cowley of misrepresentation, selective quotation, and hypocrisy, the editors declared that his position amounted to the injunction "if you can't be Stalinist, then back to the Ivory Tower with you!" The reference was apt, and it took on substance when Cowley in a second rebuke tried to turn the idea against *Partisan Review*. In that magazine, Cowley argued, there was no question of "fighting or marching or even raising money" but only an obsession with ideas. *Partisan Review* was engaged in "a retreat from practical life" into a "red ivory tower . . . as lacking in human warmth as the white ivory tower of the Symbolists."[38]

Cowley could not have known at the time just how similar his accusation was to Trotsky's charge that *Partisan Review* was creating a "cultural monastery." Trotsky had wanted direct support for his own politics from the editors; Cowley's preferences boiled down to support for the Popular Front. Both found the editors' combination of literature and independent radicalism annoying. In charging that *Partisan Review* placed its emphasis on intellectuals acting as intellectuals and not as the cheerleaders of organized politics, Trotsky and Cowley were substantially correct. Where they went astray was in suggesting that the magazine was out of touch with reality. And where they misled even themselves was in thinking that the editors had ever seriously entertained the idea of another character for *Partisan Review*.

The very anti-Stalinism that dismayed Cowley, of course, tended to satisfy Trotsky that the editors nourished at least the right hostilities. At last he supplied a contribution to *Partisan Review* in the form of a long letter published under the title "Art and Politics."[39] Yet a reapprochement of sorts with Trotsky did not mean that *Partisan Review* had narrowed its options or restricted the play of political ideas within the magazine's larger circle. In June 1938, to take a single example, *Partisan Review* published a series of letters written by Rosa Luxemburg, reflecting an interest in Luxemburg shared at least by Macdonald and Harold Rosenberg. Various members of the *Partisan Review* circle remained open to a wide range of radical ideas, most of which they found easily compatible with their anti-Stalinism.[40]

Both intellectually and institutionally, *Partisan Review* was very much an evolving organism. During the fall of 1938, *Partisan Review* was undergoing a major change in structure. George Morris had promised to provide up to three thousand dollars a year for the magazine's support. When it became clear in the summer of 1938 that expenses would push well beyond that mark, Morris reached for the emergency brake. A meeting among some of the editors and the exchange of several letters produced a number of decisions: the magazine would change printers, *Partisan Review* would in the future appear as a quarterly rather than a monthly, and the magazine's office would move to the Macdonalds' apartment to save on the cost of rent and phone. With Phillips and Dupee out of town at the time, the decision to move the office came primarily from Macdonald and Rahv, reflecting, whether coincidentally or not, their emergence as the two dominant personalities on the editorial board. Macdonald, in particular, now seemed to regard himself as the glue holding together the whole operation.[41]

Partisan Review's new complexion as "A Quarterly of Literature and Marxism" proved a benefit to the magazine's intellectual and cultural aspirations. Substantially longer than their monthly counterparts, the quarterly issues presented a greater diversity of content in criticism, poetry, fiction, philosophy, and reportage, and drew upon a wider range of contributors as *Partisan Review* attracted the positive interest of writers in both the United States and Europe. Political commentary remained visible in a new editorial section called "This Quarter"; anti-Stalinism gave a common tint to scattered articles and reviews; and an occasional essay—most notably Sidney Hook's "The Anatomy of the Popular Front"—pressed a frontal assault.[42] Yet, on the whole, politics seemed more clearly subsidiary to cultural interests in the quarterly numbers, effecting the kind of balance originally intended for *Partisan Review*. It was as if the editors, having finally vented the full bitterness of their anti-Stalinism, could heave a collective sigh of relief that all was now out in the open and go on with their business. Once a source of nail-biting anxiety, denunciations of Stalinism now became matter-of-fact.

The persisting desire in the *Partisan Review* circle to do something to combat Stalinist influence found primary outlet over the next year in a series of organizational initiatives. The effort began with a letter from Trotsky asking the editors of *Partisan Review* to publish and support a manifesto written by Diego Rivera and André Breton calling for the formation of a pro-socialist, anti-

Stalinist, International Federation of Independent Revolutionary Art (IFIRA). *Partisan Review* found little in the manifesto with which to disagree; and in the quarterly issue of November 1938, the editors printed the manifesto and their own announcement.[43] They stood ready to assist in the formation of an American body to incorporate the general aims of the IFIRA in "a program otherwise strictly adapted to American conditions." Interested parties were invited to contact the editors of *Partisan Review*. The effort proved a resounding flop. Three people responded. Macdonald reported some discouragement on the editors' part, but promised another effort soon to gather a group of writers to discuss the notion of an organization.[44]

The situation had meanwhile grown more interesting thanks to efforts by Sidney Hook to put together a similar organization, tentatively called the "League Against Totalitarianism." Where Hook's manifesto differed from that of the IFIRA was in claiming to support "no particular social philosophy" and in leaving aside all mention of classes or revolution. Macdonald, to whom Hook had sent his draft manifesto, found its greatest significance in this avoidance, declaring that the lack of concrete radical analysis led toward "amalgam at once hypocritical . . . and intellectually sleazy."[45] Other members of the editorial board and most of the close friends of *Partisan Review* seemed to share reservations about Hook's proposed group. Hook was moving away from radicalism and toward positive support for American institutions more rapidly than the majority of them could accept.[46] In early March 1939 the editors made a second attempt to pull together an organization more to their liking, beginning with a group of about thirty. After at least two meetings and much talking, a manifesto was finally approved. By the time Macdonald could send copies to Trotsky, he had to report as well that little would be done until fall. Whether this new group would have any affiliation with the IFIRA had not yet been decided.[47]

The several attempts to create new organizations generated at least mild frictions within the larger *Partisan Review* camp. Rahv reported to friends that Hook was miffed over the editors' attempt to create a new group of writers because it would compete with his own. Farrell complained repeatedly that Hook had been undemocratic in not inviting him to join his organization and in not holding meetings to discuss the objections raised by Farrell himself, Meyer Schapiro, and Rahv. The differences were real among the *Partisan Review* intellectuals, with the political spectrum ranging from confirmed followers of Trotsky—of whom Macdonald was one by

1939—to those who were only peripherally interested in politics. Yet even those who disagreed often still considered one another friends; a core of shared values and opposition to Stalinism provided the common bond.[48]

By the early summer of 1939, two groups had issued their statements and listed their members publicly: Hook's group had become the "Committee for Cultural Freedom" under the chairmanship of John Dewey, and the editors of *Partisan Review* now belonged to the "League for Cultural Freedom and Socialism." As the names of the organizations suggested, their founders still differed primarily over the issue of whether radicalism was a necessary part of resistance to cultural repression. Both, of course, saw Stalinism as the primary threat. The League's statement condemned Stalinists in dramatic terms. Sympathizers with the Soviet Union and the Popular Front had adopted a form of religion that paralleled fascism: "To the deification of Hitler and Mussolini they counterpose the deification of Stalin. . . . The mysticism of 'Aryan' supremacy they match with a national-democratic myth conjured out of America's historic infancy." *Partisan Review* writers had hinted before that Popular Front nationalism encouraged narrow prejudice, but never had the comparison with Hitler's racist mania been so strongly drawn. The League statement declared unequivocally that, among intellectuals, Communist Party organizations represented "the most active forces of reaction today."[49]

Although as yet their organizations had done little but declare their existence, anti-Stalinist intellectuals seemed eager to predict that the Popular Front would soon lose its force among writers.[50] Yet most "progressive" intellectuals seemed notably unprepared to give up their hopes for a positive Soviet role in world affairs. The foremost liberal journals reacted negatively in 1939 to intellectual manifestoes linking Stalinism with fascism. The *Nation* printed the statement of the Committee for Cultural Freedom; yet in the same issue, Freda Kirchwey—who had declined an invitation to sign the statement herself—argued in an editorial that the only real purpose of the Committee was "to drop a bomb into the ranks of the liberal and left groups." Whatever their faults (and Kirchwey admitted there were many), the Communists and the Soviet Union should not be linked with fascism, and such criticism should cease. The *New Republic*, declining to print the Committee's statement, suggested that members of the Committee were actually aiding fascism and supporting the "anti-libertarian Trotsky." When challenged by John Dewey, the *New Republic* retreated a step. Citing the appearance of the League for Cultural Freedom and Socialism, the *New Republic* snidely conceded that indeed there were no Trotskyists on the Committee because the Trotskyists were all in the League.[51]

A more formal reaction from defenders of the Popular Front came several weeks later. Some four hundred people of varying stripe signed a letter attacking the Committee for Cultural Freedom and "other committees" for encouraging the "fantastic falsehood that the U.S.S.R. and the totalitarian states are basically alike." The letter listed ten reasons why Soviet socialism differed from fascism, of which the first—ironically, as it would seem in the near future—was that the Soviet Union served as a "bulwark against war and aggression." The *New Republic*, judging from the tone of its remarks on the letter, welcomed it as an explicit response to Hook's Committee and the *Partisan Review* League.[52] The *Nation* was more guarded in publishing the letter, promising comments in the magazine's next issue. A momentous piece of news had burst upon the world just in time for shocked editorial comment: "Red Star and Swastika, once mutually exclusive symbols, have come together, and the diplomatic map of Europe has been redrawn overnight.[53] On August 23, 1939, the Nazi-Soviet non-aggression pact had become public knowledge. Denials of any link between Stalinism and fascism suddenly rang very hollow indeed. Whatever it did to the map of Europe, the Hitler-Stalin pact temporarily blasted the whole familiar terrain of left intellectual battles in New York.

The period from the revival of *Partisan Review* to the Nazi-Soviet pact covered less than two years. In the life of the magazine it was a major geological epoch. The fact that *Partisan Review* had established itself as a center for anti-Stalinist intellectuals during the late thirties became a permanent part of the magazine's identity, its most visible political brand. During these two years, the primary object of the magazine's preachments had changed. The first *Partisan Review* had seen itself as operating within a radical intellectual world, seeking to reform the revolutionary movement in literature from within. In the second *Partisan Review*—for all the continuing interest in radicalism—the overriding concern had become the position of *liberal* intellectuals. After the initial skirmishes of 1937, it was not Michael Gold or Granville Hicks or V. J. Jerome with whom the *Partisan* critics regularly crossed swords but Kenneth Burke, Malcolm Cowley, and other writers, both American and European, who visibly supported the Popular Front. Between 1937 and 1939 as well, members of the *Partisan Review* circle had begun to explore in varying ways their own continuing relation to radical ideas. This process, bounded by anti-Stalinism and a persistent critique of liberalism, would lead the magazine in time toward a new political orientation.

Chapter Six	A Flickering Vision

The characteristic stance of *Partisan Review* and its circle in the late 1930s came from the persistent effort to combine radical politics with critical support for an advanced literature and art—on this the editors of the magazine and various commentators have largely agreed. Less harmony has attended the question of whether such a combination made sense. Some of those closest to *Partisan Review* in 1937 jettisoned their hopes for a radical link between politics and culture within a decade; and by the late 1970s one critic was ready to declare that no one on the new *Partisan Review* "could explain how neo-Marxist political commentary was to be reconciled with . . . highbrow discussion of the modern masters."[1] Even ignoring the questionable tag of neo-Marxism, such a judgment reflects the hasty backward glance of a generation out of touch and out of sympathy with the aspirations of the thirties. The editors and contributors to the magazine were perpetually explaining the connections they saw; and if *Partisan Review*'s political program (beyond the idea of "independence") was sometimes vague or fragmentary and if its literary hopes remained unfulfilled, the editors' reasons for believing that radical politics and an advancing culture *ought* to reinforce one another were much in evidence.

The literary ideal of the editorial board in 1937 was not "highbrow discussion of the modern masters." At the risk of overstating for emphasis, it may be said that the editors' ideal was not modernism at all. The great wave of modernism had crested and broken before their time, and the *Partisan Review* critics assumed this from the start. Had not Edmund Wilson summed up a dying tradition in *Axel's Castle*? Was not the whole point of a radical literature in the thirties to go beyond modernism? *Partisan Review* defended literary modernism during the thirties primarily as a legacy from the past, a valuable part of the literary heritage, and certainly not as an artistic ideal. The very accomplishments of modernism were an incitement to do better.

Marxism and modernism came together for the new *Partisan Review* (as for the old) through the ideal of synthesis. If it was to move forward, literature must preserve the sophistication and boldness of modernist writing; yet it must combine with that the analysis of society inherent in Marxism, the whole package being held together by a positive sense of historical direction and purpose. Modernism alone was not enough. Radical belief alone was insufficient. *Partisan Review* combined discussions of literary craft with a concern for radical ideas because both seemed essential to the magazine's ideal of a mature and balanced literature. Much of the criticism that appeared in *Partisan Review* during the thirties made it a primary or secondary purpose to defend the viability of this ideal, indicating from early enthusiasm to later disappointment an underlying stability of literary vision.

The editors addressed directly the question of their attitude toward the modernism of the twenties in their inaugural statement. The "tradition of aestheticism," the editors declared, had "given way" to a literature that looked "beyond itself and deep into the historic process" for inspiration and justification, and that was good. Yet even if modernism had been superseded, the literary practices of the movement had been of "definite cultural value." *Partisan Review* would seek to adapt the "exacting and adventurous" standards of the modernist twenties to "the literature of the new period." Modernism was valuable but insufficient. To it, those seeking a "place in the vanguard of literature" must add a radical outlook. With a combination of high literary standards and Marxist perspective, *Partisan Review* would aspire "to represent a new and dissident generation in American letters." The echoes of earlier cultural rebellions resonant in such an ambition made it plain that at its second founding, *Partisan Review* still hoped to see its literary vision come to life in a radical future.[2]

The call for the "Europeanization of American literature" that had been issued by Phillips and Rahv earlier in 1937 rested on the belief that certain European writers stood on the threshold of an elevated culture and that, by combining the insights of those few with native patterns, American writers could help to forge a new literature. The goal was to get past the fact that there was no "revolutionary work"—that is, no outstanding token of the new age in literature —that had been written by an American and that presented "those moral and intellectual contradictions which appear in the struggle between old and new cultures." Modernism could not provide the inspiration for such a work. Modernism belonged to the final phase of the decline of the bourgeoisie, functioning at best as a transitional movement; it seemed capable of producing only negative pictures of decay rather than affirmative support for new values. To find an appropriate stimulus for American writing, Phillips and Rahv looked to European writers who seemed to promise a climb beyond modernism.

The two who received the most attention as potential pioneers of a new radical literature were Ignazio Silone and André Malraux. They belonged to the few whose work seemed for a time to balance thought and experience, abstraction and reality, through the marriage of radical politics and art. Yet the attitude *Partisan Review* took toward these writers was not one of celebration. Silone and Malraux were the closest thing to inspiring examples that Phillips and Rahv could find in 1937, and they deserved close watching; but there was little suggestion that the triumph of radical literature had arrived. Even as the new *Partisan Review* appeared, doubts were beginning to erode the magazine's confidence in Silone, and Malraux's reputation among anti-Stalinists was about to plummet.

Silone's importance to the *Partisan Review* circle was evident in the discussion of his most recent work by Lionel Abel, printed not as a review but as an essay in the first issue of the new magazine. Rahv had reviewed *Bread and Wine* for the *Nation* earlier in 1937, and his shorter commentary prefigured Abel's in a number of ways.[3] Both spoke well of Silone's previous novel, *Fontamara*, in terms that suggested why it had aroused the *Partisan* critics' interest. Rahv believed that the story was "unusual in its integration of a profound humanity with a materialistic reading of reality"; Abel stressed that its whole action had been determined by "forces flowing from the city" and that its peasant characters were in fact "very theoretical."[4] Yet the two critics seemed to agree that *Fontamara*, in Rahv's words, was not "a complete test of its author's talent." *Bread and Wine* thus came before them as an important measure of Silone's capacities and his direction. On the whole Rahv and Abel judged that Silone was going forward very well, not simply because of the quality of his writing but also (though neither critic said so directly) because Silone had moved toward anti-Stalinism.

Nevertheless, some troubling questions cast a shadow across the declarations of approval. The central problem of Silone's work involved the appropriate political and moral stance for a radical intellectual departing Stalinism. Rahv noted that Silone, with his growing respect for religion, had occasionally fallen into "idealist abstractions"; and he suggested that Silone's solution to the intellectual's dilemma was merely a narrow and personal one. Yet Rahv raised these issues only in passing. In his more extensive discussion, Abel gave doubts about Silone's evolving position a prominent place. The "human center of revolutionary gravity" had shifted for Silone, Abel thought, from "consciousness to the heart." Silone had created an "absolute contradiction" between a revolutionary party and moral values, between politics and ethics. This "grave defect" in the position of the character Spina, which had the effect of closing the door on all political organization and upsetting the possibility of synthesis, flowed "inevitably," as Abel saw it, from "Spina's attitude towards theory, which he says, bores him."

If Spina were to be taken as speaking for Silone, the *Partisan Review* critics would face an unpleasant choice: they would either have to reject one of the very few contemporary novelists who addressed as an opponent of Stalin the problems in which they were most interested, or they would have to swallow Silone's religiously oriented ethical emphasis and his repudiation of politics. What then to do with Silone? Abel provided a temporary answer, and it was quite simple. Spina did not speak for Silone. Even so, Abel's tone was uneasy as he seized upon this escape, and his words were revealing. Was Spina's position that of Silone? "I cannot think so," Abel replied. Did Spina really reject Marxism? "I prefer, since one cannot be entirely certain in such a matter, to interpret Spina's boredom with theory as something other than a rejection of Marxist theory."

The recognition that disturbing currents ran through Silone's work, coming as the new *Partisan Review* was just emerging, did not bode well for the positive literary program of the magazine. At least two ways in which that program was vulnerable were rapidly becoming apparent. First, however logical or desirable it might be, a radical literature of balance and sophistication could not be produced simply through the agency of a magazine calling for its existence. The new *Partisan Review* could not will into being the great American literature of its desires any more than the *Seven Arts* could compel its cultural vision to become reality in the teens. Nor did the *Partisan* critics expect to create *themselves* the literature they sought; there were few in the *Partisan Review* circle who were primarily creative writers. This being the case, the editors of *Partisan Review* could only urge and wait—for the one true-blue solitary rhinoceros, the pioneer of a radical literature beyond Stalinism. Such a critical position was highly susceptible to disappointment.

Second, even at the height of their enthusiasm for a pathbreaking radical literature, the *Partisan Review* critics were subject to a tension between their general literary convictions and their more immediate loyalties. The *Partisan* critics called for synthesis and balance, for giving every part of life its due, and they assumed such goals were entirely compatible with a process of "cosmopolitanization." Yet cosmopolitanism as interpreted in *Partisan Review* meant that secularism, urbanism, intellectuality, and international-mindedness would generally be taken to represent positive cultural and political values, whereas rural, religious, nationalistic, and anti-theoretical attitudes would commonly be regarded as evidence of backwardness or bad faith. A desire for openness and inclusiveness did not always blend easily with strongly held biases and convictions. The *Partisan Review* critics could not gloss over the disharmony between support for a complex and balanced literature at a general level and a sometimes heavy-handed and simplistic judgment of "good" and "bad" values in immediate encounters.

Both these weaknesses—the vulnerability of *Partisan Review*'s positive literary hopes and the susceptibility of the magazine's critics to slanted judgment—became evident in the changing evaluation of André Malraux. To Phillips and Rahv in the middle of 1937, Malraux had been, with Silone, a leader in the development of radical literature and a harbinger of better things to come. It was a measure of how quickly their hopes for particular writers could crumble that by early 1938 Malraux seemed misguided and deformed, a purveyor of corrupt values. The task of charting this decline fell to F. W. Dupee, who took Malraux's latest work as the occasion for an essay much in the mold of Abel's on Silone. But if Silone's new book allowed a general embrace while doubts were neatly sidestepped, Malraux's forced a confrontation.

Malraux's earlier writing had been commendable, as Dupee made clear. *Man's Fate* had presented a hero who balanced the "solitude of the individualist and the fraternal drive of the revolutionary collectivity"; the characters had "psychological unity" and the novel a "dramatic unity." Malraux at that point had been influenced by Trotsky, according to Dupee, and his work embodied a "semi-Trotskyist critique" of Stalinist policy. In Malraux's new novel, *L'Espoir* (*Hope*), by contrast, all was decay. The book was a work of the "higher factional publicism," Dupee announced in his first

paragraph. Malraux failed to confront problems squarely, he simplified issues, his characters were not free to develop, his message
contained "elaborate rationalizations of the left-wing *status quo*."
Man's Fate had exhibited an "artist's consciousness"; *L'Espoir* made
the revolutionary novel into "a vehicle for thinly-fictionalized reportage" and propaganda. Between them lay "the difference between
reality soundly projected and judged, and reality deformed by the
crooked glass of a reactionary dogma." Malraux, in short, had chosen
the wrong political course in following the Stalinist Popular Front,
and his literary and political degradation proceeded apace. Progressive values, Trotskyist ideas, and literary sophistication stood in
complete and convenient contrast to backward values, reactionary
Stalinism, and literary decay.

Whatever the merits of Dupee's literary evaluation of Malraux,
his essay clearly had aims that went beyond any concern with Malraux's quality as a writer. Dupee had created a confrontation between two sets of values with virtue and worth all on one side, and
he had allowed political emotions to shape his argument and his
conclusions. Until the end of the essay, Dupee had at least avoided
the cruder sorts of political name-calling. But there he slipped into
a burst of vitriol that diminished and obscured every literary argument he had made: Malraux's character Garcia was "the type of liberal Comintern lobbyist thrown up by the stooge politics of people's-
frontism. *L'Espoir*, too, comes under that head."[5] The attack was
unlike Dupee both in its crudeness and its awkwardness (the novel
itself could not be a "lobbyist"); and it represented bad tactics in
the struggle with the Stalinists as well as bad criticism. When Malcolm Cowley made Dupee's closing lines one subject of his wider
attack on *Partisan Review*'s political content, the resulting exchange
demonstrated just how easily literary issues could be obscured by
the fog of pro- and anti-Stalinist debate.[6] Coming at a time when
the editors were trying to convince Trotsky (and themselves) that
they had a clear political commitment, Dupee's tag-end remark may
have represented a self-conscious attempt at militance. If so, it demonstrated how poorly a dominantly negative belligerence related
to the achievement of a serious, sophisticated, and balanced literary criticism.

The pattern of Malraux's decline as a literary exemplar for *Partisan Review* threatened a frustration of the editors' hopes in both
politics and literature — a gradual submerging of positive vision in
the anger, pessimism, and dismay growing out of immediate experience. The expanding power of fascism and Stalin's betrayal of

revolutionary ideals threw what the editors regarded as genuine radicalism on the defensive. Within this context, the campaign of opposition to Stalinism served many needs: it gave vent to much bitterness toward the Communist Party; it filled the pages of *Partisan Review* with a sense of purpose and excitement; and it allowed the *Partisan* critics to feel they were defending the best traditions of radicalism. But anti-Stalinism could not provide positive support for the growth of radical culture. The deep emotions of the anti-Stalinist crusade interfered with even-handed judgment and at times pushed the essays in *Partisan Review* toward that use of political standards in the evaluation of literature which the magazine had set out to oppose.

If the ideal of a literature both sophisticated and radical was vulnerable to disappointment and occasional distortion, it nevertheless equipped the second *Partisan Review* with a critical stance of considerable power. The *Partisan* critics tried to write as serious advocates of literature and as radical students of society, promoting a balance between formal literary considerations and attention to social context in discussions of literary works. From one side or the other of their perspective, lesser novels might be shown up for their inadequacy in technique or values while even major works could be turned this way or that to reveal a new face.

Several pieces in the revived *Partisan Review* put the search for balance to positive use, making it a grounds for fresh investigation of familiar texts.[7] In examining Dostoevsky's *The Possessed*, for example, Rahv found two sets of characters, "one sacred and one profane, one metaphysical and one empirical." Though Dostoevsky never fully solved the problem of unifying the two, there was much to be learned from "this analyst of contradictions, who was ever vibrating between faith and heresy." Dostoevsky's work contained a greater balance than had usually been appreciated, Rahv claimed, for although Dostoevsky might have longed for the "peace of religious faith," he was driven by a "compulsion to test theory by practice," and "the infidel, the *social* philosopher in him, would not be submerged."

To find a great writer being forced by his talent and perception to present a more balanced view of life than he intended served to ratify the belief that balance and synthesis were proper ideals for a major literature. Rahv's essay depended on such exchanges of meaning and insight: the literary and political outlook of *Partisan Review* could help produce a vigorous critical reading of Dostoevsky, and Dostoevsky in turn could provide evidence to confirm the magazine in its critical stance. Rahv even saw in Dostoevsky a certain affinity with radicalism: "Reactionary in its abstract content, in its aspect as a system of ideas, his art is radical in sensibility and subversive in performance." Such claims that radical content might be found in surprising places were not some newly invented escape-hatch from the quest for a radical literature; Rahv had acknowledged in some of his earliest essays the critique of bourgeois society found in the work of modernist writers. Rather, Rahv's argument on Dostoevsky applied familiar ideas in a new way, and it demonstrated once more that the effort to combine radicalism and literary sophistication could offer a strength and unity of critical viewpoint.[8]

Writers who were safely dead made good subjects for reclamation projects. Their foibles, their imbalances, and their conscious political views could be pushed aside in favor of an emphasis on the positive insights they had achieved and the contributions they had made to the long process of unmasking bourgeois society. Living writers were another story. Failings in philosophy or execution loomed large to young critics impatient for great works, and the political adventures of living writers generated considerably more heat than the literary ashes of politics past.

The sense of standards and purpose provided by the magazine's aspirations for contemporary literature allowed judgments that were confident and firm. Reviewing Ernest Hemingway's *To Have and Have Not*, Rahv delivered a lecture to the author, who had recently allied himself with the Popular Front. In "transcending his political indifference," he had not managed to transcend his "political ignorance"; Hemingway would find, according to Rahv, that "the method of inarticulate virility" was "no substitute for consciousness." Hemingway's problem was a one-sided lack of balance, and Rahv found his critical footing in holding present work against the *Partisan* ideal.[9] The same measurement of an author against the standards of radical synthesis occurred in a far more extensive and complicated way in *Partisan Review*'s discussions of Thomas Mann. An occasion more than a cause, Mann's works served as the grounds for a critical debate that ranged across a variety of *Partisan Review*'s fundamental concerns.

Between the issues of May 1938 and Winter 1939, *Partisan Review* published five essays and a few shorter comments on Mann. Two of the essays were by William Troy, and , in general, they provided a foil against which the other writers defined their views.

The other three essays, by different members of the larger *Partisan Review* circle, demonstrated both the diversity the magazine's position allowed and the agreement on general principles it assumed, an agreement strong enough to bring contentious parties together in their differences with Troy. The first essay to appear came from Phillips, yet Phillips wrote with an acute consciousness of what Troy had already said in an article on "The Lawrence Myth" and quite probably with an editor's awareness of what Troy was about to say in his celebration of Mann. Troy had expressed approval of Lawrence's assault on "scientific rationalism," and he had appeared to be claiming that the insights of reactionary "myth" were superior to the perceptions of science in general and the social sciences in particular. Troy now stood poised to extend such arguments in what was really a rejection of most of the values that the *Partisan Review* intellectuals held dear.[10]

As Troy would make clear in the opening sentences of his discussion of Mann, the issue was one of attitudes toward modernism as a whole. "Like nearly all the more important writers of his generation," Troy began, "Thomas Mann has turned finally to the frank and open exploitation of the myth," a direction "very generally" taken by "Yeats, Joyce, Valery and the others." Mann was thus a part of a broad "movement of protest against the devastating incursion of the scientific temper in the realm of literature and the arts."[11] And Troy celebrated this movement. To the *Partisan Review* intellectuals, the "scientific temper" embodied in critical thought offered a way out of the modernist-symbolist dead end. To Troy, not literary symbolism but science rested upon an inadequate body of assumptions; the modernists, with their exploration of myth, offered the highest, most complete, and most promising approach to the contemporary world. The differences with Troy illustrated just how strongly the *Partisan* critics remained convinced of modernism's limitations and skeptical of its cultural adequacy.

Phillips found much to admire in Mann's work and in his contemporary public posture, but with the specific content of Mann's position and with his political conclusions Phillips firmly disagreed. The editors of *Partisan Review* envisioned the writer as a vanguard figure who at his best represented values that were ultimately progressive and social; Mann placed the artist permanently in opposition to society. "Paradoxically," Phillips noted, ". . . Mann regards art as a disease." Health was automatic adjustment; restlessness and dissatisfaction were ailments of the mind. Where could this lead? If Mann's argument were to be accepted, Phillips pointed out, "there can be little hope that the values of the artist will ever triumph. His martyrdom is his constant struggle against odds: the pathology of art involves a belief in the essential barbarism of man."[12]

Phillips could not accept such a view of society or of art. Mann's vision offered no hope for the future, no hope for the triumph of higher human values. In its rejection of politics and possibility, Mann's program became "static in its nobility"; it left its exemplary European man "frozen within his ideals and his fetters." Though several years would pass before the idea of art as disease was more extensively thrashed out in the pages of *Partisan Review*, Phillips in 1938 spoke for the magazine in rejecting a negative view of man and his potential, in suggesting indirectly that art could derive from healthy perception and social instincts rather than from disease and separation, and in defending the importance for intellectuals of politics and rational thought.[13]

Phillips's critique of the limitations of Mann's vision—and, by implication, of modernist writing in general—gathered steam when his essay turned in mid-course to a long panegyric to scientific thought. Mann's outlook was "incomplete," according to Phillips, because Mann had left out of his program "the most characteristic product of the European mind"—science. Phillips spoke of contemporary issues involving war and fascism as "political and economic question[s], scientific questions!"—with the juxtaposition accurately reflecting his viewpoint. To the *Partisan Review* critics, "science" nearly always referred primarily to scientific method and to the social sciences; and Phillips recounted the major contributions attributed to this sphere. First, scientific thought was the source of progressive change, which had enabled man "to overcome the conditions of [his] existence," to escape a static situation "not only in nature, but in history." Second, science was the source of rationality and system: "The extension of scientific method into history, has helped to strip it of its legends and prejudices, introducing order, direction, and law." Aiming to be scientific socialists, "we" had learned enough about the "sciences of economics and politics" to be able to see through "political rhetoric" (of the Stalinist variety in particular) and to "check political programs against social realities." A list of "scientists" explained the tradition Phillips had in mind: Aristotle, Adam Smith, Ricardo, Hegel, Marx, Lenin, Trotsky.

Third, science as both engine of change and ordering system provided a basis and an inspiration for advances in literature. The "fertility and animation of European culture were nourished by science," according to Phillips. The dynamic transformation of an agricultural into an industrial society expanded the ambitions of the European mind "until it now produces the most subtle visions out of the most solid knowledge." Just as Shakespeare and Goethe were made possible by the changes that had come about through science, "so the imagination of modern art bursts through the world-culture of Einstein and Freud." Fourth, science could contribute something more specific to literature, for science was "the avenue to the concrete observation of our surroundings." The great error of symbolism in the twenties, which Mann now seemed to embrace, was to rely too heavily on the imagination of the artist and on abstractions; this was also the classic sin of the highbrow in America. Science—the social sciences and particularly Marxism—could keep the artist linked to the reality that must always be his touchstone.

Two general claims lay behind Phillips's defense of science. Because critical thinking allowed a discovery of the realities behind appearances, Phillips held that a scientific temper had never been more needed than in the present: "To-day, even more than at any other time in the past, we must unmask our false prophets. This is a period of masquerade." In its opposition to Stalinism, *Partisan Review* claimed to stand in the great scientific tradition of bringing reality and truth to light. The second claim went to the heart of the magazine's rationale and to the fundamental tenets of its critical endorsement of synthesis. Without the insights of science to balance those of art, Phillips argued, Mann was trapped in a hopeless position, facing the "predicament of the intellectual conscience, clinging to the conditions of its own enslavement." One-sidedness crippled the artist: "Defending morality without history, art without science, culture without politics, envisioning no social action which might ensure intellectual freedom, Mann's program becomes an agony of the individual conscience—one more symptom of the tragic state of our world." Phillips had made *Partisan Review*'s literary ideal the basis for his criticism of Mann and, in the process, had offered a summary judgment on the limitations of modernist literature.

In his own discussion of Mann, Troy did not so much ignore the concerns that animated Phillips as deny their accuracy and relevance, insisting that "Mann's turning to the myth in his new work represents a synthesis between reason and experience that is full of the highest possibilities for our time." With this argument Troy not only pushed aside the *Partisan* critics' antagonism to the contemporary implications of "myth" but also disputed their notion of what constituted a proper synthesis. Mann, it seemed, was akin to Hegel and Marx in his concern for "continuous modification." Yet to carry out his aim, Troy had to argue that Mann with his myth went *beyond* Hegel and Marx, rising above the rational to encompass the *"whole* ground of human reality." Despite the fact that many of the particulars in his analysis of Mann's career were unobjectionable, this general argument of Troy's made his work as a whole extremely unpalatable to the *Partisan Review* critics.[14]

In commenting on Troy's discussion of Mann in a letter to Macdonald, Phillips remarked that Troy's specific insights were "fairly acute" but that his "premises and conclusions seem pretty phony."[15] The same broad reaction characterized the response from James Burnham that was published in *Partisan Review*. Burnham praised Troy's "integrated account of Mann's creative work" but strongly objected to his more general and sweeping claims about the value of myth. Burnham stood near the edge of the magazine's circle and did not speak for the editors on literary matters; yet he shared their allegiance to the rational intellect, and he believed as they did in the necessity of political theory and social judgment. Burnham challenged Troy's general contentions as "both false and dangerous," and in the following issue of *Partisan Review* Troy replied.[16]

As Burnham saw it, Troy appeared to argue that his own critical method (which Burnham labeled the "anthropological approach") was "the *only* basic means whereby to criticize, appreciate, and understand art," thereby committing the error of "hypostatizing a method into an Absolute." Burnham insisted on more flexibility, arguing that works of literature changed with context to "figure variously, as psychological, anthropological, sociological, economic phenomena." Troy responded by rejecting Burnham's "anthropological" label because it seemed to imply a scientific method, and he argued that science was crippled by its "fundamental inappropriateness" in the realms of art and literature. The "imponderable character" of a work of literature could only be grasped "in terms of its own inner pattern of movement," Troy maintained; a proper mode of analysis must come "from literature itself." Though Troy had earlier dissociated himself from "purely aesthetic" criticism, his position seemed to draw a line of lasting importance between critical camps.[17] In contrast to the rising wave of those who held that each art form could be properly evaluated only in terms of its internal structures and traditions, the *Partisan Review* critics maintained as a central article of faith that however much attention was given to strictly artistic considerations, literature must also be examined within a social context.

Burnham's critique also touched upon another point of fundamental importance to *Partisan Review*. In attempting to glorify Mann, Troy had asked intellectuals "to *substitute* the artist for the scientist and politician, the works of art for science and politics." If Mann was thus to be seen as the originator of a great unifying system, he must be taken whole. And Mann's politics impressed Burnham the radical as a record of compromise and convenience. Only by recognizing artistic values in Mann's work apart from social and political implication—thus repudiating Troy's notion of unifying myth—could one "continue to accept the novels." Burnham was asserting a principle of balance that Phillips and Rahv had independently come to in the first *Partisan Review*: Mann's (and Troy's) attempt to subordinate the insights of science and politics to those of literature was as distorting and dangerous as the Stalinists' attempts to make the values of art and literature subservient to the goals of politics.

Troy responded to such concerns briefly and rather weakly, suggesting that he was much more comfortable discussing the abstract opposition of myth to science than Mann's relation to contemporary politics. For the editors of *Partisan Review*, however, it was difficult to ignore the contemporary world and Mann's political adventures. An editorial comment on Mann's "career as a political thinker," written by Macdonald, charged that at present Mann was campaigning for war in the name of peace, allowing himself to seem an ally of the Stalinist Popular Front. Political embarrassments were in fact typical of Mann. Mann was constantly taking "the most extreme and reckless political positions" while also "constantly protesting his inadequate understanding of the subject, thus claiming the indulgence granted the amateur."[18] Like Phillips's earlier charge that Mann was clinging to the conditions of his own enslavement, this conclusion attributed to Mann the problem *Partisan Review* had ascribed to modern writers since 1934: for all their insights into the decay of bourgeois culture and for all their literary talent, the great modernists had failed to demonstrate an adequate grasp of political and social issues. They thus remained, as Phillips had said, "incomplete."

With several pieces already stacked up against Mann and Troy, it came as a strong confirmation of the importance that the editors attributed to the issues at stake that they should publish yet another long analysis of Mann. The new evaluation by Harold Rosenberg seemed to Macdonald "just the sort of piece PR exists to print," and such views of its quality overcame doubts about adding to the "current heavy dosage of Mann."[19] Troy had simply "succumbed to the writer he was analyzing," in Rosenberg's view, "and his study became little more than a rewording of Mann's own pretensions towards the dialectics of the Absolute."[20]

Mann, according to Rosenberg, belonged to that group of modern thinkers who believed the key to a "higher unity" had been found in "analogy," a notion that emphasized "the likeness of things apparently far removed from one another" rather than the procedures and the laws of science. Rosenberg named as examples of this school Mann, Gide, Proust, Joyce, and Pirandello, and he stressed the limitations of the reliance on analogy: "As a perspective, it shares the shakiness and intermittence of all forms of poetic and metaphorical insight, which at times lights up relations and at other times obscures them." Here, then, was another characteristic evaluation of literary modernism from the viewpoint of the *Partisan Review* circle — Rosenberg praised the specific insights of the modern artist but rejected his general perspective.[21] A broader opposition became apparent through footnotes that assigned to the analogical camp Kenneth Burke and Thurman Arnold — two quite different thinkers who had already been mauled in book reviews by Sidney Hook and James Burnham respectively. Rosenberg's critique thus applied to Mann, to many of the leading modern writers, and to social analysts who made use of similar techniques.

What did the competing ideas of Marxism and the analogical perspective offer as a solution to the modern dilemma? Marxism anticipated "the overcoming of individual alienation through the reorganization of society," and from this viewpoint science was "an indispensable instrument of the human, the weapon of its knowledge and consciousness of the world." Marxism offered change and hope — a message that had also been at the heart of Phillips's paean to science. Mann's vision, to the contrary, presented "the spiritual dilemma of present day man as an eternal situation"; there was no hope of change. It was not science and Marxism that were limited and deterministic but the whole corpus of "mythical" and analogical ideas.

To Rosenberg, analogical schemes were of little use in making concrete judgments, especially concerning politics. Mann's confrontations with Nazism, for example, had revealed a fatal weakness in his thought. Mann had shown that he could shift political direction without changing his ideas; his flight from Germany must be credited to "individual decency," for "any decision could have been made" consistent with his philosophy. The search for eternal principles, moreover, revealed the "essentially religious and idealistic nature of most analogical thinking," placing it in clear opposition to secular and materialistic thought. Marxism remained sensitive to the particular context of specific ideas and events even as it sought to give them general meaning. Analogical thinking was helpless before the unique.

Rosenberg's essay had taken the trouble to demonstrate at some length that the general perception of modern writers held by the *Partisan Review* intellectuals applied in the case of Thomas Mann. In the process of condemning the philosophical position of Mann and analogical thinking in general, Rosenberg had also reaffirmed an interpretation of Marxism that emphasized several contentions: man could hope to overcome alienation through a transformation of society; critical thought and scientific method continued to offer the best prospects for understanding and for progress; Marxism had clear values and principles, but it was a flexible method sensitive to the unique qualities of individual works of art, particular ideas, and singular events. It was because they held such a view of Marxism that the *Partisan Review* intellectuals could anticipate a fertile relationship between radicalism and literature. Their hopes for synthesis gave them much of their critical edge and led them to see not only strengths but also limitations in the work of modernists.

In criticizing works that challenged "scientific" thinking and those that seemed to ignore or mishandle social and political ideas, the *Partisan Review* intellectuals spoke with conviction and assurance. The defense of broad beliefs against clear opposition tended to emphasize basic tenets of their position, making their views appear more explicitly defined and more fixed than they actually were. Yet, though the *Partisan* critics could assert their general faith in Marxism without difficulty, they were growing increasingly sensitive to Marxism's intellectual reputation, to what they regarded as rigidifications or distortions of its ideas, and, for that matter, to all efforts to give it a clear and precise content. If their views required at times that Marxism should be defended for its broad systematizing and explanatory powers, simplifications of Marxism into stiff doctrine moved the *Partisan Review* intellectuals to insist so emphatically on the fluid and open nature of a Marxist approach that the whole idea of radical system was threatened.

An effort to defend the flexibility of Marxist criticism provided the central theme for Phillips's "The Esthetic of the Founding Fathers." Phillips repeated arguments made two and three years before by him, by Rahv, and by Farrell when he asserted that "Marx was not a literary critic," when he declared that Marx and Engels had rejected many times the simplistic interpretations of disciples, and when he accused those who preached a rigid Marxist principle in literature of tearing out one emphasis from the "many-sided theories of Marx." The chief agents of distortion were, of course, the Stalinists; and Phillips reviewed the sins of earlier "leftism" once more in well-rehearsed detail. As he turned to considering the "possibilities of Marxist criticism" in the present, Phillips played another familiar tune. Those who denied the potential of Marxist criticism did so because they simplified and dogmatized Marx, tending "to regard Marxism, on the one hand, and literature on the other as absolutes." Phillips insisted again that Marxism was not a "closed system, nor a formula" but for literature, at least, "a *method*" open to experiment.

From this point the desire for flexibility led Phillips's essay onto new ground. Far from trying to codify a new critical procedure, Phillips attempted to stretch the label of Marxism to cover nearly anything the *Partisan Review* critics might wish to do so long as it retained some interest in social context. Because Marxism was many-sided and because Marx had said little, a variety of critical procedures might claim the Marxist label. It would be best, Phillips suggested, "to speak of *Marxist criticisms* in the plural, or of *ventures in Marxist criticism*, especially since it has yet to be demonstrated that only one code of beliefs or one kind of insight into art is compatible with the philosophy of Marx."

If the beginning of Phillips's essay had reasserted the argument that Marxism was not a straitjacket, the ending opened the door to doubts that Marxism was a useful and distinctive garment at all. Yet Phillips intended no message of weakening interest at the time. Faced with the need to adjust to changing intellectual and political circumstances, Phillips found that the idea of experiments in Marxist criticism had immediate advantages. He seized upon the possibilities of the idea in two ways that were characteristic.

First, he used the idea of a rich and diverse criticism to shift the center of attention away from the creation of literature itself and toward the practice of analysis. Phillips had earlier spoken of the writer's "sensibility" as the realm within which a synthesis of aesthetic and social elements could occur; now the artist's sensibility along with his "ideas" made up a "single set of values," which it was left to the critic to reveal and explore. More than the artist himself, the critic now discharged the essential function of balancing formal qualities and social facts, literature and politics. Phillips was quite open about claiming new territories for the critical "ventures" he envisioned: "For once criticism enters into the swim of social life, once it takes up the cudgels against all modes of academicism which work to freeze the present within itself—when it seeks to affirm, in its own way, the values which literature rescues from society—criticism should share in the imaginative possibilities which literature has always enjoyed." All in all, the critic now seemed to deserve at least as high a status as the artist. Phillips was quietly claiming that the kind of criticism encouraged by *Partisan Review* stood at the center of culture in the late thirties.

The idea of diverse Marxist criticisms allowed a second use as well: it allowed Phillips to downplay critical differences with those whom *Partisan Review* wished to call friends, most notably Edmund Wilson. Wilson had begun to dismiss, as Phillips noted, "not only the isolated texts [of radical theorists] but the Marxist philosophy itself as an effective instrument of literary analysis." Indeed, in writing on Flaubert, Wilson had suggested not just that politics had little to teach literature but that literature might sometimes teach politics. He had found Flaubert superior to Marx not just because of specific judgments but because of an intellectual development rooted in rejection of the very premises of radicalism. By emphasizing the "method" of Marxism and the ideas from the radical corpus most attractive to *Partisan Review*, Phillips could claim that "despite Wilson's disavowals of 'Marxist criticism' he has certainly brought into his writing many of the values and much of the outlook of Marxism." In effect, Phillips suggested that Wilson was writing Marxist criticism without knowing it. Such was one form of latitude granted by the notion of "Marxist criticisms in the plural."[22]

Because the *Partisan Review* intellectuals placed heavy emphasis on the politics of anti-Stalinism in the late thirties and because no triumphant body of new writing appeared, it is tempting to dismiss their vision of an affirmative radical philosophy sustaining an innovative radical literature as empty or mistaken from the start—a conclusion that many have drawn. Unfulfilled dreams often prove embarrassing to those who once held them, and they make easy targets for the mockery and the smug superiority of another age. Yet occasionally the dreams deserve another look with respect for their context and aspiration. Although the present can dismiss the notion that an allegiance to Marxism was *necessary* for a new artistic outlook, the question remains whether a link between radical politics and an advancing literature was possible and whether it held any potential for fresh cultural insight. Any positive response to this question must appear rather speculative. Still, there would seem to be reasonable grounds for suggesting that behind the effort to link a radical philosophy with an evolving art lay one of the more creative impulses of the thirties.

By the early twentieth century, as many scholars have argued, older systems of religious, social, moral, and intellectual justification were unmistakably breaking down, leaving both middle-class culture and capitalism without many of their traditional legitimizing ideas. In Daniel Bell's version of the argument, the "major intellectual attack" on the older values came "from the realm of culture," from the Young Intellectuals of the teens; the economic attack grew out of the rise of mass consumption, which came into its own with the "new capitalism" of the 1920s. If these forces created greater individual and social freedom, they eroded any clear sense of community values. Liberalism was generally on the side of the transforming forces. And if liberal notions in politics could be criticized for having no distinct vision of ultimate values and ends, how much more true was this of the liberal encouragement for cultural experiment and change? A philosophy of liberation with no rationale for limits could leave both individual and society groping for meaning.[23]

The intellectual inheritance and the experience of writers in the thirties may have made some of them quite aware of the cultural problem that was emerging, however vaguely they identified its nature. The rebellion of the teens and the modernism of the twenties, the campaign against Puritanism and the assault on commercialism, were all there in the immediate past to point to the abandonment of old values and the need for new ones. The economic collapse of the Great Depression seemed to underline this need and demand the construction of a new system. The version of literary radicalism developed by the *Partisan Review* critics recognized at some level the rampaging forces of cultural and economic change and sought to read their direction. Marxism, as Phillips and Rahv understood it in their early essays, promised positive results from the transformations under way in both economics and culture. And what would guide the forces of change in such positive directions was Marxism itself, not as a source of permanent solutions or utopian doctrines, but as the inspiration for a comprehensive system of values that would follow historically the Protestant ethic, just as socialism would follow capitalism.

Radicalism, as Rahv and Phillips understood it, promised both that change would continue and that it would be contained; that the mind would have freedom but that it would also have direction; that there would be abundance and liberation but that there would also be a clear morality and accepted goals. Marxism would provide literature with a philosophical framework and a purpose. It would link experimentation to a rational and ethical system. The vision was not to become reality. The *Partisan Review* circle produced no great radical-cultural thinker. Yet given the record of American culture since the thirties, the effort of the *Partisan* critics to find a system of values that was more than an effort to resuscitate the past should not be too easily dismissed.

Granting some respect to *Partisan Review*'s aspirations allows a more generous appreciation of the pressures inhibiting a smooth romance between Marxism and literature. Certainly there were intellectual obstacles of daunting scope, and limits to the talents of those involved. Yet the attempt to develop a radical literary synthesis was never, in fact, pursued with concentration for very long or carried very far. The times were hard on the visions of intellectuals and on the expectations of the *Partisan Review* circle. By the end of the decade that had begun in radical optimism, the talk was all of endings and decay. Within months of the editors' second declaration of a new generation of writers, Philip Rahv lamented both the "ferocious surprises" in politics and the fact that "revolutionary thinking in literature has virtually come to an end." Longing to celebrate a new generative power, Rahv found himself decrying the "intellectual sterility of the age."[24]

The harsh effects of contemporary experience on their positive expectations only aggravated a problem that would have given the *Partisan Review* intellectuals trouble under any circumstances: their notion of synthesis required a degree of system and unity of which they were perpetually shy. The editors seemed most comfortable suggesting that there was, of course, a potentially rich relationship between politics and literature but that all questions remained open. Indeed, insistence on the difficulty of working out a proper synthesis became a defense against the formulas of others and an excuse for not suggesting answers of their own. In responding to Trotsky's demands on the magazine, for instance, Rahv used the claim of difficulty to deflect Trotsky's political pressure on *Par-*

tisan Review, to defend the magazine's cultural range, and to maintain a high degree of flexibility in its central conceptions.[25] Consciously or unconsciously, the editors seemed inclined to preserve an indeterminate position and to seize upon its strengths.

The *Partisan Review* intellectuals exhibited a consistent fear of fixed ideas and closed structures. Few words conveyed a stronger condemnation for them than "static." They attacked the ideas of others for assuming an "eternal situation," for freezing the present within itself, for claiming absolutes, for treating Marxism as a closed system, and on and on. They called repeatedly for "variety, curiosity, amplitude of means" in American writing.[26] The desire to preserve flexibility and openness was not simply a matter of conviction but one of basic instinct. To understand this, it is perhaps important to recall that the *Partisan Review* intellectuals had social identities as well as intellectual commitments. Especially for the children of immigrants, an open society held far more promise than one with firmly established boundaries. Belief in the positive possibilities of historical change, in values that were shaped by time and place, and in the fluid power of untrammeled thought allowed the *Partisan Review* intellectuals not only to nourish hope for mankind in general, but also to see in an evolving American culture a positive future for people like themselves.

The desire for openness and inclusiveness plainly stood at the heart of cosmopolitanism. A fundamental reason for objecting to nationalism, regionalism, nativism, "village values," and the like was that such concepts were inherently restrictive—in the process of defining those who belonged, they tended to suggest the exclusion of many others. Religious ideas, too, often encouraged parochialism, the drawing of boundaries, the fixation of belief, whereas secular scientific thought fostered a perpetual probing and skepticism that undermined convention, and encouraged change. Cosmopolitan values assumed the desirability of a society and a culture both diverse and fluid, and in this they very much belonged to the broad intellectual current of twentieth-century liberalism.

What cosmopolitanism did not and could not provide was a concrete system. When they embraced Marxism, the *Partisan Review* intellectuals hoped to find such a system that would, nevertheless, embody cosmopolitan values. The search implied a delicate balancing act that would have been difficult at any time. In the late 1930s, it proved impossible. The *Partisan Review* intellectuals could continue to insist on the virtues of Marxism *as they interpreted it*; but as their Marxism came increasingly to represent a complex of intellectual values that had many of its origins elsewhere, it lost its systematizing power, it lost its philosophical integrity, and it lost its capacity to serve literature in the way *Partisan Review* had originally imagined.

Such judgments rely on hindsight. The importance of Marxism for the *Partisan Review* intellectuals faded only slowly, and the concern with radical ideas remained strong at the end of the thirties. Yet the editors of the magazine seemed quite conscious that a great deal had changed. Many in the *Partisan Review* circle had lost confidence in organized radical politics by 1937, and by 1938 the editors had largely given up their claims that any new radical literature was emerging. Abandoning the belief that radicalism was advancing in the contemporary world meant giving up one basis for judgment; it meant losing a clear source of orientation; and it meant looking elsewhere to find a sense of purpose for a magazine like *Partisan Review*.

A greater emphasis on the existing resources of literature and critical thought, and on the responsibilities of the intellectual as intellectual, began to appear at the time of the break with the Communist Party. (Appeals to the integrity of the intellectual process carried strong ethical claims that could rival the moral appeal of radicalism.) Believing that rational thought and creative freedom were under attack on all sides by the late thirties, the *Partisan Review* intellectuals took it as their responsibility to defend the traditions of the mind and the works that had grown out of them. By the middle of 1938, William Phillips was suggesting that it was the intellectual's "vital function in society" to "safeguard the dreams and discoveries of science and art"—a rather conservative-sounding definition of the radical intellectual's responsibilities.[27] This battle of preservation did not mean a sudden shift in underlying values or standards, but it did mean that critical swords once wielded in the name of a future literature would be beaten into plowshares more fit for cultivating established literary fields.

Chapter Seven | Politics and War

If part of New York had moved to Russia in the 1930s, according to Lionel Abel's conceit, the Hitler-Stalin pact "started New York City, bitter and demoralized, back from the U.S.S.R., to America." Yet it was not just the pact that left the city "uneasy," for a series of shocks kept the ideological ground atremble. Abel himself recalled "the Russian attack on Finland, the Nazi attack on Poland, the defeat of France, the battle of Britain, the assassination of Trotsky, the Nazi attack on Russia, [and] finally Pearl Harbor." By 1940 Delmore Schwartz already took for granted a permanent change in the literary landscape, and he aspired to represent in his work "that new thing on this planet, a post-Munich sensibility."[1]

For the *Partisan Review* intellectuals, the events of 1939 and after brought a troubling series of new political challenges. Responses based on the models and theories available satisfied many for a time, few in the long run. Each person had to decide over months and years to what degree the evolving story in the world's headlines undermined or confirmed radical patterns of expectation and prophecy. Gradually, the unfolding war split the *Partisan Review* circle on the question of support and brought the magazine to a major crossroads in its history. Before 1939 the *Partisan Review* intellectuals had found in anti-Stalinism a common political purpose strong enough to override differences of personality and tactics. After the Nazi-Soviet pact—with the Communist Party's influence among intellectuals clearly weakened—opposition to Stalin no longer seemed the single most pressing concern. The brief career of the League for Cultural Freedom and Socialism made the change apparent. Finally organized to declare its opposition to Stalinism shortly before the pact, the League found itself announcing in its second (and final) statement, "War has become *the* issue."[2]

Like many other intellectuals in the United States and Europe, the editors of *Partisan Review* had shown a growing sensitivity to the threat of war well before the 1939 pact. With the Popular Front urging a united opposition to fascism by the Soviet Union and Western democracies, the magazine's early stand against war combined anti-Stalinist polemic with radical doctrine and the "lessons" of World War I. In the fall of 1938, the war question leaped to prominence in *Partisan Review* and established itself as a primary topic of the editorial "This Quarter" section for all five issues in which that feature appeared. The first such piece, triggered by the Munich Conference of late September, bitterly chastised Popular Front intellectuals for urging "the very same social-patriotic policies, the identical supra-class illusions which they claimed the catastrophe of 1914 had taught them to renounce forever." It seemed, the editors remarked with acerbity, that the intellectuals' function was "to idealize imperialist wars when they come and to debunk them after they are over."[3]

A second editorial at the beginning of 1939 illustrated the power of the war question to turn *Partisan Review*'s attention away from Stalinism for the moment and toward the views of those whom they saw as mainstream liberals. Hailing Lewis Mumford as an "anti-fascist jitterbug," the editors rejected Mumford's attribution of contemporary crises to the "pathology of the German mind" (Mumford's phrase) and equated his stance to the "Hun-baiting of 1914–1918." Mumford might be honestly horrified by Nazi racism, but he was slipping into the same "national mysticism" that provided its inspiration. "If the Nazis deduce Bolshevism from the nature of the Jewish mind, Mr. Mumford deduces fascism from the nature of the German mind." More was at stake than a set of isolated remarks. What the editors saw in Mumford was a tendency toward which the *Partisan Review* intellectuals were acutely sensitive. If the "intellectual obscenities" of condemning Jews or Germans through some myth of collective mentality represented the uglier side of the coin, the self-conscious Americanism of the Popular Front and of prewar efforts to define national virtues made up its opposite face. Believing that national myths gave rise to "racial doctrines" and repressive action, the *Partisan Review* intellectuals deeply feared the emotions of war.[4]

Given the nature of their concerns and their inheritance, it was no surprise that the editors of *Partisan Review* should turn to Randolph Bourne as a model and inspiration. Consecutive editorials in mid-1939 attempted to subject the current intellectual climate to harsh scrutiny in essays running parallel to Bourne's familiar dissections of two decades before. Macdonald's "War and the Intellectuals: Act Two" came first and made the parallel explicit. Rahv's "Twilight of the Thirties" (discussed in the next chapter) followed Bourne's "Twilight of Idols" less ostentatiously but was linked with the earlier essay in tone and purpose.

Macdonald began with a long quotation from the essay to which his title paid homage, replaying Bourne's castigation of the intellectuals of 1917; and he reminded *Partisan Review* readers of what had happened during the first war: "*The Masses* was denied the use of the mails, Max Eastman narrowly escaped lynching by some soldiers, Eugene Debs and hundreds of Wobblies and Socialists were given severe prison terms"; and when the editors of the *Seven Arts* "courageously insisted on expressing their mounting objections [to the war], their financial backing was withdrawn and the magazine died." Now in the late thirties, "all sections of the intelligentsia" were falling behind the drive toward another war, and "a whole crop of flag-waving, anti-fascist books" had appeared.

The dire warnings of coming repression that ran through Macdonald's essay looked not only to historical example but also to radical precept. A war against fascism abroad would mean "submission to the ruling class at home." Where once there had been a forward-looking interest in socialism, Macdonald now detected among the intellectuals an "anti-fascist fascism." If a "regression in liberal thought" was so obvious already, Macdonald asked, "what will happen once we go to war?" His answer took it as a given that a modern war could not be fought without severe repression: "The first result of a war against foreign fascism will be the introduction of domestic dictatorship."[5]

With such forebodings and prognostications accumulating over many months, the *Partisan Review* intellectuals were well prepared to declare their position once war actually broke out in Europe. The second statement of the League for Cultural Freedom and Socialism provided a rare collective declaration of position, carrying as it did the signatures of nearly all those who made up the magazine's circle: Lionel Abel, James Burnham, F. W. Dupee, James T. Farrell, Clement Greenberg, Dwight Macdonald, George L. K. Morris, William Phillips, Philip Rahv, Harold Rosenberg, Meyer Schapiro, and Delmore Schwartz. (Sidney Hook and Lionel Trilling, for different reasons, were not signers.)[6] One section of the statement effectively summed up what the group believed to be a proper radical position on the war: "Our entry into the war, under the slogan of 'Stop Hitler!' would actually result in the immediate introduction of totalitarianism over here. . . . The American masses can best help

. . . by fighting *at home* to keep their own liberties." The fear of repression was once again apparent. For intellectuals, American entry into the war would mean "corruption for those who accept it, spiritual if not physical imprisonment for those who do not."

What, then, should writers and artists do? The "greatest service" in a practical sense, the League statement suggested, would be to "help make articulate" the continuing opposition of the majority of Americans to entering the war. More generally—and probably of more real concern to the signers—American writers and artists should "put themselves on record against the war as a symbol of their acceptance of the responsibilities of their profession." An earlier generation had committed "spiritual suicide"; intellectuals must now avoid a repetition of that collapse, "if only for the sake of their own integrity."[7]

The *Partisan Review* intellectuals almost unanimously opposed a war against fascism in 1939, not because they doubted for a moment the danger posed by Hitler, but because they believed such a war would impose on the United States the very evils it had set out to combat. Unified on this point, their general position nevertheless allowed contrasting notions of the intellectual's obligations and varying assumptions about the future. One set of ideas emphasized opposing imperialist war in order to encourage the socialist revolutions that some continued to insist lay just around the historical corner. Other bits of analysis, as in the League statement, seemed to underline the relative political powerlessness of those who would stand opposed to war and, by implication and omission, to hold out no real hope of a mass radical uprising. The intellectual, in this view, must look to his traditions and concern himself with his own integrity and that of his "profession." Such differences created no visible conflicts in 1939, but they suggested the existence of fault lines along which tremors would soon occur under pressure of war.

The Nazi-Soviet pact, followed quickly by evidence of Russian involvement in the division of Poland and the Soviet attack on Finland, delivered a major blow to the American Communist Party and to intellectual sympathizers of the Soviet Union. A good many of the liberal friends of the Popular Front with whom the *Partisan Review* intellectuals had sparred now abandoned their confidence in the good intentions of the Soviets and sought new bearings. This did not mean that anti-Stalinism became a dead issue for *Partisan Review*—though that campaign was allowed to simmer on a back burner for a time—and it did not mean that the magazine readily embraced the chastened former sympathizers as returning prodigals. Differences tended to persist throughout the war, waiting to be brought to a boil at a later time.

At least some of those who had worked against Stalinism were perceptive enough to have mixed feelings at the news of the pact. James T. Farrell welcomed the fact that the announcement might "clarify the atmosphere" a bit, but he suggested as well that the pact was not only going to "discredit Stalinism" but would also "do severe damage to Marxism and revolutionary ideology." As Farrell reported fistfights and confusion within Communist ranks, his message to himself urged caution: "People should . . . not let emotions engendered around anti-Stalinism carry them away."[8] Yet within a month Farrell was recording with evident pleasure that he had confronted Malcolm Cowley over the pact, and he was suggesting scornfully that someone should establish an "Institution for the Moral Rehabilita[t]ion of Betrayed Stalinist Charlatans, Dupes, Hatchet-Men and Literary Hacks."[9]

Partisan Review itself proved to be none too shy about rubbing salt into the wounds of reeling Soviet sympathizers. The editors inserted in the *New Republic* an advertisement for their magazine that began, "Pardon us for pointing," and went on to say in part:

PARTISAN REVIEW is proud that—
- We were not embarrassed by the Nazi-Soviet Pact.
- We have opposed, for years and not for weeks, the corrupting influence of Stalinism on intellectual life.
- We predicted the war would not be averted by collective security.[10]

At the same time, a letter to the League of American Writers appeared in *Partisan Review*. Observing that the League had been the "most active political organization" among American writers "until August 21st, 1939" (the date when news of the pact came out), the letter noted that it had just a few months before called the Soviet Union an opponent of fascism and "the most consistent defender of peace" in the world. Where was the League now? Had it anything to say? There followed a series of specific questions concerning the League's position on the war, on the Soviet Union, and on the Communist Party, all designed to cause as much discomfort as possible.[11]

Notably, the signatures on this letter included not only the names of Rahv, Phillips, Dupee, Farrell, and Schapiro but also that of Sid-

ney Hook, who had already declared himself for American participation in a war against Stalin and Hitler. Hook could not at this
time agree with those closest to *Partisan Review* on any positive
political statement, yet he could join with them to harvest the bit-
tersweet fruit of their mutual anti-Stalinism by baiting the discom-
fited League.

The tendency of the *Partisan Review* intellectuals to be both
sharp and smug in their attitude toward disenchanted supporters
of the Popular Front had its parallel in a fresh wave of condemnation directed at the Soviet Union and the American Communist
Party. With some glee, the editors listed the successive positions
taken by the *Daily Worker* as it had squirmed to deny before the
event, and to justify after it, each step in the unwrapping of the
Hitler-Stalin agreement. For weeks there had been "ideological bedlam" among the Communists, according to *Partisan Review*, and
conflicting political lines. What did this reveal about the nature
of the Party? The editors noted that some Communists had tried
to claim that the Party's lack of preparedness for the pact demonstrated that it had no "pipeline to Moscow"; *Partisan Review* was
determined to deny this claim all credit. The important point for
the editors was that through all the shifts, the American Communist Party had "clung to Moscow."

Many would agree with the magazine's judgment that the willingness of the American Communist Party to follow the twists
and turns of Soviet policy in 1939 (as in 1941 and 1945) demonstrated that Party positions were determined more by external considerations than by indigenous American concerns. Yet the editors
of *Partisan Review* made this conclusion the basis for further declarations that simply went too far. Although the editors acknowledged a distinction between leaders (the "Party bureaucracy" that
had chosen loyalty to Moscow) and the "rank and file of the Party,"
they could see no way to explain why all Party members had not
rapidly dropped away after the pact except to exaggerate the "disciplined, monolithic character of the Party organization." The editors could see among the rank and file only a "mindless, passive
acceptance of directives, however irrational, from above" and an "ab-
dication . . . of all critical judgment."

This view of a rigidly controlled Party left unexplained the earlier talk of "ideological bedlam" among the Communists and the
stories of fistfights between Party members. It looked to the center,
to the way Party leaders represented their movement, and it denied
internal tensions and the significance of local issues. Such a view

foreshadowed — and perhaps contributed to — the damaging assumption of a unified, "monolithic" communism that fogged the vision of intellectuals and policymakers alike in the postwar decades. And the editors did not stop there. They went on to one of the most extreme statements yet to appear in *Partisan Review*: "Those who keep silent or who continue to support the policies of the Third International must from now on be called bluntly what they are: agents of the Kremlin and, for the present at least, of Hitler." This judgment was explicitly aimed not only at Communists but also at fellow-travelers and sympathetic liberals. By its logic, any of the "Cowleys and Lerners and Hickses" who now said nothing must be considered foreign "agents." Perhaps a caution is necessary: the United States was not yet at war, and the editors could not foresee what such charges might mean in the future. Nevertheless, for intellectuals sensitive to the threat of repression — who believed that the Communist Party had recently become "a prominent object of governmental persecution" — the invitation to attack Soviet sympathizers, or silent former sympathizers, as operatives of the Kremlin and of Hitler was both extraordinary and reckless.

In arguing that those who remained Communists or fellow-travelers possessed neither political nor intellectual independence, the editors in effect erected a sharp ideological boundary, denying by implication that any persistent supporter of Soviet policy could be a legitimate participant in American political life or an authentic intellectual. Yet they went on immediately to criticize liberals for simplifying the war as an "ideological conflict" between freedom and tyranny. The editors who so strongly asserted their own condemnation of Communist sympathizers rejected emphatically any attempt from other quarters to draw sharp ideological lines. They condemned the whole modern process of pumping up public loyalties in wartime even as they incited their readers to regard Communists and their supporters as foreign "agents."[12]

From those divesting themselves of Popular Front or Communist Party connections after the pact, the *Partisan Review* circle seemed inclined to demand a full confession of error and a complete renunciation of the past. The editors declared that those who had "broken with Moscow" almost immediately in 1939 had mostly done so "in a hypocritical and disingenuous way." Shortly thereafter, *Partisan Review* published an attack that condemned all those who refused to be penitent in the face of "demonstrable guilt."[13] And "guilt" was the point. From *Partisan Review*'s perspective, the evils of Stalinism had become obvious in the Popular Front years, not with the announcement of the pact. The magazine maintained an active hostility toward those who did not now agree that support of Popular Front positions had been intellectually and morally wrong.[14]

If some attacks in *Partisan Review* seemed harsh, they nevertheless touched upon legitimate questions that divided American intellectuals in the late 1930s and that have continued to be controversial into the present. Frank Warren, in his analysis of the period, has commented upon the failure of liberals, "while abandoning the Popular Front, to challenge its interpretations of events." Too many kept the same "habit of mind" after 1939 and engaged in no "wholesale reappraisal"; as a result, "most of the Popular Front beliefs stayed in place."[15] In the short run, this position included accepting the Communist version of the Spanish Civil War, continuing to believe an actual plot had triggered Stalin's purges, and discounting the level of Communist influence in various Popular Front organizations. On a more lasting basis, the argument over liberal attitudes involved such questions as whether communism should be treated as morally different from fascism, and whether liberals (by being uncritically sympathetic to communism) or anti-Stalinists (by being too virulently opposed) were offering the greatest aid to the forces threatening democratic values. All of these issues remained highly charged as the 1940s began. For the *Partisan Review* circle, the perceptions of liberal failings past and present meant that exposing the intellectual malefactions of those who appeared too forgiving of Soviet sins would remain an important theme.

The necessity of coming to terms with the challenges to theory, the political surprises, and the human horrors associated with the war had a lasting impact on the political attitudes of the *Partisan Review* intellectuals. In general the magazine's radicalism and commitment to Marxism markedly diminished during the war years, but the journeys taken by individuals varied greatly in both direction and speed of travel. The *Partisan Review* circle had never fully agreed on a positive political program, and the pressures of war drove a wedge into every perceptible crack. Growing differences did not necessarily bring an end to personal contacts or even professional cooperation; but they did reflect the weakening intellectual pulse of radicalism in the forties and its decline as a broadly unifying ideal. One of the earlier effects of the war for those around *Partisan Review* was to accelerate controversies growing out of the revaluation of Marxism.

Partisan Review stood neither at the center of nor isolated from the major reassessments of Marxism conducted by American intellectuals at the end of the thirties. Sidney Hook and James Burnham, both of whom were engaged in severe criticism of the notion of the dialectic in Marxist thought, did not publish major essays on this question in *Partisan Review*.[16] Yet the magazine clearly reflected the direction their work was taking. Burnham proclaimed in a review, for example, that the "alleged principles of dialectical materialism" were vague, could not be tested, and were "without scientific significance." Others offered similar rejections.[17]

In attacking the idea of the dialectic, most of those who contributed to *Partisan Review* did not intend to deny the value of Marxism.[18] For at least one critic, however, rejection of the dialectic was just one part of a broader questioning. Edmund Wilson had turned with great energy to studying the history of socialism in the thirties for a project that found its fruition in *To the Finland Station* (1940). As Wilson's new expertise was placed at the service of his increasing skepticism about radical ideas, the *Partisan Review* intellectuals grew more chary of his work. The editors could no longer disagree only gently with Wilson's doubts when *Partisan Review* printed "The Myth of the Marxist Dialectic."

Wilson's critique of Marxist ideas, which owed a great deal to the earlier work of Max Eastman, as Wilson acknowledged, identified the dialectic as "religious myth." Hegel's triad was really just the "old Trinity, taken over from the Christian theology, as the Christians had taken it over from Plato." The presence of this "mythical and magical triangle" in Marxist thought suggested serious limitations. Wilson raised numerous questions of theory on which he believed Marx had been vague or silent, and he emphasized contradictions and other lapses. These were not accidental flaws to Wilson; Marxism was flawed in its basic conceptions. To distance Marx from twentieth-century thought, Wilson sprinkled his essay with references to the "old German Will" and to Marx's "old Testament sternness."[19]

Unwilling to let Wilson's essay appear without comment, William Phillips offered a counterstroke in a piece placed immediately after Wilson's. Radicals could only welcome Wilson's approach, Phillips declared, as compared with the stance of those "orthodox materialists" who tended to "mummify Marxism into a system of eternal truths." Still, Wilson had landed wide of the mark; he was not "concerned with bringing Marxism up to date" but with proving "that Marxism is alien to modern thought."[20] (In a similar positioning of *Partisan Review* between the extremes of rigidification

175

and rejection, Rahv would soon place the editorial "we" of the magazine between the "revisionists," who threw away too much of Marx, and the "diehards" with their "doctrinal inflexibility."[21] Was Marxism a "static philosophy," Phillips asked rhetorically, or was Marxism to be "constantly recreated to serve the theoretical and political needs of the present?" There was, of course, no doubt about the answer in Phillips's mind. Wilson had dismissed too much; he had erred in assuming that Marxism was a unified system that would fall apart with the discovery of a major flaw. Marxism was not a "monolithic structure . . . which must be accepted or rejected in its entirety."

For all the evidence of Marx's continuing vitality and Wilson's faults that he assembled, however, Phillips alluded in passing to at least three questions that would trouble the *Partisan Review* intellectuals mightily in their ongoing assessment of Marxism. The first involved the issue of just what made Marxism special or unique once it was reduced to a method. The second concerned the role and the current consciousness of the proletariat. The third asked how Marxists should properly explain the nature of both Stalinism and fascism; Phillips conceded that the appearance of these phenomena required work on the "basic concepts" in the "economics and politics of Marxism." As the issues of war came into play, the *Partisan Review* intellectuals could agree that Marxism must neither be preserved in orthodox form nor rejected outright; they could agree that the dialectic should be discarded; and they could agree that Marxism possessed its greatest strength as a "scientific" method rooted in historical analysis. But they could not agree on just what Marxism would now mean.

The question of what made Marxism-as-method unique had lingered in the background of *Partisan Review*'s discussions throughout the 1930s. Toward the end of the decade, as those around the magazine began to discard as "dead" certain elements of Marxist theory, they created a sharper need to explain why their version of what was "living" constituted a program that was still Marxian and still special. Most revealing of the problems created by the emphasis on method, perhaps, was the often insecure effort to distinguish between the theories of Marx and the ideas of John Dewey.

For Sidney Hook there was no cause to dwell on differences. Marx and Dewey were in "fundamental agreement," he had argued in 1935, and the two could serve as compatible sources of intellectual guidance for radicals. Avoiding any direct questioning of such a rosy view themselves, the editors allowed, or more probably arranged, criticism in the book review section. Morton G. White's review of Hook's *John Dewey* (1939) suggested that Hook had been so eager to defend Dewey that he had ignored "Dewey's opposition to Marxism," which had raised "almost every charge Hook has occupied himself with refuting." White subjected Hook's claim that Dewey and Marxists could cooperate politically to a probing question: "if Dewey, operating without the *theories* of Marx and Hook, is able to come to the same political activity, what special control over affairs do any of Marx's principles effect?" If Hook was right about Dewey, why did anyone need Marx? Hook's claims seemed to blur the line between liberalism and radicalism, making it easy for Marxists to slide across the bridge of intellectual method into acceptance of the "present political framework." Most of the *Partisan Review* intellectuals were not ready to move so far—at least not yet.[22]

Criticisms of Hook's views, which were also assertions that Marxism remained a necessary and distinct perspective for radicals, came from other voices as well. Without mentioning Hook, Meyer Schapiro managed to work into a review the assertion that Marxism differed "crucially" from the views of naturalistic writers, "including Dewey," in "the deeper recognition of the extent of the conflict of group interests and its bearing on the estimation of plans for social change." Bertram Wolfe, reviewing Hook's *Reason, Social Myths, and Democracy* (1940), largely agreed. To Wolfe, the whole idea of Dewey as the inspiration for a radical mass movement seemed "faintly comic," and he insisted that any American socialist movement would have to go to Marx for "innumerable positive things" that Dewey could not provide.[23] Even so, no one rejected Dewey entirely. No one mounted a significant critique of his method or tried to distinguish it clearly from the "method" of Marxism on which so much emphasis had been laid. Marxism's identity in *Partisan Review* seemed less clearly a matter of intellectual differences from liberal theory and more precariously a matter of specific political positions that were about to be tested by war.

Challenges to radical belief were not long in coming. The developing conflict compelled radicals to consider just how strong the forces of proletarian revolt were, compared with those of both bourgeois and "totalitarian" governments. To ask this question was to face up to a very considerable weakness: there was no proletarian mass movement in sight. In the first months of European war, *Partisan Review* watched carefully for "revolutionary situations" to develop in belligerent capitals; yet even when some thought such situations existed, little happened that could be pleasing to radicals. Belief in socialist revolution carried out by the working class could persist as a matter of theory, but it grew increasingly difficult for some to find in such belief an adequate response to immediate issues. *Partisan Review* could find no formula to gloss over the difficulties and disagreements that the war helped to cause.

The degree to which doubts about the revolutionary potential of the proletariat undermined a radical anti-war position and Marxism itself for a number of the *Partisan Review* intellectuals became evident in Rahv's excisions of "dead" tissue from Marxist theory in his editorial of mid-1940, "What Is Living and What Is Dead." It was clear, Rahv declared, that the "crisis in Marxism" had been caused by the inescapable fact that around the world it was "not the social revolution but the counter-revolution which has triumphed." If being scientific implied predictive power, "then certainly the credit of Marxism, which has always insisted on being regarded as a science, is rapidly running short." Only the "negative predictions" had come true, not the positive ones; the "masses" had not risen to "reconstruct society on a more rational basis," despite the fact that international conditions had "not only been ripe but at times rotten-ripe." Without specifically repudiating the call for workers to turn imperialist war into socialist revolution, Rahv effectively declared any radical expectation of revolutionary upheaval an idle dream.

Having begun to reexamine his own position in public, Rahv was not about to exempt Marxist theory and Marxist theorists from embarrassing questions. Had Marxists "overestimated the revolutionary character of the proletariat?" How was it that "false leaders succeed in duping the workers, not once, but over and over again?" Rahv insisted that he had no desire "to deny revolutionary status to the working class"; and he declared his belief that if socialism was ever achieved, it would be "first and foremost the workers" who would achieve it. Nevertheless, he plainly believed that Marxist movements in the present had failed badly and that Marxist theory was in need of a major overhaul. Along with the other liabilities he identified, Rahv dismissed as "diseased tissue" the "theory of the dictatorship of the proletariat in its Bolshevik incarnation insofar as it negates the forms and traditions of democracy."

Through his editorial, Rahv had committed himself more directly than ever before to an emphatic position on what was "dead" in Marxism. The reality—rather than simply the threat—of war pushed Rahv to measure radical theory's reliance on socialist uprisings against the likelihood and practicality of proletarian revolts in the midst of the conflict. Rahv's reluctant questioning of elements in both Marxist and Leninist theory made Marxism seem less a ready intellectual guide in time of crisis than a crippled legacy dependent for its own political survival on new, and as yet invisible, radical formulations. Rahv admitted that he had no solutions to Marxism's problems, and he named no one else who did. Furthermore, Rahv in effect subjected Marxist theory and organization to the limits imposed by "the forms and traditions of democracy." Increasingly common in *Partisan Review* after 1939, the emphasis on democracy proclaimed the heightened fears in the magazine's circle that authoritarianism might follow revolution. Rahv had not given up on radicalism; but even in 1940, the ideas Rahv embraced as "living" betokened a severely diminished confidence in the intellectual power, the political tactics, and the contemporary importance of radicalism.[24]

Rahv's editorial, which contained several criticisms of Trotsky for his rigid adherence to doctrines that could no longer convince, reflected at a distance a major controversy among Trotsky's followers that hastened the decay of radical loyalties within the *Partisan Review* camp. Perhaps the paths followed by James Burnham and Dwight Macdonald offer the best chance to trace the splintering effects of this battle.

As a prominent Trotskyist intellectual during the second half of the thirties, Burnham took a leading role in explaining to those who would listen Trotsky's analysis of Russia under Stalin. Trotsky held that the Soviet Union remained a workers' state; that Stalinism represented reaction but not counterrevolution; that the nationalization of the means of production provided the basis for the genuine emancipation of workers in the future; and that the Soviet Union should thus receive the support of radicals in the next war. Several American writers questioned Trotsky's doctrine of "critical support," making his stance toward Russia one of the more controversial elements in the Trotskyist program. Burnham himself had raised such questions as early as 1936; yet until 1939 Burnham remained behind Trotsky in most respects.[25]

Dwight Macdonald moved most visibly toward the Trotskyist camp when in the summer of 1938, at Burnham's urging, he began contributing to the *New International*. Awkwardly enough, the same issue that carried his first article (July 1938) contained a long letter from Macdonald criticizing Trotsky's recent defense of his role in suppressing an anti-Bolshevik revolt by radical sailors at Kronstadt in 1921. Macdonald rejected Trotsky's assertion that

those who opposed the "dictatorship of the proletariat" were necessarily "opponents of the revolution"—denying, in effect, that Leninist theories made up the one true radicalism. He also termed Trotsky's self-justification an "embarrassing" piece that made it harder
to defend his ideas against those who found Trotsky "sectarian and
inflexible." For all of this, however, Macdonald moved closer to the
Trotskyists and joined the Socialist Workers Party in the fall of
1939.[26]

Within a few weeks of the outbreak of war, the idea of "critical
support" and Trotsky's rigidities became central to an explosion of
differences within the Trotskyist organization. When the Soviet
army invaded Poland, a section of the Trotskyist party led by Max
Schachtman and Burnham declared that the Soviet Union had become an imperialist power and did not deserve unconditional defense. Trotsky not only stuck to his insistence on support for the
Soviet Union, but also proclaimed that the Russian invasion of
Poland (and later the war with Finland) constituted a legitimate
extension of the revolution and a legitimate means of protecting
it. This left Trotsky in the ungainly position of holding that although Stalin's government was reactionary at home, it became the
bearer of social revolution once it crossed a Russian boundary.

Burnham opposed Trotsky's views and attempted to bring about
an open discussion of the nature of the Soviet state within the
Socialist Workers Party. Led by James Cannon, who had Trotsky's
support, the majority faction in the party moved to shut down any
public debate and to bury the issue as much as possible. The
Burnham-Schachtman minority furiously charged the majority with
organizational rigidity and authoritarianism. For six months the
battle that raged in the party's *Internal Bulletin* (as described by
one student of the party) "rose to higher and higher levels of
shrillness and sank to lower and lower levels of invective." Members of the minority who stood firm were eventually expelled in
September 1940, by which time about 40 percent of the original
party had joined Schachtman in forming a new sect.[27]

By this point Burnham had left behind more than a political party.
The quarrel with Trotsky had led him to question his whole relation to Marxist ideas. In resigning from all Trotskyist organizations
shortly after the April convention, Burnham declared abruptly that
"of the most important beliefs, which have been associated with
the Marxist movement, whether in its reformist, Leninist, Stalinist, or Trotskyist variants, there is virtually none which I accept
in its traditional form." For Burnham, the confrontation over the

nature of Stalinism brought on by the war led to a direct repudiation of Marxist ideas.[28]

Macdonald, who had joined the Trotskyist party just in time for the fight, "enthusiastically adhered" to the Burnham-Schactman faction. With characteristic energy, Macdonald churned out "three long articles" for the *Internal Bulletin,* all of which were rejected. One small piece criticizing Trotsky that reached publication brought an attack from Mexico that Macdonald reprinted with seeming pride some seventeen years later.[29] By mid-1940 Macdonald was ready to pour out a stream of essays for *Partisan Review* declaring that it had been wrong to compare the second world war to the first; he now argued that both Hitler's Germany and Stalin's Russia represented something new in history and that the United States could not defeat fascism without becoming either a fascist or a socialist state.[30] Macdonald's effort to become a theorist in his own right led to a departure from traditional Marxism, but not yet to a departure from radical ideas.

In his attack on Macdonald, Trotsky had complained of Macdonald's recent assertion in *Partisan Review* that the intellectual must practice "scepticism towards all theories, governments, and social systems." A questioning attitude toward Marxist theory itself was "scandalous" in a radical, Trotsky thundered obdurately: "He who propagates theoretical scepticism is a traitor."[31] The *Partisan Review* intellectuals rejected such attitudes. Their assumptions demanded open-ended thought and room for disagreement. When radical doctrine and party politics began to scrape against the sense of intellectual integrity and the desire for flexibility in the first years of the war, the values of the *Partisan Review* intellectuals acted to turn most of them—for good reasons or bad and at whatever speed—away from both radical politics and Marxist theory.

So, too, did yet another shock. Despite the recent differences with Trotsky, news of his assassination in late August 1940 moved many in the *Partisan Review* circle to deep emotion. Trotsky's death allowed a celebration of the intellectual symbol he had been without a restricting consciousness of particular political issues. His frequent opponent Victor Serge hailed Trotsky in *Partisan Review* as "the highest expression of a human type," representing "the flower of a half-century of the Russian intelligentsia." Paul Goodman, in a poem for the magazine, compared Trotsky to a meteor or comet and labeled him the "chief of excitement." Though sharply critical of this imagery, Delmore Schwartz had himself tried to write a poem about Trotsky around the idea that "he created, in his writing alone, a kind of international consciousness, an instrument like the electric light." James T. Farrell agreed that Trotsky's work was "more than brilliant"; it was "fertile, suggestive, illuminating." Tributes of this kind offered a reminder of the flashing freedom of intellect, the drama and the cosmopolitan breadth, that the *Partisan Review* intellectuals had hoped to find in radicalism.[32]

Now the leading symbol of that kind of radicalism—however tarnished by recent disputes—was gone. Macdonald's long valediction for Trotsky began with disbelief and asked, "How could a whole culture be murdered?" Trotsky was "the last of the giants of revolutionary Marxism," and the assassin had "set a period to a long chapter of history." It is important to note this sense of closure. From the Hitler-Stalin pact to Trotsky's death was almost exactly one year. The events of that year had shaken the Stalinists, split the Trotskyists, launched a war, engendered or intensified doubts about Marxist and Leninist ideas, and presented many intellectuals with a new political agenda. Macdonald himself worked valiantly to hang on to his radicalism. Yet what came through over and over again was his sense of how much had died—symbolically and actually—with Trotsky.[33]

If Trotsky's death further sapped for *Partisan Review* the already flickering vitality of a cosmopolitan and intellectually sophisticated radicalism, the brutality of the attack that killed him produced a surge of anger that scorched and hardened the anti-Stalinism within the magazine's orbit. There was never a moment of doubt as to who was responsible for the attack. Farrell noted that Trotsky had resisted "the despotic rulers of a great empire," who, when unable to refute his ideas, "drove a pickaxe into his brain." Macdonald spoke of the "regime of the Kremlin, whose ultimate corruption is sealed by this murder." The death of Trotsky not only took something away from any positive vision of radicalism but also concentrated the attention of anti-Stalinists on the degradations of hope, the failures of theory, and the corruptions of practice under the only existing Communist regime.[34]

Most in the *Partisan Review* circle still believed in 1940 that they wanted a reconstructed Marxism that would embody the broad humanistic goals of socialism while discarding all that they regarded as dogmatic, obsolete, or inadequate. But they did little to create such a radical stance. Macdonald and Burnham did try to construct a new explanation of fascism and Stalinism; and the two found they agreed upon the "emergence of a new non-capitalist and non-socialist form of society" (in Macdonald's statement of the common ground) and on little else. First in *Partisan Review* and then in a book, Burnham posited a "managerial revolution" sweeping the twentieth-century world and replacing capitalism with systems dominated by a new class of bureaucrats, administrators, and managers. Macdonald objected that Burnham's views made the "managerial" model "appear desirable from the standpoint of materialistic progress"; and that Burnham exaggerated the strength and internal consistency of these "totalitarian" systems.[35]

Macdonald's own attempt at definition drew an important distinction between the "bureaucratic collectivism" of Germany and Russia and the capitalism of the United States, Britain, and France. Departing from the assumptions of most Marxists in his attempt to save Marxism, Macdonald placed heavy emphasis on the centralized political power of the new societies, making economic structure secondary to political organization. His whole analysis led up to the claim that the totalitarian systems, however new and powerful, need not be regarded as stable or permanent. They were vulnerable to the "strength of the mass revolutionary forces" that might seize upon the "many 'revolutionary situations' which may be expected to rise in the next decade or two of transition." Macdonald's attempt to update and rescue radical thought led back to a reliance on social revolution as the only way to defeat fascism.[36]

Under Macdonald's auspices, *Partisan Review* devoted considerable space to discussions of the nature of fascism in 1941 and 1942 (including a favorable review by C. Wright Mills of Franz Neumann's *Behemoth: The Structure and Practice of National Socialism*, which, in arguing cogently that fascism was still a form of capitalism, directly contradicted the central thesis of both Burnham and Macdonald).[37] Yet most of those in the *Partisan Review* circle showed limited interest in the whole question. By 1943 Philip Rahv was referring to the "wild theories circulated by writers like James Burnham" and to the "elements of fantasy" in some interpretations, including Macdonald's.[38] Whatever the importance of the discussion of fascism in its own terms, its chief significance for the history of the *Partisan Review* circle was probably to demonstrate just how far the decline of faith in the interpretive powers of Marxism had gone. Neither Burnham nor Macdonald was "representative," but together they testified to the passing of a confident acceptance and assertion of traditional Marxist theory.[39] The majority of the *Partisan Review* intellectuals, sharing many of the doubts, gradually drifted away from Marxism or became silent,

neither spurning political radicalism nor demonstrating its importance to them. If one major step in the political evolution of *Partisan Review* and its circle had been taken with the coalescence
around anti-Stalinism in 1937, a second followed from the reconsideration of Marxism that was intensified by the coming of war.

In September 1939, within a few weeks of the Hitler-Stalin pact,
James T. Farrell commented in his diary: "The anti-Stalinist intellectuals who more or less came together around the time of and
through the issues involved in the Moscow trials are no[w] widen-
ing, drifting apart, and bitter cleavages are in the incipient stage."[40]
Farrell probably had in mind the differences between the anti-
Stalinist organizations put together by *Partisan Review* and by
Sidney Hook as one source of friction, and the sharp variation in
attitudes toward war as another.[41] Yet the divisions that came did
not necessarily follow the lines that Farrell might have anticipated.
In 1939 few of the *Partisan Review* intellectuals openly sympathized
with Hook's support for war, and the editorial board of the magazine seemed firmly united in its oppositionist stance. By the end
of 1941, that unity had been left in fragments. Although a supporting cast on each side stood in the background, the chief players in
the drama were Philip Rahv and Dwight Macdonald.

Rahv and Macdonald had strong personalities; their relationship
had thrown off sparks from the time of the earliest discussions over
editorial policy in 1937. Both were aggressive in argument, com-
bative by nature, and fond of their own opinions. Delmore Schwartz
noted pithily that Rahv argued "like a Mack Truck," and Schwartz's
friend James Laughlin exclaimed after his first meeting with Rahv,
"My GAWWWWD what a tank!" Another acquaintance described
Rahv's cocktail-party pronouncements as "violent rebuttals directed
at an invisible, inaudible opposition."[42] Macdonald, in turn, threw
himself into disputation with undisguised enthusiasm, sometimes
in order to search for a principle, though usually believing he had
already found one. Schwartz's fictional portrait describes the Macdonald character as driven by a "pathological excess of energy," an
energy "so great that it triumphed over reality when it was dismal
by moving forward to fresh arenas of frenzied activity." Macdonald
in later life complained to one writer that he had depicted him in
his "usual role of a stubborn Scotch argufier," but the object of this
rebuke concluded after observing Macdonald that it was "an image
he cultivated."[43]

The situation that brought the editors into serious conflict developed over many months. One early indication of trouble came during the summer of 1940 when Macdonald began talking about bringing *Partisan Review* to an end—seemingly without much consultation with his fellow editors except for a brief conversation with George L. K. Morris.[44] When he met opposition to his plans, especially from Rahv, whose work for the magazine he respected, Macdonald retreated to a proposal for "liquidating Dupee and Phillips." As new editors, Macdonald suggested Clement Greenberg and Harold Rosenberg, who he claimed were "able to write" and would "work hard." What seems apparent is that Macdonald expected political support from Greenberg and Rosenberg for advocating in *Partisan Review* what Rahv later called "an amalgam of Leninist and Luxemburgian strategies of the last war." Macdonald's plan was to shift the center of gravity on the editorial board by replacing those who supported "Rahv's over-cautious negativistic policies" with new members who would more likely support his own ideas.[45]

Macdonald had probably taken an administrative lead at the magazine for months, and some of his fellow editors may have been evading any reasonable share of the editorial burdens.[46] Nonetheless, Macdonald's proprietary tone seemed presumptuous in the extreme. In fact, Macdonald depended heavily on his friendship with George Morris, and he counted on wielding by proxy Morris's financial sword in order to control the fate of *Partisan Review*. Morris quickly made it clear to Macdonald that his money and his editorial vote were not at someone else's disposal. After throwing a good deal of cold water on Macdonald's plans, Morris suggested none too subtly that if Macdonald could not accept the current *Partisan Review*, then he would be happy to finance no magazine at all.

Macdonald protested at length, but to little avail. He settled for demanding that the magazine at least rent an office again while threatening to reduce his own role dramatically.[47] The office appeared, but little else happened immediately. Within a few months, Dupee left the magazine to take up a full-time university position, and Greenberg joined the board. The editors announced in the September–October 1940 issue that the magazine would soon change its name to the *Forties* because the old name, pertinent in 1934, had recently "led to many misunderstandings of the magazine's purpose and character." Yet by the time the change was due to go into effect, the editors announced that the plan had been "definitely abandoned" and merely published letters of comment.[48] *Partisan Review* went on very much as before; little had been resolved.

Macdonald rather suddenly gained increased control over *Par-*

tisan Review in early 1941 when Rahv married and followed his wife's work to Chicago for a time.[49] Apparently, Rahv had even planned to remove himself as an editor and had discussed possible new editors with Macdonald. Yet almost immediately upon arriving in Chicago, Rahv wrote to Macdonald asking what he was "up to on the magazine." Within two weeks, Rahv told Macdonald he had decided to "reverse my decision to take my name off the magazine," noting that this put a "new construction" on the search for additional editors. Having reclaimed his place, Rahv reviewed the prospects. Meyer Schapiro and Lionel Trilling had been asked to join the board and had declined. That left James Burnham and Paul Goodman, both of whom Macdonald had evidently once proposed. Rahv raised objections against each. Macdonald was free to search at this point, but no new editors appeared.[50]

Rahv and Macdonald were by now undergoing very different experiences that probably helped widen their differences — as yet not fully developed — over the proper response to war. In Chicago Rahv began associating with a group of "ex-Trotskyists" including Saul Bellow and H. J. Kaplan, most of whom tended to "an aid-to-England position"; he also found David Daiches "pro-war."[51] Macdonald, meanwhile, immersed himself more deeply in an analysis demanding opposition to existing governments in the name of a future revolution. His split from the Schactmanite Workers Party (into a faction of one) made Macdonald more intent on his own notions of radicalism, not less so; and *Partisan Review* became the primary outlet for his political writing.[52]

The Nazi invasion of Russia in June 1941 brought another reversal of the Soviet position, throwing Stalin into alliance with Churchill. Macdonald thought nothing had changed and felt compelled to say so. During the summer Macdonald and Clement Greenberg published "10 Propositions on the War," restating their radical position. The propositions largely followed a line Macdonald had made familiar in *Partisan Review*: the only "real solution" to the current situation was to "deflect the current of history from fascism to socialism"; isolationism was "provincial idiocy"; interventionism and support for existing governments led either toward military defeat (because fascism was more efficient) or toward a "fascist system of our own"; a social revolution would "most probably be short and relatively peaceful"; the lack of "organized leadership" for a revolutionary policy was not a "fatal" problem; and, the conclusion to which everything else led, "All support of whatever kind must be withheld from Churchill and Roosevelt."[53] In their essentials, most of these propositions did not go far beyond the basic stance against imperialist war to which all the editors had assented in 1939. Yet the war had developed a good deal since then. And opinions on all sides had been subject to the pressure of events.

Rahv was not quick to respond. The issue following the Macdonald-Greenberg statement carried no word suggesting dissent from the propositions that had seemed to represent the policy of the magazine. Yet two issues later, in "10 Propositions and 8 Errors," Rahv mounted a devastating critique that ravaged Macdonald's position and announced a major editorial split at *Partisan Review*. Macdonald and Greenberg's "dicta," Rahv declared, were "morally absolutist" and representative of an "academic revolutionism which we should have learned to discard long ago." Macdonald and Greenberg did not speak for a movement, for a party, for the working class, or even for "any influential grouping of intellectuals"; yet they wrote as if they were "backed up by masses of people" and refused to acknowledge anything that did not fit into "their apocalyptic vision of a single cleansing and overpowering event." Rahv was clearly troubled by the isolated position into which Macdonald was trying to lead *Partisan Review* and by the imperviousness of that position to events. Greenberg and Macdonald, he charged, were still offering "the same old orthodox recommendations," in which "we fail to recognize the world as we know it." Rahv was not simply rejecting Macdonald's position politically; he was also using a language that attacked a whole pattern of thought by calling up associations presumably repellent to readers of *Partisan Review*: "absolutist," "orthodox," "apocalyptic."

Rahv's own position made the destruction of fascism a precondition to any revival of radicalism; and the alliance of "Anglo-American imperialism and Stalin's Red Army" offered the only realistic hope for the military defeat of Hitler. A gross underestimation of potential allied power in Macdonald and Greenberg's propositions was matched by an absurd overestimation of the chances for socialist revolution. Their hope for revolutionary changes "in the near future" was "sheer romanticism"; their "blithely optimistic" expectation that revolution could be short and peaceful deserved no more respect than the totally empty assertion that leadership "must and will be found." Rahv insisted that he was not "arguing against a revolutionary policy in principle" but opposing such a policy under conditions in which it could only be "illusory." The defeat of Hitler and fascism could give "the labor movement" a chance to regroup.

Rahv's position combined his fear of fascism and his concern with effectiveness, his rising respect for American power and his conviction that the spirit of radicalism had sunk so low that "only a top to bottom transformation, on a world scale, of our entire moral and political environment" could restore it. Hesitations were evident in Rahv's remark that he was not urging Macdonald and Greenberg to "rush to join the war-party"; and Rahv maintained that the war was "not yet *our* war," meaning one that radicals could gladly and openly support. Yet for all his desire to maintain his sense of continuity as a radical, Rahv had taken a step of major importance in offering guarded support for the capitalist democracies in a war against fascism.[54]

Macdonald and Greenberg mounted a rather weak rejoinder to Rahv, characterized by some awkward twisting and a half-hearted effort at dismissal. Their most effective point came in the charge that Rahv was "vague" about his own ideas. If it was "not yet *our* war," whose was it, and what did Rahv's position amount to? Rahv had not been required by the occasion to develop a positive argument for supporting the war and would not prove eager to do so in the future. Wishing neither to disavow radicalism nor to take up arguments that might sound nationalistic and patriotic, Rahv and others like him were left, as Macdonald put it many years later, without "a vocabulary for a critical defense of the war." Mary McCarthy made a similar point in *The Oasis* about her barely fictionalized "realists": "To identify their survival with the arms of Western capitalism had been a natural step, but one which they took uneasily and with a certain semantic embarrassment—they showed far less constraint in characterizing the opponents of this policy as childish, unrealistic, unhistorical, etc., than in formulating a rhetoric of democratic ideals."[55]

An editorial statement in the first *Partisan Review* of 1942 acknowledged the fracture that was already much in evidence. Unable to agree themselves, the editors promised to accommodate many viewpoints in the magazine; but the awkwardness of their discord was patent.[56] Phillips lined up with Rahv against Macdonald and Greenberg on the war issue, leaving George Morris as a sometime referee. Direct American involvement after Pearl Harbor only increased the tensions on the board. Just before returning from Chicago in February 1942, Rahv wrote to a friend: "The war-atmosphere is thickening. I think we're in for some bad experiences."[57] Part of what Rahv feared was wartime censorship and the persecution of magazines (as during World War I) for publishing anti-war material. Concern over the fate of *Partisan Review* led Rahv and Phillips to resist vigorously exactly the kinds of pieces Macdonald longed to publish.

Some problems were settled amicably, if not without bruises along the way. George Orwell had begun writing a series of "London Letters" for *Partisan Review* in early 1941 (such pieces continued into 1946). Although he had at first insisted that England could not "win the war without passing through revolution," Orwell had soon declared that there did not "effectively exist any policy between being patriotic in the 'King and Country' style and being pro-Hitler." And Orwell's increasing support for the war led to ever stronger rejections of the war's opponents and of pacifists. By the summer of 1942, Macdonald was eager to publish a long letter from D. S. Savage attacking Orwell. The editors of *Partisan Review* traded conditions until they could finally agree that several complaints would be published and that Orwell would be given the chance to reply. Controversy among British intellectuals the editors could handle.[58]

Closer to home, differences arose over Macdonald's desire to publish an anti-war piece by Paul Goodman and then, almost immediately afterward, over an essay by Macdonald himself.[59] Macdonald had written, and then revised, an essay designed to expose the "bankruptcy" of American ideological justifications for the war, concentrating especially on a recent speech by Vice President Henry Wallace. Rahv and Phillips opposed printing the article "for reasons of editorial policy," Macdonald reported: "They claim it is 'anti-war propaganda,' and think that to print it will damage the magazine and possibly lead to its suppression." Macdonald complained that his two fellow editors were violating the earlier agreement to accommodate various points of view, and he appealed to George Morris for support. Though Morris saw weaknesses in the article, he did not think it subversive; and when the magazine's lawyer gave the essay a "clean bill of health" (while warning that "*any* criticism of the war" might prove "dangerous" in the future), Macdonald's article went to press. This disagreement, too, might have ended there had not Macdonald and, in this case, Phillips chosen to press their differences.[60]

Macdonald, on his side, dug up every old ax he deemed insufficiently ground and proclaimed an editorial Armageddon. The situation at *Partisan Review* was "worse than ever"; this time, Macdonald declared, "no decision can bridge the gap."[61] Phillips added to the strife by requesting that his name and Rahv's be dropped from the issue in which Macdonald's essay would appear and then re-stored to the list of editors subsequently. Macdonald first blew up over this idea but then decided that the situation presented a "heaven-sent opportunity." Why not let Phillips resign to get his name out of the current issue, he suggested to Morris, "as a means of eliminating Will from PR permanently." Macdonald threatened, as he had in 1940, to leave himself if Phillips or Rahv did not go.[62] And once again, no one left. Instead of dropping any names, the magazine added a disclaimer declaring that even articles "written by editors" represented only "the point of view of the individual author." This result could hardly have satisfied anyone.[63]

The final showdown came some months later, by which time Macdonald's ally Greenberg had left the editorial board to join the Air Force. Morris precipitated the crisis by announcing that he could no longer subsidize *Partisan Review*. Macdonald agreed with Rahv and Phillips that "the magazine had better go all one way or all the other." If Rahv and Phillips could find new financial backing, they would continue *Partisan Review*; if not, Macdonald would assume complete control on his own. Apparently confident that he would be the survivor, Macdonald drafted and sent to Rahv a statement announcing his takeover of the magazine and his plan to empha-size "political and social comment." Then, at the eleventh hour, Rahv proclaimed a "miracle." A Mrs. Norton, who liked *Partisan Review* for its "sustained contact with European literary and art ideas," agreed to provide backing for Rahv and Phillips. For reasons "including her husband's army position," Mrs. Norton asked that her support not be made public and that *Partisan Review* avoid pro-voking political controversy.[64]

Macdonald's departure was not entirely peaceful, for through-out the process he insisted on contrasting *Partisan Review* nega-tively with the kind of magazine he wanted to run. In his public letter of resignation, Macdonald asserted that *Partisan Review* had begun in 1937 as a "Marxian socialist cultural magazine" and that its political orientation had accounted for "much of the magazine's intellectual success." Now, he claimed, the "Marxist position" had been reduced "to a minority of one." Rahv and Phillips in reply pointed out that *Partisan Review* "from its inception" had been "edited mainly by literary men" and had succeeded by "combining socialist ideas with a varied literary and critical content." As for Macdonald's claim to having been the sole Marxist left on the board, the editors dismissed this as an identification of Marxism with his own politics. Macdonald had "wanted *P.R.* to take over [the] functions" of a "revolutionary movement . . . in a state of decline," and this no magazine could do. Macdonald had indicated that the magazine he hoped to start would "subordinate" cultural matters to social and political concerns. Rahv and Phillips leapt upon this remark, declaring that it was "precisely this sort of disagreement which led, in 1937, to our break with the Stalinists."[65]

On cultural issues there was as much disagreement as on political ones. Macdonald's letter of resignation complained that *Partisan Review* had become "rather academic" and expressed a preference for "a more informal, disrespectable and chance-taking magazine, with a broader and less exclusively 'literary' approach." Perhaps Morris responded most effectively to this point by reminding Macdonald that *Partisan Review* "always *was* academic and 'literary.'" Morris could think of "no instance when an experimental 'disreputable' article was turned down by the boys, that you wanted in."[66] Rahv and Phillips settled for suggesting that the indisputable contemporary significance of politics in no way made literature "less attractive or less meaningful *to those of us who respond to it*" (emphasis added).

In resigning, Macdonald could have acted far more graciously. He, in fact, drafted a sentence expressing his confidence that *Partisan Review* would "continue to be edited on a high level" and would remain of value. Then he crossed the sentence out. When Rahv and Phillips announced that they would be joined on the editorial board by "Mr. Delmore Schwartz," Macdonald exploded to Schwartz in a series of exclamations, claiming that the "Mr." betrayed a rampant academicism.[67] The cure for Macdonald's edginess was a magazine of his own, and within a few months he had it. *Politics* became the embodiment of the notions about journalism and political commentary that Macdonald had been accumulating for several years. And in *Politics* Macdonald made his own journey away from radicalism.[68]

With Macdonald's departure *Partisan Review* had lost its major political contributor of recent years; and Rahv and Phillips had accepted with their new funding some hazy limits on political debate. Yet neither of these things provided the primary reason why *Partisan Review* became a less politically active journal in the mid-1940s. More fundamental was the fact that Rahv and Phillips— as well as many of their allies and friends—had no strong interest in the positive expression of political views. The two continuing editors had moved away from Marxism, having come to doubt many of its major precepts. Rahv and Phillips insisted that they would retain an interest in "socialist ideas"; but what this seemed to mean in practice was a passion for recording the ongoing corruptions represented by Stalinism and an interest in tracing the trajectory of radical intellectuals as they fell away from systematic belief. For the articulation of the latent loyalties forced to the surface by war, most in the *Partisan Review* circle had neither vocabulary nor desire. As a result, the magazine's political voice remained clear only in the castigation of traditional enemies.

The break-up of the editorial combination that had run *Partisan Review* since 1937 reflected the intense disagreements of the wartime period. So, too, did a controversy that accompanied a series of articles under the general heading "The New Failure of Nerve." The several statements, followed by a number of replies and counter-responses, filled *Partisan Review* from the beginning to the end of 1943 and provoked discussion in other periodicals as well. Perhaps more clearly than in any other instance, the controversy of 1943 gave simultaneous evidence that the *Partisan Review* intellectuals shared a body of general values, and that common values did not of necessity lead to common opinions.

The solicited essays included contributions by Sidney Hook, John Dewey, Ernest Nagel, Norbert Guterman, Richard V. Chase, and Ruth Benedict attacking philosophical, religious, and political forms of mystical or anti-scientific thought. The common theme was that the ideas of such thinkers as Reinhold Niebuhr, Jacques Maritain, and Aldous Huxley represented a contemporary flight from rationality and from the critical traditions built up over two hundred years. Within the *Partisan Review* circle, only one of these essays attracted any substantial response — the two-part article by Hook that served as the flagship of the series.[69] Listing a whole set of movements that betokened "intellectual panic," Hook declared that liberalism, not as ideology but "as an intellectual temper, as faith in intelligence," was "everywhere on the defensive." The present "attack upon scientific method" required a campaign to "prevent intellectual hysteria from infecting those who still cling to the principles of rational experiment and analysis."

Hook's own campaign railed against what he regarded as faulty versions of radicalism. Yet Hook had little interest in discussing Marxism on this occasion, and he brushed aside the Communist Party as "little more than the American section of the G.P.U." Hook's targets were radical critics of the war and especially, it seemed, those he knew well. The remaining followers of Trotsky Hook labeled "Platonic revolutionists," calling their opposition to the war "political insanity" and "impotent fanaticism." He defined as "Bohemian revolutionists" another group opposing the war on somewhat different grounds, including under this heading Macdonald and certain "half-sober blusterers at cocktail parties" (a phrase that Farrell bitterly took as a reference to himself). Hook claimed to occupy a superior radical position with his own notions about an "independent political bloc" based on labor.[70]

Responses to Hook's essay within the *Partisan Review* circle came primarily from two directions. The first and sharper response challenged his political polemic. Apparently fearing reprisals for his anti-war views, Meyer Schapiro assailed Hook under the name "David Merian"; when Hook replied vigorously, Schapiro came back at him again. Schapiro, who had remained sympathetic to Trotsky, resented the lumping together of contemporary theologies and radical ideas. The two antagonists flew at one another over their respective positions on the war and over the validity of certain Marxist principles until each felt that he had been subjected to personal abuse and "philistine invective." The editors of *Partisan Review*, already breaking up over their own differences, were dragged into disputes over the magazine's policy on publishing such repeated thrusts. Combined with the exchange over Macdonald's resignation, the Hook-Schapiro battle offered ample evidence that there was no political consensus in the *Partisan Review* camp in 1943.[71]

The second type of response to Hook's essay questioned not his politics but the narrowness of his reliance on philosophical naturalism and the workings of human reason. Isaac Rosenfeld, for one, did not let his relative youth and recent arrival in New York circles inhibit him from suggesting that Hook's ideas suffered from a "failure of verve." Naturalism, Rosenfeld argued, needed to be "liberated, broadened, and extended" to treat man's spiritual "yearnings" and the "irrational" as both real and legitimate. Rosenfeld's remarks asserted a need for openness in culture, a resistance to an exclusive faith in method, that was characteristic of the more literary members of the *Partisan Review* circle at their best. Schapiro, too, challenged Hook's narrowness on cultural grounds. The majority of the *Partisan Review* intellectuals found Hook's ideas a poor guide to aesthetics and insisted on a more flexible and encompassing attitude toward the possibilities of life and culture.[72]

The differences among the *Partisan Review* intellectuals provided abundant grounds for sometimes heated exchanges. Yet it must also be noted that in the very act of disagreeing, members of the magazine's circle often reaffirmed their acceptance of shared values and assumptions. No one close to the magazine challenged the fundamental importance of rational analysis and scientific method, for example. What critics challenged was Hook's applications and conclusions. Even as he mounted his attack, Rosenfeld agreed that scientific method offered the only reliable way of "validating claims to knowledge," "confirming propositions," and the like. Macdonald, in offering his own late contribution to the "New Failure of Nerve" series, welcomed the "defense of scientific method" put up by Hook and others. Among the *Partisan Review* intellectuals, the tradition of critical "scientific" thought remained a common object of allegiance.[73]

Negative judgments also found common assent. Among other things, the *Partisan* critics continued to assert in chorus that religion contradicted both science and democracy. Farrell had suggested in 1940 that there was "a class struggle of the mind between religion and science"; and Rahv had declared that, examined historically, "socialism and theology turn out to be mortal enemies." When Hook attacked contemporary theologies in 1943, his critics among the *Partisan Review* intellectuals found the basic argument so far from controversial as to be almost trite. Schapiro remarked that Hook was "perfectly right in exposing for the hundredth time since the eighteenth century the illogicalities of religious thought and the reactionary part of the Church in contemporary affairs." The use of "reactionary" was no mistake. Hook had earlier opened an essay with the sentence "Catholicism is the oldest and greatest totalitarian movement in history." In 1943 Hook repeated his charge that the Catholic church was totalitarian without arousing a whimper of protest within the magazine's circle. Shared assumptions supported a significant body of shared hostilities, even as controversy raged.[74]

For the *Partisan Review* intellectuals, critical thought and democracy were natural allies: each acted to preserve the vitality of the other. Between them the two concepts contained either directly or by implication—in the eyes of the *Partisan Review* group—many of the values that made up the cosmopolitan outlook of the magazine. Critical thought must be secular, scientific, and rational; democracy must allow diversity of opinion, allegiance, and background; both must work to preserve an openness to change in political, intellectual, and social life. Yet such values, however strongly held, were inherently general. Schapiro recognized this fact on one level in his response to Hook: "when it comes to practical economic and political questions, it is misleading to speak of scientific method and naturalism as the distinctive grounds of a solution. They are only general conditions which may hold for entirely opposed views in these fields."[75] The same point extends to the realm of culture and to the guiding effects of cosmopolitan values taken whole. Shared values and shared enemies had great importance for the *Partisan Review* intellectuals, but they did not provide the "distinctive grounds" for agreement on all manner of specific questions. This, if nothing else, the political divisions brought on by the war had demonstrated vividly.

| Chapter | Literature |
| Eight | without Program |

In literature as in politics, the events of 1939 reshaped the landscape from which the *Partisan Review* intellectuals had taken their bearings. Changed surroundings left many of them unsure of their course for a time; yet the new conditions also liberated the more venturesome and allowed them to mount ambitious expeditions into fresh territory. The members of the *Partisan Review* circle had tended to fix their cultural position positively by reference to the idea of radical synthesis and negatively by their opposition to the literary activities of the Popular Front. The decline of confidence in any existing radical movement, the coming of war, and the breakup of the People's Front in 1939 demanded a shift in orientation if not in values. The chief response to this demand—a greatly heightened emphasis on intellectuals as a special social grouping, on their traditions, and on individual creativity and integrity—had been foreshadowed earlier, and it now provided both new grounds for *Partisan Review*'s sense of cultural mission and sanction for an expanding range of intellectual and critical themes.

The task of evaluating anew the intellectual's position began with pessimism, given vent in 1939 by the urge to sum up the experience of the decade. Taking stock in "Twilight of the Thirties," Philip Rahv discerned an "ebb of creative energy and a rapid decline of standards in all spheres of the intellect and of the imagination." As the "tide of patriotism and democratic eloquence" rose, one could observe the first steps toward the "withering away of literature." James T. Farrell matched Rahv's gloom in his own assessment: "Conditions for writing seem worse daily. The dangers of suppression hang over the writer. . . . There are no literary movements now."[1]

This pessimism of 1939 stood in sharp and apparent contrast to the bright hopes of the early thirties. For the editors of *Partisan Review*, such a transformation required explanation and the apportioning of blame. And, as in 1937, they fought to preserve in the midst of obvious change a sense of continuity and a belief in the relative stability of their own values. The magazine's hopes had been no mistake, Rahv insisted in an editorial, for "the idea of social revolution in its specific application to culture" had indeed "promised to re-vitalize literary expression in this decade." *Partisan Review* had supported in the early thirties the "one idea" that might have lifted culture to a new level. Unfortunately, the radical literary movement "turned into its very opposite" because from the start it had been "held in pawn by the Stalinists." The Communist influence on culture had undermined the dreams of *Partisan Review* and the future of literature in the West.[2]

Such an argument carried the benefit of requiring no repudiation of past errors by those around *Partisan Review*. Rahv's stance clearly implied that the early magazine had followed the best possible course for literature by trying to encourage an alliance between art and radical ideas. Yet having established a general claim to continuity and merit, Rahv offered as a lesson of the thirties an observation that modified the basic assumptions of the early *Partisan Review*. Politics, Rahv argued, "at first drew the literary imagination closer to social reality, enabling it to assimilate a series of fresh phenomena"; at present, politics was, "conversely, despoiling this imagination and provoking its self-destructive impulses." (The work of "marginal groupings or exceptional individuals"— some of them close to *Partisan Review*, no doubt —was exempted from this judgment.) The lesson was *not*, Rahv was careful to say, that "writers were mistaken to interest themselves in social causes or that they should stay out of politics." His message was less simple and more open-ended: "The lesson, rather, is that politics *qua* politics, as the ivory tower *qua* the ivory tower, is neither good nor bad for literature."[3]

Rahv was careful to emphasize the need to judge each case individually. Still, the earlier belief that a progressive politics and a progressing literature must go hand in hand had clearly been overthrown. Rahv's "lesson," taken as a guide for critical practice, allowed products of the "ivory tower" to be taken fully as seriously as works informed by politics. What Rahv and others had wanted for literature was the inspiration, the ideas, and the excitement of radicalism, not intellectual prescription or political control. A genuine radical movement, Rahv suggested to Farrell, helped writing, "not by its ideology, but [by] the ferment of ideas, the opening of perspectives."[4]

197

It was, in part, the desire for ferment and excitement in intellectual life, the longing for a sense of breaking down barriers and expanding the range of experience, that linked new respect for what the "ivory tower" symbolized to *Partisan Review*'s early radicalism. Given the "reactionary *Zeitgeist*" created by the "double catastrophe" of fascism and Stalinism, Rahv and most others in the *Partisan Review* circle looked more narrowly to their own kind, and more seriously than before to the past, to find support for the values they cherished. The "ivory tower" provided a convenient symbol for modern literature as a whole, and that led further, according to Rahv: "To speak of modern literature is to speak of that peculiar social grouping, the intelligentsia, to whom it belongs." The traditions of modern literature and the role of the intelligentsia became newly important centers of interest in the modification of the cultural rationale behind *Partisan Review*.

Still strongly attached to radical ideas, Rahv even managed to give the increasing interest in intellectuals and in tradition a pseudo-Marxian gloss. The intellectuals in modern society had been "restricted to the realm of technical and spiritual culture," which became, Rahv said more than once, "their only real property." According to this notion, presumably, the true interests of intellectuals lay with their "property"—that is, with the traditions of culture. Those who recognized their true interests could thus avoid close attachment to a class or movement and cultivate an independent perspective.[5]

This claim that critical detachment remained possible was central to an emerging rationale for *Partisan Review*'s cultural policies; and to some extent it helped justify a largely unstated belief that those policies were the best available substitute for political radicalism. The "self-determination" of the intelligentsia might be ultimately an illusion, Rahv argued, but it had "encouraged the creation of moral and esthetic values running counter to and often violently critical of the bourgeois spirit." The modern artist had, in fact, fled to an "obsessive introversion," an "esthetic mysticism," and a "bent toward the obscure and the morbid." But this "'anti-social' character" of much modern art, Rahv now insisted, had been the price of intellectual integrity. The ability to stand apart had become as important to Rahv as the willingness to come to grips with society.

Rahv made it plain that modern writing had generated in abundance the ferment and sense of possibility that the *Partisan Review* intellectuals had hoped to find in a budding radical culture.

At a time when fascism, Stalinism, and rising nationalism had smothered the progress of literature, those few who were "still awake," Rahv announced, had begun "to look back at the nineteen-twenties as a golden age, since that period . . . was exceedingly alive with experiment and innovation." For more than a century, in fact, modernism had blossomed with a fecundity that could be demonstrated simply by letting its stream of labels roll casually off the tongue—"romanticism, naturalism, symbolism, expressionism, surrealism, etc." The tradition of detachment and dissent had also been a tradition of diversity and vitality.

What Rahv clearly wished to do was to find in the traditions of the intelligentsia and of modern literature some sustaining power to carry *Partisan Review* through a period of radical collapse and world conflagration. Optimism was not a possibility. Rahv could bring himself no longer to proclaim a new radical generation or an imminent breakthrough—announcements that in effect assumed an immediate ability to continue the tradition and to build beyond modernism with radical ideas. Yet all was not lost for those who took the right inspiration from the past. Despite many pressures, Rahv declared with feeling, "a literary minority can still maintain its identity," and "what it can do is to warn." Intellectuals could remain true to their traditions and uphold their integrity by seizing "the possibilities of individual and group secession from, and protest against, the dominant values of our time." By doing so, they might not just save themselves (though that obviously was a matter of great concern), but also keep open the possibilities of future revival.[6]

Rahv's arguments in 1939 have the air of a conscious attempt to assess the cultural position of *Partisan Review* and to lay down a rationale suited to a dramatically altered contemporary situation. Rahv leaned heavily on the idea of group identity and group values as a source of strength. In 1937, as they moved toward open anti-Stalinism, the editors of *Partisan Review* had consciously worked to build up a group of intellectuals who would provide both contributions for the magazine and social and psychological support for one another. In the period from 1939 to 1941, a similar cultivation of a sense of group identity and purpose seemed to be taking place. The idea of being a "literary minority" defending through storm and stress the modern intellectual heritage provided both a source of collective identity and a fountain of justification for those around *Partisan Review*. Perhaps a set of remarks taken from an essay by Lionel Trilling can stand as sufficient testimony to this:

"here we are, a very small group and quite obscure; our possibility of action is suspended by events; perhaps we have never been more than vocal and perhaps soon we can hope to be no more than thoughtful; our relations with the future are dark and dubious. There is, indeed, only one connection with the future of which we can be to any extent sure: our pledge to the critical intellect."[7]

The tendency among the *Partisan Review* intellectuals to define themselves as a group of superior critical perspective sounded to some ears self-congratulatory and even self-righteous. There was justice in such reactions. The questions provided in 1939 for the first major *Partisan Review* symposium, "The Situation in American Writing," fairly begged in a number of cases for agreement with editorial assumptions and applause for the magazine's work. James Agee for one reacted to the questions with remarks he later called "intemperate." Intemperate or not, Agee had not imagined the tone in *Partisan Review* that irritated him.[8]

The note of self-celebration in the magazine belonged intrinsically to that process of reinforcing group identity, of defending cultural values, and of assuring each other of the capacity to survive and develop, that occupied many of the *Partisan Review* literary intellectuals as war settled on the world. The members of the magazine's circle felt that they possessed greater intellectual integrity than most of those around them, and it showed; yet their deep sense of anxiety was as responsible for their tone as any solid confidence. The prevailing mood may have been most accurately conveyed in Rahv's private comment that "we're half dead. Most of the people today are all dead."[9] The attitudes expressed in the magazine were neither empty bluster nor simple arrogance. Rather, they combined genuine loyalty to values under seige with the cultivation of an image — the image of a detached and alienated intelligentsia holding the line against corruptions of mind and spirit. As Rahv's whole analysis had tended to suggest, in periods of distress and anxiety a certain amount of posing could supply intellectuals with a "necessary myth."[10]

Rahv's 1939 assessment of the cultural situation found the chief threat to literature in a rising tide of nationalistic feeling and pro-war sentiment. At one level, this new source of corruption represented a familiar menace to art; the *Partisan Review* critics accused pro-war liberals of applying political tests to literature much as both fascists and Stalinists had done. At a deeper level, the fundamental objections that the *Partisan Review* intellectuals raised against many liberal writers had their roots in elemental cultural differences that once again brought their basic values into play.

With the outbreak of war in Europe, liberal intellectuals sympathetic to a crusade against fascism began to decry the disillusion and doubt that had followed World War I and to resuscitate the language of democratic idealism. Pro-war critics and literary nationalists tended to look back to an American past of farms and villages and to reject the skeptical and "negating" ethos of modernism. The *Partisan Review* circle found in such views an attack on the highest traditions of culture and thought, and they replied with various barbs at those who had "proven in the liberal weeklies that culture is subversive." Archibald MacLeish, Lewis Mumford, Dorothy Thompson, Waldo Frank, and "all the university presidents" served as targets.[11]

The sallies from *Partisan Review* grew into a campaign after MacLeish, recently installed as the Librarian of Congress, published a number of new essays, most particularly *The Irresponsibles*. MacLeish attacked intellectuals for failing to rise earlier to the battle against fascism; for writing with neutrality about the "discreditable"; for refusing to carry their words "to the barricades of intellectual warfare"; for having been seduced by the appeal of "objectivity and detachment." Speaking longingly of the intellectual climate "a century ago, two centuries ago," MacLeish proclaimed an "obligation to defend the inherited culture." Combined with the nationalistic bent of other essays appearing at roughly the same time, the message of *The Irresponsibles* seemed to herald a narrowing of intellectual life under patriotic pressure, much as *Partisan Review* had been predicting. The fact that MacLeish now wrote as a government official, who reputedly had the President's ear, did nothing to ease the magazine's fears.[12]

In its first two numbers of 1941, *Partisan Review* published an extended dissection of the life and work of "The Poet on Capitol Hill" by Morton Dauwen Zabel, a Chicago critic with whom Rahv was becoming friendly. Zabel referred to MacLeish as a "patriotic orator" and "an officer of the state" whose indictment of modern intellectuals could be compared to "the maledictions of Hitler and Goebbels." There had indeed been much "raw egotism" following World War I, Zabel agreed; but the twenties had also produced "a profound critical alertness to public values . . . , and an extreme suspicion of their professional advocates." If anything could save the present, the rescue would come "exactly through the operation of such a critical faculty in men, classes, and nations." The danger,

Zabel declared, came from those who promised salvation "through appeals to race, blood, and religious hatred, through contempt for intellect and thought." It was MacLeish, not modern values, that Zabel found threatening.[13]

MacLeish's condemnation of "irresponsible" intellectuals made his name one of a pair that soon came to symbolize for the *Partisan Review* intellectuals an uncritical nationalism applied to culture and a rejection of the best traditions of modern thought. With an open and explicit attack on literary modernism in September 1941, Van Wyck Brooks emerged as the other incubus of the "Brooks-MacLeish Thesis." Brooks had already attracted a good deal of attention from *Partisan Review*, in part because he touched the magazine's sympathies in a way that demanded an explanation of his behavior. Brooks himself had been associated with the emergence of the "typically modern" in America; it was in the teens, Rahv suggested, that "a separate intellectual class emerged conscious of itself as standing apart from society and as possessing special and superior interests and ideals."[14] For Brooks now to seek refuge in a provincial past made him a special challenge to the increasing emphasis in the *Partisan Review* circle on the modern tradition in literature and on the role of an intelligentsia.

The most substantial discussion of Brooks to appear in *Partisan Review* before his frontal assault on modernism, F. W. Dupee's "The Americanism of Van Wyck Brooks," measured Brooks by the cosmopolitan standard that *Partisan Review* associated with the best traditions of modern intellectual life. In his early prime, Brooks had been the "spokesman of a city culture which was then just emerging in its strength" among intellectuals. More than any other person at the time, "unless it was Randolph Bourne," Brooks valued the development of intellectuals as a self-conscious grouping in America. The Brooks of the teens had been a "cosmopolitan critic of American letters." Yet Brooks had always been of divided mind, it seemed, and Brooks as "myth maker" won out over Brooks as "sceptic." He proved a "type of native mind," "a spiritual New Englander," who could not escape the restrictions of an older tradition, though he had once recognized it as "at best a sectional phenomenon" that had "come to block the growth of a larger intellectual consciousness in America." Brooks had embraced "anti-modernism" on his way to glorifying the "pre-metropolitan half-agrarian universe of Concord and Boston." Brooks now reveled in "bellicose" allusions to national identity and practiced the "snobbish mystification" of some "secret Yankee language."[15]

As Dupee's analysis suggested, by 1941 those around *Partisan Review* had regarded Brooks as an opponent of cosmopolitan values and of modernism for some time. Yet it was one thing for Brooks to reject modernity in praising an earlier tradition, quite another for him to mount a bitter attack on modern literature. In "Primary Literature and Coterie Literature," Brooks contrasted writers who had believed in progress and developed the "great themes" (virtually all of whom were safely dead) with writers of a "secondary" sort whose technique was brilliant but who lacked positive substance (a group including virtually all major writers of the twentieth century). Brook's opening paragraph might well have stirred alarm in many an intellectual circle: "primary" literature followed the "biological grain," he suggested, and was conducive to "race-survival." Proper literary content, which derived from "responsible living," Brooks deemed impossible for those who "spent their lives in countries not their own."[16]

Responses to Brooks's essay came from many quarters, and perhaps none were stronger or sharper than those in *Partisan Review*. William Phillips replied in an essay that on its surface seemed only tangentially related to the Brooks affair, though a few brief passages toward the end of his argument made it apparent that the whole discussion provided grounds for rejecting all that Brooks had said. "The Intellectuals' Tradition," as the title suggested, gave great weight to the "distinct group culture" of the "intelligentsia" as a source of art. Phillips placed particular emphasis on the idea that only a "unified and self-perpetuating group" could provide the individual artist with a "sustaining tradition"; it was almost an "esthetic law" that "continuity is the condition for creative invention." The idea of an intellectuals' culture was leading toward one of the most familiar themes of the early Van Wyck Brooks — the lack of continuity and sustaining tradition in American literature.

Phillips followed Brooks closely as he lamented the American pattern of "momentary efforts by solitary writers or by intellectual groups . . . with the inevitable petering out, and the necessity for a fresh start all over again." Adding a touch characteristic in the *Partisan Review* circle, Phillips attributed some of the problem to the weakness in American culture of "the city, as the symbol of modern civilization," with the consequent dominance of the "atomizing influence of ruralism." Yet in the twentieth century an intelligentsia had appeared; and in the 1920s it gave rise to the "provocations of modernism," a movement that offered better hope for a sustaining continuity than either "regional nostalgia" or orthodox Marxism. Unfortunately, the country now faced attempts "to frame a new cultural myth" that were "patently a negation of everything the 20's stood for." Who but Van Wyck Brooks had called for a purge of "the truly characteristic works of the modern tradition"? The rising "epidemic of literary nationalism" with its "militant provincialism" represented a new abandonment of "the values of group-detachment" on the part of American writers. It was a new break with the intellectuals' tradition that could not but "thwart the production of a mature and sustained literature." By the time Phillips's argument reached this phrase, he had accomplished at least two things: Phillips had neatly accused Brooks of undermining the most cherished goal of his early literary vision, and Phillips had himself reaffirmed that goal.[17]

Phillips mounted his critique of Brooks on intellectual and literary grounds, with hardly a whiff of politics. He kept his attention centered on the American situation—not that of the world at large—and treated Brooks as simply an "advanced case" of the current fever. Even the threatened break in the developing modern tradition seemed, in Phillips's analysis, to portend little more than another cycle in a frustrating American pattern. Dwight Macdonald could accept no such restricted view of the danger.

In "Kulturbolschewismus Is Here," Macdonald argued a connection between Brooks's attack on modern literature and the repressions of Nazism. This theme took its strength from two sets of ideas that did not always mesh smoothly in Macdonald's analysis. The first supported a critique of Brooks on cultural and intellectual grounds and found a similarity to Nazi attitudes in his hostility toward rational, cosmopolitan values. Brooks had rejected the modern writer as "a doubter, a scorner, a sceptic, expatriate, highbrow and city slicker"—a list of terms that Macdonald fully intended should sound not negative but positive by cosmopolitan standards. Brooks spoke for "totalitarian cultural values," according to Macdonald, and the "note of xenophobia" running through his remarks and his "chauvinistic leanings" threatened a dramatic narrowing of American culture. Against this limiting nationalistic appeal the editors of *Partisan Review* stood united, and for this part of his message Macdonald found only support.

The other set of ideas that Macdonald used to tie Brooks to fascism suggested a closer and more ominous link bursting with political implications. Macdonald distinguished early in his essay between an anticipated "swing back to bourgeois values" and the more dangerous tendency "to rally to the concepts of Hitler's (and

Stalin's) 'new order.'" Goebbels himself could "applaud" not only the target of Brooks's attack but also "the very terms of the argument," Macdonald insisted. Brooks's position embodied "the specific cultural values of Stalinism and the specific methods of the Moscow Trials." Macdonald was suggesting quite clearly that Brooks and MacLeish should be read as harbingers of an American turn toward official repression akin to that of totalitarian societies. Such a development was predictable according to Macdonald's anti-war analysis.[18]

In the political side of his assessment of Brooks, Macdonald was out of step with his fellow editors and with most who offered an evaluation of his essay for an attempted symposium. Fewer than half of the writers asked to comment chose to do so; and of the eight who did respond, several showed little sympathy with Macdonald's assertion that it was a matter of "cultural life or death" to resist the "drift toward totalitarianism" represented by Brooks. Perhaps Lionel Trilling caught the spirit of many respondents most concisely. Trilling accepted the cultural side of Macdonald's critique, remarking that Brooks wanted "religion and not literature at all" and pronouncing Macdonald's essay "very just so far as its literary judgment goes." The political judgments were another story, as Trilling made abundantly clear: "I do not share his feelings about the political importance of Brooks's recent attitudes. . . . And I do not share Macdonald's assumption that socialism promises a moral and literary regeneration."[19] Like Phillips, Trilling treated Brooks's attack on modern literature as a sign of cultural retreat without reading into it any sweeping political import.

Macdonald, in attempting to preserve and give substance to a radical political perspective, fell easily into arguments that seemed to prove its power; literature became, when he was not careful, a direct reflection of politics. Yet Macdonald did not really want to go this far. At the end of his essay on Brooks, his main emphasis fell on an assessment of the cultural situation with which his editorial colleagues could largely agree. Looking back over the history of *Partisan Review*, Macdonald declared himself impressed with "how continuously we have been fighting a rear-guard action against this growing official esthetic," first as manifested in the "Stalinist writers' front" and more recently as exhibited by the nationalist war camp. Macdonald insisted that the great modern writers were "an end and not a beginning," that they belonged to the past. Yet even as he clung to his belief that socialist revolution might produce a "new esthetic tendency," he admitted that the forces capable of bringing this about were "frozen and impotent." To say this was to admit that modernism remained "the most advanced cultural tendency that exists." From there it was a short step for Macdonald to a striking claim about modern literature: "in a reactionary period it has come to represent again relatively the same threat to official society as it did in the early decades of the century."[20]

Macdonald's final argument provided better support for the position of his rival editors than it did for his own more political stance. An editorial comment in the letters column of the same issue quoted Macdonald and went on to declare, "It is coming to be something of a revolutionary act simply to print serious creative writing."[21] The general cultural retreat, from this point of view, had placed the rear-guard in the van once again. The great virtue of this perspective for many of those around *Partisan Review* was that it allowed writers and critics to maintain a sense of integrity and even of continuing radicalism while they moved away from Marxist politics. It enabled them to align themselves with the idea of an "advanced" culture even as they gave increasing attention to the literature of the past. It permitted the belief that the values of critical thought and cosmopolitanism retained their forward-moving, "progressive" edge even as those same values came to require, for more and more of them, giving support to the general political arrangements of established democratic societies. The notion that printing "serious creative writing" made a direct contribution to the literary intelligentsia's long tradition of detachment and dissent suggested that *Partisan Review*'s revised rationale — the rationale that would serve the magazine through the years of war — was reaching mature form. And Macdonald, for all his desire to put politics before literature in these years, accepted a large part of that rationale and most of the values behind it.

The work of defending modern culture in *Partisan Review* opened new doors for the editors even at the peak of their war-climate jitters. Though the magazine continued to pay close attention to the present, the presumption of a literary slump and the belief that previous writing had been endowed with a new vitality by its enemies encouraged a harvesting of the past to find grist for criticism and models of a vibrant literary life. At the same time, the wider separation of culture from politics implied by Rahv's "lesson," combined with the conviction that "advanced" literature lay under siege, allowed and promoted the building of a broader base among contemporary writers and critics who shared a respect for cultural modernism. *Partisan Review* in the thirties had spoken mainly to the New York literary left. In the forties it would move toward a stronger national, and even international, appeal.

Partisan Review sharply increased its efforts to reach both backward and outward during the years from 1939 to 1941. The editors seemed eager to create a sense of direct involvement in an ongoing cultural enterprise, to prove continuity with the twenties, and to evoke a feeling of intellectual spiritedness. The magazine developed a rather sudden attraction to memoirs that, at one level or another, could do each of these things. Louis MacNeice described the birthplace of the Auden generation in "Oxford in the Twenties"; Eugene Jolas contributed a piece on "My Friend James Joyce"; and Marianne Moore recalled earlier ferment in "The Dial: A Retrospect."[22] The editors also sought to bring American intellectuals closer to their European contemporaries as the war descended. In 1939 *Partisan Review* carried André Gide's "Pages from a Journal" and in 1940 Stephen Spender's "September Journal"—both of which were heavy with the weight of world events. Letters from writers abroad, originating primarily in Paris and London, delivered direct reports on developments in literature and politics. At times the news was reduced to listing the names and locations of artists and writers under such titles as "What Has Become of Them?"[23]

Partisan Review's publication of this material declared the editors' values and loyalties as loudly as any direct statement. The memoirs, the journals, the reports, all assumed the existence of that "peculiar social grouping" called the intelligentsia. Together, they asserted as well that modern culture was emphatically international. Many of those around *Partisan Review* had lost any earlier sense that radical ideas and politics provided a living tie to an international intellectual force. By emphasizing the cosmopolitan nature of modern culture, they could identify themselves as part of a great network of writers and artists, tied together amid the extremities of the present, and stretching supportively into the past.

The editors affirmed in a variety of ways their conviction that American culture had shared in the modern experience. The list of participants in the magazine's 1939 symposium on American writing suggested a diverse national contribution to twentieth-century literature: John Dos Passos, Allen Tate, James T. Farrell, Kenneth Fearing, Katherine Anne Porter, Wallace Stevens, Gertrude Stein, William Carlos Williams, John Peale Bishop, Harold Rosenberg, Henry Miller, Sherwood Anderson, Louise Bogan, Lionel Trilling, Robert Penn Warren, Robert Fitzgerald, R. P. Blackmur, Horace Gregory. The editors were attempting to make *Partisan Review* a center for the continuing cultivation of modern writing—in the broadest sense—and of the values they associated with it. They wanted the best writers and critics of the day to be conscious of *Partisan Review* and to see it as an important cultural institution.

The editors worked diligently to bring into the magazine a greater variety of authors and materials. Along with the symposium, which itself served this end, *Partisan Review* published in the last two issues of 1939 a batch of poems largely by younger writers, who contributed to its expanding literary base. Randall Jarrell would soon become a regular contributor. Two other young poets who would have more to offer after the war, John Berryman and Theodore Roethke, signaled *Partisan Review*'s connection—primarily through Delmore Schwartz—with an emerging circle of poets who followed each other's work closely. *Partisan Review* would publish others from this grouping (especially Robert Lowell) over the next few years, as well as poets from outside this network (such as Karl Shapiro). Looking to secure itself as a literary center, the magazine had made early contact with several of the best American poets of the next two decades.[24]

The editors were also reaching out to still another literary grouping—the body of contemporary writers and critics who emphasized their origins in the South. The "Agrarians," who in the late 1930s had particular ties to the *Southern Review*, included Allen Tate, Robert Penn Warren, and Cleanth Brooks, all of whom contributed to *Partisan Review*. The *Partisan* circle tended to reject those views for which the southerners came to be best known among a wider public: a social emphasis on the virtues of a regional and agrarian culture (which the magazine had earlier called reactionary) and a literary emphasis, through a "new criticism," on the rigorous examination of texts with limited reference to their environment. Yet the *Partisan Review* critics found much that was positive among the southerners as their own concern shifted toward the defense of literary sophistication and cultural modernism.

The relations between Allen Tate and the *Partisan Review* circle can stand as an example of the mutual respect that developed at certain levels. In reviewing Tate's novel *The Fathers* in late 1938, Lionel Trilling commented on the "factiousness and even the dangers of Mr. Tate's intellectual position," yet he treated his work with the greatest seriousness and praised its precision. Tate disagreed with a part of Trilling's analysis but called the review "the ablest and most interesting I have seen." He went on to suggest that Tril-

ling had proven conclusively "that it is possible for a critic to examine a work whose author holds fundamentally opposite views,
and yet convince that author, by moderation and intelligence, that
the critic is disinterested." The next year, when reviewing Tate's
poetry for the *Southern Review*, Delmore Schwartz took the occasion to compare Tate's "whole view" with the "whole view of Marxism" and to find a "common denominator of human values" that
made "the disagreement . . . less than the agreement." Tate began
contributing to *Partisan Review* in 1939 and by 1941 was comfortably airing in its pages his complaints against the *Nation* and *New
Republic*.[25] Personal relationships developed alongside professional
ones. Rahv first approached Tate in the fall of 1938, seeking material
for *Partisan Review* with a "Dear Mr. Tate" letter that was rather
formal; by the end of the next year it was "Dear Allen," and the
letter had a casual, friendly tone. Rahv asked Tate in both 1939 and
1942 to serve as one of his references in applying for a Guggenheim
Fellowship.[26] *Partisan Review* also published a poetic blast by Tate
directed at the Brooks-MacLeish position, which Rahv called in a
letter to Tate "the first really meaningful poem on the war written
in America."[27]

Common enemies, respect, and even friendship did not, of course,
eliminate disagreement. Yet *Partisan Review* gained confidence and
strength from its ties to southern writers and critics. Along with
the Europeans, the veterans of the twenties, and the emerging poets
and novelists to whom the editors reached out at the end of the
thirties, the "Agrarians" helped provide the *Partisan* critics with a
sustaining network of intellectual and social ties as their bonds to
the left unraveled.

The criticism that came out of the *Partisan Review* circle from the
late thirties to the end of the war reflected a belief that literature
should be at once intellectually engaged with contemporary affairs
and partially detached from them. Writing was simultaneously a
matter of ideas, rooted in the climate of the times, and a matter
of craft, nourished by the traditions and standards of the art. For
those around the magazine, such notions allowed ample room for
both older and newer themes to find a voice in their essays. Greater
emphasis on the relative social independence of a modern intelligentsia and its literature did not replace established values so much
as it added to them, making the *Partisan* critics, if anything, more
sensitive to questions of balance and more skeptical of what they
regarded as limiting or extreme ideas.

Efforts to counterpoise seemingly conflicting notions of the character and obligations of literature were much in evidence at the close of the thirties. Delmore Schwartz made it a point in writing about Yeats to explain the poet's "equivocal attitude" as a desire to be both in the world and apart from it. Schwartz's suggestion that the writer might profit from hearing the opposing calls of the world and the tower found a parallel in F. W. Dupee's assessments of contemporary criticism. Reviewing in 1941 a book of statements by four major critics, Dupee paired his subjects to argue that, "from the point of view of 'ideal' criticism," each had gone too far in one direction; he implied that a fully satisfying criticism would need to achieve a better balance. Dupee expressed admiration for the achievements of those who concentrated on the "internal" qualities of literature, yet his concluding remark held that "perhaps it is only by reference to the historical situation in which literary works are produced that you *can* interpret them as wholes."[28]

In using the notion of an "ideal" criticism to mount a critique of every existing "program," Dupee relied on a familiar pattern from the past. Yet something was missing. An earlier confidence had drained away, leaving his critical tone noticeably flat. There was no affirmation of the vision of an ideal, no sense that it might be achievable; his essay was summed up in the "perhaps" of the final sentence. Like Dupee, a number of others associated with *Partisan Review* seemed uncertain about just what should give direction to their criticism at the beginning of the forties. It was not that they had turned away from the cultural values that fueled their sureness in negative judgment—these remained—but that they had lost their faith in the ready applicability of Marxism to literature and were struggling anew over the relation of art to politics.

Reviewing a new novel by Ignazio Silone in 1942, for example, Phillips spoke with confidence and even cockiness in rejecting Silone's attempt to salve the ethical wounds inflicted by Stalinized socialism through an immersion in peasant life and religion. Silone's position amounted to a "repudiation of city culture" in favor of "peasant stoicism"; and his "obsessive interest in rural life" explained his religious turn, since the village was a "breeding ground for every conceivable variety of mystification." When asserting his own secular and cosmopolitan values, Phillips played upon familiar themes with assurance. The difficulty came in talking about the problem behind Silone's work. Phillips found no reason for radical hope either in traditional Marxism or in Silone's ethical quest. Yet he could offer no alternative. If Silone's "spiritual vision" failed to be convincing, it was "not because we have at hand a more acceptable solution," Phillips conceded: "In this sense, Silone has actually put the mirror once more to those radical intellectuals who have largely given up Marxism as a system of thinking, yet still cling to its optimism of progress." Phillips slid on to other topics, leaving behind a naked admission that he was philosophically adrift. For his more general beliefs, Phillips now seemed unable to find satisfactory justification.[29]

An equivalent uncertainty about the fundamental basis for criticism revealed itself in a quite different way in the writing of Clement Greenberg. The question of the relation of the masses and of socialism to "advanced art," for instance, troubled his 1939 essay, "Avant-Garde and Kitsch." Greenberg placed great emphasis on the wide gap under industrialism between the high culture of intellectuals and the popular culture of the masses. An appreciation of superior art, he argued, depended upon an understanding of the traditions of the art form itself; art was "one of the most artificial of all human creations," requiring "leisure, energy and comfort" to train for its enjoyment. Greenberg left open the possibility of wider appreciation if the "problems of production" could be solved "in a socialist sense," but his emphasis on the intellectual difficulty of modern art effectively torpedoed dreams of mass support.

Much of Greenberg's argument seemed to imply an even sharper division between culture and politics than Rahv was suggesting at this time; yet wanting to preserve a cultural argument in favor of radicalism, Greenberg moved in his last few lines back past Rahv and toward a rather awkward stance. "Advances in culture," he claimed, were a "threat" to capitalism—even though he denied that "a superior culture is inherently a more critical culture." With little explanation, he went on: "Today we no longer look towards socialism for a new culture—as inevitably as one will appear, once we do have socialism. Today we look to socialism *simply* for the preservation of whatever living culture we have right now."[30] Greenberg was trying to defend both the need for radicalism and the vitality of existing art. Like Macdonald in his attack on Van Wyck Brooks, Greenberg suggested simultaneously that radicalism could inspire a new art and that existing traditions of modern art were already radical.

Greenberg's criticism in other essays made it obvious that he felt the pull of incompatible notions about the relation of art and politics. Writing about painting, which would become his major subject in the future, Greenberg defended the relative isolation of artists and their "escape from ideas" into the values of their discipline. Yet writing about poetry a few months later, he demanded a "return to politics" and mocked those who claimed to be "for culture" but had no political opinions.[31] In the early 1940s Greenberg was uncertain of his ground, and it showed.

To argue that the declining persuasiveness of radicalism, combined with the pressures applied by fascism and war, created some critical insecurity among the *Partisan Review* intellectuals only acknowledges what might well seem a predictable consequence of the period. American intellectuals of varying perspectives found it necessary to reconsider their political and cultural ideas in the late 1930s or during the decade that followed. The test that individuals faced was not whether they could avoid uncertainty amidst the "shocks" and "surprises" of the period, but whether they could remain thoughtful, discriminating, and productive at all. For at least two of those among the literary intellectuals associated with *Partisan Review*, the years from 1939 to 1945 were among the richest in their careers. Philip Rahv and Lionel Trilling shared the capacity to turn doubt and disappointment to advantage. Their essays from the war years represent two overlapping and yet quite different solutions to the problem of critical direction.

Rahv's "Twilight of the Thirties" provided not only a modified rationale for *Partisan Review* but also a logical basis for the criticism he was already beginning to write. From his disappointment over the dimming of radicalism and the decline of cultural promise, Rahv turned to the analysis of literary tradition with surprising energy, offering no strikingly original interpretations but applying a familiar set of ideas in stimulating and fruitful ways. Beginning in 1939, Rahv published essays in the major literary journals of the day—the *Southern Review* and *Kenyon Review* as well as *Partisan Review*. At one time or another before 1941, he planned books on American literature, on Kafka, and on "Literature in a Political Age."[32]

Rahv's surge of interest in American literature at the end of the thirties grew out of a general move within the *Partisan Review* circle toward exploring the national tradition.[33] Rahv launched his own assessment with an essay fundamentally dependent on the early Van Wyck Brooks. Finding that the terms "highbrow" and "lowbrow" had become "much too general and popular" by 1939 (as Rahv later put it in acknowledging Brooks's work), Rahv chose a "more indigenous nomenclature" in titling his essay "Paleface and

Redskin."[34] The paleface ("a 'high-brow'") had as his weaknesses a hankering after "religious norms," a "refined estrangement from reality," and a capacity at his lowest level to be "genteel, snobbish, and pedantic." The redskin (or "low-brow") accepted his environment even "to the degree of fusion with it" and, at his worst, was "a vulgar anti-intellectual, combining aggression with conformity." (Rahv undoubtedly had some contemporaries under consideration as he described the types.) Making his emphasis accord with his earlier work, Rahv defined the "dichotomy" in the American mind as one between "experience and consciousness."[35]

As his basis for comparison, Rahv relied (as had Brooks) on Europe. The break between paleface and redskin, between the "fatal antipodes" of Henry James and Walt Whitman, stood "without parallel in any European country." The problem for American writers had consistently been to escape the "blight of one-sidedness." The goal remained a literature of "mature control" and balance. Nowhere did Rahv call upon radical ideas to provide the inspiration for a new literature, yet the goal he espoused for American culture differed little from that which had stood behind much of his writing throughout the thirties. Rahv was establishing his critical footing by bringing to the fore an analysis that, on literary issues, had always provided the foundation beneath his radicalism.

Rahv posited a chronological divide in American literature: the palefaces dominated in the nineteenth century, "but in the twentieth they were overthrown by the redskins." Redskins had habitually gloried in their "Americanism," according to Rahv; and their "worst tendencies" had been aggravated by the "popular political creeds of our time" (a catch-all reference to the Popular Front–nationalist–war liberal continuum against which *Partisan Review* primarily defined itself). Even as circumstances were rapidly changing, Rahv's essay thus carried forward the argument summed up earlier in the call for "Europeanization"–the claim that contemporary American writing exhibited an extreme emphasis on raw experience at the expense of intellectual consciousness.[36]

The identification of a broad shift in American literature from the nineteenth to the twentieth century and the general dichotomy he had described gave Rahv his themes. In another essay, "The Cult of Experience in American Writing," Rahv built upon his outline while elaborating a sophisticated case emphasizing what American writers had in common. He also applied his general scheme in judgments of the teens, the twenties, and the thirties that sounded forceful and fresh at many points.[37] Yet for all the new twists, he remained constant in seeking a balance that would lift American writing toward greater sophistication and maturity and in suggesting the limitations of even the modernist past. The persistence of Rahv's values and cultural goals brought him once again at the end of his essay—almost shyly—to what amounted to a message of hope. Throughout its history, American literary life had been "largely determined by national forces"; now "international forces" had "begun to exert a dominant influence." In this "historic change" lay a promise Rahv would not relinquish for "the future course of American writing."[38] The literary radical vision, though chastened, remained a source of guidance and hope.

Rahv built into his interpretation of American literature a theme that touched the lives of many of those around *Partisan Review*— "the historical theme of the American character in its approach to art and experience." This theme encompassed for Rahv that "painful doubleness" in Hawthorne that reflected the tension between provincial New England values and "the world." The same theme found perhaps its highest artistic expression in Henry James, whose ability to present conflict deeply impressed Rahv.[39] Rahv mocked attempts to reject James as too European and agreed with Edmund Wilson that America had the better of it in James's work; yet the question of James's "ultimate loyalty" to one or the other was not the central issue to Rahv. The "valuations of Europe and America" offered by James were "not the polar opposites but the two commanding centres of his work"—the two sides that James balanced to make "mutual assimilation feasible." Rahv saw in James's treatment of the fundamental American theme a cosmopolitan answer by which the "heritage" of both old world and new could be brought to the creation of a richer cultural vision.[40]

Such answers contained immediate relevance. Many in the *Partisan Review* circle faced considerations of identity and loyalty anew in the 1940s, prompted by the question of support for the war, by the fate of European Jews, and by the pressures of the postwar situation. The most common pattern for explaining the relationship between writer and citizen, between Jew and American, between American identity and the international culture of the West, was the cosmopolitan one: there could be two centers, and a determination of "ultimate loyalty" was beside the point; not total acceptance of one side or the other but "mutual assimilation" was the essential goal. Rahv might speak pessimistically of the contemporary literary situation in the early 1940s, but beneath the snows he clung to an expectation that cosmopolitan values would win out in American culture. (It was this belief that allowed him without a hint of self-consciousness to speak of "our literature.")[41] Threatened by disorientation, Rahv found the strength to remain creative and productive by cultivating more intensely a critical tradition and a version of cosmopolitanism that were emphatically American.

In his occasional pieces on modernist writers as well, Rahv worked hard to preserve under trying circumstances many of the essential features of his literary vision. Because modernism now seemed central to an intellectuals' culture facing crisis, Rahv was determined to see in modernism at its best a coherent and even a responsible tradition that ultimately stood—when properly interpreted—on the side of secular, rational, and cosmopolitan values. In one essay on Kafka, Rahv rejected emphatically the suggestion that religion could be the bedrock of Kafka's art or his meaning, and then he flirted with an emphasis on Kafka's "uniqueness."[42] Not content with this, he soon produced a second and more substantial essay on Kafka in which he attempted "to see him ideologically."[43]

In "The Death of Ivan Ilyich and Joseph K.," Rahv compared novels by Kafka and Tolstoy, asserting by the very act of comparison Kafka's continuity with literary tradition. Kafka and Tolstoy shared above all a "common ideological tendency"—a tendency "against civilization, against the heresies of the man of the city whose penalty is spiritual death." Implicit in such a perspective was a critique of bourgeois life; yet Rahv recognized that a critique on such grounds pointed away from the values of cosmopolitanism and critical thought. In rejecting civilization, the present, and the city in favor of religion, the past, and the country, "Tolstoy and Kafka rejected rationalism and all its works." The problem was again to justify a high valuation of the insights of modern literature without accepting the "reactionary" conclusions modern writers tended to reach.

Rahv's solution was to argue that these writers had not fully understood the nature of their target: "Tolstoy and Kafka were really protesting against the irrational masquerading as the rational," for "to believe in the genuine rationality of the bourgeois pattern is a profound illusion." The bourgeois era had increased "man's control over nature," Rahv readily admitted, but behind the "facade of official rationality, anarchy still reigns in fact." The neat suggestion nestled in Rahv's claim was that modern literature actually stood on the side of the "right" values if correctly understood. The exponents of a "radical secularism," with whom Rahv identified himself, took a "positive attitude" toward the workings of rationalism: "They hold that in order to resolve the conflicts of modern times, it is not necessary to get rid of modern acquisitions—the machine, science, the city. To them the reverse is true, for they value these acquisitions as the tangible prerequisites of human freedom." As in his discussions of American writing, Rahv seemed able in thinking about modernism to reconcile a standing allegiance to secular, rational, urban values with his changing critical interests —preserving all the while a confidence that the modern world (and the American environment) offered at least the "prerequisites" for "human freedom" and for the further advance of literature.⁴⁴

In comparing Kafka to Tolstoy, Rahv had consciously set out to rescue Kafka from the judgment that his "innovations" had left him detached from literary tradition. For Rahv, a study of "the relation between tradition and individual talent" showed that a "surplus of originality is more often a sign of weakness than of strength." Working from the same assumptions, Rahv could only judge Henry Miller a fringe figure. Because he followed through the possibility of "nihilism" and "total Negation" so completely, Miller rated as an important "literary character"; yet Rahv (following Orwell) judged his importance as "more symptomatic than substantial." Miller had thrown aside all traditions of writing to create not the "work of art as a whole" but fragments; he could no longer make "the continual sacrifice of personality that the act of creation requires." This is an important phrase for understanding Rahv's values. Art, or culture more broadly, could not welcome a totally unfettered expression of personality; it demanded, instead, a curb on extreme individuality, a sense of balance. To the extent that modernism in some of its forms encouraged simple license, Rahv grew uneasy.⁴⁵

In evaluating younger writers working in the shadow of modernism, Rahv returned again and again to his theme that literature must preserve an ability to make distinctions—a sense of values and a framework of control. Rahv complained, for example, that the New Directions series suffered from a "much too ungraded enthusiasm for the 'new.'" In another essay, he mounted a criticism of Kafka's recent imitators as "one-sided and even inept." Rahv's lecture was firm: "To know how to take apart the recognizable world is not enough, is in fact merely a way of letting oneself go and of striving for originality at all costs." The "genuine innovator," like Kafka, was no mere destroyer: "at the very same time that he takes the world apart he puts it together again. For to proceed otherwise is to dissipate rather than alter our sense of reality, to weaken and

216

compromise rather than change in any significant fashion our feeling of relatedness to the world." Reality must function as the *"discipline of fiction."*[46] There was no attempt now to make Marxism the key to such discipline. Notions of the "sacrifice of personality" and of a coherent tradition were being asked to provide the check on literary extremism once expected from radicalism. In a period of diminished expectations, the critic could be, if nothing else, a conservator of the vision of what was possible in art.

By the early 1940s, Rahv was making a conscious attempt to concentrate his attention on criticism and the defense of cultural values.[47] Although his political hopes had been frustrated both philosophically and practically, he refused to lose his literary voice. The critic, Rahv now declared, could not "afford metaphysical commitments." The possibility of "succumbing to metaphysical leanings —either of the spiritualist or materialist variety"—threatened to freeze the critic's insights and to rob him of his *"ideal aloofness* from abstract systems."[48] Rahv could not fill the gap left by the disillusionment with radical politics, but he could deny its significance to his life as a critic and press on. If this meant in the long run that Rahv undertook no fundamental reconsideration of his beliefs that might have sustained intellectual growth in the years beyond the war, it gave him in the short run a stability of standards and values, and a capacity to blend new concerns with old, that provided the undergirding for a period of vigorous and substantial work.

Lionel Trilling stands, by general though not unanimous consent, as one of the two or three major American critics of the mid-twentieth century.[49] It is simply a token of his stature that Trilling's work has spawned a host of commentaries by literary scholars offering a variety of perspectives on his outlook and his achievements.[50] Considerations of Trilling as an individual tend to emphasize those qualities which separated him from any group; yet he associated himself with *Partisan Review* and its concerns quite closely in the late 1930s and early 1940s. Perhaps the most telling evidence for this conscious tie is the record of regular and substantial contributions to the magazine—some thirteen pieces in a span of seven years.[51] Both anti-Stalinism and the cultural values he shared with others in the *Partisan Review* circle deserve recognition as major influences on Trilling's developing criticism.[52]

Even so, occasional comments in Trilling's writing and the general tenor of his prose gave evidence that he was following his own course. No issue was more central to the *Partisan Review* intellectuals as a group at the end of the thirties than the question of how to respond to the Stalinist degradation of radical politics and ideas. Macdonald tried to insist that radical theory could be rescued and that political discussion should become the dominant concern for *Partisan Review*. Rahv eased away from Marxism without wanting to admit how far he had gone and built his criticism around established ideas. Trilling, more readily than almost anyone else close to the magazine, moved to distance himself from radicalism and, indeed, to turn skepticism against the fundamental assumptions of the left. A sense of the limits of human vision, an emphasis on difficulty and at the same time on possibility, a caressing fondness for ambiguity, increasingly occupied Trilling's prose. (In the early 1940s, he began publishing the kinds of pieces that would later be collected in *The Liberal Imagination*.) Trilling reacted to the Stalinist corruption of radical politics by calling into question a whole tradition; and this questioning, growing distinctly out of the experience of the thirties, would become the foundation for his postwar reputation.

In one essay Trilling combined for analysis V. L. Parrington's *Main Currents in American Thought*, with its "militant Jeffersonian populism," and the work of the "Marxist" critic Bernard Smith, whom Trilling accused of compounding the errors and ignoring the weaknesses of Parrington's aesthetic judgments. The point was to suggest that common assumptions lay behind the politics of the Popular Front and the dominant strain of American liberalism. In the Smith-Parrington distortions of literature and the procrustean standards of their criticism, moreover, Trilling saw the influence of an outdated nineteenth-century science in which "things are what they are and nothing else," and reality appeared "solid and irrefutable." Such assumptions made Trilling very skeptical indeed about talk of the "scientific method in literature." Only a few things in literature could be measured or accepted with certainty: "a meaning is not indisputable, nor a quality either, and we find ourselves in a realm in which science cannot apply." Twentieth-century scientific thought was more to his liking: "Would it not . . . be borrowing one of the virtues of science to remember that the object changes as we change the instrument by which it is observed?" To acknowledge the limitations of human understanding without giving up the attempt to make sense of past and present would be to learn a proper lesson from science.[53]

In an essay on Eliot published a few months later, Trilling expanded his critique.[54] Eliot belonged, according to Trilling, to the "romantic line" of the nineteenth century, which had mounted a protest against the "philosophical assumptions of materialistic Liberalism"; Trilling wished to "recommend to the attention" Eliot's "religious politics." Trilling was careful to stress that he did not recommend Eliot's ideas to the "allegiance" of his readers. Indeed, quoting Matthew Arnold, he suggested that in the "practical sphere" such ideas were "maleficent." Nevertheless, Trilling chose to read a lesson from Eliot on the intellectual limitations of the radical-liberal tradition.

The emphasis in Eliot that touched on the contemporary need for a "whole new intellectual world" was his fundamental concern with morality. Trilling distanced himself from Eliot's belief that morality was absolute, but he applauded the centrality of the question "What should man become?" The targets of the lecture began to become clear when Trilling suggested that Eliot's way of considering morality had advantages over "Trotsky's way or the Marxist way in general." The "social imagination" of contemporary radicals, he argued, was distinctly inferior to the speculations of the "preparatory days of revolution" in the eighteenth century. Trilling attributed the decline in part to the "heightened tempo of events." He charged a greater responsibility to Marx who—"with his claim to a science of society, with his concept of materialistic and dialectical causation," and with his general scorn for "considerations of morality"—made concern with immediate issues, not with ultimate ends or human dignity, "seem unavoidable." Yet the fundamental error leading to a "diminished ideal" of man lay more deeply buried. It lay in the view that "man was very simple and individually of small worth in the cosmic or political scheme," a view that Trilling saw as "shared alike by Liberal manufacturing Whig and radical philosopher."

Trilling was doing at least two things that challenged common assumptions on the left, including those held within the *Partisan Review* circle: he was calling into question the sufficiency of the materialist, rationalist, and scientific tradition; and, as in his Parrington-Smith essay, he was treating middle-class liberals and Marxist radicals as if the views they shared were more important than their differences. Trilling was less interested in either a continuing radical critique of bourgeois society or an intellectual dissection of Marxism than in a basic reconsideration of liberal-left belief. This became clearest, perhaps, when he assailed the influence of the idea of progress—"a belief shared by the bourgeois and

219

the Marxist"—in drawing attention away from the consideration of "moral possibility." Trilling condemned as an "absolute" the Marxist certainty of what "higher" and "better" meant, and he declared "untenable" any notion that the history of art or of human relations revealed a "definable progress and improvement." If many others in moving away from Marxism had clung to an "optimism of progress," Trilling called into doubt even the sustaining hope that progress was possible and challenged all efforts to believe that the future might redeem the present. Such ideas might well have pushed him away from *Partisan Review* if singly and wholeheartedly embraced, but they were not.

Trilling framed his discussion of Eliot's "religious politics" and of moral possibility within a context of allegiance to the broad tradition he wished to criticize. He had spoken of Eliot's ideas "with respect," Trilling remarked, because they suggested "elements which a rational and naturalistic philosophy, to be adequate, must encompass." The argument was for a more inclusive and more balanced rational philosophy, not for the rejection of rationalism.[55] Such a pattern was everywhere apparent. In "The Sense of the Past" in 1942, Trilling expressed some sympathy for the current critical revolt against that historical study of literature which had "allied itself with the science of the 19th century." Yet Trilling came down firmly on the side of a more sensitive historical criticism and against the new critics who made "the elucidation of poetic ambiguity a kind of intellectual calisthenic ritual." The argument was again for balance—for balance within the rational, secular, broadly alert tradition of critical thought to which the *Partisan Review* intellectuals felt they belonged.[56]

Trilling combined the theme of balance in his essays with an appeal for cosmopolitan openness and diversity. Bernard Smith had claimed to stand for the "broadest possible democracy," but to Trilling his ideas implied not "the greatest number of kinds of people but rather the greatest number of people of one kind thinking the same thing." To find simple answers or to create simple patterns, Trilling suggested many times, destroyed the complexity of life and threatened a distorting (and at least potentially repressive) narrowness. Because Trilling became so closely associated with such a message after publication of *The Liberal Imagination*, it is easy to overlook the ties between his stance in the 1950s and the critical spirit of *Partisan Review* at the end of the thirties. Yet the editors of the magazine as early as February 1938 had called for greater "variety, curiosity, and amplitude of means" in American writing;

and the familiar emphasis on "consciousness" in the work of Rahv and Phillips had urged a heightened awareness of the difficult and the complex. Trilling added to a common stock of concern among the *Partisan* critics when he summed up the message in his essay on Eliot: "What is meant negatively is that man cannot be comprehended in a formula; what is meant positively is the sense of complication and possibility, of surprise, intensification, variety, unfoldment, worth." Trilling became a specialist in the demand for complexity; but the fundamental resistance to formula and closed system, the essential concern with openness and possibility, reflected values Trilling shared with other literary intellectuals in the *Partisan Review* circle.[57]

Despite the political differences of the war years, the *Partisan Review* intellectuals continued to find common ground in their cultural concerns and to share the same general antipathies. They stood together for a criticism that considered history and social meaning in interpreting works of art, without neglecting aesthetic values or applying political formulas. Although there was much room for variation within this stance, the *Partisan Review* circle created a center of opposition to the "new criticism" on one side and to the Brooks-MacLeish, social responsibility groups on the other. In this process, Trilling was a leading actor properly identified with the *Partisan Review* camp.[58]

The literary intellectuals associated with *Partisan Review* shared something else as well: a skepticism burned deeply into their minds by the fate of radicalism in the thirties; an inability to accept any systematic philosophy or to articulate directly a structure of positive beliefs. Trilling played one creed off against another in the forties, working to challenge political idealisms in particular and to deflate postures of certainty. The task of revealing the inadequacies of established assumptions gave Trilling the theme for his fiction as well as his criticism, beginning with two stories written during the war, both of which were published in *Partisan Review*. In "Of This Time, Of That Place," Trilling by his own later description placed the "judgment of morality" in conflict with the judgment "of science," allowing clear superiority to neither. In "The Other Margaret," he attacked liberalism's belief in social determinism and its moral apologias for the disadvantaged. Trilling's one novel, *The Middle of the Journey*, aimed to show up the self-deceptions of fellow-traveling liberals, the inadequacy of an escape from politics to religion, and even (with a more tender touch) the shallowness of cultural bohemianism. In all three pieces of fic-

221

tion, the author's representative in the narrative feels all the tensions between beliefs but remains apart from positive advocacy or commitment.[59]

Trilling made himself a connoisseur of tension and ambivalence, leaving the task of reconciling "dissimilar modes of judgment" to the individual imagination.[60] His own thought, "which at once overrode and abjured systems," became in the mind of one Trilling scholar "more decisively influential . . . than systems customarily are." Perhaps; though as the same scholar readily admits, Trilling provided no intellectual perspective from which others could "easily borrow either parts or techniques," and those disciples he had were "errant."[61] Trilling found his way to a considerable personal achievement, but he could not help the *Partisan Review* intellectuals find a new clarity of belief in the forties.

During 1944 and 1945, both Rahv and Phillips reviewed new books by Arthur Koestler and, in so doing, offered glimpses into the state of their own ideas. Both detected a lack of true seriousness and genuine intellectual achievement in Koestler, yet both found positive qualities as well. The positive contribution grew out of the fact that Koestler addressed, in Rahv's words, "the world-historical theme of the breakdown of the socialist-revolutionary cause," especially as that breakdown was "reflected in the disillusionment and frustration of its intellectual adherents." This was a theme in which Rahv and Phillips obviously had a good deal of personal interest. In their reactions to Koestler, the two editors put on display their own strategies for dealing with the frustration of radical hopes.[62]

Rahv remarked in commenting on *Arrival and Departure* that the "political-minded individual who is so unfortunate as to have been deprived of his faith" must go through the "supremely painful experience of locating himself anew" in the world; he must face the task of discovering "a way of life that will enable him to redefine his true identity." Although this was an exaggerated version of Rahv's own dilemma, its relevance to his political posture became clear when he addressed the problem faced by Koestler's hero in reconciling "radical convictions" with support for "values gone musty." The "answer"— in Rahv's response to the book as in his life — was that "even if in the dynamics of history the bourgeois democracies act not as the engine but the brake, there is real need for a brake when the engine begins running wild." This seemed a good enough reason "for a policy of strategic expediency in supporting the democratic war against fascism in order to obtain a second chance for socialism."

In reviewing *The Yogi and the Commissar* for *Partisan Review*, Rahv went out of his way to argue that the "democratic institutions of the West" were "just as much worth defending" as nationalized property in Russia. Not only economic arrangements but also "social, political and ethical conditions" must serve as the measure of society. Rahv insisted on the need to uphold the "original definition of socialism": "Socialism is above all libertarian. Socialism is incompatible with an hierarchical organization of society. Socialism is freedom, democracy, and equality." The conjunction between justifications for the defense of Western institutions and this paean to the ideal of socialism revealed much about the explanations Rahv offered to himself in 1945.[63]

Phillips's review of the same Koestler essays followed Rahv's quite closely in many of the specific points it made, but the framing of the discussion was different. Phillips offered a nod to Koestler's argument that "the very idea of socialism becomes meaningless if divorced from the idea or practice of democracy," and he welcomed Koestler's "humanism" as an "important counter-balance to the current fetish of political and economic 'laws.'" Phillips, however, made no effort comparable with Rahv's to claim a continuing loyalty to radical ideas, and he directed far more attention to the sins of the "avowed liberals" who used Koestler's shortcomings as a justifica tion for "their own fuzzy progressivism and illusions about the nature of Soviet Russia." To those who attacked Koestler as merely a disillusioned skeptic, Phillips replied: "True enough, Koestler has not come up with a positive, buoyant resolution of the contemporary dilemma. But, in all honesty, who has?" The lack of "answers" seemed to suit Phillips just fine.[64]

Rahv, Phillips, and Trilling responded to the "breakdown of the socialist-revolutionary cause" in different ways. Of the three Rahv, who had been the most political to begin with, worked hardest to maintain a sense of radical identity, an often subterranean faith in historical direction, and a belief that attempts to provide "answers" to intellectual dilemmas were important. Trilling's response carried him to a questioning of the basic assumptions of liberal and radical thought, and he came to insist on a degree of complexity in human life that seemingly defied all but individual and temporary resolutions. Phillips fell somewhere in between, exhibiting limited interest in either justifying or reconsidering the grounds for his opinions. Despite these differences, all three shared a conviction of major significance in 1945: the conviction that there was no available system of ideas or method of analysis that offered the disillusioned radical (or anyone else) an immediate grip on the problems of the age or comprehensive intellectual guidance. If the "end of ideology" was not yet in vogue, the attitudes behind the phrase were already gathering strength in the realm of literary criticism.

Chapter Nine | *Partisan Review* and the New York Intellectuals

The influence of *Partisan Review* was on the rise by the early 1940s. Although differences within the magazine's inner circle threatened to destroy the whole enterprise, those same difficulties contributed to a sense of breadth, of struggle, and of vitality in the magazine. By the second half of the decade, *Partisan Review* had become sufficiently established among American intellectuals to attract both inflated praise and immoderate attack. For opponents especially, the magazine had come to stand for a whole set of ideas and attitudes associated not just with *Partisan Review* but with a larger circle of writers and scholars whose views found their most telling expression in its pages. This group would come to be known in time as the "New York Intellectuals."

The pillars of the community, the models of what a New York Intellectual should be and do, came largely from that group which had gathered around *Partisan Review* in 1937. Anti-Stalinism had been the cause that brought them together, and out of the battles of the late 1930s came a sense of shared experience strong enough to override many of the differences of the next decade. Out of the fight against Stalinism, too, came some of the New York Intellectuals' most enduring legends—legends of fearless truth-seeking, intellectual courage, and the heroic defense of values. It was a flattering self-portrait. Adherence to the anti-Stalinist position and loyalty to the legends of the thirties were touchstones for the type.

In June of 1939 James T. Farrell recorded a comment from a friend that *Partisan Review* had "the chance to assume the intellectual leadership of America."[1] Such encouragement helped create a sense of common purpose and group support around the magazine; at the same time, it both reflected and reinforced a level of ambition that put considerable pressure on editors and contributors alike. The dream of "intellectual leadership" justified a demanding standard and a critical dissection of each other's work that could too easily slide from ideas to personalities. From the early years of the New York Intellectuals onward, a tension between mutual support and critical evaluation, between intellectual respect and competitive rivalry, regulated the character of the group and shaped its patterns of exchange. If the results were sometimes destructive or the controversies trivial, the tension and the high ambition more often gave *Partisan Review* a tone of intellectual audacity and importance—especially in the early years.

It was, in part, this tone that attracted to the magazine's circle an energetic body of younger recruits who would add considerably to its strength. These younger writers and critics had histories of their own and were not simply followers of some *Partisan Review* line; yet they looked to that magazine as the most stimulating voice of the intellectual world they sought to enter and felt the pull of its principles and its passions.

Some of these potential recruits were already gathered in clumps on a few college campuses during the late 1930s and practicing their politics there. At the City College of New York, two alcoves of the lunchroom were dominated by rival left factions, one sympathetic to Stalin and the other anti-Stalinist. The anti-Stalinist group numbered in its ranks young Trotskyists like Irving Howe and Irving Kristol, the social-democratic Daniel Bell, and others, including Nathan Glazer, Melvin J. Lasky, and Seymour Martin Lipset—all of whom would be tied to the New York Intellectuals to varying degrees in coming years. At the University of Chicago another clump had gathered, including Saul Bellow, Isaac Rosenfeld, and Leslie Fiedler, a graduate student at the University of Wisconsin, that was less political than the City College group but tinged with Trotskyism and clearly anti-Stalinist nonetheless. For both groups *Partisan Review* was a periodical of major importance.[2]

The younger intellectuals, growing up as anti-Stalinists, had not for the most part felt the strong pull of the Communist movement in the depths of the depression; they had not generally undergone a confrontation with their own political pasts or faced the threat of isolation; they would be free in the 1940s to choose whether and what to remember about the battles of the thirties, in a way that the older veterans of that decade were not. To say this is not to question the sincerity of the newer arrivals, but it is to suggest that a part of their radical experience was vicarious. *Partisan Review* offered them a tie to battles already waged. The break from the Communist Party in 1937, support for the Dewey Commission, condemnation of the Moscow Trials, the prestige of having been "right" about Stalinism *before* the Nazi-Soviet pact, were all theirs—in part by virtue of their anti-Stalinist politics, but more keenly through intellectual identification with *Partisan Review* and with the older men and women who had given the magazine life. Not just opposition to Stalinism but a collective loyalty to the memory of that opposition helped tie the New York Intellectuals together.

William Barrett, who remained largely in the background as a friend of Delmore Schwartz before 1945, suggests in his memoirs the depth of feeling that the image of the *Partisan Review* circle could arouse. On meeting the editors in 1937, it was not their individual strengths that aroused "awe and admiration" in Barrett but the sense of what they represented as a group: "Theirs was the world of bohemia and the arts, of political movements and counter-movements, bold and sweeping ideologies; and they were the intrepid spirits who bravely walked within that world. They were therefore beings invested in my eyes with a strange and mysterious glamour; and I felt tongue-tied and stupid in their presence." Barrett acknowledges that he was "young and ready for hero-worship"; later, in describing Schwartz, Philip Rahv, and the whole *Partisan Review* circle after 1945, Barrett's attitude is anything but one of veneration. Yet he protects and treasures the legend of the thirties. As a group, Barrett insists, the editors of 1937 "deserved this admiration" for their "courage." In politics they were "fighting the Stalinist tide," attacking the Moscow Trials, criticizing the Soviet Union "from the point of view of a purer Marxism," all of which was commendable. In culture *Partisan Review* undertook a "battle to champion the cause of modern literature and art." For the young student, it was "a bracing challenge to be on the side of the difficult and rare," defending, along with *Partisan Review*, the artist's right to be complex.[3]

The impact the magazine had on young minds favorably disposed to receive it is confirmed by a variety of sources. Irving Kristol sounds much like Barrett in recalling that *Partisan Review* was an "intimidating presence" among his college friends: "Even simply to understand it seemed a goal beyond reach. I would read each article at least twice, in a state of awe and exasperation—excited to see such elegance of style and profundity of mind." Like Barrett, Kristol hints that youthful innocence and inexperience lay behind his admiration—forty years later he can see "limitations then not visible to me." Yet Kristol, too, endorses the imposing reputation of *Partisan Review* in the years after 1937 and largely justifies his awe: the pursuit of radicalism in both politics and culture "established a dialectic of challenge and response that released the finest creative energies. . . . *Partisan Review* in its heyday was unquestionably one of the finest American cultural periodicals ever published —perhaps even the very finest."[4]

One of the interesting things about this pattern of discussion among the New York Intellectuals is how early the pattern emerged, how quickly the magazine's contributions of the late thirties were raised to special eminence while its policies over time were subjected to critical dissection. The pattern began to take form as early as 1942 in an essay by Irving Howe. Howe's piece was primarily a ringing attack from a Trotskyist perspective on *Partisan Review*'s waffling over the issue of war. Yet it began by paying tribute to the magazine's "valuable services" a few years before: "It served as a center for those intellectuals who broke from Stalinism. . . . It opened its pages to obscure young writers and its editors exhibited that catholicity of taste and sympathy for innovation and experimentation that is essential for a left wing literary journal. . . . it brought literature and aesthetics a bit closer to the politics of the revolutionary movement."[5] Already in 1942, Howe's list held up the *Partisan Review* of the late 1930s as exemplary, and it emphasized anti-Stalinism and the fruitful combination of literature and politics as sources of the magazine's appeal.

There was also something more at work. *Partisan Review* in its early years was a young person's magazine. The openness to new ideas and new writers to which Howe testified provided an important sense of opportunity and then achievement for a number of talented young intellectuals. If the older members of the *Partisan Review* circle had a certain body of work behind them by 1940, they too were still in early stages of their careers for the most part, firmly established only in the minds of their younger counterparts. The New York Intellectuals of both age groups could feel bound together in the early 1940s by an invigorating sense of intellectual power and promise.

For all of this, the pattern of the memoirs clearly suggests the presence of complex and divided attitudes toward *Partisan Review*. Those trying to recapture and explain the mixed feelings of the time have found it difficult to convey the ways in which enthusiastic support and vivid interest blended with doubt, resistance, and an exuberance of disputation. More than contemporary ambivalence or personal idiosyncracy or the vagaries of memory is involved here; the question of what *Partisan Review* meant to its supporters goes quickly to the problem of identity for the New York Intellectuals.

228

Perhaps a comment of Leslie Fiedler's offers one way to understand the memoirs and grants some insight into the particular conditions of coherence for the New York group. In dealing with *Partisan Review*, Fielder wrote, "I have the sense of beginning my own autobiography, or, more precisely, of treating that part of my life which is typical rather than peculiar: my life as an urban American Jew, who came of age intellectually during the Depression: who discovered Europe for the imagination before America: who was influenced by Marxist ideas, Communist and Trotskyist; who wanted desperately to feel that the struggle for a revolutionary politics and the highest literary standards was a single struggle (but who had more and more trouble believing it as the years went on); whose political certainty unraveled during the second World War."[6] This broad collective experience, "typical" for a specific group, seems inescapably tied up with the whole task of discussing *Partisan Review*. What drew people into the *Partisan Review* circle was not the chunk of their lives that remained distinctive; they could cultivate individuality and deny conformity to their hearts' content. What made them New York Intellectuals to begin with was a body of general values, a set of shared experiences, and a belief in the importance of those experiences. *Partisan Review* gave institutional form to the collective history and left a record of it for which there was no equivalent.

Fiedler's list of traits that tied his own life to the history of *Partisan Review* began with his identity as an "urban American Jew." Most of the New York Intellectuals shared this identity. At some levels of intellectual sympathy and personal understanding, a common Jewish heritage almost certainly worked to draw many of the wider group together into a cluster. Yet testimony about exactly what Jewishness meant to individuals and to the group must be taken with a large grain of salt. To most of the New York Intellectuals and to many others, for instance, Alfred Kazin's emphasis on the importance of being Jewish in his several volumes of memoir seems clearly the product of a later sensitivity, not an accurate record of his consciousness in the 1930s and early 1940s.[7] Kazin's case is but one example of the problems that may arise in weighing testimony delivered long after the fact. Such things as the changing status of Jews and of Jewish intellectuals, the need to come to grips with the shock of the Holocaust, and the struggle to establish Israel as a state created a very different context for the discussion of Jewish identity after the mid-1940s and placed every comment on past or present attitudes within a new web of meaning.

Consider, for example, two accounts of the New York Intellectuals offered in the 1960s. Norman Podhoretz, who identifies himself as a member of the "third generation" within the group, suggests several differences between the "first generation" of the 1930s and the "second generation" that came to maturity during or after World War II. In the second generation, Podhoretz claims, "those who were Jewish tended to be more comfortable with that fact than their elders had been." In part, the argument goes, this was the result of an intellectual progression "from Marx to Freud, from self-transcendence to self-acceptance." There was also a larger circumstance affecting both generations, "Hitler's altogether irrefutable demonstration of the inescapability of Jewishness."[8] The second explanation would seem to offer a powerful reason why intellectual Jews of any age would give more public attention to the nature of their Jewish identity in the 1940s, but Podhoretz seems much fonder of his first idea. He wants to insist that the older *Partisan Review* intellectuals with their attraction to Marxism were less comfortable being Jews than their younger colleagues.

Irving Howe, of the "second" generation, provides a more careful and complex analysis of the New York Intellectuals' relation to Jewishness by describing the historical context that gave rise to an understandable enthusiasm for "the idea of discarding the past, breaking away from families, traditions, and memories." Yet Howe also remarks in a superior tone, "That this severance from Jewish roots and immigrant sources would later come to seem a little suspect, is another matter." And he goes on to declare that "precisely at the point in the thirties when the New York Intellectuals began to form themselves into a loose cultural-political tendency, Jewishness as idea and sentiment played no significant role in their expectations."[9] The implication seems to be that the whole attitude toward ethnicity in the older group was "a little suspect."

Both Podhoretz and Howe posit a change in attitude from the first to the second generation of New York Intellectuals, a desirable change that gave a more prominent place to Jewishness in the work of the younger writers. Yet to say that Jewishness was discussed more openly and more extensively in the 1940s than in the 1930s need not lead to negative judgments of the older intellectuals. There seems to be at work in the arguments of Podhoretz and Howe a modest degree of tension between generations and the strong influence of later perspectives. Although the two analyses are as different in detail as the later views of the two men, both assume a certain superiority to the first generation rooted in a sense that younger New York Intellectuals were more comfortable being Jews and identified themselves as such more honorably. A post-Hitler sense of obligation to Jewishness is involved here. So, too, it is tempting to argue, is the self-esteem of the younger intellectuals: if their elders laid permanent claim to integrity for their early opposition to Stalinism in the thirties, the younger writers could lower the fathers by suggesting a failure on matters of Jewish identity. Elders who were less comfortable being Jewish and a little suspect in their attitudes allowed those who arrived after the thirties their own rectitude and their own legend.

Yet the investigation must not stop there. The summary judgment that "Jewishness as idea and sentiment played no significant role" for the *Partisan Review* circle must be weighed against the evidence of other testimony, including Howe's own. Howe comments in the same essay that "there was something decidedly Jewish about the intellectuals who began to cohere as a group around *Partisan Review* in the late thirties." Elsewhere he has suggested that the early *Partisan Review* is full of "Jewish references, motifs, inside jokes, and even explicit themes." And in describing the appearance of Delmore Schwartz's story "In Dreams Begin Responsibilities," Howe has testified to the power of these specific cultural references to cut through the whole ethos of radical politics and highbrow ideas for younger intellectuals attracted to *Partisan Review*. Those reading the story were "stunned." Schwartz's tone was "distinctly urban," and it spoke both of "Jewish immigrants" and of "their son, proudly moving toward the culture of America." Young intellectuals "heard a voice that seemed our own, though it had never really existed until Schwartz invented it."[10] Surely this suggests that young people were in some cases drawn toward *Partisan Review* by more than the pull of a "loose cultural-political tendency." Taken together, Howe's several declarations would seem to indicate that Jewishness did indeed play a significant if muted role in shaping the discourse and in defining the contours of the *Partisan Review* circle.[11]

Nevertheless, the problem of defining the attitude of the early New York Intellectuals toward Jewishness remains. The argument here will be, as it has been throughout, that those in the *Partisan Review* circle who were Jewish demonstrated a continuing consciousness of that fact and responded to it in reasonable and creative ways. Their stance has been challenged and it has been reduced to a mood or a series of gestures, but seldom has it been taken seriously as a substantial position on Jewish identity. In fact, there would seem to be grounds for claiming that the position established by the first generation remained quite stable, even into the postwar period, and that the links between the older and younger New York Intellectuals on the matter of Jewish identity were more impressive than the differences. A few things must first be said about the consciousness of Jewish identity among the *Partisan Review* intellectuals.

During the late thirties and early forties, *Partisan Review* devoted little space to discussing the fate of Jews in Europe, to probing the nature of anti-Semitism (this came later), or to exploring any other issue that clearly and explicitly involved a question of Jewish identity. Among those on the left in whose circles *Partisan Review* had most of its limited circulation in the thirties, there was little need to spell out the belief that fascism and anti-Semitism were undesirable. Moreover, for journalistic coverage of the growing Nazi threat other periodicals on the anti-Stalinist left were better suited.

Some of these were certainly read by *Partisan Review*'s editors and supporters, and to some they contributed. In late 1938, for instance, Sidney Hook began a guest column in the Social Democratic *New Leader* with the sentence "The tragedy of German Jewry is one of the darkest shadows on our century." Hook went on to attack the effort of the Communist Party to pose as the defender of "persecuted Jews everywhere in the world," predicting a Stalinist shift toward anti-Semitism if a rumored Nazi-Soviet agreement came about. Hook's column manifested a clear sensitivity to the fate of Jews. It also demonstrated that for him a true defense of Jewish interests and the interests of all minorities was intimately tied up with opposition to Stalinism—the central political cause of the *Partisan Review* intellectuals.[12]

There is considerable evidence that the *Partisan* intellectuals were alert to the instances and effects of anti-Semitism in their private discussions as well. Several of the conversations James T. Farrell recorded in his diary in the spring of 1939 made this concern apparent. (That non-Jews like Farrell were partners in such conversations demonstrates emphatically that anti-Semitism was a fundamental concern in the *Partisan Review* circle, not some grievance whispered about privately by Jews uncomfortable with their identities.) In early May, for example, Farrell recorded a conversation with Meyer Schapiro about a *New Masses* attack on a former Soviet agent that both found anti-Semitic, and he noted the opinion of another friend that the same attack was "one of the worst pieces of jew-baiting he had encountered and that it belonged in an organ such as *Volkischer Baeobachten* [*sic*]."[13] As in Hook's column for the *New Leader*, Farrell and his friends tied together Nazi and Stalinist tactics, saw anti-Semitism as a tool used by both, and, thus, made opposition to such prejudice a function of a general left anti-Stalinist position.[14]

Farrell also made note of a conversation with Lionel Trilling concerning his recent promotion to assistant professor at Columbia. Trilling's case has become a reminder of the prejudice against Jews in American universities during the twenties and thirties. Young Jewish intellectuals in those years faced a troubling question, Diana Trilling has since remarked: "Could a Jew realistically plan on a university career? The consensus was that especially in certain fields he could not." There were exceptions to the rule by the late thirties, including Sidney Hook and Meyer Schapiro; and opposition to Nazi ideology as well as the arrival of several established Jewish scholars from Germany helped to open up more opportunities. Yet English departments remained notorious bastions of Anglo-Saxon prejudice. Forced to run the gantlet of such prejudice, Trilling became in 1939 the first Jew to serve as a regular member of the English department at Columbia only after the direct intervention of President Nicholas Murray Butler.[15] For teachers and students alike, university life regularly reminded them that immigrant backgrounds and Jewishness mattered, whether they felt immediately oppressed by their environment or not.[16]

The evidence that those *Partisan Review* intellectuals who were Jewish remained quite aware of that fact and alert to the effects of anti-Semitism may seem to suggest only a natural and private consciousness separated from the essential ideas and public attitudes of the older New York Intellectuals. Yet when the evidence of Jewish consciousness is put in its rightful context, it appears as an integral part of a logical and consistent position on the place of ethnicity. At the core of *Partisan Review*'s position stood an adherence to cosmopolitan values. Those values, to restate their import, assumed the desirability of a broad and inclusive culture. No individual or group was to be scorned or excluded on the basis of heritage; instead, social and cultural differences were to be esteemed for what they could bring to the general perspective and to a more comprehensive understanding of experience. Such values presumed an open society in which free discussion was possible and in which ideas and individuals could succeed through merit.

What the *Partisan Review* intellectuals rejected in the name of cosmopolitan values was, as they saw it, the cultural blight of parochialism, narrowness, and prejudice.

The standard laid down by the acceptance of cosmopolitan values was evident throughout the early history of *Partisan Review*. When considered in light of this standard, the various indications of the older New York Intellectuals' relation to Jewishness take on a new coherence. Jews and other minorities should defend the idea of an open democratic society (which did not necessarily mean the existing institutions of the United States) by opposing both fascism and Stalinism. A young writer like Delmore Schwartz should bring his particular heritage to the service of a larger cultural purpose. Such values did not require an abandonment of Jewish identity. They did require that Jewishness as an element in the public lives of intellectuals contribute to a broader and richer cultural understanding and inform the defense of those principles that made the exchange of ideas possible.

In the 1940s the *Partisan Review* intellectuals began to discuss the nature of Jewish identity more explicitly at both a personal and a general level. There were many variations in tone and texture; yet in their central thrust these discussions affirmed and elaborated earlier positions, demonstrating the stability and primacy of cosmopolitan values among the New York Intellectuals into the postwar years.

The *Contemporary Jewish Record* gathered one set of statements in "Under Forty: A Symposium on American Literature and the Younger Generation of American Jews" (1944). Among those participating were Alfred Kazin, Lionel Trilling, Clement Greenberg, Delmore Schwartz, and Isaac Rosenfeld. (For the same issue Harold Rosenberg and Saul Bellow did book reviews, and the managing editor of the moment was Philip Rahv; a fair representation of New York Intellectuals appeared in this issue of a clearly labeled Jewish magazine to discuss, in most cases, issues involving their Jewishness.) The published comments came in response to questions sent out by the magazine's regular editors that clearly affected the tone and content of replies. The editors announced first that "American Jews have reached the stage of integration with the native environment." They went on to speak of Jewish heritage as being "so remarkable" and "so significant on every level of existence" that the American Jewish writer could not help but be affected by it, and asked whether each writer had "formed a conscious attitude toward his heritage." In seeming to celebrate both the "native environment"

234

and Jewish distinctness, the editors, remarkably enough, managed to sound as if they approved of *both* cultures that *Partisan Review* intellectuals had rejected as limiting and parochial.[17]

Lionel Trilling's response both acknowledged the influence of Jewishness and limited its importance. "It is clear to me that my existence as a Jew is one of the shaping conditions of my temperament," Trilling wrote, "and therefore I suppose it must have its effect on my intellect." Yet nothing in his "professional intellectual life" struck Trilling as specifically Jewish: "I do not think of myself as a 'Jewish writer.' . . . I should resent it if a critic of my work were to discover in it either faults or virtues which he called Jewish." Trilling aspired to be a writer and critic within a national and international culture, not an ethnic one. In his "life as a citizen" the situation was somewhat different. There, Trilling testified, "my being Jewish exists as a point of honor," meaning that "I would not, even if I could, deny or escape being Jewish." If this "minimal" position took on "a certain gracelessness" when formulated, that was better than "merely symbolic action" or "mere guilty gesture."

As Trilling's response continued, both his sharp rejection of the editors' premises and his reliance on cosmopolitan values became more obvious. Trilling did not attack a heritage of traditional Jewish culture; he rejected as culturally inadequate the *American* Judaism the editors had seemed to be praising. Though sympathetic to the suffering of European Jews, Trilling avowed "no feeling of guilt toward the American Jewish community," which found itself at an "impasse of sterility." American Judaism lacked positive force. "Modern Jewish religion at its best may indeed be intelligent and soaked in university knowledge, but out of it there has not come a single voice with the note of authority—of philosophical, or poetic, or even of rhetorical, let alone of religious, authority." The whole idea of "Jewish self-realization" encouraged a willingness to be "provincial and parochial." The bottom line was damning: "As the Jewish community now exists, it can give no sustenance to the American artist or intellectual who is born a Jew. . . . I know of writers who have used their Jewish experience as the subject of excellent work; I know of no writer in English who has added a micromillimetre to his stature by 'realizing his Jewishness,' although I know of some who have curtailed their promise by trying to heighten their Jewish consciousness." Such sentiments clearly reflected the cosmopolitan position. A particular ethnic experience could enrich an effort to deal with broad cultural themes; immersion in that experience alone led nowhere.[18]

Trilling's critics have noted that specific references to Jewishness are neglected or submerged in his work after the later 1920s in favor of more general ideas.[19] There is a positive way of explaining this shift. Trilling's own comments about his experience with the *Menorah Journal* suggest that he found at this point in his life a way in which Jewishness could be seen in the context of larger social issues. "The discovery, through the *Menorah Journal*, of the Jewish situation had the effect of making society at last available to my imagination," Trilling wrote in a sentence that conveyed after forty years the remembered feelings of a youth before whom vistas of understanding seemed to be opening. "Suddenly it began to be possible—better than that, indeed: it began to be necessary—to think with categories that were charged with energy. . . . One couldn't, for example, think for very long about Jews without perceiving that one was using the category of social class." And the question of class quickly led Trilling beyond the "general concept of Jewishness that had at first claimed one's recognition and interest."[20]

It was not that Trilling suddenly turned against his Jewish birth. Rather, in a manner appropriate to the workings of cosmopolitan values, Trilling came to his general position *because* of his Jewishness. The leap toward "categories" and a culture beyond either Jewish or American parochialism promised an opportunity for intellectual growth and significance that the *Menorah Journal* position could not begin to match. And so the scope of Trilling's interests changed. Having worked his way to a cosmopolitan position through an early consideration of Jewishness, he seldom looked back.

Alfred Kazin did look back. After Trilling's death he would write that Trilling had always considered him "too Jewish" and "too full of my lower-class experience"; Kazin in turn pictured Trilling as a vain, ambitious, cautious sort who "would always defend himself from the things he had left behind." (One critic has commented that Kazin's "drama of the pariah-Jew at war with the gentleman-Jew belongs to the world of social comedy.")[21] Trilling and Kazin would thus seem to represent very different attitudes toward Jewishness. Yet in Kazin's own contribution to the "Under Forty" symposium, the similarity of his position to Trilling's was striking.

Although Kazin declared that he appreciated certain features of Jewish tradition and felt vaguely "influenced as a writer and a person by the idea of them," he nevertheless made his basic position emphatic: "I have never seen much of what I admire in American Jewish culture, or among Jewish writers in America generally." The

American Jew tended to exist in an "unhappy limbo" in which even his suffering was "sterile": "what a pity that he should feel 'different,' when he believes so little." Kazin rebuffed the assertion that Jews had become "full participants" in American cultural life, insisting that it was "about time we stopped confusing the experience of being an immigrant, or an immigrant's son, with the experience of being Jewish." The dissociation from American Jewish culture, the denial of its intellectual viability, and the rejection of the editors' premises put Kazin squarely in agreement with Trilling.

His own struggle, Kazin maintained, had been against a "merely imposed faith" and a "sentimental chauvinism." Too many confused "timidity with devotion" and "parochialism . . . with a conscious faith." The mention of timidity, parochialism, and chauvinism marked Kazin's rejection of cultural traits antithetical to cosmopolitan values; his declaration of literary loyalties exhibited the positive side of the same perspective. Kazin had learned "to accept the fact that I was Jewish," yet he had also learned as a writer "to follow what I really believed in" not "naive community feelings." Kazin's list of those who had influenced him included "Blake, Melville, Emerson, the seventeenth-century English religious poets, and the Russian novelists." Whatever the reconstructions of Kazin's later career, his position of 1944 was one based on cosmopolitan values and similar in most respects to Trilling's.[22]

Clement Greenberg had come to the *Partisan Review* circle later than the stalwarts of 1937, falling in this respect between the magazine's "generations." Perhaps that position helped to make the views he expressed in the "Under Forty" symposium a mixture of concerns and themes. Greenberg's comments served to link the responses of older and younger representatives of the New York Intellectual camp, demonstrating that a common allegiance to cosmopolitan values lay behind obvious differences in tone and emphasis.

Elements of kinship with Trilling and Kazin were not hard to find in Greenberg's response. His opening sentence challenged the bias toward positive Jewish consciousness contained in the editors' symposium questions: "This writer has no more of a conscious position toward his Jewish heritage than the average American Jew— which is to say, hardly any." At the same time, Greenberg expressed a conviction that the Jewish heritage ("is *heritage* the right word?") inescapably influenced his work through a "quality of Jewishness" that was "very informal, being transmitted mostly through mother's milk and the habits and talk of the family." These comments followed the pattern found in Trilling and Kazin of denying an affirmative consciousness of Jewishness while acknowledging some personal imprint. The common ground was extended by the fact that American Jewish culture was subjected in Greenberg's remarks to a familiar condemnation for its parochialism and its inability to sustain serious writing. And in noting with approval his parents' belief that "to change one's name because it is too Jewish is shameful," Greenberg suggested a position compatible with Trilling's "point of honor."[23]

From a cosmopolitan perspective, the international traditions of Western culture, the broad insights of social and political theory, and the patterns of modern life that could be generalized offered the writer far more than did immersion in a narrow culture based on ethnic or nationalistic feeling. Greenberg spoke forcefully to this theme, tying many of the present failings of Jewish writers to an inability to escape their ethnic heritage. In the process, Greenberg made use of two ideas that were growing in popularity among the New York Intellectuals. These ideas in combination paved the way for a more direct and more positive consideration of Jewishness among younger members of the New York group (though Greenberg did not go this far). The first idea was that the writer had to create his own identity and that this meant reaching some understanding of his own experience. The second was that the Jew, and particularly the Jewish writer, was representative of the modern condition. Neither idea conflicted with cosmopolitan values. Indeed, the uses to which they were put served those values well and exercised some of the possibilities inherent in the cosmopolitan framework.

The Jewish writer's need to create a sense of cultural identity was not a new theme. Kazin suggested as much in commenting that "like many another American, I have had to make my own culture."[24] Kazin and Trilling had "made" their sustaining culture out of the resources of Western literature. Other writers had tried another route. Greenberg concentrated on those who had exhibited a "preoccupation with the autobiographical" by tracing their "flights" from immigrant neighborhoods to the "wide open world." Such writers touched upon more than one "great American theme," but they faced special difficulties because of the parochial limits of Jewish culture in America: "The Jewish writer suffers from the unavailability of a sufficient variety of observed experience. He is forced to write, if he is serious, the way the pelican feeds its young, striking his own breast to draw the blood of his theme." The writer needed, in Greenberg's mind, to identify himself with a broader community, to expand the range of his experience, and to find ideas and standards that could serve as a basis for social criticism. All these things pointed away from self-conscious Jewishness and toward cosmopolitan values.

Greenberg's use of the idea that the writer must create his own identity and his own culture emphasized the problems involved — especially for the Jewish writer — rather than the possibilities. Yet within Greenberg's discussion there was steady reference to a second idea that tended to turn his argument into a grounds for hope and ambition. Each of the difficulties of Jewish writers discussed by Greenberg had been presented as a more acute version of a general problem, an intensification of wider patterns. Greenberg's analysis made the Jewish writer's struggles as a writer pertinent to the history of American and Western culture as a whole. The Jewish writer as Jew could make a similar claim to representativeness, it seemed. The "Jew's chronic conception of himself as a wanderer" and an outsider had become a pathway toward typicality. The Jewish writer's plight, Greenberg declared, "becomes like every other plight today, a version of the alienation of man under capitalism; all plights merge, and that of the Jew has become less particular because it turns more and more into an intensified expression of a general one." Because alienation could be seen as the characteristic fate of modern man (and not just in Marxist terms), the Jewish writer turned out to be not just typical in his experience but especially well situated to explore the modern condition through his own "intensified" version of the general plight.[25]

Greenberg did not explicitly turn his suggestions of representativeness into a claim for the positive value of Jewish birth; that use of the argument was left to others. Greenberg's response was a bridge between the contributions of Trilling and Kazin and those of two younger writers who contributed to the "Under Forty" symposium. Delmore Schwartz and Isaac Rosenfeld both sought to identify themselves with a broader, more general culture that was not specifically Jewish, just as Trilling and Kazin had done; but both younger men were determined to use autobiographical materials and the idea of Jewish representativeness in order to achieve cosmopolitan identity.

To be "the child of immigrants from Eastern Europe" might provide the author with "a heightened sensitivity to language," Schwartz remarked, but it was also likely to produce a certain verbal insecurity and a critical perspective toward the parental culture. The heritage of the Jewish past was reduced for the child to the need to memorize "certain passages in a dead language." Jewish tradition and American Jewish life were not, to Schwartz, an adequate basis for a complex living culture. On this there was only agreement among the New York Intellectuals.

There was also widespread agreement in the *Partisan Review* circle that Jewishness was defined in large part by anti-Semitism. Trilling, Kazin, and Greenberg had all referred to hostility toward Jews in trying to clarify their own positions. Schwartz made anti-Semitism a major theme in his story of growing awareness as a writer, echoing in some respects Trilling's account of his growth away from the *Menorah Journal* position. "Social anti-Semitism" had always been a part of his experience, Schwartz testified, but it had led toward no sophisticated understanding of the situation of Jews. It was the "revival of political anti-Semitism" that put his mind to work:[26] "the fact of being a Jew became available to me as a central symbol of alienation, bias, point of view, and certain other characteristics which are the peculiar marks of modern life, and as I think now, the essential ones." Jewishness was thus an "ever-growing good," a "fruitful and inexhaustible inheritance" for the author.[27]

Schwartz's affirmation of the positive value of Jewishness came fully within a framework of cosmopolitan values. Jewish particularity mattered to Schwartz primarily as a symbol of more general experience, as a way of comprehending the "essential" patterns of modern life. Schwartz's position differed from that of some of the older New York Intellectuals not through any departure from cosmopolitanism but in the belief that the Jew might be supremely well-situated to apprehend and to analyze modern experience. In Isaac Rosenfeld's remarks, claims for the advantages to the writer of being Jewish became dominant.

Rosenfeld, too, worked from ideas common to the New York Intellectuals, giving them his personal twist. When he declared that a "conscious member" of a minority group in the United States was "distressed by differences which in a healthy society would be considered healthful," the model of a "healthy" society to which he referred was a cosmopolitan one. To Rosenfeld, being Jewish "should occupy no more of a man's attention than any ordinary fact of his history." An artist in positive surroundings should have "the security of a dignified neutrality"; he should be a "representative even if extraordinary individual." Unfortunately, in the unhealthy world of the early 1940s, the Jewish writer had to live with the threat that he might be "called to account not for his art, nor even for his life, but for his Jewishness."

Even so, the position of Jewish artists and intellectuals was "not entirely an unfortunate one": "For the most part the young Jewish writers of today are the children of immigrants, and as such—not completely integrated in society and yet not wholly foreign to it— they enjoy a critical advantage over the life that surrounds them." Jews were particularly suited to carry forward a cosmopolitan intellectual perspective, for as "marginal men," they were "open to more influences than perhaps any other group." These urban barometers of modernity, Rosenfeld emphasized again and again, were "centrally exposed to all movements in art and in thought." The Jewish writer was the beneficiary of a wonderful paradox: "Since modern life is so complex that no man can possess it in its entirety, the outsider often finds himself the perfect insider."[28]

The claim of a central position for the Jewish intellectual based on his marginality seemed to inspire Rosenfeld to develop yet another argument for representativeness around the theme of alienation. "As a member of an internationally insecure group," Rosenberg declared, the Jewish writer had become a "specialist in alienation (the one international banking system the Jews actually control)." Alienation put the Jewish writer in touch "with his own past traditions, the history of the Diaspora; with the present predicament of almost all intellectuals and, for all one knows, with the future conditions of civilized humanity." Contemporary culture—"thought, creation, perception"—stood "alienated from the society," pushed into that outsider's territory where Jews were the experts. And here a second invigorating paradox could come into play: "alienation from society, like the paradox of the outsider, may function as a condition of entrance into society." The "moral discoveries" of the Jewish writer would "indict the world," but they might also be "crucial to its salvation." For Rosenfeld, alienation served as the touchstone, as the framework for analysis, and even as the wellspring of hope that socialism had been for the *Partisan Review* in the thirties.

Rosenfeld was quick to add that he did "not want to make too much of alienation." The concept would lose much of its power if it came to seem too positive. Alienation was "the only possible condition, the theme we have to work with," but "undesirable" in falling short of the "full human range." In closing, Rosenfeld allowed himself a moment of tender optimism for the old cosmopolitan dream of an integrated and diverse society friendly to intellectuals: "in every society, in every group, there are what Saul Bellow has called 'colonies of the spirit.' Artists create their colonies. Some day these may become empires."[29] The vision of a new cultural empire, so important to *Partisan Review* in the thirties, did not die easily.

Similarities of aspiration and commitment, of course, did not necessarily lead to harmonious styles or identical choices. Yet for all the apparent range of tone and attitude in the "Under Forty" symposium, the responses of older and younger writers from the New York circle suggested a shared cultural outlook that provided a link between them. The ideas and the positions developed in the individual symposium pieces of 1944 grew out of a perspective that was already well established and that would continue to be elaborated and defended in the immediate postwar period. It may be useful to glance briefly at three continuing themes of the New York Intellectuals to suggest the ways in which Jewishness shaped—and, yes, "intensified"—their adherence to cosmopolitan values.

The idea of the intellectual as outsider had, in one form or another, a very long history; so, too, did the idea of the Jew as exile or wanderer. Those among the New York Intellectuals who were Jews took their bearings from the sense that they stood outside *two* cultures. It was Jewishness that allowed them to claim, with some accuracy, that their plight was a heightened form of the typical plight of intellectuals. It was Jewishness that made possible the assertion of a double exile that promised exceptional insight.

The work of the New York Intellectuals in the late forties demonstrated a continuing consciousness of their relation to two cultures. Some used the concept of the outsider and the idea of an intensified Jewish plight to make an explicit case, as Rosenfeld had done. In one title that summarized most of his message—"The Lost Young Intellectual: A Marginal Man Twice Alienated"—Irving Howe managed to squeeze together both notions and to suggest a new "lost" generation in the process. Others filed no such brief but still exhibited a consciousness of two cultures tied to cosmopolitan assumptions. In 1949 Lionel Trilling declared that he disliked both the flattering generalizations about Jews he had heard in the "intimate culture" of his childhood and the hostile ones of the larger society. He set himself apart, in other words, from two traditions. What he embraced was the seeming contradiction of being at once distinct and representative that lay at the heart of the cosmopolitan position.[30]

A second continuing theme revolved around the intellectual's need to create his own culture and to define his own identity. Such issues had played a part in the cosmopolitan perspective from the first. Yet the New York Intellectuals came under a new kind of pressure to defend their values and to define their position more explicitly when the question of Jewish identity burst into prominence after World War II. Three essays by Sidney Hook, Clement Greenberg, and Harold Rosenberg appearing in 1949 and 1950 demonstrated, for all their differences in focus and tone, certain patterns that reflected a solid core of shared assumptions. All three opposed the efforts of self-consciously "Jewish" groups to define Jewish identity and to push some form of one-hundred-percent Jewishness. (Rosenberg's opposition might be described as gentle but firm; Hook's and Greenberg's was very sharp indeed.) All three criticized, as well, any attempt to deny Jewish identity, to seek full assimilation, or to escape the fact of being a Jew. Each one, therefore, characteristically defined his position as one that fell between extremes.

In the problem of identity, each author saw grounds for reasserting the importance of openness, diversity, and choice. Hook argued that differences among Jews undercut any notion of a single group identity, asserted the importance of a democratic pluralism, and submitted a plea for the right of all people "to freely determine themselves as Jews or Gentiles, as citizens of one country or another, as cultural heirs of Socrates or Aquinas or Dewey." Greenberg called for a Jewishness that might "liberate rather than organize us" and declared that he wished to "feel free to be whatever I need to be and delight in being as a personality without being typed or prescribed to as a Jew or, for that matter, as an American." Rosenberg underlined the "*voluntary* aspect of modern identity," particularly in an "open community" like the United States, and stressed the need to recognize the "varying and oscillating presence" that Jewishness might be. The question of Jewish identity led all three men to declare more openly and to advocate more emphatically the values of a cosmopolitan position that had long been theirs.[31]

A third theme in the work of the New York Intellectuals—the defense of a rational, secular culture—was so basic to a cosmopolitan position that it may at first seem to have little about it that was related to Jewishness or distinctive to a particular group. Yet for many in the *Partisan Review* circle, rational and secular values were not just necessary to a sophisticated culture; they were also intimately tied up with resistance to anti-Semitism.[32] This became clear in the late 1940s when leaders of the New York camp undertook to defend their values against renewed religious interest among both Christians and Jews. In considering the persistence of anti-

Semitism, Sidney Hook attributed it primarily to the Christian tradition of the Jew as Christ-killer; and he defined anti-Semitism as "not so much an opinion as a *passion*," placing it in clear opposition to rational thought. Religion should be only a "private matter," Hook argued, and "secular humanism" was "a safer, as well as truer, philosophy for democratic life" than Christian humanism.

Postwar Jewish self-consciousness and militance disturbed Hook no less than what he regarded as reactionary Christianity. It seemed to him that Jews "were out to prove that they are like everyone else —inconsistent, fanatical, atavistic." Such behavior seemed especially inappropriate for a people that had, "by and large, been rational and pacific." By implication as well as by direction, Hook called upon Jews to embrace secular, democratic, cosmopolitan values as the best means of bringing about a society in which anti-Semitism had no place.[33]

The question of anti-Semitism in the Western literary tradition led several of the New York Intellectuals to affirm their values in a 1949 symposium. The discussion grew out of an essay by Leslie Fiedler that described the "rich alienated art" of modernity as a product of "secularization" among both Christians and Jews: the belief in "universal reason" at the time of the Enlightenment had brought "the dream of a 'human' culture, available to Jew and Gentile alike." Fiedler quite obviously embraced this dream. To counteract lingering anti-Semitic stereotypes in literature, he proposed the creation of "rival myths of our meaning for the Western world" built around the idea of the Jew as a central modern figure. What was necessary to overcome literary anti-Semitism, therefore, was a continuation of the secularizing process to allow Jews to stand increasingly for common human experience.[34]

The responses included contributions from William Phillips, Philip Rahv, Paul Goodman, Isaac Rosenfeld, Diana Trilling, Harold Rosenberg, Irving Howe, Saul Bellow, Alfred Kazin, and Lionel Trilling, all of whom gave evidence of their loyalty to reason and "the ideals of common humanity."[35] Perhaps the strongest assertion of the link between a secular, rational cosmopolitanism and resistance to anti-Semitism came from Rahv. Rahv agreed with Fiedler that Jewish entry into Western culture was "coincident with its secularization," but Rahv wanted to assert the connection between this modern process and a positive environment for Jews even more strongly: "to complete that historical proposition one must go on to state that to the degree that this secularization is weakened, debilitated by the reanimation of the Christian myth, precisely to that degree does the position of the Jew become precarious and in the long run intolerable." The future of Jews within the "Anglo-American culture milieu" clearly lay, in Rahv's mind, with "an even more radical secularizing and internationalizing of culture"; the task must be to "bring a halt to the de-secularization of culture so frivolously attempted by the reactionary intellectuals." Rahv's cosmopolitan loyalties were open and emphatic.[36]

There was, then, a continuity of perspective in the work of the New York Intellectuals running through the 1930s and 1940s. To say this is not to claim that there was no development over time in the attitudes or the viewpoint of the *Partisan Review* circle, nor is it to deny differences over political, philosophical, or literary issues within that circle. The argument does claim that the New York Intellectuals embraced cosmopolitan values, that their loyalty to those values was intensified by their consciousness of being Jewish, and that such a consciousness helped to make the *Partisan Review* variant of cosmopolitanism a discrete intellectual position. Eric Bentley emphasized this distinctiveness when he hailed *Partisan Review* in 1947 as "the voice of the New York ghetto, a magazine one can speak of as a unit because it has a definite attitude, a tone of voice." Yet Bentley also recognized that *Partisan Review* belonged in a larger company of those who were "for the breaking of barriers"; who tried to be "urbane, cosmopolitan, and catholic" in an age of "provincialism, nationalism, and specialization"; who practiced "cross-fertilization" in an age preaching "purity of race"; and who remembered "our common humanity" in an age praising the "common man."[37] The New York Intellectuals had succeeded, to Bentley's mind, in speaking with a particular voice that had general significance. And that was a fitting tribute to the values for which they stood.

Looking at the most visible evidence of the nature of personal relationships within the *Partisan Review* camp, it might be tempting to conclude that disagreement, incivility, prickliness, and blood-letting dominated the group's behavior. There is considerable evidence in the published sources alone to support Irving Howe's contention that New York Intellectual existence came "closer to the vision of life we associate with Hobbes than with Kropotkin."[38] Even in 1937 there was contention and strife: and when Philip Rahv wrote to an old colleague in 1952, "I don't know whether PR can survive the personality wrangles that are catching up with it," he was summarizing a long and continuing history of Hobbesian quarrels.[39]

245

An expanding body of memoirs tends to confirm in many cases an image of flashing knives and acid tongues. Some narratives show the clear marks of continuing effort to settle scores or diminish rivals—as other veterans of the New York camp are quick to point out. Indeed, the counter-volleys of differing memoirs and the reactions to each flurry of recollection often mix present and past disagreements in one contentious stew.[40] The private papers of those in or near the *Partisan Review* circle present a more varied picture of personal relationships, but one that has its share of backbiting and vituperation. If much of the correspondence between members of the New York group was perfectly normal, a few exchanges seem so abrasive that only a rampant destructiveness is readily visible. The sniping between Dwight Macdonald and Delmore Schwartz built to a climax of mutual recrimination in the middle of 1943 that would be hard to exaggerate.[41]

It seems only reasonable to ask why this aggressive temper in personal relationships should have been so strong. Perhaps the background of many of the New York Intellectuals had something to do with it. The majority were fighting their way upward from lower- or lower-middle-class origins, competing for recognition and status through the strenuous exercise of intelligence, as they had from their early school days. Some had received a higher training in the methods of stripping and gashing opponents from such teachers as City College's Morris R. Cohen, whose students would later insist that they had been "slashed, stabbed, scrubbed, and seared for their own good."[42] Factors of this kind could hardly explain the whole phenomenon, however; Dwight Macdonald, the Yale man, would yield to few in his love of the battle, and Mary McCarthy made veteran warriors tremble with the sharpness of her tongue.

Some of the New York Intellectuals abrasiveness was a function of personality and of the atmosphere created when particular personalities came together. Not everyone accepted the need for cutting attack or adopted a style that broadcast its aggressive intent: both F. W. Dupee and Lionel Trilling well knew how to make strong partisan arguments, but both generally avoided in published works and in private correspondence the tendency to excoriate and degrade. Those who dipped their pens in acid on occasion probably did so because they were pleased with the results. A number of the New York Intellectuals were so exuberant in their exercise of mind, so in love with the evidences of wit, that they seemed unable to resist the clever retort, the colorful remark, the apt phrase. What one had said others were prone to repeat in a process that celebrated the sharp sting of originality. Proud of his special talent for the game, Delmore Schwartz once reminded Dwight Macdonald of the "immortal epigram" that "Dwight is in search of a disciple who will tell him what to think." Schwartz circulated examples of his own ingenuity with the eagerness of a public relations man.[43] Some in the *Partisan Review* circle proved rather thin-skinned, and over the years long memories filled themselves up with a bitter harvest of bruises and slights.

At least one other concern quite likely contributed to the constant agitation among the New York Intellectuals. Again and again in recollections and post mortems, *Partisan Review* writers have tried to express their mixed feelings in the forties and since about being closely identified with the magazine. Coining one of those catchy phrases that the New York writers loved, Harold Rosenberg captured the paradoxical impulses among his peers in the title "The Herd of Independent Minds."[44] However much they might share, the New York Intellectuals wanted to claim originality of thought; they wanted to be recognized for personal, not group, achievement. The very quarrelsomeness of the *Partisan Review* group and the sharp exchanges over ideas helped to assure the New York writers that they remained independent, free-thinking individuals, just as the recounting of splits and bickering in the memoirs served at times to downplay the unity of the group and to deny that it ever operated as an intellectual establishment. If contentiousness was natural and perhaps unavoidable, it also had its utility.

The Hobbesian picture of personal relationships in the *Partisan Review* camp is not enough, however. Dissension provides a more colorful topic than agreement, friction is easier to describe than amity, yet too great an emphasis on swordplay and skirmishing leaves a one-sided portrait that misses the importance of positive social ties among the New York Intellectuals. They did, after all, have to attend meetings and parties together over a good many years to generate enough grist for the memoir mill. At these gatherings, as in the correspondence and elsewhere, there was often no simple and clear line between friendliness and hostility.

Examples of a certain level of congeniality abound. James T. Farrell, for all his criticisms of Sidney Hook's tactics and ideas, wrote after one exchange: "I find that Sidney is very appealing personally, and it is impossible for me to get angry with him."[45] Schwartz's characterizations of his friends were wonderfully humorous and observant in an affectionate way as often as they were biting or brutal; again, the line between the two voices was often blurred.[46] In describing an editorial meeting at *Partisan Review* in which Alfred Kazin became the object of various witticisms, William Barrett has commented that although Kazin was "not a personal favorite" of the editors, he was respected as a writer. Thus, the jocularity of Rahv and Schwartz and Phillips (Barrett does not mention his own level of involvement) was "so exuberant that it was almost free from any malice, and even carried a certain affection for the victim." Such shared good humor helped the editors live with their dislikes and differences.[47]

A view of personal relations among the *Partisan Review* intellectuals must also acknowledge the simple fact that members of the group sometimes provided a good portion of each other's day-to-day social lives. They met informally, they corresponded when apart, they visited each other's homes; by choice they sought one another out for companionship as well as for professional reasons. Perhaps Farrell's diary by its very nature records the range and frequency of contacts most clearly, though the patterns are evident in a variety of sources. Farrell's entries are filled with comments denoting the rhythms of everyday life: "Phil Rahv came around last night, and after him, Sidney and Ann Hook"; "Rahv came around about ten last night, and we went down to Pete's Tavern"; "William Phillips called me up and said he was depressed. Fred Dupee dropped in"; "Party at Dwight MacDonald's [*sic*] last night. Weldon Kees, . . . Clement Greenberg, Herbert Solow, Philip Rahv, William Phillips, . . . some others, including Lionel Trilling"; "Saturday night, at a party at Jim Burnham's, I had a talk with Clement Greenberg"; and many times, with varying names and topics, the form "Mike Schapiro says Sidney Hook . . ." believes this or takes that position. All this is aside from such entries as Farrell's long and enthusiastic description of a baseball game between "The Studs Lonigan A.C." (his team) and "The Marxist Maulers." The list could go on and on.[48]

Saul Bellow has recalled that when he arrived in New York in the 1940s a sense of community existed among the writers around *Partisan Review* and that he rapidly came to enjoy the "open spirit of easy fraternization" he found. Bellow's new associates "were not always friendly friends, but they were always stimulating friends."[49] The *Partisan Review* intellectuals often goaded one another with teasing or critique, and yet there was also public praise. The habits of attacking one another and quoting one another really made up two sides of the same intense interest in work coming out of their own circle. The New York writers were "nervously alert to one another's judgments," and they made up each other's primary audience much of the time.[50] The rapt attention paid to others in the circle, the conjoining of intellectual and personal affairs, and the smoothly functioning network of gossip and contacts have all been evoked more than once through the metaphor of a New York literary stock market, churning out a daily report on the ups and downs of intellectual reputation.

As a community of sorts, the New York writers had their sense of standards—a sense that was strengthened by the general identification of their own work with the virtues and the reputation of New York as a cultural center. What the standards entailed was succinctly suggested by Rahv in a report from Chicago on Saul Bellow and Harold Kaplan: "I am quite enthusiastic about these two youngsters—they are the Delmore Schwartz type: brilliant and yet at the same time methodical and responsible."[51] Rahv expected a deft handling of ideas, yet he also wanted regular and reliable writers whose pieces would hold together logically. Such concerns were not uncommon in an editor, but among the New York Intellectuals a series of similar expectations added up to the one basic question of whether a person was "our" kind of writer. Occasionally even someone with ties to the group would fall short and be pushed to the fringes.[52]

A group that could exclude could also include and protect. The New York circle provided some with a social identity; it offered all a definite and distinctive context for intellectual work. *Partisan Review* gave the writers in its camp a secure outlet to the world, an increasingly prestigious place to publish, and a pathway to other opportunities. When books by members of the magazine's circle appeared, they were generally greeted in *Partisan Review* with a serious, carefully critical, and distinctly friendly reception. Reviewers in these situations were chosen carefully. In the occasional instance when the review produced was clearly negative, it might even be rejected and a more positive one prepared. Such was the case when Lionel Trilling's *Matthew Arnold* was treated roughly by its assigned reviewer; the piece was withdrawn and William Phillips took over the task, delivering a friendlier and, in this case, probably a fairer review.[53]

The *Partisan Review* circle was a haven and a support. From the time it came into being in 1937, it served to assure many of its members that they were not alone in the world, that sympathetic intellectuals existed in sufficient number to provide them with social and professional moorings. Individual situations varied, but many of the *Partisan* writers shared experiences that underlined the need for mutual reinforcement. The New York Intellectuals showed themselves much concerned in the 1940s with questions of isolation, homelessness, and separation from the mass. All the while, midst storm and strife, they were tolerably pleased with the comfort, support, and stimulation they gained from one another.

Chapter Ten	A Tolerable Place to Live

Between the early 1930s and the end of the 1940s, a majority of the New York Intellectuals made the political trek from self-conscious radicalism to Cold War liberalism. The early positions —whether Communist, Trotskyist, or other—shared a faith in socialism and a harsh critique of capitalist society; the positions of the fifties had in common a sharp hostility to the Soviet Union and (in general and with qualifications) a positive attitude toward the United States of America. The shift was not a matter of sudden conversion but of gradual migration. Few in the *Partisan Review* circle fit the image of the transformed radical who became in the fifties a raging conservative or a professional ex-Communist.[1] Many, in fact, demonstrated a considerable consistency in values and intellectual loyalties even as their attitudes toward American society underwent an apparent transformation. To stress this continuity is not to deny the political shift, but to suggest a context within which it can be better understood.

Some explanations would place the course taken by the New York Intellectuals within a very general pattern. Youth is idealistic and subject to fits of rebellion, a familiar argument holds, while age brings a greater acceptance of the world. Exile leads logically to return, rebellion to later acceptance. Such an explanation is not without its appeal, but the temptation to embrace this established model must be held at bay. The notion that rebellion is cured by age robs radicalism of its power and significance; an assumption that exile precedes integration saps the meaning from exclusion and isolation. In their very generality, moreover, such ideas fail to say much about specific historical situations or particular people; the pattern invites assertion: it does not encourage investigation.

Two other general explanations for the political shift in the *Partisan Review* camp point toward more substantial encounters with a distinct historical experience. One would underscore the importance of national and international events, making shifts in political perspective a reasoned response to a changing world. The other would emphasize the acquisition of property and status, asserting that a capitalist America became increasingly attractive to writers on the make. Both of these explanations are too narrow in themselves, but each may reasonably contribute to a more complex account.

Between 1930 and 1945 young intellectuals were forced to confront a series of events that pushed and tugged at their ideas and values from several directions. The depression threatened frustration for a whole generation of young people trying to begin adult careers. Personal experience made it easy to believe that capitalism in general had failed, that the economic collapse represented the unraveling of a whole system. Those with a literary bent, already steeped in a critique of commercialism and business civilization, were particularly prone to adopt the language of radicalism to carry that critique to a new level and to celebrate the downfall of Babbittry. Individual and social ambitions, attraction to the explanatory power of Marxism, a humane response to the depression's effects, sensitivity to questions of prejudice and discrimination, and the values associated with literary sophistication all seemed to push young intellectuals toward the adoption of a radical political posture in the 1930s.

The rise of National Socialism in Germany pressed intellectuals to come to terms with a horrific politics and an ever more ominous series of events. At first fascism served only to strengthen the appeal of the left; yet Hitler stirred up sensitivities among the New York Intellectuals that ultimately contributed to the disintegration of their radicalism. Nazism helped create a heightened awareness at the first *Partisan Review* of attitudes, ideas, and values that the editors saw as regressive. The increasing use of terms associated with fascism to develop a critique of the Communist Party marked Phillips's and Rahv's pathway toward an anti-Stalinist position. Moreover, fascism drew attention to the dangers of a highly centralized and dictatorial government, to the dark possibilities of mass parties and movements, to the repressions of a closed system, in ways that could not ultimately flatter Stalin and the Soviet Union. Indeed, the regimes of Hitler and Stalin gradually came to be joined in the concept of totalitarianism. In moving toward greater acceptance of existing political arrangements in the United States, the New York Intellectuals were in part recognizing their own government's importance in resisting both Hitler and Stalin.

When *Partisan Review* turned against the Communist Party in 1937, it did not abandon radical politics but took up an independent radical position leaning heavily toward Trotsky—a position regarded at the time as a break to the left. Yet the example of the Soviet Union continued to weigh heavily on all radical thought, and for most of the New York Intellectuals the road to the left led back eventually toward the center. The Soviet example posed a number of difficult questions that many found it enervating even to consider. Was Soviet communism a natural and logical outcome of Marxism? Did the socialist vision necessarily point toward a "totalitarian" state? Did Stalinism make belief in the original promise of the Russian Revolution impossible? Were all ideological commitments dangerous? The *Partisan Review* intellectuals for the most part answered these questions in the negative before 1945, and some continued to do so thereafter, but the need to answer them at all revealed a radicalism on the defensive, drained of its positive energies. Interest in socialism simply began to "wither away," according to William Phillips, and gradually it came to be assumed "that the verdict of history was in—against socialism."[2]

Partisan Review's hostility toward the Communist Party grew out of a cumulative experience. If the break in 1937 was not quite the example of fierce courage and pure principle that the legend upholds, it was an act that did require a considerable amount of nerve and one that was rooted in a solid allegiance to intellectual and cultural values. The Communist Party did indeed try to repress its opponents; it did make its cultural policies the tail on a political dog that changed directions regularly; it did demand that the actions of the Soviet Union be weighed on a different scale from those of other nations, if they were weighed at all. The *Partisan Review* intellectuals confronted the implications of the Moscow Trials and the Popular Front at a time when most writers on the left did not; they upheld the belief that critical thought must be directed toward all systems and ideas, even if their practice was imperfect.[3] One need not defend the later tendency among many New York Intellectuals to press the anti-Stalinist campaign when Communist-baiting had become something of a national sport in order to believe that the migration away from Stalinism and toward greater acceptance of America was a reasonable and intellectually consistent response to domestic and international events.

It is possible, then, to explain *Partisan Review's* course as a series of reactions to the momentous historical developments of its formative period. In considering the magazine within this context, arguments implying that its editors and supporters were more intelligent and virtuous at one time than another fall flat. The assumption that during their radical years the New York Intellectuals were truants or callow youths who came to their senses only when they got an early start on the Cold War carries no more weight than the belief that they were courageous and insightful radicals in the thirties who lost all integrity and judgment when they discovered substantial merit in the American system. An explanation from events suggests that it made about an equal amount of sense for the *Partisan Review* writers to embrace radicalism and to let it go, regardless of later feelings about those decisions. A similar conclusion might be reached after looking at the case for the influence of prosperity and status.

The argument that the New York Intellectuals turned away from radicalism when they began to prosper in the forties may carry a good deal of credibility. Who, after all, would deny the power of self-interest? And who would argue that prosperity and growing recognition are true friends of radicalism? The United States after 1940 was a country on its way toward a long economic boom. Although this future was not always obvious along the way, and although writers and intellectuals experienced no sudden rush to wealth, economic recovery and expansion opened up an ever wider set of opportunities that brought benefits trickling into the lives of most. The gains were hardly overwhelming by the standards that would be established in coming years, but then it did not take much to give someone who had been on the Federal Writers' Project a sense of greater well-being.

Money was seldom the direct measure of this growing success. Although Philip Rahv had married a woman of means in 1940, he was clearly delighted to be paid $125 a month to write a column for the *American Mercury* in 1943. Rahv had nothing against money, yet he probably treasured the recognition and the sense of an expanding cultural purview even more.[4] The New York Intellectuals were beginning to be acknowledged for their work and employed to continue it. Academic jobs opened up for some in the forties: F. W. Dupee went permanently into university teaching; Delmore Schwartz did so fitfully; others, including William Phillips, had their hopes.[5] Novels, stories, and poems appeared from many to whom the *Partisan Review* circle could lay some claim: Delmore Schwartz, Saul Bellow, Mary McCarthy, Elizabeth Hardwick, Isaac Rosenfeld, Paul Goodman, Harold Rosenberg, and even Lionel Trilling. Trilling was rapidly becoming a leading critic, and Alfred Kazin had made an impressive start with *On Native Grounds*. The New York Intellectuals during the forties were clearly beginning to benefit from the network they had created around *Partisan Review* as individual accomplishments and the successes of the magazine fed each other in a process that pushed ahead the whole group's reputation.

As a general proposition, then, it might be only reasonable to suggest that a trend toward increasing opportunity, recognition, and reward made it considerably easier for the New York Intellectuals to find something good about American society. Yet any attempt to tie this improving status to specific stages in the drift away from radicalism quickly runs into trouble. Such explanations also flounder when they imply a moral failing. If a responsiveness to economic pressures, an alertness to professional opportunities, and a pattern of changing political views add up to a moral failing, then such a failing existed at the time the New York group took up radical politics as much as at the time their radicalism weakened.

Either an explanation from events or an explanation from self-interest can tell only part of the story behind *Partisan Review*'s changing attitude toward American society. Both explanations assume too narrow a range of human motivation, and neither gives sufficient attention to particular ideas and values. For the *Partisan Review* circle, the conception of themselves as intellectuals mattered a great deal. Ideas were important to them. If they were sometimes subject to intellectual fads, if they felt the breezes of international politics and tasted the first fruits of a ripening success, they did not cast aside their basic values in a headlong rush toward the attractions of the moment. The more significant changes in attitude that did occur had to be justified, at least to themselves, in terms consistent with ongoing commitments and loyalties. This was true for the break with the Communist Party in 1937, and it was true for the increasing receptiveness toward America in the 1940s.

The nature of *Partisan Review*'s early critique of American culture deserves another look. Harsh words were directed toward what the United States presently was, not toward its inherent potential. Even before 1937, Phillips and Rahv had found reason for optimism in American conditions; and despite a sincere radicalism, many of *Partisan Review*'s complaints rested on values and goals that were not inherently radical. American culture was attacked in the 1930s because it was parochial, because it carried a strong strain of nativism, because it seemed limited by a rural mentality, because it was hostile to ideas; in short, because it did not measure up at all well by cosmopolitan standards. The vision of an integrated society welcoming diversity and encouraging a sophisticated art was the goal embodied in the idea of synthesis, and it provided an effective critical platform. But there was, from the start, plenty of room short of that goal for the image of a parochial American society to change. When in the early 1940s America began to look better to the New York Intellectuals, it was not simply because their viewpoint was changing but because the national culture was changing as well.

Daniel Aaron has written that "The Jewish intellectual's disenchantment with the Soviets . . . happened to coincide with a small but perceptible lessening of discriminatory practices and the opening of opportunities in letters, the arts, and education."[6] Just at the time the *Partisan Review* intellectuals were losing any solid base in a radical movement, in other words, American society was moving slowly toward that tolerance of ethnic diversity which was basic to cosmopolitanism. Few could have anticipated the scope of the changes that would come. The decline in discrimination began at a time when anti-Semitism was highly visible in its most virulent forms, and the widespread collapse of that prejudice in the postwar period was, as John Higham has noted, "totally unforeseen by the social science of the 1940s and 1950s." Yet Higham has pointed out as well that anti-Semitic agitation from the late thirties on was "more than counter-balanced by the rise of the broadest, most powerful movement for ethnic democracy in American history."[7] Jewish intellectuals were a part of this movement, and they knew they were not alone in opposing discrimination. No one would have claimed that a full acceptance of diversity had arrived, but cosmopolitan values did seem to be gaining strength in American culture.

The changing ethos in many universities required the New York Intellectuals to modify one of the favorite negative presumptions of the literary radical tradition—the prejudice against the academic. The "academic" had generally been associated with writing that was by definition dry and dull, that failed to engage the vital ideas of the present, and that was unbearably conservative either by intent or through lack of imagination. In the first *Partisan Review*, Phillips and Rahv had spoken of academic writing as "not so much a quality of style as a content marginal to important literary problems: a pedantic treatment of minor ideas with the emphasis placed on 'data' rather than on analysis."[8] Moreover, the academy had seemed a bastion of genteel parochialism.

Change came to academia in the 1940s for many reasons. A generation of immigrant children was coming to full intellectual maturity. World War II played havoc with the normal enrollments, courses, and student bodies at many universities. In the postwar period veterans' benefits and other forces fed a major expansion of higher education, opening up jobs for a wider range of faculty in an increasing number of specialties. As many of the New York Intellectuals began to gravitate toward the universities, they not only helped to change the academic environment by their presence but also learned through direct contact that all was not as bleak as it had seemed. Irving Howe later remarked that the group had "discovered that scholarship could have a value and dignity of its own, and that if there were professors—good lord, plenty of them!—as small-minded and arid as we had supposed, others really cared about ideas and possessed a quiet learning that made our own absorption in the contemporary seem provincial."[9] As the universities came to seem more diverse and enlightened, the idea that American culture was dominated by a parochial tradition had to give way at the very least to a more complex view. There was room in America, it seemed, for intellectual sophistication and variety. How else could the New York Intellectuals explain their own growing success, or that of *Partisan Review*?

American society also gained credibility simply by surviving depression and war roughly intact. That was not what radical doctrine had predicted. Capitalism was supposed to die in the depression; governments were expected to fall; a capitalist democracy could not fight a war against fascism without becoming fascist itself. As such predictions fell flat, radicalism seemed increasingly tired, unable to generate a significant body of work in either literature or social thought.[10] Even those who continued to call themselves radicals found it hard to deny that American society had demonstrated an unexpected vitality.

The increased consciousness of civil liberties brought about by Hitler and Stalin did much to alter *Partisan Review*'s negative judgment of American conditions. True socialism, as the New York Intellectuals understood it, promised an invigoration of intellectual life, an opening up of culture to a larger audience, and the free circulation of ideas. Stalinism had demonstrated how thoroughly this vision could be corrupted and how easily cultural life could be restricted in the name of radicalism. Hitler, meanwhile, had brought under attack some of the most basic values of modern thought and demonstrated the consequences that a denial of civil liberties might

257

have, especially for Jews. Having assumed from the start the desirability and the prevalence of civil liberties and rational public discussion, the New York Intellectuals were forced by the late 1930s to conclude that such things were hardly secure. The same American society that had seemed a corrupting environment for intellectual life in the early thirties was beginning to look like the best the world had to offer a decade later. Despite a marked sensitivity around *Partisan Review* to restrictions on speech or political opinion during World War II, what seemed most impressive over time was that the United States went through the war with liberties largely preserved.

Philip Rahv observed after the war that "in America we are in an especially favorable position" to oppose the antics of reactionaries, "since the American concept of nationality is built on political rather than on ethnic or religious foundations." Like Randolph Bourne, Rahv apparently believed that cultural and political loyalties could be separated, and he wished to emphasize the virtues of a concept of nationality "political to the core."[11] In the American case, this seemed a guarantee of diversity. The sense of a provincial, nativist cultural tradition suffocating intellectual life had been substantially modified in Rahv's view.

Behind Rahv's cautiously positive evaluation of the American scene lay a whole set of changing conditions that made not only the national setting but also the immediate cultural prospects more attractive to the New York Intellectuals. Some of these changes were difficult to measure or define in precise terms, but they were nevertheless clearly felt. Irving Howe has recalled, for instance, that during the forties there was "a change of style and tone in the life of the New York middle class. . . . Culture was coming into fashion as a sign of a more comfortable and refined mode of living."[12] The New York Intellectuals told themselves as well that the prestige of business had been dealt a serious (not crippling) blow by the depression, allowing a greater variety of influences to have some impact. Echoes of a notion that cultural power would accompany American political power after the war also surfaced occasionally in *Partisan Review*, providing additional, if vague, reason for optimism about the future of intellectuals in America.

The New York Intellectuals were themselves making a respectable contribution to a longterm shift in the cultural climate. Under way since the late nineteenth century, the gradual American growth from provincialism toward equivalency with European cultures reached fruition in the 1940s. William Phillips recognized the trend shortly after the birth of *Partisan Review* when he acknowledged the "cosmopolitanization" of American culture achieved in the 1920s. Rahv and Phillips sought to continue the process when they urged "Europeanization" in the mid-1930s. *Partisan Review* promoted in particular the ideas of Marx and Freud, the works of modern literature, an interest in European politics, and a consciousness of postwar movements, including existentialism. The New York Intellectuals helped to create an awareness of European ideas in America just as they brought American intellectual life to the attention of Europeans.

Even as the *Partisan Review* circle was doing its bit to make American culture more cosmopolitan, major forces were at work toward the same end. Thanks primarily to Hitler, a remarkable flood of scientists, artists, musicians, philosophers, writers, and political theorists crossed the Atlantic to enrich the life of the new world. H. Stuart Hughes has called this migration "the most important cultural event—or series of events—of the second quarter of the twentieth century"; it produced a "shift in intellectual weight that made the former pattern of deference toward the Old World no longer necessary or appropriate." Two-thirds of the intellectual migrants were Jewish.[13] The United States was serving as a haven for a European intellectual elite, and in the process American culture was gaining that equivalency with Europe that had long been a dream. The New York Intellectuals were far from insensitive to such changes.

Indeed, the increasing intellectual prominence of America was concentrated and even exaggerated for many members of the *Partisan Review* circle by the transformations in their immediate environment. Generally preoccupied with New York and convinced that the city represented the American cultural future, they gave singular attention to New York's status in national and world affairs. Already a city of international significance, New York grew in stature in the 1940s both because of domestic trends and because of the influx of intellectual immigrants. Yet what changed New York's *international* position most dramatically was the crippling of European centers by the war. New York seemed to shine more brightly as the lights of its rivals were obscured.

In commentaries on the fate of European culture, Paris received special attention. Paris was "the 'eye' of modern European civilization," the editorial column of *Partisan Review* noted in 1939. Central to developments in politics as well as in the arts for more than a century, Paris was "the expression of the best integrated culture of modern times," a culture now under serious threat.[14] A year and a half later, Paris had indeed fallen to fascism. Harold Rosenberg gave vivid expression to the sense of intellectual loss in the opening sentence of his obituary essay: "The laboratory of the twentieth century has been shut down." The culture of Paris had been international, and Rosenberg proclaimed its contribution in emphatically cosmopolitan terms: "Because Paris was the opposite of the national in art, the art of every nation increased through Paris. No folk lost its integrity there; on the contrary, its artists, renewed by this magnanimous milieu, discovered in the depths of themselves what was most alive in the communities from which they had come." Paris had seemed to embody the intellectual and cultural values most precious to the New York Intellectuals, and its loss added to the feeling at the dawn of the forties that the best traditions of Western civilization were under siege.

But was there not a ray of hope? Might not another city play the role in the future that Paris had played in the past? Rosenberg was cautious in declaring at the end of his essay, "No one can predict which city or nation will be the center of this new phase"; yet the effect of this statement was to focus attention exactly on the question of what new center of cultural and political ideas might arise. Rosenberg's analysis seemed to offer clues. Paris had risen "not because of its affirmative genius alone, but perhaps, on the contrary, through its passivity, which allowed it to be possessed by the searchers of every nation." (In what country was there a city relatively free of an oppressive national tradition and possessed by peoples of many lands?) Again, Rosenberg insisted that an international center could not rise "by its own genius alone" but only as a result of "currents flowing throughout the world." (And where were such powerful currents depositing migratory intellectuals in the 1940s?) Rosenberg spoke directly only once. From the anti-Stalinist viewpoint, the response of the "Paris Left" to the events of the late 1930s had demonstrated an abandonment of intellectual principles. It was in another country that the best traditions of modern intellectual life had been upheld: "during the Moscow Trials we learned with surprise and alarm that it was here, in America! that the greatest opposition to the criminal burlesque was being voiced." Rosenberg's analysis seemed to suggest on each of these points that Paris might well be replaced as the leading center of intellectual life in the West by his own New York—New York, which had long been open to the people of many nations and subject to their influence; New

York, which was a magnet for Europe's intellectual refugees; New York, which had led the opposition to the Moscow Trials.[15]

The New York Intellectuals' "surprise" that France should fail the intellectual tests of the thirties and that America should pass them suggested a repetition in the *Partisan Review* circle of what was becoming a familiar pattern. Writers of the twenties, in going to Europe, had often discovered America. So too, the New York Intellectuals, in their attentiveness to European cultural developments, found that America measured up surprisingly well. At a personal level, contact with European intellectuals who came to New York tended not only to boost the confidence of the *Partisan Review* circle but also to remind its members, through differences of manners and tastes, of just how American they were.[16] When after the war some of the younger New York Intellectuals began to go to Europe for extended visits, testimony on the surprising discovery in oneself of a strong American identity, sparking a new interest in American culture, became a common form.[17]

In trying to explain the development of a more positive attitude toward American society and culture among the New York Intellectuals, then, movements occurring on two fronts must be kept in mind. Many intellectuals were shifting ground in their views of the American environment; the environment was also changing and moving in a direction that made it more attractive to the *Partisan Review* circle. The two processes were intertwined and mutually reinforcing. Sharply conscious of "the sudden emergence of America as the repository of Western culture in a world overrun by Fascism," the New York Intellectuals harkened well to the appeal of what Alfred Kazin called in 1942 "the pride of helping to breed a new cosmopolitan culture."[18]

By no means all of the New York Intellectuals rushed to embrace America in the 1940s, but many were increasingly ready to see the United States as the chief defender of the cultural traditions they treasured and as the strongest proponent of those civil liberties on which freedom of thought must rest. New York—their city —had become the center of American culture, and it seemed for a moment to be just possibly the next great center of Western civilization. This did not mean that the old literary radical dream of a sophisticated and well-integrated culture had come to pass, but it did mean that the dream was passing. The growing belief that American culture had gained equivalency in the contemporary world with the cultures of Europe, and the evidence that a cosmopolitan society was now emerging, took much of the edge off a vigorous tradition of cultural complaint.

The conditions of the 1940s that had given New York its special prominence proved in time to be a passing thing. European cities recovered from the war and re-established their cultural importance, though none could claim the dominance of an earlier Paris. Within the United States institutions of learning and the arts flourished in a number of cities, bringing about a decentralization of high culture over a period of two or three decades. The New York Intellectuals themselves were a part of this process. Though many clung to familiar turf, others heeded the call of universities and migrated North and West. The national and international forces that had helped to create the New York of the forties later worked to diminish that city's supremacy.

As the patterns growing out of World War II gradually broke down the physical unity of the New York Intellectuals, the political and cultural issues of the postwar period led to division of another kind. Continuing agreement on opposition to Stalinism and the Soviet Union meant less and less once those attitudes had become the norm. The New York camp found itself more and more divided over just how eagerly Cold War policies should be embraced, over just how far the critique of liberalism should go, and especially over just how much of a threat domestic communism posed. These later divisions make the early to middle forties a time in between. The New York Intellectuals were carrying on a balancing act in these years. Still very much attached to ideas and values brought with them out of the thirties, they were nevertheless aware of new possibilities. Having been in their own eyes an embattled minority, they were on their way to becoming in the eyes of others an "establishment." It was a time when tensions and ambiguities in the outlook of the New York Intellectuals ripened within forms both old and new.

The need to balance ideas and loyalties that were not in natural harmony had been evident from the first. The young *Partisan Review* intellectuals sought to combine within some broader vision a commitment to a sophisticated literature and an interest in radical politics; a loyalty to rational, scientific thought and a belief in the powers of artistic insight; a sense of themselves as Jews (in the majority of cases) and an identity as Americans. Though the balancing of such ideas went on with varying degrees of success, claims of synthesis achieved did not dominate their thought so much as consciousness of the oppositions in art and experience. This was true of the mature criticism of the New York Intellectuals as much as it was true of their youth, and it applied whether the discussion was of doubling or the dialectic, of repression or negation.[19] In the forties, as new wine began to mingle with old among the New York Intellectuals, some of the vessels designed to balance the ferment of ideas proved supple and equal to the task; others began to split at the seams.

One of the most successful devices for the containment of opposing ideas was the concept of alienation. The idea offered sweeping explanatory powers: alienation provided a general theory purporting to deal with great chunks of modern experience, and at the same time it invited application to the details of individual existence. In the New York camp, it furnished an umbrella under which discussion from either a Marxist or a Freudian perspective might take place, probably blurring the lines between them and allowing some to migrate more easily from one to the other. Both society and art could be discussed in the language of alienation, preserving the belief that politics and literature could be dealt with from a unified perspective. Discussions of alienation might be hardheaded and rationalistic in tone, or they might involve a rather romantic treatment of the loneliness of the modern artist. Alienation allowed New York writers to indulge both the penchant for finding world-historical significance in their own experience and the taste for abstract theoretical debate. The concept of alienation seemed to provide the New York intellectuals with both power and flexibility in ideas, the combination they had consistently sought.

That was not the end of it. With its claim that existing institutions had not earned the intellectual's support—indeed, had pushed him away—the idea of alienation provided a ready justification for standing apart. The writer could declare himself alienated from America, from Jewish culture, from the war, or from radical politics with equal facility, using the concept as selectively as he wished. Yet the whole idea suggested not some simple escape but a conscious effort to come to grips with problems of both politics and culture. To call oneself "alienated" was to suggest a heightened awareness, to imply a sophisticated analysis of one's social and intellectual position that was the first step toward solving the problems that had created alienation. The alienated were thus superior to the well-adjusted; they could even be an intellectual elite and a cultural avant-garde. By the 1940s, for the most part, the New York Intellectuals had given up the notion that the moment for

radical synthesis was at hand; but through the concept of alienation, they continued not just to condemn the inadequacies of established society but to make the implicit claim that the future
belonged to them.

Alienation, as the idea was used by the New York Intellectuals,
was not the same thing as true isolation from society or total rejection of it. The alienated could live neither with existing culture
nor without it. This relationship of awkward dependency lay at the
root of Isaac Rosenfeld's lovely paradoxes: the outsider was sometimes the "perfect insider," and alienation from society could function "as a condition of entrance into society." Like the claims of
writers in the 1920s that they were a lost generation, the declarations by the New York Intellectuals that they were alienated represented both a serious idea and a conscious pose. The language of
alienation allowed the New York Intellectuals to have it both ways:
they could continue to think of themselves as outsiders and radicals even as they began to experience intellectual, political, and
economic integration into American society. It was not at all clear
in the 1940s whether this integrating process would continue; the
concept of alienation helped the New York intellectuals maintain
a certain distance in a period of flux and kept their options open.

Even in the heyday of alienation, what remained basic to many
of the New York Intellectuals' judgments were those cosmopolitan
values that had also stood behind their Marxism in the thirties.
(The writer was alienated in part because the society fell short of
the cosmopolitan community that would make him feel at home.)
This cosmopolitan perspective continued to give the New York Intellectuals some sense of common values and some of their critical bite. Yet the years of hot and cold war revealed limitations as
well as strengths—weaknesses in the cosmopolitan viewpoint itself and in the New York Intellectuals' ability to abide by its tenets.

Tension between principle and practice emerged, for example,
over matters of intellectual and political tolerance. Cosmopolitanism assumed a context within which a free exchange of ideas was
the norm; and *Partisan Review* had generally defended the principles of openness and diversity, first within the Communist Party
and later against the repressive tendencies of both fascism and Stalinism. Even as the editors of *Partisan Review* split over the proper
attitude to take toward World War II, they were able to agree that
the magazine's main task must be "to preserve cultural values
against all types of pressure and coercion," which meant a defense
of "the fullest freedom of expression on political matters."[20]

Yet there was a contrary pattern as well. In their actual political commitments and in their stance toward opponents of varying stripes, the New York Intellectuals often revealed an outlook not so much pluralistic as Manichean. They seemed happiest when presenting political issues as a struggle between the forces of light and the forces of darkness. Before 1937 *Partisan Review* divided the world primarily between radicalism and reaction. In the late 1930s, the forces of light dwindled to the limited circle of the anti-Stalinist left. During the war — or afterward for some — the United States became the chief defender of political good, and evil was increasingly embodied in a Janus-faced totalitarianism looking to both right and left. The emphatic, emotionally charged, often moralistic positions that the New York Intellectuals established, and the tendency to identify their own views with fundamental intellectual integrity, worked against the commitment to openness and free thought proclaimed in their public statements and implicit in their attachment to cosmopolitan values.

The multiple pressures of the early 1940s pushed to the fore a growing contradiction in the way the New York Intellectuals saw themselves. The pages of *Partisan Review* tended to convey an image of rebel intellectuals defending a minority position and upholding the best traditions of radicalism. In 1942 the editors launched a column called "Dangerous Thoughts" with the presumption that an open intellectual forum would, in itself, help to sustain "democratic civilization" and threaten repressive power.[21] In 1944 Philip Rahv put the magazine on the side of "cultural bolshevism" and reminded readers of its opposition to the "world-wide campaign . . . against all cultural forms of dissidence and experiment."[22] The New York Intellectuals continued in the 1940s to see themselves as dissenters and to emphasize the importance of a wide latitude for ideas. Yet this same group had begun to convey a different message based on a different self-perception. Unrelenting in their opposition to the Communist Party and its liberal sympathizers, the New York Intellectuals moved in the 1940s toward ever fiercer condemnation. Angered by the news of Trotsky's death in 1940, William Phillips wrote that "some kind of moral and intellectual pogrom should be started against the Stalinists." Philip Rahv suggested in mid-war that a particular opponent was "really getting out of bounds and should be stepped on." Sidney Hook called in 1945 for *Partisan Review* to "meet the challenge of Stalinist totalitarianism head-on and plan for concentrated fire in each issue on some phase or other of the theme."[23] None of these remarks clearly called for repressive measures, and all might be individually explained as demands for a kind of vigorous intellectual attack not incompatible with the notion of full and free expression; yet such comments reflected a desire not simply to refute opponents but to discipline and subdue them that had little to do with cosmopolitan tolerance.

The language of pogroms and concentrated fire did not suggest activities to be undertaken by a dissident minority but the campaigns of a group with considerable intellectual power. Even as they cultivated the image of radical dissenters, some in the *Partisan Review* circle were beginning to feel their oats and to enjoy the fact that in their relations with the Stalinist intellectuals, they were now on top. The tensions between a pluralistic and a dualistic view of politics, between a belief in tolerance and a desire to push political opponents beyond the pale, and between the image of themselves as a rebellious minority and the willingness to speak like cultural and political enforcers testified to the difficulties the New York Intellectuals met in trying to maintain a coherent intellectual position against the corroding effects of their own illiberal impulses. Values consistent with cosmopolitanism remained dominant in the war years, but evidence was already appearing that the language of diversity, free expression, and tolerance might all too easily survive while the spirit behind it decayed. When the defense of an open society began to grow for some into a rationale for repression, cosmopolitan values were being perverted, not fulfilled.

The New York Intellectuals fell short of their own ideal in another sphere as well. Secure in the worldiness and breadth of their own urban perspective, members of the *Partisan Review* circle remained largely insensitive to the possibility that they were nourishing a parochialism of their own. Quick to condemn the narrowness of other American viewpoints, they refused to credit the evidence that New York for all its varied life was a province with its own limitations. Attacks on *Partisan Review* and its supporters —whether launched by midwestern radicals in the thirties or rival literary critics in the forties—were often exaggerated and unfair, but they were usually rooted in a legitimate resentment of the New Yorkers' assumption that they held a monopoly on intellectual sophistication. If the attitude of the New York Intellectuals mellowed with time and their own dispersion, the feelings expressed all too vigorously by Philip Rahv in the early 1940s never quite went away:

If you lived in Chicago for a while you'd realize the importance of PR: it's like an island of culture in an ocean of barbarism. In New York our friends no less than we tend to take the magazine too much for granted; once, however, you step out of the charmed circle it comes to you as a revelation that this little magazine is in fact the only decent organ of American writing today. (And don't tell me about the Kenyon Review and the Southern Review!)[24]

This extravagant assertion had little in common with a spirit of cultural openness and receptivity.

It was not merely that on this occasion or that one the New York Intellectuals failed to show respect for ideas and traditions running counter to their own. It was not simply that they sometimes fell short of the cosmopolitan ideal. Rather, they had a blind spot, a deep-seated prejudice, built into their very notion of cosmopolitanism. And in this case the problem was not theirs alone but part of a whole inheritance. The assumption that rural America and its traditions were hostile to intelligence, rationality, and sophistication had become a critical commonplace by the nineteen twenties, just in time for the older New York Intellectuals to imbibe it with their first long draught of literary ale. In the thirties, the sense of a great gulf between the urban and the rural intensified within the *Partisan Review* camp: the rural was now associated with nativism, anti-Semitism, nationalism, and fascism as well as with anti-intellectualism and provincialism; the urban was associated antithetically with ethnic and cultural tolerance, with internationalism, and with advanced ideas. New York as the largest city, the most open and diverse, was presumed to be the most distant from rural norms. The New York Intellectuals simply *began* with the assumption that the rural—with which they associated much of American tradition and most of the territory beyond New York—had little to contribute to a cosmopolitan culture.

Such a view closed the minds of the *Partisan Review* circle on too many questions and cut off that searching inquiry and rich borrowing of ideas that should have been a cosmopolitan strength. The New York Intellectuals, for example, could never get past their negative assumptions about the native radical tradition in order to see it clearly; because it was rural, it simply must be narrow and reactionary. It was no accident that members of the New York group later associated McCarthyism with populism in the expectation that each would discredit the other. Populism meant rural anti-intellectualism and nativist prejudice to *Partisan Review* from the beginning, and those things were what many feared in McCarthyism. Though they might disagree emphatically over the need for a domestic security campaign in the early 1950s, few of the New York Intellectuals were immune to the pleasures of distinguishing between their own sophisticated anti-communism and the crude rural variety of McCarthy and his kind. Defining the issues in this way reaffirmed standing cultural assumptions. At the same time, it provided a convenient shelter within which a good many intellectuals could avoid reconsideration of their own attacks on "totalitarian liberals" and the like. By interpreting cultural and political issues through the urban-rural lens, writers could even mask assertions of superiority and expressions of anti-democratic sentiments as the judgments of an objective expertise.[25] Invidious distinctions between urban and rural were so familiar to a wide intellectual audience that few questioned them or challenged their implications.

If there were failures to fulfill the ideals of tolerance, openness, and full inquiry, there was also a weakness at the heart of cosmopolitan theory. The notion of a cosmopolitan culture assumed that it would be continually enriched by contributions from people of different national and ethnic traditions. When Randolph Bourne was writing about trans-nationalism and when *Partisan Review* was getting under way in the thirties, there seemed little reason to doubt the existence or the strength of multiple cultures within the United States. In the years following World War II, however, after two or three decades with immigration much reduced and assimilation proceeding apace, the question could be asked of those taking a cosmopolitan position: what will preserve the ongoing vitality of those particularistic cultures on which cosmopolitanism draws? The New York Intellectuals were vulnerable on this point when it came to discussions of Jewish identity in the 1940s. The position defined by Bourne had tried to stake out a territory between assimilation and cultural pluralism; yet in the absence of strong ethnic enclaves, a cosmopolitan position would rapidly become the equivalent of an assimilationist stance, leading toward that drabness and lack of variety that Bourne abhorred. It gradually became apparent in the postwar period that, as an understanding of the place of ethnicity, the cosmopolitanism of the New York Intellectuals could remain viable only if a good many people rejected it.

For all that can be said about the limitations of the New York Intellectual brand of cosmopolitanism—whether those limitations were inherent in the perspective itself or products of an imperfect application of it—the ideas that came out of the *Partisan Review* circle formed one of the richer patterns in American culture during the late 1930s and the 1940s. There was a spirit of serious intellectual aspiration around the magazine that refused to be stifled, and there was serious accomplishment. If the editors and their associates sometimes fell short of their own ideals, they also managed to embody those ideals and to give them life in one campaign after another. The values of cosmopolitanism were generous ones, and ones to which the *Partisan Review* intellectuals clung with more than customary consistency and integrity. In their finer moments, they stood as an American presence speaking out against narrowness, confinement, dogma, and fraud. And it was especially at such moments that they gave substance and meaning to the fundamental impulses of the cosmopolitan vision.

Epilogue

Between 1934 and 1945, the circle of writers and critics associated with *Partisan Review* established a collective presence in American intellectual life that made their ideas and experiences a center of discussion in the postwar period. During these years — for all the individual variations that might be noted — a set of interrelated goals, assumptions, and biases gave particular character and special flavor to the work of the *Partisan Review* intellectuals. Now, as the magazine moved into its period of greatest fame, the hopes and commitments that had their common foundation in a loyalty to cosmopolitan values were noticeably fading; and the political, cultural, and social campaigns tied up with the magazine's history and identity were losing much of their intellectual power and urgency.

In politics, with anti-Stalinism becoming a national sentiment after 1945, *Partisan Review* spoke more often in the voice of habit and fixed opinion than in a spirit of fresh analysis. In culture, the vitality and sense of mission spun off in earlier years by the vision of a new literature survived in no recognizable form, and vehemence in defending high culture seemed increasingly less necessary. By 1952 the editors of *Partisan Review* were declaring without hesitation that "most writers no longer accept alienation as the artist's fate in America," suggesting a transformation in the magazine's view of the society. Philip Rahv noted the postwar "*embourgeoisement* of the American intelligentsia"; and a later critic detected a "massive embourgeoisement of Jews in America" by the same period.[1]

What all of this meant was that the abundant vitality and ambition of *Partisan Review*'s early years were being fenced in and domesticated by pressures from at least two directions. On one side, the collapse of exalted hopes for radicalism and for literature crushed the more speculative, aspiring, forward-looking projections of *Partisan Review*'s cosmopolitanism from which so much critical energy

270

had flowed. On the other, the force of an increasingly prosperous, internationalized, and less discriminatory culture sapped the strength of cosmopolitan critique by diminishing the grounds for complaint, especially among intellectuals. Cosmopolitan values remained significant, but their significance was now moderated, confined, tamed into a defense of virtues newly discovered or comforts recently gained. Once an engine of rebellion, cosmopolitanism was now a settled tradition.

A positive commitment to cosmopolitan values had provided a reservoir of affirmation behind the attacks and the oppositional campaigns of *Partisan Review*'s early history. As the meaning of that commitment narrowed in the postwar years, negativity was too often left holding the field alone. Philip Rahv recognized as much when he contrasted the "old anti-Stalinism" of the late 1930s and early 1940s with the postwar variety that had "lost its bearings" and begun to mouth its denunciatory politics with a "deadly sameness." Effective opposition to Communist ideology, Rahv insisted, must proceed from "more enlightened assumptions" and "with positive ends in view."[2] Daniel Bell, too, was eventually troubled by the "exhaustion of political ideas in the fifties"; even as he spoke favorably of "The End of Ideology in the West," Bell pointed to the need to "begin anew the discussion of utopia." There was "now, more than ever," according to Bell, "some need for utopia, in the sense that men need . . . some vision of their potential, some manner of fusing passion with intelligence."[3] Neither Bell nor Rahv suggested any second thoughts about the cut of his politics, yet both acknowledged that postwar thought lacked a vitality and balance that were much to be desired.

Such qualities had lived for a time in the youthful *Partisan Review*. Postwar intellectuals often seemed to be trying to recall the flavor of that stew even as they applied a greater energy to denying that its ingredients should ever have been combined. Yet the magazine had been quite intentionally an arena for the bouts of contradictory impulses. The editors felt, and sought to recognize, both an urge toward creativity, rebellion, and idiosyncrasy and the pull of tradition, order, and moral meaning. The caution and ambivalence with which they handled any single tendency, or the claims of any one sphere, reflected a positive desire for inclusiveness that was central to the cosmopolitanism of *Partisan Review*'s first decade. Balance, in the early magazine, meant an attempt to deal with powerfully attractive forces whose claims on the mind created a constant tension.

271

By the early 1950s this sense of striving for comprehension, of grappling freshly with experience, had drained away among the New York Intellectuals, unable to survive on the sympathy of a few or a fitful rejuvenation. For many, no doubt, the work of consolidation and the satisfactions of being "responsible" and "mature" were more than adequate compensation for what had been lost. For others, the intermittent tuggings of memory and desire suggested that, between the destruction of some hopes and the satisfaction of others, intellectuals had let too much of their proper quest atrophy and decay. Perhaps with this in mind, it is not too much to suggest that the history of *Partisan Review* sounded a recurring American theme—that success in the wider world may exact as its price a transformation of character. Such, too, was the fate of cosmopolitan values.

Notes
Bibliographic Note
Index

Notes

Introduction

1 Melvin Maddocks, "Field Trips Among the Intellectuals," *Sewanee Review*, 90 (1982), 570.

2 The sociologist Charles Kadushin has noted as the first distinct characteristic of intellectual circles that they have *"no clear boundaries, and the dividing line between the center and the periphery is often arbitrarily drawn."* Kadushin adds, in what must stand as a warning against the claims of memoir and memory, that "because the boundary lines are not especially clear and because any individual member of a circle can 'see' only his immediate surrounding contacts, 'natives' of circles frequently have only fuzzy, if not totally incorrect, notions of what their circle looks like." "Networks and Circles in the Production of Culture," *American Behavioral Scientist*, 19 (1976), 770–771.

3 James Burkhart Gilbert, *Writers and Partisans: A History of Literary Radicalism in America* (New York, 1968).

4 A list of the major contributions to the literature of memoir and autobiography would include at least the following: Norman Podhoretz, *Making It* (New York, 1967); Alfred Kazin, *A Walker in the City* (New York, 1951), *Starting Out in the Thirties* (Boston, 1965), and *New York Jew* (New York, 1978); William Barrett, *The Truants: Adventures Among the Intellectuals* (Garden City, N.Y., 1982); William Phillips, *A Partisan View: Five Decades of the Literary Life* (Briarcliff Manor, N.Y., 1983); Sidney Hook's forthcoming memoirs, of which a piece appeared as "The Radical Comedians: Inside *Partisan Review*," *American Scholar*, 54 (1984–85), 45–61; and, in somewhat different veins, Lionel Abel, *The Intellectual Follies: A Memoir of the Literary Venture in New York and Paris* (New York, 1984); and Irving Howe, *A Margin of Hope: An Intellectual Autobiography* (New York, 1982). There have also been many ventures in recollection and reminiscence appearing as short pieces, essays, and parts of books; those pertinent to this study are cited throughout in the notes.

5 *Anti-Intellectualism in American Life* (New York, 1963), 394.
6 Grant Webster, *The Republic of Letters: A History of Postwar American Literary Opinion* (Baltimore, 1979), 210; Stephen A. Longstaff, "The New York Intellectuals: A Study of Particularism and Universalism in American High Culture" (Ph.D. dissertation, University of California, Berkeley, 1978).

Chapter One

1 Alfred Kazin, "The Jew as Modern Writer," in *The Ghetto and Beyond: Essays on Jewish Life in America*, ed. Peter I. Rose (New York, 1969), 423.
2 Irving Howe, *World of Our Fathers* (New York, 1976), 115–116.
3 John Higham, "Social Discrimination Against Jews, 1830–1930," *Send These to Me: Jews and Other Immigrants in Urban America* (New York, 1975), 167.
4 David A. Hollinger, *Morris R. Cohen and the Scientific Ideal* (Cambridge, Mass., 1975), 19.
5 Joseph Freeman, *An American Testament: A Narrative of Rebels and Romantics* (New York, 1936), 21–22; Norman Podhoretz, *Making It* (New York, 1967), especially chap. 1, "The Brutal Bargain," 3–19. Freeman should not be considered a "New York Intellectual" in the restrictive sense, though this does not discount the representative nature of his early experiences, which reflect common patterns described in a variety of sources. Freeman's story is discussed at length, and perhaps too sympathetically, in Daniel Aaron, *Writers on the Left* (New York, 1961).
6 See, for example, Irving Howe, "A Memoir of the Thirties," *Steady Work: Essays in the Politics of Democratic Radicalism, 1953–1966* (New York, 1966), 354–355. Many of Howe's earlier pieces of memoir, including this one, were incorporated into *A Margin of Hope: An Intellectual Autobiography* (New York, 1982). See also on the sense of a double life Alfred Kazin, *Starting Out in the Thirties* (Boston, 1965), 48.
7 Howe, *World of Our Fathers*, 251.
8 Alfred Kazin, "Under Forty: A Symposium on American Literature and the Younger Generation of American Jews," *Contemporary Jewish Record*, 7 (Feb. 1944), 11.
9 Jews were expected to work on their own Sabbath while remaining idle on that of Protestants and Catholics; public schools forced Christian beliefs on Jewish children through insistence on reciting the Lord's Prayer and the like; movements based on Protestant morality, like prohibition, threatened religious customs, including the ceremonial use of wine. See, for example, Daniel J. Elazar, "American Political Theory

and the Political Notions of American Jews: Convergences and Contradictions," in *The Ghetto and Beyond*, ed. Rose, 213–214. If the more general frictions between cultures were not enough, there were conflicts in the streets between gangs of boys — in Joseph Freeman's neighborhood they were known as the Jews and the Micks (meaning, in this case, gentiles of any race); in William Phillips's, it was Jews versus Italians — and there were openly anti-Semitic comments from teachers or other students at school. Freeman reports that his French teacher once shouted at him in class: "What do you want to go to college for? American colleges should be for Americans! You're not even a European; you're an Oriental — a Jew!" See Freeman, *American Testament*, 18–19, 42; William Phillips, *A Partisan View: Five Decades of the Literary Life* (New York, 1983), 21.

10 Higham, "Social Discrimination Against Jews," 161.

11 Alan Lelchuk, "Philip Rahv: The Last Years," in *Images and Ideas in American Culture: The Functions of Criticism: Essays in Memory of Philip Rahv*, ed. Arthur Edelstein (Hanover, N.H., 1979), 204. See Hollinger, *Morris R. Cohen*, 25; for other examples of the enthusiasm with which some young Jews approached Western ideas.

12 Kazin, "The Jew as Modern Writer," 429.

13 Podhoretz, *Making It*, 32–33.

14 Leon Wieseltier, "Only in America," *New York Review of Books* (July 15, 1976), 25.

15 Thorstein Veblen, "The Intellectual Pre-Eminence of Jews in Modern Europe," *Political Science Quarterly*, 34 (March 1919), reprinted in *Contemporary Jewish Record*, 7 (1944), 565, 567.

16 Robert E. Park, "Human Migration and the Marginal Man," *American Journal of Sociology*, 33 (1928), 891–892, quoted in Allen Guttman, *The Jewish Writer in America: Assimilation and the Crisis of Identity* (New York, 1971), 137.

17 Irving Howe, *Commentary*, 2 (1946), 361–367. In *The Jewish Writer in America*, Allen Guttman proclaimed: "Every Jew in Christendom knows what many Christians never know—that there is more than one answer to life's ultimate questions. The intellectual of Jewish origin knows still more. He knows that there are at least two answers and that neither one of them will do" (136–137).

18 A sophisticated discussion of the problem of identity for Jews in America may be found in Harold Rosenberg, "Jewish Identity in a Free Society," *Discovering the Present: Three Decades in Art, Culture, and Politics* (Chicago, 1973), 259–269.

19 Irving Howe, "New York and the National Culture," *Partisan Review*, 44 (1977), 175–176; Kazin, "The Jew as Modern Writer," 426.

20 Howe, "A Memoir of the Thirties," 352–353.

21 Lionel Abel, "New York City: A Remembrance," *Dissent*, 8 (1961), 251. Irving Howe has noted as well that young radicals and intellectuals often felt "that only here, in New York, could one bear to live at all." See "A Memoir of the Thirties," 351.

22 Podhoretz, *Making It*, 3.

23 Abel, "New York City," 251–252.

24 Alfred Kazin, *On Native Grounds: An Interpretation of Modern American Prose Literature* (New York, 1942), 166. The quotation in the following sentence may be found on page 168.

25 Intellectuals of the teens have sometimes been treated as mere sparks thrown off by the Progressive movement. As Henry May and others have insisted previously, the rebellion took shape in opposition to many dominant political values. Paul F. Bourke discusses the inadequacy of political categories for dealing with these intellectuals in "The Social Critics and the End of American Innocence: 1907–1921," *Journal of American Studies*, 3 (1969), 57–61. The standard account of intellectual life in this period is Henry F. May, *The End of American Innocence: A Study of the First Years of Our Own Time, 1912–1917* (New York, 1959). Arthur Frank Wertheim, *The New York Little Renaissance: Iconoclasm, Modernism, and Nationalism in American Culture, 1908–1917* (New York, 1976), is also useful and provides a good recent bibliography. Kenneth S. Lynn has offered what he intends as a corrective and somewhat debunking account in "The Rebels of Greenwich Village," *Perspectives in American History*, 8 (1978), 335–377.

26 Harold Rosenberg, "The Education of John Reed," *Partisan Review*, 3 (June 1936), 28. Meyer Schapiro makes a similar point about the ashcan artists of the period; see "Rebellion in Art," in *America in Crisis*, ed. Daniel Aaron (New York, 1952), 241. For a recent account, see Leslie Fishbein, *Rebels in Bohemia: The Radicals of "The Masses," 1911–1917* (Chapel Hill, N.C., 1982).

27 See Daniel Aaron's discussion of different groupings in the teens in *Writers on the Left*, 23–29.

28 Claire Sprague, ed., "Introduction," *Van Wyck Brooks: The Early Years: A Selection from His Works, 1908–1921* (New York, 1968), xx–xxi. Other sources include different names or reject some of these. Aaron in *Writers on the Left* includes Lewis Mumford as a close associate of the group led by Brooks and Bourne (26) while labeling Sherwood Anderson "unclassifiable" (29).

29 In addition to sources already cited, this discussion of Brooks makes use of William Wasserstrom, *The Legacy of Van Wyck Brooks: A Study of Maladies and Motives* (Carbondale, Ill., 1971); Paul Francis Bourke,

"Culture and the Status of Politics, 1907–1917: Studies in the Social Criticism of Herbert Croly, Walter Lippmann, Randolph Bourne, and Van Wyck Brooks" (Ph.D. dissertation, University of Wisconsin, 1967); and James Hoopes, *Van Wyck Brooks: In Search of American Culture* (Amherst, Mass., 1977).

30 Van Wyck Brooks, "America's Coming of Age," in *Van Wyck Brooks*, ed. Sprague, 82–83. This long essay, originally published separately in 1915, was issued later as part of *Three Essays on America* (New York, 1934); in the Anchor paperback edition of 1958, *America's Coming of Age* became the title of the whole volume. Sprague notes in her "Introduction" that Brooks is responsible for the "subsequent intellectual currency of the terms 'highbrow' and 'lowbrow' if not for their coinage" (xviii).

31 Sprague, "Introduction," x–xi, points out that use of a dialectical pattern was common in the period, and suggests that Brooks may have come to the method through Carlyle or Coleridge rather than through Hegel directly.

32 The tradition to which Brooks attached himself stretched from John Ruskin and Matthew Arnold, through William Morris, to H. G. Wells and George Bernard Shaw. Though Brooks did not fully understand the transition from a concern with industrialism's erosions of culture to an openly socialist stance leaning heavily on economic insights, he found a combination of ideas in Wells and his predecessors that gave him sustenance and helped to provide the language for his own critique of America. See Van Wyck Brooks, *The World of H. G. Wells* (New York, 1915), and "America's Coming of Age"; Sprague, "Introduction," esp. viii; Wasserstrom, *The Legacy of Van Wyck Brooks*, esp. 21.

33 Van Wyck Brooks, "On Creating a Usable Past," *Dial*, 64 (1918), 337–341, reprinted in *Van Wyck Brooks*, ed. Sprague, quotations from 225–226, 223.

34 Brooks showed somewhat less enthusiasm for the role of immigrant groups in the cultural transformation of America than did Bourne, but he believed that living cultures were borrowing cultures, since "every people selects from the experiences of every other people whatever contributes most vitally to its own development" ("On Creating a Usable Past," 224). See on this point Hoopes, *Van Wyck Brooks*, 119.

35 See David A. Hollinger, "Ethnic Diversity, Cosmopolitanism, and the Emergence of the American Liberal Intelligentsia," *American Quarterly*, 27 (1975), 133–151, for a fuller view of the multiple sources and instances of the new ethic among intellectuals. Hollinger notes: "Since Bourne was destined to become a cultural hero to so many intellectu-

als, his advocacy of this view is especially pertinent to an inquiry into the development of the intelligentsia" (133n).

36 Randolph S. Bourne, "The Jew and Trans-National America," *Menorah Journal*, 2 (1916), 277–284; "Trans-National America," *Atlantic Monthly*, 118 (July 1916), 86–97; both reprinted in *War and the Intellectuals: Essays by Randolph S. Bourne, 1915–1919*, ed. Carl Resek (New York, 1964); quotations here are from 124, 125, 117–118, 123, 122 in the Resek volume.

37 Bourne, "The Jew and Trans-National America," 128; Bourne referred specifically to Kallen's articles in the *Nation* in 1915.

38 Higham, "Ethnic Pluralism in American Thought," *Send These to Me*, 212, 207.

39 Bourne, "The Jew and Trans-National America," 131.

40 Bourne, "Trans-National America," 123; Bourne probably italicizes "intelligentsia" in recognition of its largely foreign reference at the time.

41 Brooks, *The World of H. G. Wells*, 68–69. See the discussion of Brooks's attitudes toward pragmatism in Bourke, "Culture and the Status of Politics," esp. 178–184.

42 Randolph S. Bourne, "Twilight of Idols," *War and the Intellectuals*, ed. Resek, 63.

43 Van Wyck Brooks, "Our Lost Intransigents," *Freeman*, 3 (August 10, 1921), reprinted in *Van Wyck Brooks*, ed. Sprague, quotation on 240.

44 Hollinger, "Ethnic Diversity," 138.

45 Malcolm Cowley, *Exile's Return: A Literary Odyssey of the 1920's* (1934; reprint ed., New York, 1951), 110–111.

46 See T. S. Eliot, "Tradition and the Individual Talent," in *The Norton Anthology of English Literature*, rev. ed., ed. M. H. Abrams et al. (New York, 1968), 1813, 1808. Eliot published the essay in the *Egotist* (1919) and later in *The Sacred Wood* (1920).

47 For a discussion of the reaction of Brooks and others in the *Seven Arts* group to the modernist writing of the early twenties, see Aaron, *Writers on the Left*, 77–80.

48 See William Wasserstrom, *The Time of the "Dial,"* (Syracuse, N.Y., 1963), 71–77, on the relationship between the *Seven Arts* and the *Dial*; the "without politics" phrase, uttered by S. Foster Damon, is quoted in Wasserstrom's discussion.

49 Sherman Paul, *Edmund Wilson: A Study of Literary Vocation in Our Time* (Urbana, Ill. 1965), 28.

50 Edmund Wilson, "Imaginary Dialogues: The Delegate from Great Neck," *The Shores of Light: A Literary Chronicle of the Twenties and Thirties* (New York, 1952), 143–144, 149, 150.

51 Paul, *Edmund Wilson*, 32, 36, 34–35. Wilson's debt to Brooks comes

across as a persistent theme in Paul; see also 44, 46, 80, 93, for examples of the connections Paul sees.

52 In Malcolm Cowley's list of 236 cultural figures born between 1891 and 1905, only Wilson is awarded the title of "man of letters." *Exile's Return*, 311–316.

53 Edmund Wilson, *I Thought of Daisy* (New York, 1929). See Sherman Paul's discussion of *Daisy* in *Edmund Wilson*, 53–76.

54 Edmund Wilson, *Axel's Castle: A Study in the Imaginative Literature of 1870–1930* (1931; reprint ed., New York, 1959), 2, 19.

55 Of the other writers covered, Proust, Joyce, and Yeats were "modern heroes . . . not so much to be argued with as explained," and Valery and Stein were cases of one-sidedness and excess. Paul, *Edmund Wilson*, 86.

56 See Wilson, *Axel's Castle*, 99, 111, 112, 114, 124, for Wilson's positive assessments of Eliot.

57 On Wilson's preoccupation with Eliot, see Paul, *Edmund Wilson*, 84. Paul also notes that in *Axel's Castle*, "Wilson is speaking to the theme of Brooks's *Letters and Leadership* (1918)" (80).

58 Wilson, *Axel's Castle*, 102, 105, 126.

59 Ibid., 119–126.

60 Ibid., 294–297.

61 Ibid., 293.

62 William Phillips, "The Wholeness of Literature," *American Mercury*, 75 (Nov. 1952), 107.

63 Lionel Trilling, "Edmund Wilson: A Backward Glance," *A Gathering of Fugitives* (Boston, 1956), 49, 50.

64 Abel, "New York City," 255.

65 Elazar, "American Political Theory and the Political Notions of American Jews," 213.

66 Nathan Glazer, *The Social Basis of American Communism* (New York, 1961), 130. The high visibility of Jewish radicals could at times create friction both between Jews and surrounding communities and among Jews themselves. Both kinds of tension are apparent in James Rorty's description of the University of Wisconsin, Madison, 1934: "Very undeveloped socially and politically. Radicals are New York Jews and sneered at as such. . . . Madison Jewish merchants called radical Jewish students together and asked them to sacrifice their idealisms a little because they were giving Jews a bad name." James Rorty to Winifred Rorty, November 5, 1934, Rorty Papers, University of Oregon Library, Eugene, Oregon.

67 Daniel Bell, "The Mood of Three Generations," *The End of Ideology: On the Exhaustion of Political Ideas in the Fifties*, rev. ed. (New York,

1962), 299; Howe, "A Memoir of the Thirties," 350. A few attempts have been made to downplay the importance of radicalism in the Jewish community. Lewis Feuer, for instance, has denied that he saw much of radicalism growing up on the Lower East Side. Even Feuer, however, admits that he saw socialist parades and demonstrations, suggesting a consciousness of radical parties not characteristic of every American boy. See "The Legend of the Socialist East Side," *Midstream*, 24 (1978), 23–35.

68 Quoted in Daniel Aaron, "Some Reflections on Communism and the Jewish Writer," in *The Ghetto and Beyond*, ed. Rose, 264.

69 Many have noted the continuity of this literary tradition. See, for instance, T. B. Bottomore's comment that "the vogue of Marxism in the United States was chiefly among the literary intellectuals, who seem to me to have continued, in another fashion, that alienation from American society which had begun towards the end of the nineteenth century." *Critics of Society: Radical Thought in North America* (New York [Vintage Books ed.], 1969), 39.

70 Recalling an "anti-evictor . . . praising someone for being a 'crackerjack Marxist,'" Lionel Abel has remembered his interest in the question of whether he should become a Marxist in order to win such admiration. He was not alone: "The thought . . . entered into the minds of most of the people I knew, and soon a moment came when there was no longer any question as to whether we were going or not going to be Marxists. The only remaining question was: which of us would be crackerjacks?" Abel, "New York City," 256–257.

71 Aaron, *Writers on the Left*, 207.

72 See Aaron's account of this period in *Writers on the Left*, 193–200; also Walter B. Rideout, *The Radical Novel in the United States, 1900–1954: Some Interrelations of Literature and Society* (Cambridge, Mass., 1956), 128–131. The differences between Gold and the "liberals" on the early *New Masses*, and the ill-feeling that accompanied Gold's take-over of the magazine, are discussed in an unpublished autobiographical manuscript by James Rorty, "It Has Happened Here: The Memoirs of a Muckraker," Rorty Papers. There is also among Rorty's papers a copy of a seven-page attack on Gold and his quest for control, addressed "To the Executive Board of the New Masses" (undated correspondence file).

73 Quoted in Aaron, *Writers on the Left*, 98, 204.

74 Richard Pells, *Radical Visions and American Dreams: Culture and Social Thought in the Depression Years* (New York, 1973), 167; Gold is quoted in Aaron, *Writers on the Left*, 164.

75 Quoted in Aaron, *Writers on the Left*, 164, 188.

76 Rideout, *The Radical Novel*, 226.

77 Granville Hicks, "The Crisis in American Criticism," *New Masses*, 8 (Feb. 1933), 5; quoted in Rideout, *The Radical Novel*, 226.

78 *New Masses*, 6 (Dec. 1930), 22, quoted in Aaron, *Writers on the Left*, 209.

79 Granville Hicks, *Part of the Truth* (New York, 1965), 100, 101.

80 Edmund Wilson, "An Appeal to Progressives," *New Republic*, 65 (1931), 235, 236, 237, 238; reprinted in *The Shores of Light*, 518–533.

81 Ibid., 238.

82 Wilson, "The Literary Consequences of the Crash," *The Shores of Light*, 497, 499.

Chapter Two

1 Other magazines begun with Reed Club sponsorship include *Folio* (Los Angeles), *Leftward* (Boston), the *Cauldron* (Grand Rapids, Michigan), *Midland Left* (Indianapolis), the *New Force* (Detroit), *Left Review* (Philadelphia), the *Hammer* (Hartford, Connecticut), and the *Partisan* (Hollywood and Carmel, California). Various other radical periodicals, such as *Anvil, Dynamo, Revolt,* and *Rebel Poet,* reflected the same enthusiasm and enjoyed the same transitory existence.

2 There are differing accounts of *Partisan's* founding, depending largely on the varying memories of the participants. Those interested may consult Aaron, *Writers on the Left*, 298; Gilbert, *Writers and Partisans*, 119–120; and their references. Freeman and Phillips have even disagreed over who wrote the first editorial.

3 William Phillips, "How *Partisan Review* Began," *Commentary* 62 (Dec. 1976), 43. The characterization of Strachey as "suave" is from William Phillips, "On *Partisan Review*," in *The Little Magazine in America: A Modern Documentary History*, ed. Elliott Anderson and Mary Kinzie (Yonkers, N.Y., 1978), 133. On salaries, Phillips elsewhere comments that although the early *Partisan Review* had "no rent or staff, . . . as I recall, Rahv got twelve dollars a week to do the production, though I helped too" ("On *Partisan Review*," 133). Rahv and Phillips also seem to have indicated to James Gilbert that Strachey's lecture provided funds to cover two months of publication rather than a year (*Writers and Partisans*, 120). Such discrepancies are not signs of dishonesty or of any unique failing, but are the typical products of memory and a warning to historians on the problems inherent in such sources.

4 Phillips, "How *Partisan Review* Began," 44. In addition to Rahv and Phillips (who appears until 1935 as "Wallace Phelps"), the other editors listed were Nathan Adler, Edward Dahlberg, Joseph Freeman, Sender Garlin, Alfred Hayes, Milton Howard, Joshua Kunitz, Louis Lozowick,

Leonard Mins, and Edwin Rolfe. Several of Phillips's pieces on *Partisan Review*, including the one cited here, were later incorporated into *A Partisan View*.

5 "How *Partisan Review* Began," 42. Phillips's comment that his "literary and intellectual development was rooted in the 20's" should be balanced against his statement two paragraphs earlier that "intellectually speaking, I, too, was born in the 30's."

6 Ibid.

7 William Phillips [W. Phelps], "*Class*-ical Culture," *Communist*, 12 (Jan. 1933), 93–95.

8 For the "non-Marxist" label, see Phillips, "How *Partisan Review* Began," 43.

9 William Phillips, "Categories for Criticism," *Symposium*, 4 (Jan. 1933), reprinted in William Phillips, *A Sense of the Present* (New York, 1967), 140, 144–146.

10 William Styron, remarks at the Brandeis University memorial service for Philip Rahv (Feb. 2, 1974), quoted in Andrew James Dvosin, "Literature in a Political World: The Career and Writings of Philip Rahv" (Ph.D. dissertation, New York University, 1977), 12–13; Mary McCarthy, "Philip Rahv, 1908–1973," *New York Times Book Review* (Feb. 17, 1974), reprinted in Philip Rahv, *Essays on Literature and Politics, 1932–1972*, ed. Arabel J. Porter and Andrew J. Dvosin (Boston, 1978), vii, viii. McCarthy's picture of at least two distinct sides of Rahv's personality is supported in Irving Howe, "Philip Rahv: A Memoir," *American Scholar*, 48 (1979), 487–488.

11 Rahv was born Ivan Greenberg in the town of Kupin in the Ukraine on March 10, 1908. After experiencing pogrom and war, the young boy lived for short times in Vienna, Providence, Rhode Island, Palestine, and Oregon before finding his way to New York. Dvosin, "Literature in a Political World," 13–16.

12 Phillips, "How *Partisan Review* Began," 43.

13 Philip Rahv, "For Whom Do You Write," *New Quarterly*, 1 (Summer 1934), 12; Gilbert, *Writers and Partisans*, 113.

14 Conroy, "On *Anvil*," in *The Little Magazine in America*, ed. Anderson and Kinzie, 119–120, describes Rahv as "superrevolutionary" and offers a jaundiced account of the young Rahv's leading a superheated faction to dominance over the magazine *Rebel Poet* and destroying it in the process.

15 Philip Rahv, "An Open Letter to Young Writers," *Rebel Poet*, no. 16 (Sept. 1932), 3–4.

16 Philip Rahv, "For Whom Do You Write," 12.

17 Philip Rahv, "The Literary Class War," *New Masses*, 8 (Aug. 1932), excerpts reprinted in Rahv, *Essays on Literature and Politics*, 381.

18 Philip Rahv, "You Can't Duck Hurricane Under Beach Umbrella," *Daily Worker* (May 5, 1934), reprinted as "F. Scott Fitzgerald on the Riviera," in Rahv, *Essays on Literature and Politics*, 24; McCarthy, "Philip Rahv," viii.

19 Phillips, "On *Partisan Review*," 133. A comment that follows this remark—that *Partisan Review* was begun "in opposition to the *New Masses*"—is not justified by the contemporary evidence, though *Partisan Review* sought to become the dominant magazine of Marxist criticism, and "opposition" emerged fairly quickly.

20 Phillips, "How *Partisan Review* Began," 45.

21 Ibid., 43.

22 Granville Hicks, *Where We Came Out* (New York, 1954), 43–44.

23 Rahv, "The Literary Class War," 281.

24 Howe, "A Memoir of the Thirties," 358, 360.

25 Mary McCarthy, "No News, or, What Killed the Dog," *On the Contrary: Articles of Belief, 1946–1961* (New York, 1962), 32–33.

26 Kazin, *Starting Out in the Thirties*, 15.

27 Lionel Trilling, "A Novel of the Thirties," in *The Last Decade: Essays and Reviews, 1965–75*, ed. Diana Trilling (New York, 1979), 7.

28 Abel, "New York City," 257.

29 Ibid., 256. One ex-Communist remarked to Daniel Aaron: "They really meant 'solidarity forever,' especially second generation Jews who were cut off from their Yiddish speaking parents and the outside world in general." Quoted in Daniel Aaron, "Some Reflections on Communism and the Jewish Writer," in *The Ghetto and Beyond*, ed. Rose, 258.

30 Philip Rahv, "Proletarian Literature: A Political Autopsy," *Southern Review*, 4 (1938–39), 618.

31 Joseph Freeman concluded on visiting Russia that the Soviets had eliminated all traces of ghettos and pogroms, the hated symbols of Czarist rule. Mike Gold reported from a Soviet conference in 1930 that whereas the revolutionary felt like "a nut, a rebel, an outcast" under capitalism, he felt immediately at home, part of a "common world" in the Soviet Union. In 1935 Gold quoted approvingly Isaac Babel's comment to him that "in the Soviet Union, one forgets one is a Jew." For Freeman's view, see Aaron, *Writers on the Left*, 132; for Gold's remarks, see Aaron, 220 and 305. Joshua Kunitz in *Russian Literature and the Jew* (New York, 1929) worried about the persistence of negative Jewish stereotypes, and Freeman later bitterly remembered undercover anti-Semitism among radicals in both Russia and America (Aaron, 132n).

32 Kazin, *Starting Out in the Thirties*, 88–89; Phillips, "How *Partisan Review* Began," 43; see also Howe, "A Memoir of the Thirties," 351.

33 William Phillips [Wallace Phelps] and Philip Rahv, "Problems and Per-

spectives in Revolutionary Literature," *Partisan Review*, 1 (June–July 1934), 3. See also Kazin, *Starting Out in the Thirties*, 80–81.

34 Rahv, "An Open Letter to Young Writers," 3.

35 William Phillips [Wallace Phelps], "Three Generations," *Partisan Review*, 1 (Sept.–Oct. 1934), 49, 52.

36 Granville Hicks, "Our Magazines and Their Functions," *New Masses*, 13 (Dec. 18, 1934), 22–23; reprinted in *Granville Hicks in the "New Masses,"* ed. Jack Alan Robbins (Port Washington, N.Y., 1974), 263–266.

37 Fred R. Miller, "The *New Masses* and Who Else," *Blue Pencil*, 2 (Feb. 1935), 4–5.

38 Other battles over opportunity on the left developed, ironically enough, over the question of how federal money and jobs should be allocated to unemployed radicals. See Jerre Mangione, *The Dream and The Deal: The Federal Writers' Project, 1935–1943* (Boston, 1972), 33–37. When the Federal Writers' Project was finally established, a good many radicals, including Phillips, Rahv, and Rosenberg, accepted jobs with little apparent fear that "double-dealing" would corrupt their morals. In New York at least, the Project seems to have lived on very close terms with the Communists, with the government thus aiding the Party in maintaining its reputation for opportunity. Talking with James T. Farrell in September 1936, Rosenberg "referred to the Communist Party as having become a job hunting and a job finding agency. He said that the C. P. had more influence in the W.P.A. here than Tammany Hall." James T. Farrell, personal diary, entry for September 5, 1936, James T. Farrell Papers, Special Collections, Van Pelt Library, University of Pennsylvania, Philadelphia, Pennsylvania (henceforth cited as Farrell Diary).

39 See Glazer, *The Social Basis of American Communism*, 138; and Kazin, *Starting Out in the Thirties*, 122. John Higham mentions competitive civil service examinations as putting a damper on discrimination and thus allowing bright second-generation Jews easier access to public jobs than to private ones. Higham, "Anti-Semitism and American Culture," *Send These to Me*, 190–191.

40 Lionel Trilling has noted the ambivalence among his own friends of the decade: "In the ethos of the time, the idea of 'integrity' had great coercive power and it was commonly supposed that success indicated an integrity compromised or even wholly lost. . . . This did not, of course, make success any the less interesting and attractive, and those who constituted the circle . . . wanted it for themselves, chiefly in the form of fame through literary achievement." "A Novel of the Thirties," 6.

41 Edmund Wilson, "The Literary Consequences of the Crash," *The Shores of Light*, 498–499, 493.

42 Phillips, "Three Generations," 50.

43 "Editorial Statement," *Partisan Review*, 1 (Feb.–March 1934), 2.

44 Philip Rahv, "Marxist Criticism and Henry Hazlitt," *International Literature*, 2 (1934), 112–113.

45 Rahv, "Marxist Criticism and Henry Hazlitt," 115; see also William Phillips [Wallace Phelps], "The Anatomy of Liberalism," *Partisan Review* 1 (Feb.–March 1934), 51.

46 "Editorial Statement," 2; Phillips and Rahv, "Problems and Perspectives in Revolutionary Literature," 10.

47 See, for instance, Rahv's use of the familiar Communist "out" on the question of freedom, Engels's remark that "freedom is the recognition of necessity," in "The Literary Class War," 283; and Conroy's claim that in 1934 Phillips and Rahv sought to bring up the New York editor of *Anvil* before the John Reed Club on charges of having published fiction by a Lovestoneite, in "On *Anvil*," 123.

48 Philip Rahv, "How the Waste Land Became a Flower Garden," *Partisan Review*, 1 (Sept.–Oct. 1934), 41.

49 Ibid., 42.

50 In looking back on their early years from the vantage point of the 1940s, Phillips and Rahv would observe, "we were far more responsive to Marxism as a method of analysis than to organizational pressures and maneuvers." Some coyness about earlier political activities enters into such self-explanation, yet the contemporary evidence confirms this claim that Marxism was more important to the editors of *Partisan Review* intellectually than it was politically. William Phillips and Philip Rahv, "In Retrospect: Ten Years of *Partisan Review*," in *The Partisan Reader: Ten Years of "Partisan Review," 1934–1944: An Anthology* (New York, 1946), 680–681.

51 Marshall Berman, "'All That Is Solid Melts into Air': Marx, Modernism and Modernization," *Dissent*, (Winter 1978); reprinted in *Twenty-Five Years of "Dissent": An American Tradition*, ed. Irving Howe (New York, 1979), 341. See also the fuller discussion in Berman's *All That Is Solid Melts Into Air: The Experience of Modernity* (New York, 1982).

52 Stephen Spender, "Moderns and Contemporaries," in *Literary Modernism*, ed. Irving Howe (Greenwich, Conn., 1967), 44; Irving Howe, "Introduction: The Idea of the Modern," ibid., 14–16. Howe's essay has appeared elsewhere under the title "The Culture of Modernism"; the book as a whole has been reissued with the title *The Idea of the Modern in Literature and the Arts* (New York [Horizon Press ed.], 1967).

53 William Phillips and Philip Rahv, "Private Experience and Public Philosophy," *Poetry*, 48 (May 1936), 104.

54 William Phillips, "The Last Platonist," *Partisan Review*, 3 (April 1936), 26; Phillips and Rahv, "Private Experience and Public Philosophy," 104.

55 William Phillips [Wallace Phelps], "Form and Content," *Partisan Review*, 2 (Jan.–Feb. 1935), 31–33, 38–39.

56 Philip Rahv, "The Novelist As a Partisan," *Partisan Review*, 1 (April–May 1934), 50.

57 Phillips, "The Anatomy of Liberalism," 49.

58 Hollinger, *Morris R. Cohen*, 59.

59 William Phillips [Wallace Phelps] and Philip Rahv, "Criticism," *Partisan Review*, 2 (April–May 1935), 21–22, emphasis in original.

60 Phillips and Rahv, "Private Experience and Public Philosophy," 105.

61 Phillips and Rahv were not easily discouraged, however. In early 1937, on the eve of their break with the Communist Party and with their magazine in a state of indefinite suspension, Phillips and Rahv nevertheless termed disparagement of Marxism "short-sighted" and offered a restatement of their belief in its systematizing power. See William Phillips and Philip Rahv, "Some Aspects of Literary Criticism," *Science and Society*, 1 (1937), 214.

62 The best scholarly discussion of cosmopolitanism and its importance is Hollinger, "Ethnic Diversity, Cosmopolitanism and the Emergence of the American Liberal Intelligentsia." Like many other terms, "cosmopolitanism" has been put to various and contradictory uses, some of which carry implications this study would strongly disavow. As Hollinger points out, for example, the concept of the "cosmopolitan Jew" has "long been a stereotype of adulation . . . and of anti-Semitism" (138n). What attracted Randolph Bourne to Jewish intellectuals would clearly repel a nativist. Negative uses should not eliminate the word from our vocabulary, however. "Cosmopolitanism" remains the best available term to describe the positive values that attracted many intellectuals. It suggests the possibilities of ideas and cultures mixing without merging; its use has been established by Bourne and by Hollinger; and no other term offers an advantage of either tradition or clarity.

63 Hollinger, *Morris R. Cohen*, 59.

64 Phillips, "Three Generations," 52–53; Phillips, "Categories for Criticism," 147–148; Phillips and Rahv, "Problems and Perspectives in Revolutionary Literature," 9.

65 Phillips and Rahv, "Problems and Perspectives in Revolutionary Literature", 7–9. See also the comment by Phillips and Rahv: "There is no use whatsoever in talking about the usable past if we assume beforehand that nothing is usable save that which is near-Marxian" ("Criticism," 24). The editors saw no contradiction between this position and the belief expressed by Phillips that the "unified outlook" of the "Marx-

ian philosophy" held the key to a "systematic approach to the usable elements in our literary heritage" ("Form and Content," 32). Obviously *Partisan Review*'s discussion of the problem of literary tradition, even in the magazine's most radical phase, was much influenced by the language provided earlier by Brooks.

66 Phillips and Rahv, "Problems and Perspectives in Revolutionary Literature," 8–9.

67 Phillips and Rahv, "Some Aspects of Literary Criticism," 218.

68 Rahv, "The Novelist As a Partisan," 51–52; Phillips, "Form and Content," 37; Phillips and Rahv, "Private Experience and Public Philosophy," 104. See also William Phillips [Wallace Phelps], "Sensibility and Modern Poetry," *Dynamo*, 1 (Summer 1934), 22.

69 Phillips and Rahv, "Problems and Perspectives in Revolutionary Literature," 4, 8; Phillips and Rahv, "Private Experience and Public Philosophy," 103; Phillips and Rahv, "Criticism," 16.

70 Daniel Aaron, to take one instance, presents Mike Gold as a man with a religious background and a fondness for Hebrew hymns, a man inclined to make statements that appealed openly to religious sentiment: "Masses are never far from heaven"; "The Social Revolution . . . is the religion of the masses"; "The Revolution . . . is thereby worthy of the religious devotion of the artist." Gold himself provided in *Jews Without Money* a model of the conversion experience that was to become formulaic in proletarian novels as he rhapsodized on his last page: "O workers' Revolution, you brought hope to me, a lonely, suicidal boy. You are the true Messiah." Aaron's Granville Hicks, with his two years of graduate theological training, speaks in a "subdued evangelical tone" in one volume, suggesting his "prior religious orientation." Aaron, *Writers on the Left*, 88, 355; Rideout, *The Radical Novel*, 152, discusses Gold's *Jews Without Money*.

71 Rahv, "How the Waste Land," 38.

72 Phillips and Rahv, "Criticism," 21.

73 Sidney Hook, *Towards the Understanding of Karl Marx: A Revolutionary Interpretation* (New York, 1933), 5, ix, 16, 98. See Pells, *Radical Visions and American Dreams*, 131–140.

74 Hook mentions Phillips's presence in his 1933 class at New York University in a note to Dwight Macdonald attached to proof pages from *Politics* and marked by Macdonald "1944–1949?" Dwight Macdonald Papers, Yale University Library, New Haven, Connecticut. See also Phillips, *A Partisan View*, 30.

75 See Hook, *Towards the Understanding of Karl Marx*, 6–7.

76 Bourne, "Twilight of Idols," 62–63.

77 Phillips declared Dewey's approach to the form-content question at-

tractive but inadequate because Dewey remained on the "plane of categorical relations." The categorizing stultified the relationship of form and content in art, which Phillips proposed to understand through the free-floating prism of the artist's "sensibility." Hook came under fire for treating forms too independently, as if they were merely neutral means. What Phillips was effectively saying was that Dewey and Hook were presenting too closed and fixed a view of art, a view that certainly applied intelligence but that fell short of "intelligence suffused by feeling." Phillips, "Form and Content," 32, 37–38.

Chapter Three

1 Kazin, *On Native Grounds*, 401–407.
2 The discussion that follows is based on Phillips, "Three Generations," 49–54.
3 Rahv, "How the Waste Land," 41, 42.
4 William Phillips and Philip Rahv, "Some Aspects of Literary Criticism," *Science and Society*, 1 (1937), 213.
5 Philip Rahv, "T. S. Eliot," *Fantasy*, 2 (Winter 1932), 17–20.
6 William Phillips [Wallace Phelps], "Eliot Takes His Stand," *Partisan Review*, 1 (April–May 1934), 52–54.
7 Phillips and Rahv, "Problems and Perspectives in Revolutionary Literature," 6; Phillips, "Three Generations," 53.
8 Phillips and Rahv, "Problems and Perspectives in Revolutionary Literature," 4,5.
9 Ibid., 6.
10 Philip Rahv, "Valedictory on the Propaganda Issue," *Little Magazine*, 1 (Sept.–Oct. 1934), 2.
11 Phillips, "Three Generations," 54.
12 The two uses of "gush" appear in Phillips, "Three Generations," 54, and in Phillips and Rahv, "Problems and Perspectives in Revolutionary Literature," 5. Phillips and Rahv elsewhere complained of the "leftists'" "vociferous aversion to theoretical analysis," which amounted to "carrying over the poorest, rather than the best, traditions of bourgeois critics" and which they insisted was "not based on Marxian principles but on what is known as the 'pragmatic American temper.'" "Criticism," 17.
13 Phillips and Rahv, "Criticism," 17–19, 24–25.
14 Philip Rahv, "A Season in Heaven," *Partisan Review and Anvil*, 3 (June 1936), 14.
15 Phillips and Rahv, "Problems and Perspectives in Revolutionary Literature," 8; Phillips and Rahv, "Criticism," 22. See also Phillips and Rahv, "Private Experience and Public Philosophy," 104.

16 Rideout, *The Radical Novel*, 228–229; "National John Reed Club Conference," *Partisan Review*, 1 (Nov.–Dec. 1934), 60–61.

17 "National John Reed Club Conference," 61. The degree to which decisions made in the Soviet Union influenced the course of American radical writing has always been the subject of some debate. While many American scholars tend to emphasize the absence of rigid controls, a British scholar has recently argued that "the experience of the left in American literature is scarcely comprehensible without a firm grasp of the ways Soviet literary policy was emulated," and has charged that Richard Pells in *Radical Visions and American Dreams*, for example, "seriously underestimates the Russian influence." Eric Homberger, "Proletarian Literature and the John Reed Clubs, 1929–1935," *Journal of American Studies*, 13 (Aug. 1979), 244.

18 "The Coming Writers Congress," *Partisan Review*, 2 (Jan.–Feb. 1935), 94.

19 These specifics on the dissolution of the New York Reed Club, based on a letter from Walter Snow to Jack Balch dated February 6, 1935, are reported in Gilbert, *Writers and Partisans*, 135n; see also the discussion of the termination of the clubs in Aaron, *Writers on the Left*, 280–283.

20 Arvin's and Hicks's remarks appear as "Discussion" of Phillips and Rahv's article, "Criticism," in *Partisan Review*, 2 (April–May 1935), 25–27, 28–30.

21 Recollections by Malcolm Cowley and Phillips may be found in "Symposium: Thirty Years Later: Memories of the First American Writers' Congress," *American Scholar*, 35 (1966), 495, 499–500; Granville Hicks, who also participated in this symposium, commented in *Where We Came Out* that it was taken for granted that the Communist Party would control Popular Front organizations (45).

22 See Henry Hart, ed., *American Writers' Congress* (New York, 1935).

23 See Rideout, *The Radical Novel*, 243–244.

24 Malcolm Cowley would later claim that the turn away from younger lower-class writers of immigrant background in 1935 launched "a new war between literary generations." Cowley, "Thirty Years Later," 512–513. Cowley's recollections of the First Writers' Congress were later written up as "1935: The Year of Congresses," *Southern Review*, 15 (April 1979), and published again as part of his *The Dream of the Golden Mountains* (New York, 1980).

25 When Philip Rahv reviewed Nelson Algren's *Somebody in Boots*, for instance, his remarks had less to do with the book itself than with the neglect in radical circles of "the first novel of a young writer whose literary efforts originated and took on definite shape inside the revo-

lutionary movement." Philip Rahv, "The Lower Depths," *Partisan Review*, 2 (July–Aug. 1935), 63. See also William Phillips, "Marking Time?" *New Masses*, 21 (Dec. 22, 1936), 23–24; the soul-searching in Alan Calmer, "Portrait of the Artist as Proletarian," *Saturday Review of Literature*, 16 (July 3, 1937), 14; and the later views of the 1935 shift in Rahv, "Proletarian Literature: A Political Autopsy," 616, and James T. Farrell, The End of a Literary Decade," *American Mercury*, 48 (1939), 411–412.

26 Editorial Notes, *Partisan Review*, 2 (July–Aug. 1935), 2.

27 Discussions about *Partisan Review* in the League executive committee were reported in the committee's minutes for December 11, 1935, as quoted in Gilbert, *Writers and Partisans*, 142. The editors of *Partisan Review* quite clearly knew something of such discussions. On February 14, 1936, James T. Farrell noted in his diary that Rahv was "worried lest they put the clamps down on The Partisan Review and Anvil." (Entries in the diary are quoted as they appear—in this case without the addition of italics for the magazine titles.)

28 When *Partisan Review and Anvil* was being planned, Trachtenberg apparently made clear what he wanted to see from the new publication—a literary magazine that would follow quite closely the Party line. If this was indeed still another attempt to put Phillips and Rahv on a political leash, it worked no better than any other: in Conroy's bitter words, "not a merger but a takeover had occurred." Conroy, "On *Anvil*," 125–217. Conroy's account depends upon his own letters discussing the prospective merger and on a letter written by Clinton Simpson (a member of the merged editorial board friendly to Conroy) for Trachtenberg's expectations.

29 Waldo Frank, "The Writer's Part in Communism," *Partisan Review and Anvil*, 3 (Feb. 1936), 17; Carl Van Doren, "To the Left: To the Subsoil," ibid., 9; James T. Farrell, "Theatre Chronicle," ibid., 29.

30 On Farrell's earlier relations with the *New Masses* and the Party, see Alan Wald, *James T. Farrell: The Revolutionary Socialist Years* (New York, 1978), 27–35.

31 Michael Gold, "Papa Anvil and Mother Partisan," *New Masses*, 18 (Feb. 18, 1936), 22–23.

32 The book began as an essay, became a booklet some fifty-seven pages long, and then kept growing until it was more than two hundred pages in length. The pattern of growing personal anger and frustration, as well as of increasing opposition to Popular Front policies, may be followed in Farrell's diary entries for January 12, 17, 18, 20, 22[?], and February 1, 9, 1936.

33 James T. Farrell, *A Note on Literary Criticism* (New York, 1936), 11–

13, 29–31. Farrell quotes several sentences from one of Phillips and Rahv's attacks on "leftism" as part of his argument (128).

34 Alan Calmer, "Down with 'Leftism,'" *Partisan Review and Anvil*, 3 (June 1936), 7–9.

35 Farrell Diary, June 15, 16, 1936.

36 Isidor Schneider, "Sectarianism on the Right," *New Masses*, 19 (June 23, 1936), 23–25; Granville Hicks, "In Defense of James Farrell," *New Masses*, 20 (July 14, 1936), 23; James T. Farrell, "Farrell Rebuts," *New Masses*, 20 (Aug. 18, 1936), 22–23.

37 Daniel Aaron in *Writers on the Left* suggests that the crusade against "leftism" started too late, holding up for support V. F. Calverton's contemporary claim that Party critics after 1935 no longer had to minimize aesthetic values (302). See also Gilbert, *Writers and Partisans*, 152, which suggests that "leftism" was really a dead issue.

38 "What is Americanism?: A Symposium on Marxism and the American Tradition," *Partisan Review and Anvil*, 3 (April 1936), 3.

39 Newton Arvin, ibid., 4–5.

40 William Troy, ibid., 12–13.

41 Philip Rahv, "An Esthetic of Migration," *Partisan Review and Anvil*, 3 (April 1936), 28–29.

42 Alan Calmer, "MacLeish and Proletarian Poetry," *Partisan Review and Anvil*, 3 (May 1936), 20–21.

43 See William Phillips, "Dixie Idyll," ibid., 26–27.

44 Phillips and Rahv, "Criticism," 22.

45 Rahv, "A Season in Heaven," 11–14.

46 The discussion that follows is based on William Phillips and Philip Rahv, "Literature in a Political Decade," in *New Letters in America*, ed. Horace Gregory and Eleanor Clark (New York, 1937), 172–180.

47 Phillips had, by this time, attributed religious patterns and motives to "leftist" proletarian novels: "the poverty of much revolutionary fiction in America comes from an attempt to construct a fabulous Christian world where political virtue triumphs over political evil, where neon signs point the moral, and conversion is swift and miraculous." This language does run parallel to the kind of attack Phillips had earlier leveled at the religious themes in Eliot and Tate, strengthening the sense that arguments earlier directed toward the right were now coming into play against the presumptive left. But Phillips at this point emphasized the simplistic nature of these patterns in line with the continuing assault on "leftism" as unsophisticated, rather than openly suggesting that Communist politics were themselves religion-like and, therefore, reactionary. William Phillips, "The Humanism of André Malraux," *Partisan Review and Anvil*, 3 (June 1936), 18.

Chapter Four

1 See Aaron, *Writers on the Left*, 311–312.
2 On the Hicks-Arvin concerns, previously discussed in Chapter One, see Hicks, *Part of the Truth*, 100–101. Phillips, Hicks, et al., "Thirty Years Later," 502, 505–506; see also Phillips, "How *Partisan Review* Began," 44.
3 Phillips, "How *Partisan Review* Began," 45; Phillips, "Thirty Years Later," 500, 510; Joseph Freeman is quoted in Aaron, *Writers on the Left*, 311.
4 Farrell Diary, August 14, 1936.
5 Ibid., August 20, 1936; August [21, 1936].
6 Ibid., September 17, 18, 1936; Gilbert, *Writers and Partisans*, 153, reports the details of the League proposals and notes discussion of the venture in executive committee minutes for September 8, 21, and October 15, 1936.
7 Farrell Diary, October 10, October 14, October 16, 1936.
8 Gilbert, *Writers and Partisans*, 153, notes that the minutes of the League executive committee of October 15, 1936, reported that Phillips and Rahv were reconsidering affiliation.
9 Farrell Diary, December 31, 1936; January 6, 1937.
10 Ibid., January 6, 1937.
11 Ibid., January 18, 22, 1937.
12 Ibid., February 1, 7, 9, 20, 1937.
13 Ibid., March 23, 1937.
14 "Dupee, Frederick Wilcox," in *Twentieth Century Authors*, ed. Stanley J. Kunitz, 1st supplement (New York, 1955), 291–292; Phillips, Hicks, et al., "Thirty Years Later," 511.
15 Dwight Macdonald, "Politics Past," in *Memoirs of a Revolutionist: Essays in Political Criticism* (New York, 1957), 6, 8.
16 Dwight Macdonald, "*Fortune* Magazine," *Nation*, 144 (1937), 528; "The Communist Party," *Fortune*, 10 (Sept. 1934), 159; F. W. Dupee to Dwight Macdonald [October 21, 1936], Macdonald Papers; Macdonald commented in "Politics Past," 6–7, that he had "first read Marx" at thirty, which would have been in 1936.
17 Phillips, "Thirty Years Later," 510.
18 Dupee to Macdonald, [shortly after March 30, 1937], Macdonald Papers.
19 Macdonald, "*Fortune* Magazine," 529–530.
20 See Constance Ashton Myers, "American Trotskyists: The First Years," *Studies in Comparative Communism*, 10 (1977), 142–143.
21 Mary McCarthy, "My Confession," *On the Contrary: Articles of Belief, 1946–1961* (New York [Noonday ed.], 1962), 93–101; like Macdonald,

McCarthy had been prepared to vote for Browder in 1936. Farrell is identified as the novelist friend who put McCarthy on the spot about Trotsky in "Mary McCarthy" (Interview), *Paris Review*, 27 (1962), 73.

22 On the selection of the commission, see Alan Wald, "Memories of the John Dewey Commission: Forty Years Later," *Antioch Review*, 35 (1977), 441; the characterization of Dewey is from Farrell's memoir "Dewey in Mexico," in James T. Farrell, *Reflections at Fifty* (New York, 1954), 99; Sidney Hook, "Some Memories of John Dewey, 1859–1952," *Commentary*, 14 (1952), 250. A report on the hearings of the Dewey Commission was published as *The Case of Leon Trotsky* (New York, 1937), and the commission's judgments appeared in *Not Guilty* (New York, 1938; reprint ed., 1972).

23 McCarthy, in "Mary McCarthy" (Interview), 73. Macdonald was privately asked by George Novack to recommend "one or two trustworthy people" to give a "substantial contribution to the work of the Dewey delegation" (Novack to Macdonald, March 25, 1937, Macdonald Papers); Macdonald later received thanks from Felix Morrow for his own contribution (with a receipt from Suzanne LaFollette, who was the Committee Treasurer and a member of the Dewey Commission) and a request to appeal himself to the friend he had recommended as a donor (Morrow to Macdonald, April 19, 1937, Macdonald Papers).

24 Dupee to Macdonald, [shortly after March 30, 1937], Macdonald Papers; McCarthy, "My Confession," 102; Phillips to Macdonald, July 17, 1937, Macdonald Papers.

25 Macdonald to Dinsmore Wheeler, [May 7, 1937], Macdonald Papers.

26 Farrell Diary, May 31, 1937; Phillips, "Thirty Years Later," 509. The others present at the May 27 meeting were Eleanor Clark, James Rorty, Herbert Solow, Bruno Fischer, and Margaret Marshall.

27 See the account in Gilbert, *Writers and Partisans*, 174, based on an interview with Dupee.

28 Henry Hart, ed., *The Writer in a Changing World* (New York, 1937), 225; Hicks, "Thirty Years Later," 509–510.

29 Farrell Diary, June 8, 10, 1937.

30 Granville Hicks, *Part of the Truth*, 148.

31 Phillips, "How *Partisan Review* Began," 45; Phillips, "On *Partisan Review*," 134.

32 Glazer, *The Social Basis of American Communism*, 160. John Higham remarks that after the publication of Horace Kallen's *Culture and Democracy in the United States* in 1924, "cultural pluralism remained in suspension until liberal intellectuals, in the late 1930's, reverted to Americanism." "Ethnic Pluralism in American Thought," *Send These to Me*, 213.

33 David Hollinger commented briefly on the *Partisan Review* board in "Ethnic Diversity," 145.

34 "McCarthy, Mary," in *Twentieth Century Authors*, ed. Kunitz, 1st supplement, 608. See also Mary McCarthy, *Memories of a Catholic Girlhood* (New York, 1957). McCarthy has written that she was accepted, "unwillingly, as an editor because I had a minute 'name' and was the girl friend of one of the 'boys,' who had issued a ukase on my behalf." (The friend—perhaps the only one in the group prepared to hand down a ukase—was Rahv.) The stylish, attractive, and quick-witted McCarthy added a special vibrance to the magazine's circle, though she served as an editor for only three issues, departing Rahv and the magazine in 1938 to marry Edmund Wilson. Her contributions but not her editorial status would later return. Mary McCarthy, "Introduction," *Mary McCarthy's Theatre Chronicles, 1937–1962* (New York, 1963), ix–x. For a fictional view of the relationship between McCarthy and Rahv, see Delmore Schwartz, "Mary, Philip, Wilson" (draft of a story), Delmore Schwartz Papers, Collection of American Literature, Beinecke Rare Book and Manuscript Library, Yale University, New Haven, Connecticut.

35 Morris to Macdonald, June 29 [1937], Macdonald Papers. Reviewing his papers many years later, Macdonald penciled in "1938?" on this letter, but references to opening offices for *Partisan Review* in August and to Nancy Macdonald's recent selection fix the letter clearly in 1937.

36 For general background on the Communist Party in America and its factional tendencies, see Theodore Draper, *American Communism and Soviet Russia: The Formative Period* (New York, 1960), and Irving Howe and Lewis Coser, *The American Communist Party: A Critical History* (New York, 1962). On Trotskyism, see Constance Ashton Myers, *The Prophet's Army: Trotskyists in America, 1928–1941* (Westport, Conn., 1977), and the same author's "American Trotskyists."

37 Alan M. Wald, "The Menorah Group Moves Left," *Jewish Social Studies*, 38 (1976) 290–293. The *Menorah Journal* writers included, in addition to those named in the text, Clifton Fadiman, Henry Rosenthal, Tess Slesinger, Anita Brenner, and Louis Berg.

38 Ibid., 294–301.

39 Lionel Trilling, "Some Notes for an Autobiographical Lecture," in *The Last Decade*, ed. Trilling, 237; Trilling, "A Novel of the Thirties," 18–19. The account to which Trilling responded was Murray Kempton's in *Part of Our Time* (New York, 1955).

40 See especially Myers, "American Trotskyists," 137–141; Wald, "The Menorah Group Moves Left," 304–309; Gilbert, *Writers and Partisans*, 165–167.

41 Myers, "American Trotskyists," 141–142. Wald notes in "The Menorah

Group Moves Left" that most of the group did not go along with the merger of 1936 (310).

42 Representatives of several anti-Stalinist positions joined in early 1937 to bring out the *Marxist Quarterly* as a journal of scholarly socialist thought free of factional ties. Many of its articles were of high quality, but the telltale reduction of its editorial board before the second issue signaled the disputes over ideology that brought the effort sputtering to a halt by the summer. See the three issues of *Marxist Quarterly* and the "Introduction" by Michael Harrington in the Greenwood Press reprint edition (Westport, Conn., 1968).

43 Rahv to Macdonald, July 30, August 4, 1937, Macdonald Papers.

44 Dupee to Macdonald, [early September 1937], Macdonald Papers; William Phillips to James T. Farrell, July 28, 1937, Farrell Papers; see also Farrell Diary, October 17, 1937, on Phillips's complaints.

45 Dupee to Macdonald, July 9, [1937], Macdonald Papers; Rahv to Macdonald, July 30, 1937, Macdonald Papers; Phillips to Farrell, July 28, 1937, Farrell Papers; Rahv to Macdonald, August 4, 1937, Macdonald Papers; Dupee to Macdonald, [August 1937], and September 18, 1937 [date added, probably by Macdonald], Macdonald Papers.

46 On this rocky relationship in 1937, see Farrell Diary, June 20, 1937; Phillips to Farrell, July 28, 1937, Farrell Papers; Dupee to Macdonald, [early September 1937] and September 18, 1937, Macdonald Papers.

47 Two letters from Dos Passos to Rahv—one responding to the invitation to contribute, one congratulating Rahv on the first issue of the new *Partisan Review*—are quoted in full in Dvosin, "Literature in a Political World," 60–62.

48 Rahv to Macdonald, August 4, 1937, Macdonald Papers; McCarthy discusses the Vassar literary magazine in her *Paris Review* interview, 71; Dupee to Macdonald, [early September 1937], Macdonald Papers, mentions McCarthy's lunch with Rukeyser and the promise of a poem.

49 For Phillips's generally positive comment on Schwartz a year before he had met him, see his *New Masses* review of the *New Caravan*, edited by Alfred Kreymborg, Lewis Mumford, and Paul Rosenfeld, "Marking Time?" 23. For Schwartz's first contacts with the editors of *Partisan Review* and their later characterizations of him at this time, see James Atlas, *Delmore Schwartz: The Life of an American Poet* (New York, 1977), 97–103.

50 Philip Rahv, Letter to the Editor, *New Masses*, 23 (March 30, 1937), 21.

51 Philip Rahv, "The Revolutionary Conscience," *Nation*, 144 (1937), 412; "Torrents of Spring," ibid., 733.

52 Philip Rahv, "Summer Fiction," *Nation*, 145 (1937), 79; "Shorter Notices," ibid., 156–157; "Sojourn in Sodom," ibid., 174–175; "You Read as You

Please," ibid., 244; "Golden Calves," ibid., 326; "Europa in Melodrama," ibid., 354.

53 "Falsely Labeled Goods," *New Masses*, 24 (Sept. 14, 1937), 9–10.

54 Dupee to Macdonald, [early September 1937], Macdonald Papers.

55 William Phillips and Philip Rahv, "A Protest," and the editorial response, "We Reply," *New Masses*, 25 (Oct. 19, 1937), 21.

56 Gold's attack appeared in the *Daily Worker* for October 12, 1937. Granville Hicks, "Those Who Quibble, Bicker, Nag, and Deny," *New Masses*, 25 (Sept. 28, 1937), 22–23. This essay, several reader responses, and Hicks's reply are collected in *Granville Hicks in the "New Masses,"* ed. Robbins, 382–406.

57 Farrell Diary, October 16, November 30, 1937. Farrell also noted on October 16 that Alan Calmer was giving up some of his friendships (particularly with Phillips and Rahv) to stay in the Party.

58 Dupee to Macdonald, [early September 1937], Macdonald Papers.

59 Farrell Diary, November 1, 16, 30, 1937.

60 Michael Gold, "Migratory Intellectuals," *New Masses*, 21 (Dec. 15, 1936), 27–28; "Notes on the Cultural Front," Literary Supplement to *New Masses*, 25 (Dec. 7, 1937), 1–5.

61 "The *Nation* and Trotsky," *New Masses*, 21 (Nov. 10, 1936), 11–12; Granville Hicks, "A *Nation* Divided," Literary Supplement to *New Masses*, 25 (Dec. 7, 1937), 8–11.

62 McCarthy, "Introduction," *Theatre Chronicles*, vii–viii.

63 Dupee to Macdonald, September 18, 1937, Macdonald Papers.

64 McCarthy, "Introduction," *Theatre Chronicles*, ix–x; Dupee to Macdonald, September 29, 1937, Macdonald Papers, tries to reassure Macdonald.

65 Dupee to Macdonald, September 18, 1937, Macdonald Papers.

66 Phillips and Rahv, "Literature in a Political Decade," 174.

Chapter Five

1 "Editorial Statement," *Partisan Review*, 4 (Dec. 1937), 3–4.

2 Phillips would later admit that perhaps he and Rahv had been too cautious, tending "too much toward sobriety," feeling more acutely than the others the pressures of a "constant state of siege" and the threat of Communist "sabotage." Phillips, "How *Partisan Review* Began," 45.

3 Rahv to Macdonald, July 20, 1937, Macdonald Papers. Gide contributed a later comment on his disillusionment with the Soviet Union to *The God That Failed*, ed. Richard Crossman (New York, 1950).

4 Dupee to Macdonald, [early September 1937], mentions receiving permission from Gide; Dupee to Macdonald, September 18, 1937, Macdonald Papers.

5 Philip Rahv to André Gide, November 25, 1937, and letter (no author) to Gide, January 6, 1938, cited in Gilbert, *Writers and Partisans*, 197–198; and S. A. Longstaff, "*Partisan Review* and the Second World War," *Salmagundi*, no. 43 (Winter 1979), 118n. In relying on recollections of the participants and the timing of the letters to Gide, the Gilbert and Longstaff accounts suggest a simpler progression of editorial opinion, more consistent individual views, and a longer delay before the decision to publish was made than do the contemporary manuscript sources now available. Farrell Diary, November 30, December 10, 1937.

6 "Ripostes," *Partisan Review*, 4 (Dec. 1937), 74–75. Just possibly, the comments in "Ripostes" were stimulated in part by a common defensive strategy of leading Party opponents in the late thirties — to seek publicity for the most extreme attacks to create a form of protection through notoriety.

7 Lionel Trilling, "Marxism in Limbo," *Partisan Review*, 4 (Dec. 1937), 70–72. The title given this piece underscored its political implications.

8 Sidney Hook, "The Technique of Mystification," *Partisan Review*, 4 (Dec. 1937), 57–62. Here again, the title of the piece is indicative of *Partisan Review*'s concerns, emphasizing the anti-rational tendency that Hook found in Burke.

9 Farrell's diary indicates that the December 1937 *Partisan Review* was out by November 14, and Phillips was still telling Farrell on November 30 that Gide was too political for publication; Phillips reported the decision to publish only on December 10.

10 André Gide, "Second Thoughts on the U.S.S.R.," *Partisan Review*, 4 (Jan. 1938), 21–23, 28.

11 Kenneth Burke, "Is Mr. Hook a Socialist?" and Sidney Hook, "Is Mr. Burke Serious?" *Partisan Review*, 4 (Jan. 1938), 40–47. Among other things, Hook attacked the "literary pogroms of the Communist Party." The word "pogrom" was, of course, an emotionally laden term with special connotations for Jewish intellectuals on both sides of the rising political barricades.

12 "Ripostes," *Partisan Review*, 4 (Jan. 1938), 61–62.

13 Dupee to Dinsmore Wheeler, December 20, 1937, Macdonald Papers.

14 Paul N. Siegel, ed., *Leon Trotsky on Literature and Art* (New York, 1970), 45–54, quotations at pages 54, 49. A substantial portion of *Literature and Revolution*, first published in English in 1925, is combined in this collection with a number of Trotsky's other writings on culture.

15 William Phillips, "What Happened in the 30's," in *A Sense of the Present*, 21–22; Philip Rahv, "The Great Outsider," review of *The Prophet Outcast* by Isaac Deutscher, in the *New York Review of Books* (Jan. 23,

1964), 4–5; McCarthy's comments are part of her entry in *Twentieth Century Authors*, ed. Kunitz, 1st supp., 609.

16 Macdonald to Trotsky, July 7, 1937, Macdonald Papers. By coincidence, Macdonald visited James T. Farrell on the day he wrote this letter and discussed with him the plans for *Partisan Review*. Farrell's reactions, recorded the next day, strengthen the evidence of uncertainty found in the Trotsky letter. Of Macdonald, Farrell noted: "Not clear on ideas for Partisan Review," and, later, "His concepts are not clear and well formed either." Farrell Diary, July 8, 1937.

17 Trotsky to Macdonald, July 15, 1937, Macdonald Papers.

18 Rahv to Macdonald, August 4, 1937, Macdonald Papers; Dwight Macdonald, "Politics Past," 4.

19 Macdonald to Trotsky, August 23, 1937, Macdonald Papers.

20 For a defense of the intellectual's separation from day-to-day politics in order to concern himself with more abstract issues, see Randolph Bourne's "The Price of Radicalism" in *War and the Intellectuals*, ed. Resek, 139–141; the distinction between the writer as craftsman and the writer as citizen was a staple of Edmund Wilson's criticism in the late twenties.

21 Trotsky to Macdonald, September 11, 1937, Macdonald Papers. For an example of the combination of frustration and elation that Trotsky generated in the editors, see Dupee to Macdonald, September 18, 1937, Macdonald Papers.

22 Myers, "American Trotskyists," 143–144. Myers discusses relevent tensions within the Trotskyist camp between the "city intellectual" wing (which was augmented by the Young Socialists) and the "trade union activist" or "proletarian" wing. A conversation with Norman Thomas recorded by James T. Farrell at the time suggests that there may also have been tensions, even at the height of their cooperation, between the "city intellectual" camp and the Socialist leaders. Thomas felt that the Trotskyists did "some good theoretical work," but that they were "too 'theological' and 'Talmudic,'" and that they had "the psychology of a merely oppositionist group." Farrell Diary, January 22, 1937.

23 "Ripostes," *Partisan Review*, 4 (Feb. 1938), 61–62. The original criticism appeared in the December 4, 1937, issue of the *Socialist Appeal*.

24 Ibid., 62–63.

25 Trotsky to Macdonald, January 20, 1938, Macdonald Papers. This letter has been published in full in Siegel, ed., *Leon Trotsky on Literature and Art*, 101–103. Siegel declares Trotsky's doubts about *Partisan Review* "justified," since the magazine did become, in Siegel's view, a "small cultural monastery." Despite the later desire of some of the editors to keep apart from certain elements of the world, this characterization

accurately describes the position of *Partisan Review* neither at its beginning nor over time.

26 Philip Rahv to Leon Trotsky, February 21, 1938, Macdonald Papers.

27 Trotsky to Macdonald, January 20, 1938, Macdonald Papers. Isaac Deutscher has commented that "the fact that *Partisan Review* intended to start its 'new chapter' by questioning the validity of Marxism did not recommend it to Trotsky." *The Prophet Outcast, Trotsky: 1929–1940* (New York, 1963), 430n. To many politically oriented radicals then and since, raising questions about any part of Marxism has meant challenging its validity as a whole. Proposed contributors to the symposium included Harold Laski, Sidney Hook, Ignazio Silone, Edmund Wilson, August Thalheimer, John Strachey, Fenner Brockway, Boris Souvarine, and Victor Serge—a diverse, partially literary, and conspicuously international group. How many of these people were actually contacted is unclear, since the project developed only in pieces.

28 F. W. Dupee to Dwight Macdonald, July 9, [1937], from "Grand Haven," Macdonald Papers; William Phillips to Dwight Macdonald, July 27, 1937, Macdonald Papers; William Phillips to James T. Farrell, July 28, 1937, Farrell Papers; Philip Rahv to Dwight Macdonald, July 20, 1937, Macdonald Papers.

29 William Phillips, "The Esthetic of the Founding Fathers," *Partisan Review*, 4 (March 1938), 16.

30 Dwight Macdonald, "Laugh and Lie Down," *Partisan Review*, 4 (Dec. 1937), 45; Mary McCarthy, "Theater Chronicle," ibid., 56.

31 James Burnham, "Capitalism, American Style," *Partisan Review*, 4 (March 1938), 52; Meyer Schapiro, "Architect's Utopia," ibid., 42–45; Meyer Schapiro, "Populist Realism," *Partisan Review*, 4 (Jan. 1938), 57.

32 Phillips, "The Esthetic of the Founding Fathers," 12–13; Hook, "The Technique of Mystification," 59.

33 Philip Rahv, "Two Years of Progress—From Waldo Frank to Donald Ogden Stewart," *Partisan Review*, 4 (Feb. 1938), 22–30.

34 Philip Rahv, "Trials of the Mind," *Partisan Review*, 4 (April 1938), 3–11. In referring to Marxism's "Russian captivity" and the killing of the "firstborn of October," Rahv may or may not have intended consciously to call upon the story of the Jewish people enslaved in Egypt, but these references and others suggest that Biblical knowledge was a more important part of Rahv's educational heritage than he commonly professed.

35 Phillips and Rahv, "Literature in a Political Decade," 179; Rahv, "The Great Outsider," 4; Alfred Kazin, *Starting Out in the Thirties*, 153–154. Other quotations in this paragraph are from "Trials of the Mind."

36 Macdonald to Harold Rosenberg, June 7, 1938, Macdonald Papers.

37 Malcolm Cowley, "Partisan Review," *New Republic*, 96 (1938), 311–312.

38 "A Letter to the New Republic," *Partisan Review*, 6 (Fall 1938), 124–127; Malcolm Cowley, "Red Ivory Tower," *New Republic*, 97 (1938), 22–23. Privately, Rahv commented that though Cowley's attack was a "factional document," it was "better than the bleak silence of last year." Rahv to Allen Tate, October 24, 1938, Tate Collection, Princeton University Library, Princeton, New Jersey. Published with permission of Princeton University Library.

39 *Partisan Review*, 5 (Aug.–Sept. 1938), 3–10.

40 Rosenberg to Macdonald, June 14, 1938, and September 4, 1939, Macdonald Papers.

41 George L. K. Morris to Macdonald, August 8, 9, 22, 1938, Macdonald Papers. Macdonald added to the financial reasons for moving the office the argument that it would be easier for him to work at home than to travel downtown (Macdonald to Morris, August 17, 1938, Macdonald Papers). Phillips, out of town for some time and quite far removed from the magazine's operations at this point, seems to have accepted all the changes calmly (Phillips to F. W. Dupee, August 22, 1938, F. W. Dupee Collection, Columbia University Library, New York). Dupee, on the other hand, bristled over the fact that he had not been consulted, objected to the office decision, and pointed out that what was easier for Macdonald was considerably more difficult for everyone else (Dupee to Macdonald, September 8, 1938, Macdonald Papers).

42 *Partisan Review*, 6 (Spring 1939), 29–45.

43 Trotsky to Philip Rahv, July 30, 1938, Macdonald Papers; André Breton and Diego Rivera, "Manifesto: Towards a Free Revolutionary Art," *Partisan Review*, 6 (Fall 1938), 49–53; Macdonald to Trotsky, August 16, 1938, Macdonald Papers.

44 The editors' invitation appeared as the opening section of "This Quarter" in *Partisan Review*, 6 (Fall 1938). The three responses came from Bertram Wolfe, John Wheelwright, and a Paul Dobbs. Macdonald to Paul Dobbs, November 27, 1938; Macdonald to Trotsky, December 19, 1938, Macdonald Papers.

45 Macdonald to Hook, December 6, 1938, Macdonald Papers. Attached to this letter is a draft copy of the "League Against Totalitarianism" manifesto signed by Hook, John Dewey, and Eugene Lyons, and marked "confidential."

46 Rahv reported a few weeks after Macdonald's letter that the Trotskyists had "excommunicated Hook for his 'deviations,'" but that the heretic seemed "quite happy in his final exclusion from the orthodox fold." Rahv was clearly not sympathetic to the Trotskyists here; but neither was he ready to support Hook's new organization. Rahv to Robert Penn Warren, February 23, 1939, *Southern Review* Papers, Collection of Amer-

ican Literature, Beinecke Rare Book and Manuscript Library, Yale University, New Haven, Connecticut.

47 Macdonald to Trotsky, March 5, 1939, and a later, undated letter; Macdonald to Harold Rosenberg, March 12, 1939, Macdonald Papers. James T. Farrell reported on the two meetings in his diary (March 2, 18, 1939), expressing pessimism after the first and commenting about the second, "The door is open for the nuts."

48 Farrell repeated Rahv's report in his diary, March 14, 1939; Farrell's criticisms of Hook's behavior appear in diary entries for [April 26, 1939 (date supplied)], May 26, and September 25, 1939.

49 "Statement of the L.C.F.S.," *Partisan Review*, 6 (Summer 1939), 125–127. In addition to the names of all five of *Partisan Review*'s editors at this time (Phillips, Rahv, Dupee, Macdonald, Morris), the signatures on the statement included the names of Lionel Abel, James Burnham, James T. Farrell, Clement Greenberg, Harold Rosenberg, Meyer Schapiro, Delmore Schwartz, and other friends of the magazine. V. F. Calverton and James Rorty signed Hook's manifesto as well as the League's.

50 Philip Rahv, "Where the News Ends" (guest column), *New Leader*, (Dec. 10, 1938), 8; Philip Rahv, "A Variety of Fiction," *Partisan Review*, 6 (Spring 1939), 108; Farrell Diary, April 6, May 26, June 7, June 9, and June 25, 1939.

51 Freda Kirchwey, "Red Totalitarianism," *Nation*, 148 (1939), 605–606; "Manifesto," ibid., 626; see also the "Reply" from Sidney Hook and the "Rebuttal" from Kirchwey, ibid., 710–711; "Liberty and Common Sense," *New Republic*, 99 (1939), 89–90; "Still Another Committee," ibid., 144; letter from John Dewey and reply, ibid., 161–162; see also the letter from the League and reply, ibid., 336.

52 "To All Active Supporters of Democracy and Peace" (text of the letter with some signatures), *Nation*, 149 (1939), 228; "In Reply to a Committee," *New Republic*, 100 (1939), 63.

53 "Red Star and Swastika," *Nation* 149 (1939), 211–212. The letter appeared in the same issue on 228. By the next issue, an editorial note declared that events had made "lengthy discussion seem unnecessary." Ibid., 231.

Chapter Six

1 Frederick Crews, "The Partisan," review of Philip Rahv, *Essays on Literature and Politics*, ed. Porter and Dvosin, *New York Review of Books* (Nov. 23, 1978), 3. Crews later announced that the *Partisan* intellectuals' political and literary views were united by their "animus against the bland middle class" and their "equidistance from Iowa"; the magazine, therefore, was "held together by elitism" (4). There was clearly

a hostility toward blandness, the genteel middle class, nativism, and "Iowa" at *Partisan Review*, but Crews distorted these attitudes and ignored their context in his failure to take the magazine's rationale seriously. Christopher Lasch called Crews to account for his remarks in "Modernism, Politics, and Philip Rahv," *Partisan Review*, 47 (1980), 185–188 (the present argument would not, however, endorse all of Lasch's conclusions).

2 "Editorial Statement" of December 1937, 3–4.

3 Rahv's review appears under the title "The Revolutionary Conscience" in *Nation*, 144 (1937), 412.

4 Lionel Abel, "Ignazio Silone," *Partisan Review*, 4 (Dec. 1937), 33–39.

5 F. W. Dupee, "André Malraux," *Partisan Review*, 4 (March 1938), 24–35.

6 Cowley first charged that Dupee had dismissed Malraux himself as a "liberal Comintern lobbyist." The editors of *Partisan Review* in a reply called this a "flat misquotation" and claimed accurately that the particular phrase had been applied to Garcia. Cowley then responded by arguing that the characterization of the novel directly involved Malraux. Both sides were less than scrupulous in their argumentation, and the exchange on this particular issue had little point except to display their mutual hostility. Cowley, "Partisan Review," 311; "A Letter to the New Republic," 126; Cowley, "Red Ivory Tower," 22.

7 Such a technique could, of course, be turned to a variety of ends. In the first issue of the new *Partisan Review*, Edmund Wilson, writing on Flaubert, and William Troy, reviewing Zola's *Germinal*, both made a point of discovering unexpected balance in a major writer's work, though both were beginning to move in directions that took them away from the primary values of the magazine. Edmund Wilson, "Flaubert's Politics," *Partisan Review*, 4 (Dec. 1937), 13–24; William Troy, "The Symbolism of Zola," ibid., 64–66.

8 Philip Rahv, "Dostoevsky and Politics: Notes on 'The Possessed,'" *Partisan Review*, 5 (July 1938), 25–36.

9 Philip Rahv, "The Social Muse and the Great Kudu," *Partisan Review*, 4 (Dec. 1937), 64.

10 William Troy, "The Lawrence Myth," *Partisan Review*, 4 (Jan. 1938), 8–9, 12–13.

11 William Troy, "Thomas Mann: Myth and Reason," *Partisan Review*, 5 (June 1938), 24.

12 William Phillips, "Thomas Mann: Humanism in Exile," *Partisan Review*, 4 (May 1938), 3–10.

13 Wilson made the relation of art and disease a leading topic of *The Wound and the Bow: Seven Studies in Literature* (Boston, 1941), often speak-

ing indirectly but generally suggesting that great art depended on disease or pain. Lionel Trilling challenged this belief in Wilson and in the culture generally through his well-known essay "Art and Neurosis," discussing art as a product of health. That Wilson was a primary object of Trilling's attentions was more apparent in his original piece, "A Note on Art and Neurosis," *Partisan Review*, 12 (Winter 1945), 41–48, than in the final version of the essay published in *The Liberal Imagination* (New York, 1950). See also Robert Gorham Davis, "Art and Anxiety," *Partisan Review*, 12 (Summer 1945), 310–320.

14 Troy, "Thomas Mann: Myth and Reason," June 1938, 24–32, and July 1938, 51–64.

15 Phillips to Macdonald, August 20, [1938], Macdonald Papers.

16 James Burnham, "William Troy's Myths," *Partisan Review*, 5 (Aug.–Sept. 1938), 65–68; William Troy, "A Further Note on Myth," *Partisan Review*, 6 (Fall 1938), 95–100.

17 Troy speaks of the missteps of the "purely aesthetic critic" in "The Lawrence Myth," 5.

18 "This Quarter: Reflections on a Non-Political Man," *Partisan Review*, 6 (Fall 1938), 14–16. Surviving correspondence between Dwight Macdonald and Harold Rosenberg indicates that Macdonald was the author of the editorial remarks on Mann. Rosenberg to Macdonald, October 15, 1938; Macdonald to Rosenberg, October 22 [1938], Macdonald Papers.

19 Rosenberg had originally submitted his essay elsewhere, sending a copy to Macdonald for comment and possible later use in case it was not accepted elsewhere. Macdonald showed the piece to Rahv and Dupee on his own initiative and reported a collective response before the essay was actually available. There had been some friction between Rosenberg and the "Rahv-Phillips camp" (as Macdonald called it), and Macdonald was eager to announce that Rahv had been enthusiastic about Rosenberg's piece; he noted as a point in Rahv's favor, "I have never known him to let his personal feelings interfere with his editorial judgment." Macdonald also made a direct appeal to Rosenberg that suggested the minority-camp mentality and the sense of alliance on principle that characterized the *Partisan Review* intellectuals in this period: "it seems a great pity, considering how few really good minds 'our' group (I say 'our' since, politically and intellectually, you seem to have much the same outlook as we of PR do) can command—it seems too bad to have you split off from us by personal animosities" (Macdonald to Rosenberg, June 7, 1938, Macdonald Papers). When Rosenberg's essay on Mann appeared, the editors identified Rosenberg in part by noting that "his reviews appeared frequently in the old *Partisan Review*," a remark that

tried hard to emphasize continuity in his relationship with the magazine. "Contributors," *Partisan Review*, 6 (Winter 1939), 2.

20 Harold Rosenberg, "Myth and History," *Partisan Review*, 6 (Winter 1939), 19–39. In this criticism of Troy, Rosenberg repeated a part of the critique he had earlier outlined in a letter to Macdonald. Rosenberg saw Troy as "caught up with the 'myths' of Mann and Lawrence." To evaluate such ideas, Rosenberg argued, it was "necessary to cut across them with new values," which Troy did not do. The idea that new values (derived from Marxism) provided the "necessary" tool for evaluating the great modern writers linked Rosenberg with the editors of *Partisan Review*. Rosenberg to Macdonald, June 14, 1938, Macdonald Papers.

21 Rosenberg added in a footnote a comment on the direction of Mann's thought that also followed patterns seen before in *Partisan Review*. Rosenberg claimed that in turning from the present situation of modern man to "eroded images of the past," Mann was moving "toward the right." So long as Mann dealt with the modern world, his analysis "could not escape the *radicalism* of the middle class—historic destroyer of all Values." Thus, as Rosenberg made the common point, Mann's earlier work had developed radical insights "in spite of the most conservative intentions." When he turned to the distant past and to the right, Mann discarded "the hard substance of contemporary life," and the loss was felt "in the relaxed and bulbous quality of his prose." In linking a turn away from the present to a loss of insight, to a move toward conservatism, and to a decline in prose style, Rosenberg drew a picture of Mann's career that had resemblances to other analyses in *Partisan Review* and to Rahv's 1932 description of T. S. Eliot's glory and decline.

22 Phillips, "The Esthetic of the Founding Fathers," 11–21.

23 Daniel Bell, *The Cultural Contradictions of Capitalism* (New York, 1976), 46–61, 65–72, 74. Scholars who disagree with Bell on specific points, or who reject the conclusions he directs at the present, often make the same general argument about the shifts in twentieth-century American culture.

24 Rahv, "Two Years of Progress," 22, 28; and "Trials of the Mind," 3, 11.

25 Rahv to Trotsky, February 21, 1938.

26 "Ripostes" ("Is Naturalism Exhausted?"), *Partisan Review* 4 (Feb. 1938), 60–61.

27 Phillips, "Thomas Mann," 3.

Chapter Seven

1 Abel, "New York City," 258; Schwartz to Dwight Macdonald, [probably September 1940 (Macdonald's dating)], Macdonald Papers.

2 "War Is the Issue!" *Partisan Review*, 6 (Fall 1939), 125.

3 "This Quarter: Munich and the Intellectuals," *Partisan Review*, 6 (Fall 1938), 7–10.

4 "This Quarter: Anti-Fascist Jitterbug," *Partisan Review*, 6 (Winter 1939), 4–6. This piece was probably written by Rahv.

5 Dwight Macdonald, "War and the Intellectuals: Act Two," *Partisan Review*, 6 (Spring 1939), 3–20.

6 Other signatures were also present, of course. Signers included anti-Stalinist political allies like George Novack, James Rorty, Anita Brenner, Bertram Wolfe, and V. F. Calverton; a variety of those who had published in *Partisan Review*, including Kay Boyle, Eleanor Clark, Kenneth Patchen, Kenneth Rexroth, Louise Bogan, and Robert Fitzgerald; and, perhaps most interestingly, William Carlos Williams.

7 "War Is the Issue!" 125–126.

8 Farrell Diary, August 22, 23, 24, 25, 1939.

9 Ibid., September 21, 1939.

10 *New Republic*, 101 (Nov. 15, 1939), ii (inside front cover).

11 "A Letter to the L. A. W.," *Partisan Review*, 6 (Fall 1939), 127–128.

12 "The War of the Neutrals," *Partisan Review*, 6 (Fall 1939), 3–5.

13 Ibid., 11; Frank Trager, "Frederick L. Schuman: A Case History," *Partisan Review*, 7 (March–April 1940), 143–151. See also the editors' sharp reply to a letter defending Schumann in *Partisan Review*, 7 (May–June 1940), 248 and inside back cover.

14 See especially James T. Farrell, "The Cultural Front," *Partisan Review*, 7 (March–April 1940), 139–142. Farrell took the occasion a year later to demand a refund from the *Nation* when its foreign correspondent of the late thirties, Louis Fischer, admitted that he had suppressed negative information about the Soviet Union. Farrell's letter was printed in *Partisan Review*, 8 (July–Aug. 1941), 349.

15 Frank A. Warren, III, *Liberals and Communism: The "Red Decade" Revisited* (Bloomington, Ind., 1966), 209–215.

16 See John P. Diggins, *Up from Communism: Conservative Odysseys in American Intellectual History* (New York, 1975), esp. 59–66, for a discussion of the attack on the dialectic. Those interested may trace Hook's many articles through the bibliography compiled by John Dennis Crowley in *Sidney Hook and the Contemporary World*, ed. Paul Kurtz (New York, 1968).

17 James Burnham, "A Belated Dialectician," *Partisan Review*, 6 (Spring 1939), 120–123. See also Eliseo Vivas, "The Dialectic According to Levy," *Partisan Review*, 4 (May 1938), 51–54.

18 See Diggins, *Up from Communism*, 65, which suggestively contrasts American views of Marxism circa 1940 with those of the emigre Frank-

furt School, whose members looked to Hegelianism to preserve Marxism.

19 Edmund Wilson, "The Myth of the Marxist Dialectic," *Partisan Review*, 6 (Fall 1938), 66–81.
20 William Phillips, "The Devil Theory of the Dialectic," *Partisan Review*, 6 (Fall 1938), 82–90.
21 Philip Rahv, "What Is Living and What Is Dead," *Partisan Review*, 7 (May–June 1940), 175.
22 M. G. White, "From Marx to Dewey," *Partisan Review*, 7 (Jan.–Feb. 1940), 62–67.
23 Meyer Schapiro, "The Revolutionary Personality," *Partisan Review*, 7 (Nov.–Dec. 1940), 478; Bertram D. Wolfe, "The Light That Failed," *Partisan Review*, 8 (Jan.–Feb. 1941), 71–72.
24 Rahv, "What Is Living and What Is Dead," 175–180. In taking stock of Marxism's condition, Rahv declared that "it remains the greatest contribution to social science and to the technique of social action made in modern times." Marxism deserved continuing credit for its interpretation of history; for "the theory of the class struggle, of the state, of bourgeois economy, of imperialist conflicts"; for "the theory and strategy of internationalism"; and for "the analysis of reformist movements." Significantly, Rahv's list read more like an acknowledgment of the historical contributions of Marxism to general social theory than a defense of a contemporary radical position.
25 Diggins, *Up from Communism*, 179–184; Myers, "American Trotskyists," 145.
26 Macdonald chose to reprint his letter on Kronstadt in *Discriminations: Essays and Afterthoughts, 1938–1974* (New York, 1974), 355–359; See the discussion in Macdonald, "Politics Past," 15–19; and Diggins, *Up from Communism*, 183–184.
27 Myers, "American Trotskyists," 145–147; Diggins, *Up from Communism*, 184–186; Deutscher, *The Prophet Outcast*, 471–477. Trotsky's contributions to the battle in the American party are collected in *In Defense of Marxism* (1942; reprint ed., New York, 1973).
28 Diggins, *Up from Communism*, 186–189; Deutscher, *The Prophet Outcast*, 476. Burnham's resignation letter appears in Trotsky, *In Defense of Marxism*, 207–211.
29 Macdonald, "Politics Past," 18–19.
30 Macdonald's first efforts along these lines came in "Notes on a Strange War," *Partisan Review*, 7 (May–June 1940), 170–175; and in "National Defense: The Case for Socialism," *Partisan Review*, 7 (July–Aug. 1940), 250–266.
31 Leon Trotsky, "American Problems," in *Writings of Leon Trotsky [1939–*

40] (1969; reprint ed., New York, 1973), 340–341; originally published as "Discussion with Lund" in *Discussion Bulletin* (Socialist Workers Party), 3 (Sept. 1940). Trotsky was quoting from Macdonald, "National Defense: The Case for Socialism," 266.

32 Victor Serge, "In Memory: L. D. Trotsky," *Partisan Review*, 9 (Sept.–Oct. 1942), 389–390; Paul Goodman, "The Death of Leon Trotsky," *Partisan Review*, 7 (Nov.–Dec. 1940), 425–429; Schwartz to Dwight Macdonald, May 1, 1940, September 11, 1940, Macdonald Papers (in a letter to Macdonald probably written in May 1941, Schwartz assails Goodman for "that poem in which Trotsky is the chief of excitement and the Russian Revolution becomes by obvious implication an amusement park"); James T. Farrell, "The Cultural Front: Leon Trotsky," *Partisan Review*, 7 (Sept.–Oct. 1940), 388.

33 Dwight Macdonald, "Trotsky Is Dead," *Partisan Review*, 7 (Sept.–Oct. 1940), 339–342. Macdonald referred to Trotsky at one point as a "sixty-one year old Jewish exile named Lev Davidovitch Bronstein." Others also called attention to Trotsky's Jewishness in *Partisan Review*. Goodman's poem, cited earlier, referred to him as "Lev Davidovitch" and bore one section entitled "A Hebrew Song, in Memory of L. T."

34 Farrell, "The Cultural Front: Leon Trotsky," 388; Macdonald, "Trotsky Is Dead," 340.

35 James Burnham, "The Theory of the Managerial Revolution," *Partisan Review*, 3 (May–June 1941), 181–197, and *The Managerial Revolution: What Is Happening in the World* (New York, 1941); Dwight Macdonald, "The Burnhamian Revolution," *Partisan Review*, 9 (Jan.–Feb. 1942), 76–84.

36 Dwight Macdonald, "The End of Capitalism in Germany," *Partisan Review*, 8 (Sept.–Oct. 1941), 426–430.

37 C. Wright Mills, "The Nazi Behemoth Dissected," *Partisan Review*, 9 (Sept.–Oct. 1942), 432–437. Other pieces on fascism included J. R. Stanwell, "Something New on the New Order," ibid., 437–440; Paul Mattick, "How New Is the 'New Order' of Fascism?" *Partisan Review*, 8 (July–Aug. 1941), 289–310; "A Letter from Victor Serge," *Partisan Review*, 8 (Sept.–Oct. 1941), 418–422; Marceau Pivert, "Fascism and Capitalism," ibid., 423–426; and Clement Greenberg, "Venusberg to Nuremberg" (a review of Peter Viereck's *Metapolitics: From the Romantics to Hitler*), *Partisan Review*, 8 (Nov.–Dec. 1941), 509–512.

38 Philip Rahv, "Utopians, Left and Right," *American Mercury*, 57 (1943), 498–499. Rahv had earlier suggested in a letter to Macdonald, written before he had read Burnham's book and before Macdonald had published his own major piece in *Partisan Review*, that what he was reading about

the "Italian situation" made "all this stuff about 'a new order' seem rather silly" (April 9, 1941, Macdonald Papers).

39 To Trotsky loyalists, it has always seemed clear that those who strayed from the fold in 1939–1940 were abandoning Marxism. Isaac Deutscher has accused the Burnham-Schactman group of joining the "Retreat of the Intellectuals" that the two leaders had themselves attacked in early 1939 (*The Prophet Outcast*, 472). George Novack has called the "convulsive events" at the beginning of the war the "great turning point" in the political "devolution" of a whole band of his former Trotskyist friends; "Introduction," Greenwood reprint ed. of *New International* (New York, 1968), 3.

40 Farrell Diary, September 11, 1939.

41 See Farrell Diary, October 15, 29, 1939, July 14, September 12, 1940, for comments on Hook, mostly negative.

42 Schwartz's remark is written on an undated scrap of paper, Schwartz Papers; Laughlin to Schwartz, [mid-1943], Schwartz Papers; Dorothea Straus, "Many Mansions," in *Palaces and Prisons* (Boston, 1976), 67–68.

43 Delmore Schwartz, "New Year's Eve," in *In Dreams Begin Responsibilities and Other Stories*, ed. James Atlas (New York, 1978), 94, 100; James Atlas, "Unsentimental Education," *Atlantic Monthly*, 251 (June 1983), 90. In her satirical novel *The Oasis* (which many of *Partisan Review*'s friends found excessively harsh), Mary McCarthy caricatured Rahv and Macdonald as the leaders of opposing factions labeled the "realists" and the "purists." *The Oasis* (New York, 1949), 7–26, passim.

44 Farrell noted in July that Macdonald did not think *Partisan Review* would survive "more than another issue" and that Macdonald had claimed the editors did not have "much interest in going on." Apparently Macdonald had sent the same message to Delmore Schwartz, who soon asked about the deadline for the "last" issue so that he could appear in it, "partly as a matter of sentimentality." Morris wrote to Macdonald about material for the "last" issue as well, commenting that their earlier conversation had made a gathering to "discuss whether to continue or not," which Dupee had by now suggested, "hardly necessary." Farrell Diary, July 29, 1940; Schwartz to Macdonald, August 12, 1940, Macdonald Papers; G. L. K. Morris to Macdonald, September 4, [1940], Macdonald Papers.

45 Macdonald to Morris, September 2, 1940, Macdonald Papers; Philip Rahv, "10 Propositions and 8 Errors," *Partisan Review*, 8 (Nov.–Dec. 1941), 501.

46 James T. Farrell observed in his diary in 1939 that William Phillips had "developed a whole system of not working" and went on to offer some thumbnail analysis (January 5, 1939). Some of Phillips's own letters

in this period seem to support the charge that he was quick with excuses; see Phillips to Farrell, "received August 15, 1942," Farrell Papers.

47 The preceding discussion is based on Morris to Macdonald, September 7, [1940], and Macdonald to Morris, September 9, 1940, Macdonald Papers.

48 The announcement of a new name appeared inside the front cover of the magazine. Letters of comment and the disavowal of the change came in *Partisan Review*, 8 (Jan.–Feb. 1941), 79–80.

49 Rahv married Nathalie Swan, an architect. Farrell noted almost immediately in his diary (March 13, 1941) that *"Partisan Review* will now be completely in the hands of Dwight Macdonald, seconded by Clement Greenberg"; and he later reaffirmed (May 2, 1941) that the magazine was "practically in the hands of Dwight Macdonald." Farrell had been highly sensitive to what he believed were personal and professional slights from Rahv and some of the other editors in early 1941 and was shortly to move away from the magazine's circle. See Farrell Diary, January 3, 10, 11 and April 20, 24, 1941.

50 Rahv to Macdonald, March 18, 30, 1941, Macdonald Papers. Rahv's eagerness to keep tabs on *Partisan Review* and New York happenings is also apparent in Rahv to Farrell, March 18, 1941, Farrell Papers; and Rahv to Dupee, April 5, 1941, Dupee Collection.

51 Rahv to Macdonald, March 30, 1941, Macdonald Papers. Kaplan, mentioned here under the pseudonym "Scope," is identified in Rahv's follow-up letter of April 9, 1941. Rahv was perhaps sensitive as well to the fact that Macdonald's anti-war declarations were strongly shaping the image of the magazine with people like Stephen Spender, with whom Macdonald had a run-in over the war in 1940. See Stephen Spender, "September Journal," *Partisan Review*, 7 (March–April 1940), 92; Macdonald, "Notes on a Strange War," 173–174; Stephen Spender and Dwight Macdonald, "The Defense of Britain, A Controversy," *Partisan Review*, 7 (Sept.–Oct. 1940), 405–408.

52 See Macdonald, "Politics Past," 20–21, and the discussion of this period in Stephen J. Whitfield, *A Critical American: The Politics of Dwight Macdonald* (Hamden, Conn., 1984), 18–30.

53 Clement Greenberg and Dwight Macdonald, "10 Propositions on the War," *Partisan Review*, 8 (July–Aug. 1941), 271–278. It is perhaps worth noting that Greenberg did not share Macdonald's belief that German fascism constituted a "new order" and that the two defined socialism as "collectivised property plus political democracy."

54 Philip Rahv, "10 Propositions and 8 Errors," 499–506.

55 "Reply by Greenberg and Macdonald," *Partisan Review*, 8 (Nov.–Dec. 1941), 506–508; Macdonald's later comment is quoted by Longstaff in

"Partisan Review and the Second World War," 121n; McCarthy, *The Oasis*, 19.

56 "A Statement by the Editors," *Partisan Review*, 9 (Jan.–Feb. 1942), 2.

57 Rahv to Dupee, February 16, 1942, Dupee Collection. Rahv was eager to leave "this dismal place" (Chicago) and to get back to New York, where he wanted "to live in the village" (Greenwich Village).

58 See especially George Orwell, "London Letter," *Partisan Review*, 8 (March–April 1941), 108–110; and D. S. Savage, George Woodcock, Alex Comfort, George Orwell, "Pacifism and the War: A Controversy," *Partisan Review*, 9 (Sept.–Oct. 1942), 414–421. Orwell's remark that pacifists were "objectively pro-Fascist" received special attention. Discussions over printing the controversy were reported in Macdonald to Morris, June 25, [1942], Macdonald Papers.

59 The editors consulted a lawyer before agreeing to publish Goodman; Macdonald to Morris, June 25, [1942]. Goodman's statement appeared as "Better Judgment and 'Public Conscience,'" *Partisan Review*, 9 (July–Aug. 1942), 348–351.

60 Macdonald to Morris, June 25, [1942]; Morris to Macdonald, June 29, [1942]; Macdonald to Morris [undated; probably July 1 or 2, 1942]; Macdonald Papers.

61 Macdonald to Morris, June 25, [1942].

62 Macdonald to Morris, [undated; probably July 1 or 2, 1942]. Macdonald repeated in this letter the substance of his earlier complaints against Phillips: "Will for years has contributed nothing to the magazine, and lately his attitude has been utterly negativistic. He's just a shadow of Phil—except that sometimes his neurotic fears drive him to take even more super-cautious positions than Phil."

63 Statement on the contents page, *Partisan Review*, 9 (July–Aug. 1942). Morris had agreed with Macdonald's suggestion that if Phillips wanted his name removed, he should resign for good (Morris to Macdonald, dated July 5, 1940, but clearly 1942). Phillips may well have upset Macdonald's plans by simply deciding to accept the publication of his article, with the disclaimer, rather than resign.

64 Macdonald to Delmore Schwartz, July 21, [1943]; Macdonald to Rahv, [June 1943]; Rahv to Macdonald, [late June 1943]; Macdonald to Rahv, July 3, [1943]; Macdonald Papers.

65 "Letters," *Partisan Review*, 10 (July–Aug. 1943), 383–384. Both Rahv and Phillips felt Macdonald had misrepresented their position in his letter and attacked *Partisan Review* unfairly, and they told him so. See Rahv to Macdonald, July 28, 1943; Phillips to Macdonald, "Thursday" [July 1943]; Macdonald Papers.

66 Morris to Macdonald, August 10, [1943], Macdonald Papers.

67 Macdonald, draft of resignation letter, July 3, 1943; Macdonald to Schwartz, [late July or early August, 1943], Macdonald Papers.

68 See the discussion in Richard King, *The Party of Eros: Radical Social Thought and the Realm of Freedom* (Chapel Hill, N.C., 1972), 31–45; and in Whitfield, *A Critical American*, 43–52. Macdonald's own account is in "Politics Past," 25–31.

69 The essays by those named appeared in the first two issues of *Partisan Review* for 1943, with a part of Hook's essay accompanying each group; Sidney Hook, "The New Failure of Nerve" and "The Failure of the Left," *Partisan Review*, 10 (Jan.–Feb. and March–April 1943), 2–23, 165–177. The phrase "failure of nerve" was borrowed from Gilbert Murray's *Four Stages of Greek Religion*, and whether Hook had properly applied it became a minor issue in the debate over his essay.

70 Ibid., 2–4, 8, 166–169, 175–176; Wald, *James T. Farrell*, 166, n. 14.

71 Meyer Schapiro [David Merian], "The Nerve of Sidney Hook," and Sidney Hook, "The Politics of Wonderland," *Partisan Review*, 10 (May–June 1943), 248–262; and a further exchange, "Socialism and the Failure of Nerve," *Partisan Review*, 10 (Sept.–Oct. 1943), 473–481. Several letters refer to the editorial discussions over publishing the second Schapiro response: five between Rahv and Macdonald, two between Schwartz and Macdonald, one from Morris to Macdonald, and one from Schapiro to Macdonald; all are from July and August 1943, and may be found in the Macdonald Papers.

72 Rosenfeld's "Philosophical Naturalism: The Failure of Verve," originally published in the *New Republic* of July 19, 1943, appears in Isaac Rosenfeld, *An Age of Enormity*, ed. Theodore Solotaroff (Cleveland, 1962), 58–62; Schapiro, "The Nerve of Sidney Hook," 249.

73 Rosenfeld, "Philosophical Naturalism," 60; Schapiro, "The Nerve of Sidney Hook," 250–251; Dwight Macdonald, "The Future of Democratic Values," *Partisan Review*, 10 (July–Aug. 1943), 321.

74 James T. Farrell, "Mortimer J. Adler: A Provincial Torquemada," *Partisan Review*, 7 (Nov.–Dec. 1940), 453–455; Philip Rahv, "Modernizing James," *Kenyon Review*, 7 (1945), 315; Schapiro, "The Nerve of Sidney Hook," 249; Sidney Hook, "The Integral Humanism of Jacques Maritain," *Partisan Review*, 7 (May–June 1940), 204.

75 Schapiro, "The Nerve of Sidney Hook," 255.

Chapter Eight

1 Rahv, "Twilight of the Thirties," *Partisan Review*, 6 (Summer 1939), 4–5; James T. Farrell, "The End of a Literary Decade," *American Mercury*, 48 (1939), 414.

2 Rahv, "Twilight of the Thirties," 6; see also Philip Rahv, "Proletarian Literature: A Political Autopsy," *Southern Review*, 4 (1938–39), 616–628. Rahv began thinking about a piece on the decline of revolutionary literature that would point the finger at the Stalinists (and defend the early hopes of *Partisan Review*) as early as the fall of 1937, though his argument was still evolving; see Rahv to Editor [Robert Penn Warren], October 17, 1937, *Southern Review* Papers.

3 Rahv, "Twilight of the Thirties," 8.

4 Farrell Diary, August 19, 1939; Farrell, "The End of a Literary Decade," 409–411.

5 Rahv, "Twilight of the Thirties," 10–11. Rahv also made reference to culture as the intellectuals' "only real property" in "Trials of the Mind," 9.

6 Rahv, "Twilight of the Thirties," 3–15.

7 Ibid., 14; Lionel Trilling, "Elements That Are Wanted," *Partisan Review*, 7 (Sept.–Oct. 1940), 368.

8 "The Situation in American Writing," *Partisan Review*, 6 (Summer 1939), 25–26; Agee included his reply in James Agee and Walker Evans, *Let Us Now Praise Famous Men* (New York [Ballentine paper ed.], 1973), 318–325.

9 Recorded in Farrell Diary, August 19, 1939.

10 The phrase comes from a letter by Delmore Schwartz. It is interesting to compare Schwartz's explanation of his attitude toward the war in 1942 with Rahv's earlier notions of the intellectual's role. Schwartz offered his comments as a defense against Dwight Macdonald's complaint that he had not spoken out against the war: "The initial assumption is that no political position is possible for intellectuals at present. Second, the intellectuals must, as a necessary myth, conceive of themselves as a class, or rather a club, or at any rate, a group which, by the very nature of their profession, have a vested interest in truth, an interest which must be defended more than ever in wartime. . . . This does not strike me as particularly original or enthralling as a stand; but it is workable, as is made evident by the fact that some fall back on it naturally and of necessity. It is also a position from which one can advance to a political stand whenever such a one is made possible by the movements of the well-known masses." Schwartz to Macdonald, October 5, 1942, Macdonald Papers. Some of Schwartz's letters to Macdonald and others have been published in *Letters to Delmore Schwartz*, ed. Robert Phillips (Princeton, N.J., 1984).

11 James T. Farrell, "The Cultural Front," *Partisan Review*, 7 (July–Aug. 1940), 311–313; James Burnham, "God Bless America," *Partisan Review*, 7 (Nov.–Dec. 1940), 479.

12 Archibald MacLeish, *The Irresponsibles: A Declaration* (New York,

1940), esp. 21, 30–34; MacLeish collected a group of his essays in *A Time to Speak* (Boston, 1941).

13 Morton Dauwen Zabel, "The Poet on Capitol Hill," *Partisan Review*, 8 (Jan.–Feb. and March–April 1941), 2–8, 132–138; James Rorty added to Zabel's attack on MacLeish his own argument that MacLeish was hypocritical or worse in a letter published in *Partisan Review*, 8 (March–April 1941), 160.

14 Rahv, "Twilight of the Thirties," 11–12.

15 F. W. Dupee, "The Americanism of Van Wyck Brooks," *Partisan Review*, 6 (Summer 1939), 69–85.

16 Brooks's essay was originally delivered as a paper at a Columbia University conference on September 10, 1941. A published version is perhaps most readily available in Jack Salzman, ed., *The Survival Years: A Collection of American Writings of the 1940's* (New York, 1969), 185–203.

17 William Phillips, "The Intellectuals' Tradition," *Partisan Review*, 8 (Nov.–Dec. 1941), 481–490.

18 Dwight Macdonald, "Kulturbolschewismus Is Here," *Partisan Review*, 8 (Nov.–Dec. 1941), 442–451.

19 Seven comments were published together in "On the 'Brooks-MacLeish Thesis,'" 38–47; a late reply from T. S. Eliot appeared as "A Letter to the Editors," *Partisan Review*, 9 (March–April 1942), 115–116. Among the responses, only that of James T. Farrell was generally supportive of Macdonald's political viewpoint.

20 Macdonald, "Kulturbolschewismus Is Here," 451.

21 Reply by the editors under "P.R.'s Literary Principles," *Partisan Review*, 8 (Nov.–Dec. 1941), 519.

22 These three pieces appeared respectively in *Partisan Review*, 7 (Nov.–Dec. 1940), 430–439; 8 (March–April 1941), 82–93; and 9 (Jan.–Feb. 1942), 52–58.

23 William Petersen, "What Has Become of Them? A Check-List," *Partisan Review*, 8 (Jan.–Feb. 1941), 59–62. Petersen was one of two business managers of *Partisan Review* at this time, which made his information gathering an emblem of the magazine's concern.

24 On the relations among many of the younger poets mentioned, see Atlas, *Delmore Schwartz*, and Eileen Simpson, *Poets in Their Youth* (New York, 1982).

25 Lionel Trilling, "Allen Tate as Novelist," *Partisan Review*, 6 (Fall 1938), 111–113; Allen Tate, letter addressed to Philip Rahv, printed in *Partisan Review*, 6 (Winter 1939), 125–126; Delmore Schwartz, "The Poetry of Allen Tate," *Southern Review*, 5 (1939–40), 437–438; Allen Tate, "The Double Agents: Provocateur," *Partisan Review*, 8 (Jan.–Feb. 1941), 67–

69. Rahv had also shown great respect for Robert Penn Warren's first novel, *Night Rider*, suggesting that Warren had "attained in one bound a leading position among American novelists." Rahv, "A Variety of Fiction," 112.

26 Philip Rahv to Allen Tate, September 16, 1938; November 28, 1939; November 16, 1942; Tate Collection.

27 Allen Tate, "Ode: To Our Young Pro-Consuls of the Air," *Partisan Review*, 10 (March–April 1943), 129–132; Rahv to Tate, March 1, 1943, Tate Collection. There had even been a proposal earlier for a book of responses to Brooks and MacLeish supported jointly by *Partisan Review* and the *Southern Review*. See Macdonald to Robert Penn Warren, February 21, 1942, Southern Review Papers.

28 Delmore Schwartz, "The Poet as Poet," *Partisan Review*, 6 (Spring 1939), 55–56; F. W. Dupee, "The Discussion Was Lively," *Partisan Review*, 8 (Nov.–Dec. 1941), 512–513.

29 William Phillips, "The Spiritual Underground," *Partisan Review*, 9 (Nov.–Dec. 1942), 529–531.

30 Clement Greenberg, "Avant-Garde and Kitsch," *Partisan Review*, 6 (Fall 1939), 34–49.

31 Clement Greenberg, "Towards a Newer Laocoon," *Partisan Review*, 7 (July–Aug. 1940), 301, 310; and "The Renaissance of the Little Magazine," *Partisan Review*, 8 (Jan.–Feb. 1941), 76. On Greenberg's later work, see Donald B. Kuspit, *Clement Greenberg: Art Critic* (Madison, 1979).

32 Rahv worked on outlines for books on Kafka and on literature in the thirties when preparing a Guggenheim application in 1939 (Rahv to Morton Dauwen Zabel, August 11, 1939, Zabel Papers, Newberry Library, Chicago). "The Dark Lady of Salem" was presented in *Partisan Review*, 8 (Sept.–Oct. 1941), 362–381, as a chapter from a forthcoming book on American fiction (362n).

33 In deciding for various reasons to study American writers more deeply, the *Partisan* critics seemed to respond to a common impulse as the forties approached. F. W. Dupee announced that he had been "reading Americana" and thinking about writing articles or a book to cover the "literary history of the 20's," while going back "as far as Whitman and Howells." Lionel Trilling, planning to teach a course on American literature, indicated that he expected to "immerse" himself in it. Delmore Schwartz named as a possible contribution to *Partisan Review* an essay on *The Portrait of a Lady*, which he called "one of the greatest novels ever written, I am sure." The magazine had published an Edmund Wilson essay on Henry James the year before, and Trilling was soon sending references on James to Dupee, who, along with Rahv, would be a leader of the coming James revival. Dupee to Macdonald, September 8, 1938, Macdonald Papers; Trilling to Dupee, May 23, 1939,

and postcards dated October 11 and October 20, 1940, Dupee Collection; Schwartz to Dupee, postcard dated March 14, 1939, Dupee Collection; Edmund Wilson's "The Last Phase of Henry James" was published in *Partisan Review*, 4 (Feb. 1939), 3–8.

34 Rahv's references to Brooks's terms and to his own may be found in "In the American Grain," *American Mercury*, 57 (1943), 247.

35 Rahv was insistent on the value of the cultural analysis growing out of the teens and on the usefulness of Brooks's view of American letters in particular. Reviewing Edmund Wilson's *The Shock of Recognition*, a gathering of critical pieces on American writing from two centuries, Rahv rejected Wilson's claim that the highbrow-lowbrow division was coming to an end when Brooks first described it in 1915. The cleavage constituted a kind of "cultural schizophrenia" that had actually "gotten worse in the past decade," Rahv declared, defending in the process the continuing viability of Brooks's analysis and his own adaptations of it. To replace some of the "dreary stuff" Wilson had included in his collection, Rahv recommended "one of Randolph Bourne's examinations of the American scene" or perhaps "Brooks's chapter on 'Our Poets' from his *America's Coming of Age*" which had been "immensely influential." Ibid., 247–248.

36 Philip Rahv, "Paleface and Redskin," *Kenyon Review*, 1 (1939), 251–256. Rahv made a few minor changes in wording before publishing this essay in *Image and Idea* (1949; rev. ed., Norfolk, Conn., 1957), and such changes have been followed in quotation here. Interestingly, one change replaced a use of "lowbrow" in the original with "redskin," suggesting just how close Rahv understood the terms to be.

37 Christopher Lasch has found in Rahv's remarks an early version of one of his own major themes: "No other critic wrote more perceptively than Rahv about the 'cult of experience' in American literary thought or understood so clearly—and so far ahead of his time—the ideology of personal liberation it encouraged." Lasch, "Modernism, Politics, and Philip Rahv," 184.

38 Philip Rahv, "The Cult of Experience in American Writing," *Partisan Review*, 7 (Nov.–Dec. 1940), 412–424.

39 See Rahv, "The Dark Lady of Salem"; "The Heiress of All the Ages," *Partisan Review*, 10 (May–June 1943), 227–247; "Attitudes to Henry James," *New Republic*, 108 (1943), 220–224.

40 Rahv, "The Heiress of All the Ages," 231.

41 Rahv, "Modernizing James," 311.

42 Philip Rahv, "Franz Kafka: The Hero As Lonely Man," *Kenyon Review*, 1 (1939), 60–74.

43 Rahv to R. P. Warren, November 29, 1938, Southern Review Papers. Kafka's work came to most critics of the late 1930s as a new discovery.

The first of his books to appear in translation in the United States was *The Castle* (1930), but it was not until the publication of *The Trial* in 1937 that attention seemed to blossom. *Partisan Review* published a review of *The Trial* by F. W. Dupee, and William Phillips reviewed the book for the *Nation*. In mid-1938 *Partisan Review* carried a section from the biography of Kafka by Max Brod, Kafka's friend and literary executor, and the magazine also managed to obtain and publish three of Kafka's stories in 1939, 1941, and 1942. William Phillips, "Everyman," *Nation*, 165 (1937), 448–449; F. W. Dupee, "The Fabulous and the Familiar," *Partisan Review*, 4 (Dec. 1937), 66–69; Max Brod, "Kafka: Father and Son," *Partisan Review*, 4 (May 1938), 19–29; the stories published in *Partisan Review* were "Blumfeld, an Elderly Bachelor," "In the Penal Colony," and "Josephine, the Songstress, or, The Mice Nation."

44 Philip Rahv, "The Death of Ivan Ilyich and Joseph K.," *Southern Review*, 5 (1939–40), 174–185.

45 Ibid., 174; Philip Rahv, "The Artist as Desperado," *New Republic*, 104 (1941), 557–559.

46 Philip Rahv, "Souvenirs and Experiments," *Kenyon Review*, 4 (1942), 238; "On the Decline of Naturalism," *Partisan Review*, 9 (Nov.–Dec. 1942), 485–486.

47 Rahv wrote to Lionel Trilling shortly after Hitler's invasion of the Soviet Union that he had been reading the news instead of doing his work and expressed some regret for his continuing susceptibility to an immersion in politics. Rahv to Trilling, June 24, 1941, Lionel Trilling Papers, Columbia University, New York.

48 Rahv, "On the Decline of Naturalism," 484.

49 See, for instance, the discussion of Trilling as one of three exceptional postwar critics in A. Walton Litz, "Literary Criticism," in *Harvard Guide to Contemporary American Writing*, ed. Daniel Hoffman (Cambridge, Mass., 1979), 80–83.

50 Studies of Trilling include the following: Robert Boyers, *Lionel Trilling: Negative Capability and the Wisdom of Avoidance* (Columbia, Mo., 1977); William M. Chace, *Lionel Trilling: Criticism and Politics* (Stanford, Calif., 1980); four essays by Mark Shechner, Joseph Frank, Robert Langbaum, and Helen Vendler, plus a symposium in which Trilling participated, in *Salmagundi*, no. 41 (Spring 1978); essays by Jacques Barzun, Quentin Anderson, and Stephen Marcus in *Art, Politics, and Will: Essays in Honor of Lionel Trilling*, ed. Quentin Anderson, Stephen Donadio, and Steven Marcus (New York, 1977); Denis Donoghue, "Trilling, Mind, and Society," *Sewanee Review*, 86 (April–June 1978), 161–186; and, an attempt at a debunking piece, Roger Sale, "Lionel Trilling," *Hudson Review*, 26 (Spring 1973), 241–247.

51 Trilling himself pursued the relationship actively enough that only six months after one of his essays had appeared in *Partisan Review*, he commented that he had done nothing recently for the magazine and asked Dwight Macdonald to think of things he might do (Trilling to Macdonald, October 3, 1942, Macdonald Papers). The association with the magazine was no small matter for Trilling in 1939; he was then a young scholar who was subsidizing the publication of his first book, not the established critic of later years. The terms for publication of *Matthew Arnold* are discussed in Lionel Trilling to W. W. Norton, June 30, 1938, W. W. Norton Collection, Columbia University, New York.

52 For an example of the harsh language Trilling directed against Popular Front liberals, see Lionel Trilling, "Hemingway and His Critics," *Partisan Review*, 6 (Winter 1939), 52–60.

53 Lionel Trilling, "Parrington, Mr. Smith and Reality," *Partisan Review*, 7 (Jan.–Feb. 1940), 24–40.

54 Trilling, "Elements That Are Wanted," 367–379. Trilling originally planned to include this essay, renamed "T. S. Eliot's Politics," in the book that became *The Liberal Imagination* (see Trilling to W. W. Norton, April 16, 1942, Norton Collection).

55 In the preface to *The Liberal Imagination*, Trilling would write of the need for "a criticism which has at heart the interests of liberalism" to keep its ideas and assumptions from becoming "stale, habitual, and inert." He introduced his arguments with a quotation from Mill that he had also used at the beginning of his essay on Eliot. Lionel Trilling, *The Liberal Imagination: Essays on Literature and Society* (New York, 1950), x.

56 Lionel Trilling, "The Sense of the Past," *Partisan Review*, 9 (May–June 1942), 230–231.

57 Trilling, *The Liberal Imagination*, xv; "Ripostes" ("Is Naturalism Exhausted?"), 61; Trilling, "Elements That Are Wanted," 376.

58 In his relations with the editors of *Partisan Review*, Trilling seemed happy to stress areas of mutual respect and agreement. Reviewing *For Whom the Bell Tolls* in 1941, Trilling took obvious pleasure in citing two of Rahv's critical essays and in making use of Rahv's ideas in his own analysis. The two critics shared not only general values but also a good many specific opinions in the early forties. Dwight Macdonald differed more sharply from Trilling in his interests and temperament, yet these two also found opportunities to agree. Macdonald congratulated Trilling in 1942 on a piece attacking the "'social responsibility' school of literary criticism," noting the compatibility between Trilling's ideas and his own position and even admitting that Trilling said "much

I could have, should have said in my job on Brooks." Trilling replied with thanks and an agreement that "In literature we often start at opposite ends . . . and come out at much the same place." This he found "encouraging." Lionel Trilling, "An American in Spain," *Partisan Review*, 8 (Jan.–Feb. 1941), 63–67; Dwight Macdonald, "Reading From Left to Right," ibid., 24–33; Macdonald to Trilling, September 30 [1942], Trilling Papers; Trilling to Macdonald, October 3, 1942, Macdonald Papers.

59 Lionel Trilling, "Of This Time, Of That Place," *Partisan Review*, 10 (Jan.–Feb. 1943), 72–81, 84–105; *The Experience of Literature* (New York, 1967), 784; "The Other Margaret," *Partisan Review*, 12 (Fall 1945), 481–501; *The Middle of the Journey* (New York, 1947).

60 Trilling, *The Experience of Literature*, 784.

61 Chace, *Lionel Trilling*, 1.

62 Philip Rahv, "Lost Illusions," *Kenyon Review*, 6 (1944), 288–292; William Phillips, "A Tract for the Time," *Kenyon Review*, 7 (1945), 705–709.

63 Philip Rahv, "Testament of a Homeless Radical," *Partisan Review*, 12 (Summer 1945), 398–402.

64 Phillips, "A Tract for the Time," 705–709.

Chapter Nine

1 Farrell Diary, June 16, 1939.

2 Irving Kristol, "Memoirs of a Trotskyist," *New York Times Magazine* (January 23, 1977), 55–56. Some of the young Trotskyists who moved into New York Intellectual circles had been among those captured from the Socialist Party in the "French turn"; they belonged to the "city intellectual" wing that followed Max Shachtman during the major Trotskyist split in 1940. See Myers, "American Trotskyists," 144–147.

3 William Barrett, *The Truants: Adventures Among the Intellectuals* (Garden City, N.Y., 1982), 7–9. Barrett's self-consciously mature voice finds in the attraction to radical purity a "hankering after self-righteousness," and he assumes the incompatibility of radical politics and avant-garde art. Yet, rather typically for those among the New York Intellectuals who have grown quite conservative, Barrett avoids grappling with his contradictory attitudes toward the positions of the late 1930s.

4 Kristol, "Memoirs of a Trotskyist," 57.

5 Irving Howe, "The Dilemma of Partisan Review," *New International*, 8 (Feb. 1942), 24, 20.

6 Leslie Fiedler, "Partisan Review: Phoenix or Dodo?" *To the Gentiles* (New York, 1972), 41; originally published in *Perspectives USA* (1956).

7 Kazin himself suggests a change in his attitude toward being Jewish

at the end of *Starting Out in the Thirties,* as he describes sitting in a London theater in 1945 watching "the first films of newly liberated Belsen" (166). Allen Guttman comments that it was a "single emotional step" for Kazin from a new awareness of Bergen-Belsen to "nostalgic" memoir (*The Jewish Writer in America,* 92). Irving Howe has remarked that "Kazin's affectionate stress on the Jewish sources of his experience is mainly a feeling of retrospect," not an accurate picture of the young intellectual's emotions in the thirties, however "typical" the general experiences might be. "The New York Intellectuals," *Decline of the New* (New York, 1970), 216; originally published in *Commentary,* 46 (Oct. 1968), 29–51. In his own memoirs, William Barrett offers a passing devaluation of Kazin in warning the reader, "I am not a walker in the city seeking narcissistically to capture myself" (*The Truants,* 24). For a skeptical treatment of Kazin's reliance on the theme of Jewishness, see Mark Krupnick, "An American Life," *Salmagundi,* nos. 44–45 (Spring–Summer 1979), 197–204.

8 Podhoretz, *Making It,* 91–92. Podhoretz's use of "generation" is clearly a matter of convenience, not an attempt to use the concept of generations in any significant way.

9 Howe, "The New York Intellectuals," 215–216.

10 Ibid., 214–215n; "New York and the National Culture," 175–176 (a fuller version of Howe's remark appears in Chapter One); "Foreword," in Schwartz, *In Dreams Begin Responsibilities and Other Stories,* ed. Atlas, vii–ix.

11 Others have confirmed this picture. William Barrett, for instance, announces early in his memoir that "in the New York intellectual circle in which I was to move, the background was subtly but nonetheless pervasively Jewish." Barrett, *The Truants,* 24.

12 Sidney Hook, "Where the News Ends," *New Leader* (November 26, 1938), 8. Hook quoted "Walter Duranty, the Kremlin's ace reporter," as having written (in an effort "to overcome Nazi reluctance" to a deal with Russia) that "Stalin has killed more Jews in the last two years than Hitler has since he came to power."

13 Farrell Diary, May 6, 11, 1939. The entries referred to the case of General Krivitsky, who had been publishing revelations about Communist attempts to destroy other loyalist groups in Spain. The *New Masses* had charged Krivitsky with being a phony whose real name was "Shmelka Ginsberg." For two editorial paragraphs attacking Krivitsky's credibility, see the *New Republic,* 99 (1939), 2, 31. Frank A. Warren discusses the *New Republic*'s resistance to any reconsideration of the Stalinists' role in Spain after the Krivitsky testimony, and especially that of Malcolm Cowley, in *Liberals and Communism,* 139–141, 211.

14 Other evidences of the group's alertness to the various manifestations of anti-Semitism are scattered through these same diary pages. Farrell took note of the story from William Phillips that while watching a Stop Hitler parade, Phillips had heard a "raggedy Irishman" proclaiming "there [sic] all dictators. Over there, they got a Dutchman. Here we got a Jew dictator." Anita Brenner of the old *Menorah Journal* crowd repeated to Farrell the rumor that "a lot of the cops—1000 in NY City—were Silver Shirts." The diary also suggests that personal contact with refugee intellectuals, many of whom were Jewish, kept the issue of anti-Semitism squarely before the eyes of those around *Partisan Review*. Farrell Diary, April 5, March 2, May 31, June 3, 1939.

15 Farrell Diary, June 7, 1939; Diana Trilling, "Lionel Trilling, A Jew at Columbia," *Commentary*, 67 (March 1979), 40–46; Sidney Hook, "Anti-Semitism in the Academy: Some Pages of the Past," *Midstream*, 25 (Jan. 1979), 49–54. Hook gives himself a major role as an advisor to Trilling, whereas Diana Trilling does not mention his involvement; Hook also places more emphasis on anti-Semitism as an issue in the 1936 dismissal and rehiring. There is little disagreement about the general situation, however, or about the importance of President Butler to Trilling's eventual appointment. Trilling himself wrote of his experience at Columbia: "for some time my career in the College was conditioned by my being Jewish" ("A Novel of the Thirties," 13). For Delmore Schwartz's encounters with anti-Semitism at Harvard, see Atlas, *Delmore Schwartz*, 81, 162–63, 165–66, 195.

16 See, for example, Podhoretz, *Making It*, 31–32, 35–36, on the "conversion" that Columbia attempted to bring about.

17 "Under Forty: A Symposium," 3. The editorial board at the time of the symposium (February 1944) included Morris D. Waldman, John Slawson, and Harry Schneiderman; Adolph S. Oko served as editor and Harold J. Jonas as associate editor. The magazine, something of a forerunner of *Commentary*, was published by the American Jewish Committee.

18 Lionel Trilling, "Under Forty: A Symposium," 15–17.

19 Without questioning Trilling's integrity, Mark Shechner has suggested that "Trilling's break with the Jewish past, which apparently accompanied his break with *The Menorah Journal*, was more thorough-going and permanent than was the rule among second generation Jewish intellectuals." Shechner's argument is that a "denial of Jewishness" occurred as Trilling created for himself a "prosthetic identity," proving able to deal with Jewish experience "only by way of the general idea, and that only through its literary sublimations." William M. Chace agrees with Shechner that the maturing Trilling tended to embrace general ideas at the expense of specific social and political detail. He

remarks, however: "Where Shechner sees Trilling's energies channeled into 'suppression,' I see them given over to transcendence." Chace distinguishes between early and later attitudes toward Jewishness in Trilling's work: in the *Menorah Journal* stories, "the context is Jewish displacement; later the context will become general. Jewishness as a consideration will become blurred and the weight of its specificity will be lifted." Mark Shechner, "Psychoanalysis and Liberalism: The Case of Lionel Trilling," *Salmagundi*, no. 41 (Spring 1978), 29–31; Chace, *Lionel Trilling*, 13n, 25.

20 Trilling, "A Novel of the Thirties," 14–15.

21 Alfred Kazin, *New York Jew* (New York, 1978), 46–47; Krupnick, "An American Life," 199. Kazin's picture of Trilling has engendered a host of responses denying the accuracy of Kazin's portrait. William M. Chace has said bluntly that Kazin's "notion that the self 'left behind' by Trilling was somehow more real and authentic than the one to be found in his writings seems to me idle and incorrect" (*Lionel Trilling*, 18n). See the letters of complaint from Robert Penn Warren and from a group of nineteen others concerning Kazin's treatment of Trilling in the *New York Times Book Review*, June 25, 1978, 56.

22 Alfred Kazin, "Under Forty: A Symposium," 9–11.

23 Clement Greenberg, ibid., 32–33.

24 Kazin, ibid., 11.

25 Greenberg, ibid., 32–34.

26 Schwartz's distinction between kinds of anti-Semitism suggests an effort in New York Intellectual circles to come to grips conceptually with this most conspicuous problem for Jews. The distinction is fundamentally the same as that made by John Higham between "social" and "political or ideological" anti-Semitism (*Send These To Me*, 120).

27 Delmore Schwartz, "Under Forty: A Symposium," 12–14.

28 Rosenfeld got so carried away with the idea that the Jewish writer had access to the full range of human experience that he even tried to suggest that through "cultural retention" the young writer might still understand the "character and traditions" of "rural life." This rang false, given his critical stance toward Jewish culture, his emphasis on city life, and the general insensitivity of the New York Intellectuals to rural society.

29 Isaac Rosenfeld, "Under Forty: A Symposium," 34–36. See the reference to a "colony of the spirit" in Bellow's *Dangling Man* (1944; reprint ed., New York [New American Library Plume ed.], 1974), especially 38–40.

30 Howe's essay, cited earlier, appeared in *Commentary* in October 1946; Lionel Trilling, contribution to a symposium on "The Jewish Writer and the English Literary Tradition," *Commentary*, 8 (Oct. 1949), 368–

369. Trilling went on to suggest that "if we stand for a cultural pluralism we must suppose that each of its components has enough reality
to tempt discourse" and "we must expect tension." Though "cultural
pluralism" affirmed certain aspects of cosmopolitanism, Trilling's remarks raised some important questions about the vision of an integrated
culture and the intellectual's relation to specific "components" (including the writer's relation to Jewishness, for instance) that it is not clear
Trilling saw or was prepared to answer.

31 Sidney Hook, "Reflections on the Jewish Question," *Partisan Review,*
16 (May 1949), 463–482; Clement Greenberg, "Self-Hatred and Jewish
Chauvinism," *Commentary,* 10 (Nov. 1950), 426–433; Harold Rosenberg, "Jewish Identity in a Free Society," 259–269, first published in *Commentary,* 9 (June 1950).

32 James T. Farrell, in an opinion that was almost certainly not his alone,
suggested in 1939 that attacks on Jews were attacks on the evolution
of intellectual values in the modern world: "the real attack which the
anti-Semitic fascists are making is an attack on the ideals of the French
Revolution, on the liberal mind." It was an attack not just on Jews but
on "Rousseau, Voltaire, Diderot, Condorcet, Thomas Jefferson, Thomas
Paine." Farrell Diary, November 15, 1939.

33 Hook, "Reflections on the Jewish Question," 466–472.

34 Fiedler wrote that "in this apocalyptic period of atomization and
uprooting, of a catholic terror and a universal alienation, the image
of the Jew tends to become the image of everyone; and we are perhaps
approaching the day when the Jew will come to seem the central symbol, the essential myth of the whole Western world." Leslie Fiedler,
"What Can We Do About Fagin?: The Jew Villain in Western Tradition,"
Commentary, 7 (May 1949), 411–418.

35 The quoted phrase is from Trilling's response, previously cited, which
appeared in part two of the symposium. William Phillips gave very direct
expression to the sense of opposition between cosmopolitan values and
prejudice against Jews when he advocated "a truly cosmopolitan literary tradition that cuts under the shabby myths of anti-Semitism." "The
Jewish Writer and the English Literary Tradition," *Commentary,* 8 (Sept.
1949), 210.

36 Philip Rahv, ibid., 361–362. It should be noted once again, perhaps, that
the cosmopolitan position did not mean a denial of the Jewish cultural
heritage. Rahv commented in the midst of his argument, "Nor is it true
that the secularizing and internationalizing of culture must necessarily involve us in that nihilistic rejection of national and religious traditions of which the old-time Marxists and rationalistic liberals have been
rightly accused. It is entirely possible to maintain a fairly complete

sense of the meaningfulness of myth and tradition, Christian or otherwise, while transcending them in a secular spirit."

37 Eric Bentley, "Little Magazines," *Kenyon Review*, 9 (1947), 283, 285–86.

38 Howe, "The New York Intellectuals," 213.

39 Rahv to Dupee, December 15, 1952, Dupee Collection.

40 There is an adequate supply of examples in works previously cited. See as well the exchange between William Phillips and Lionel Abel in the "Letters" section of *Partisan Review*, 51 (1984), 159–160; and Phillips's response to Sidney Hook's "The Radical Comedians: Inside *Partisan Review*," *American Scholar*, 54 (1984–85), 45–61, in "Stalinism of the Right," *Partisan Review*, 52 (1985), 169–171.

41 The immediate issue at the height of the exchange involved a vitriolic attack by Schwartz on Paul Goodman and the question of whether Schwartz had or had not demanded that Macdonald ban Goodman from his new magazine before Schwartz would contribute to it. Other matters dating back at least to Macdonald's 1940 assertion (which he later acknowledged to be mistaken) that Schwartz wrote undergraduate criticism and should leave that field alone fed the flames of accusation. When Macdonald did not respond to his culminating tirade, Schwartz commented, "Your silence strongly suggests that you like to write angry or denunciatory letters, you do not like to receive them" (September 21, 1943). Macdonald was goaded to respond, "I didn't reply to your letter of August 30 because it was so malicious and so clearly designed simply to hurt and humiliate me that there seemed little point in answering" (September 30, 1943). Schwartz wrote back in a tone that must have galled Macdonald even more, "If I must choose between friendship and saying what I think (rightly or not), I choose friendship" (October 3, 1943). All existing letters in the correspondence are in the Macdonald Papers.

42 Hollinger, *Morris R. Cohen*, 73–75. Hollinger quotes widely from recollections by Cohen's students, including Paul Goodman and Sidney Hook, the latter of whom recognized, amidst praise for Cohen, his old teacher's "persistent cruelty." Hollinger also notes the "negative" quality of Cohen's style (76) and suggests, following others, a certain pleasure among the anxious Jewish students of the thirties in giving and receiving punishment (74).

43 Schwartz to Macdonald, August 30, 1943, Macdonald Papers. Schwartz's own papers in the Beinecke Library at Yale contain many scraps that he apparently used to practice or preserve his "epigrams." Schwartz seems to have claimed this one for himself in writing to Macdonald, though others have attributed it to William Phillips. Atlas, *Delmore Schwartz*, 208.

44 "The Herd of Independent Minds," which originally appeared in *Commentary* in September 1948, has been reprinted in Rosenberg, *Discovering the Present*, 15–28. Rosenberg also used the phrase as a section title in *The Tradition of the New* (New York, 1959).

45 Farrell Diary, June 20, 1939, Farrell Papers.

46 Schwartz declared in one letter to Macdonald that he was in the middle of a story "which Sir Clement Greenberg (O.M., Ph.D., D.Litt. (Horizon), W.C. (Oxon.), PMLA, DT. will first maintain ought not to be accepted and then will decide ought to be revised in the light of his critical standards as communicated to the author, thus enacting a superiority ritual"—all this in a single set of parentheses. The tone here was mocking but neither unfriendly nor unkind. Schwartz to Macdonald, December 19, 1942, Macdonald Papers; all punctuation or lack thereof follows the original.

47 Barrett, *The Truants*, 46–47. Barrett notes that when "animosities were pushed aside," Rahv and Schwartz could enjoy each other's humor and intellect "enormously."

48 Farrell Diary, May 26, June 11, August 19, September 3, 25, all 1939; September 19, 1940; February 17, 1941.

49 Michiko Kakutani, "A Talk with Saul Bellow: On His Work and Himself," *New York Times Book Review* (Dec. 13, 1981), 29.

50 Howe, "The New York Intellectuals," 214.

51 Rahv to Dupee, April 5, 1941, Dupee Collection.

52 Paul Goodman may serve as an example here; he was perhaps "brilliant" enough to measure up in Rahv's eyes, but he was also erratic. When *Partisan Review* published Goodman's story, "The Mean, the Maximum and the Minimum" (Sept.–Oct. 1940), one reader wrote that he resented being "deliberately confused by a work of supposedly lucid art" and suggested that Goodman was a notorious adopter of conflicting intellectual positions. Goodman replied that any contradictions among the doctrines he had preached "have managed to thrive in my own head without the least pause to my animal spirits." "Letters," *Partisan Review*, 8 (Jan.–Feb. 1941), 78. Neither the story nor the answer made Goodman look very good by Rahv's standards. Once Rahv returned from Chicago and Macdonald's short-term control over *PR* was broken, Goodman largely vanished from the magazine's pages.

53 See John Peale Bishop to Dupee, February 26 , 1939, Dupee Collection. Bishop, the first reviewer, expressed his distaste for the book in this letter, which accompanied his review. Dupee at some later point summarized the affair on the reverse of the sheet. Apparently Edmund Wilson had suggested Bishop as the reviewer and then later arranged for him to withdraw his review. Wilson himself reviewed *Matthew Arnold*

elsewhere, causing Trilling great concern when he heard rumors that the piece was rather cold. Trilling was entirely pleased when he actually saw the review, however, for Wilson, like Phillips, was very friendly to his work. See Trilling to Dupee, March 9, [1939], and March 16, 1939, Dupee Collection.

Chapter Ten

1 The obvious exception here might be James Burnham. The trajectory of Burnham's career brought him into the larger *Partisan Review* circle for a time, but he broke with the magazine in the early fifties as he moved rapidly rightward.

2 Phillips, "What Happened in the 30's," 23.

3 Some recent scholars have made a case for the positive contributions of Communist activity in certain spheres. The relation of the Party to labor, for example, has been newly examined in Roger Keeran, *The Communist Party and the Auto Workers Union* (Bloomington, Ind., 1980), and Harvey A. Levenstein, *Communism, Anticommunism, and the CIO* (Westport, Conn., 1981). The arguments of these books are not easily transferable to the realm of culture, however. Attempts to claim that the Communist Party's cultural apparatus was autonomous, open to free debate, or untainted by the need to apologize for Stalin's activities have been weak and unconvincing. On recent scholarship discussing the Communist Party, see Kenneth Walzer, "The New History of American Communism," *Reviews in American History*, 11 (1983), 259–267.

4 Rahv described the offer in a letter to Dwight Macdonald written in late June or very early July, 1943 (Macdonald Papers). For Rahv's marriage to Nathalie Swan, see Dvosin, "Literature in a Political World," 103–104. Dvosin quotes William Barrett as remarking that "in Nathalie he had a perpetual Guggenheim." Perhaps, but again this did not stop Rahv from continuing to seek a real Guggenheim—presumably not just for the money.

5 Phillips had taught at New York University briefly before the founding of *Partisan Review* and showed interest in returning to teaching from about 1940 on. A letter from Rahv to F. W. Dupee in 1945 suggests the significance that even a very limited academic appointment might have, in psychological more than monetary terms: "Did you hear of William's resurrection? He's teaching the summer session at Columbia and getting $1600 for it. . . . I have no doubt that this event will do no end of good to his ego. Miracles will happen!" Rahv to Dupee, June 29, 1945, Dupee Collection.

6 Aaron, "Some Reflections on Communism and the Jewish Writer," 264.

7 John Higham, "Anti-Semitism and American Culture," in *Send These To Me*, 193, 191.

8 Phillips [Phelps] and Rahv, "Criticism," 17. Later, when Phillips suggested gently in a review that Lionel Trilling's *Matthew Arnold* was too long and rather diffuse, Trilling agreed and blamed these faults on "the dead hand of academicism." Trilling to Dupee, May 23, 1939, Dupee Collection.

9 Irving Howe, "Mid-Century Turning Point: An Intellectual Memoir," *Midstream*, 21 (June–July 1975), 26.

10 On the lack of Marxist-inspired social thought and the limited impact of Marxism on the social sciences in the thirties, see T. B. Bottomore, *Critics of Society*, passim.

11 Rahv, "The Jewish Writer and the English Literary Tradition," 362.

12 Howe, "Mid-Century Turning Point," 25.

13 H. Stuart Hughes, *The Sea Change: The Migration of Social Thought, 1930–1945* (New York, 1975), 1–4.

14 "This Quarter," *Partisan Review*, 6 (Winter 1939), 3.

15 Harold Rosenberg, "On the Fall of Paris," *Partisan Review*, 7 (Nov.–Dec. 1940), 440–448. New York's centrality to American intellectual life was seldom questioned by the New York Intellectuals. They generally believed, as Dwight Macdonald commented in discussing the "intellectual atmosphere" of two different periods, that "in this context, New York is America, as Paris is France." "Politics Past,"4.

16 Norman Podhoretz testified to a pattern of clustering by custom in his recollection of "Hannah Arendt's annual New Year's Eve party, where the German-speaking contingent, arriving promptly at 9:30, would congregate in one room with the marzipan and the liqueurs, and the family [the New York Intellectuals], filing in toward midnight, would segregate itself in another with the bourbon and the Scotch." *Making It*, 247–248.

17 See the examples provided by Leslie Fielder in the "Innocence Abroad" section of *An End to Innocence: Essays on Culture and Politics* (Boston, 1955). The fourth of these essays, "Looking Backwards: America from Europe," begins with the sentence, "The end of the American artist's pilgrimage to Europe is the discovery of America" (124). Accounts written considerably after the fact, like Norman Podhoretz's in *Making It* (61–69), reflect a variety of later concerns but leave the basic pattern of discovery quite visible.

18 Kazin, *On Native Grounds*, 488.

19 In many cases, it is quite obvious that essays by various New York Intellectuals are built around the idea of forces in opposition; Philip

Rahv's "Paleface and Redskin" can stand as an example. Scholars study-ing particular members of the circle have often found such a design to be pervasive: William Chace in *Lionel Trilling* has made the con-cept of the "double" a major theme in interpreting Trilling (20–30 and passim); and Donald B. Kuspit has found a reliance on dialectical pat-tern in both Clement Greenberg and Meyer Schapiro. See Kuspit's *Clem-ent Greenberg*, especially 20–29; and his "Dialectical Reasoning in Meyer Schapiro," *Social Research*, 45 (Spring 1978), 93–129.

20 "A Statement by the Editors," *Partisan Review*, 9 (Jan.–Feb. 1942), 2.

21 "Dangerous Thoughts," *Partisan Review*, 9 (March–April 1942), 172–173.

22 Philip Rahv, "The Progress of Cultural Bolshevism (cont'd)," *Partisan Review*, 11 (Summer 1944), 361.

23 Phillips to Farrell, August 22, 1940, Farrell Papers; Rahv to Macdonald, August 16, 1943, Macdonald Papers; Hook to Rahv, August 15, 1945, quoted in Longstaff, "*Partisan Review* and the Second World War," 128.

24 Rahv to Macdonald, April 9, 1941, Macdonald Papers.

25 There was nothing new about urban-rural distinctions functioning in this way. Paul A. Carter has noted, for instance, that "Walter Lipp-mann . . . readily embraced a rural-vs.-urban interpretation of Funda-mentalism as the most practical way of arguing it down without fall-ing into the illiberal assumption that the people ought to be governed by their betters." "The Fundamentalist Defense of the Faith," in *Change and Continuity in Twentieth-Century America: The 1920's*, ed. John Braeman, Robert H. Bremner, David Brody (Columbus, Ohio, 1968), 201.

Epilogue

1 "Our Country and Our Culture" (editorial statement), *Partisan Review*, 19 (May–June 1952), 284; Rahv, "Our Country and Our Culture" (in-dividual response), 304–305; Mark Shechner, "Isaac Rosenfeld's World," *Partisan Review*, 43 (1976), 525.

2 Rahv, "Our Country and Our Culture," 307–308. Rahv was, of course, calling up the negative connotations of stasis familiar in the early *Par-tisan Review* when he spoke of a "deadly sameness" and when he la-beled his targets the "petrified anti-Stalinists." He also suggested that some had retreated to positions "so safe-and-sound as to be devoid of all moral or intellectual content." See also Irving Howe's comments on Rahv's role in encouraging Howe's well-known 1954 piece, "This Age of Conformity," in "Philip Rahv: A Memoir," *American Scholar*, 48 (1979), 490–491.

3 Bell, *The End of Ideology*, 405.

Bibliographic Note

The volumes of *Partisan Review* issued between 1934 and 1945 are obviously of central importance to this study. Other periodicals from roughly the same period, ranging from the familiar and readily available (*New Republic, Nation*) to the more obscure and difficult to find (*Rebel Poet, Dynamo*), contain additional materials and provide some of the context for *Partisan Review*'s early history. Several of the people close to the magazine in the 1930s or beyond have in recent years offered the public their reminiscences and interpretations of New York intellectual life. Scholars, meanwhile, have built up, according to their ways, substantial deposits of books and articles on American literary and political life in the first half of the twentieth century. All of these are published sources, and specific citations of pertinent materials are available in the notes.

Among the unpublished sources, two archival collections stand out in their importance: the Dwight Macdonald Papers in the Sterling Memorial Library at Yale, and the James T. Farrell Collection in the Van Pelt Library at the University of Pennsylvania. The Macdonald Papers are as rich as they are because Macdonald was a saver: he kept letters from others, copies of his own outgoing correspondence, and items of various sorts spun off by his whirl of activity. This passion for saving, which Macdonald sometimes made fun of in himself, is of special importance for those interested in *Partisan Review* during the late 1930s. As is indicated in the text, the magazine's office was in the Macdonalds' apartment for approximately two years, between August 1938 and September 1940. It seems clear from the materials in the Macdonald Papers that a good deal of correspondence connected with *Partisan Review* merged with Macdonald's own files during these years. To take one example, the Macdonald Papers include Macdonald's own letters to Leon Trotsky on behalf of *Partisan Review*, the letters written to Trotsky by Philip Rahv, and all of Trotsky's replies. In a different vein, the collection contains both sides of the correspondence between Macdonald and George L. K. Morris, in which Macdonald filled in his friend on the business of the magazine and poured out his frustrations. These letters and others in the Macdonald Papers provide the most detailed evidence available on the tensions leading to the breakup of the editorial board in 1943. The Macdonald Papers are of fundamental importance for studying the history of *Partisan Review* before 1945.

The Farrell Collection offers treasure of a quite different sort. Although a few pieces of correspondence hold some interest, the gem of the collection (so far as *Partisan Review* is concerned) is the diary Farrell kept throughout the thirties. Farrell recorded meetings with friends, lines of discussion, the nature of the socializing that went on, rumors and gossip he heard, instances of political friction between rival camps on the left, the plans of various associates to do this or adopt that strategy, and so on and so on—all mixed together with the unvarnished expression of his own opinions. Because Farrell became friendly with Philip Rahv and William Phillips before their break from the Communist Party, the diary offers a striking contemporary record of their jagged path toward anti-Stalinism. It also suggests the complex array of social and political contacts within New York intellectual circles better than any memoir has been able to do. The diary has its biases, of course, but they do not damage its standing as a unique and valuable source.

The F. W. Dupee Collection at Columbia University contains scattered letters to Dupee from several others in the *Partisan Review* circle that are sometimes of considerable interest. The Delmore Schwartz Papers in the Beinecke Rare Book and Manuscript Library at Yale include two or three partial story drafts, a few items of correspondence, and a number of notes scrawled on scrap paper that touch on matters considered here. Several letters from different editors of *Partisan Review* may be found among the Lionel Trilling Papers at Columbia. The James Rorty Papers at the University of Oregon offer some unusual materials on the internal politics of the *New Masses* in the late 1920s and a variety of letters, research notes, and drafts of articles that follow Rorty's activities into the postwar period.

Correspondence from Philip Rahv may be found in the Macdonald, Dupee, and Trilling collections, as well as in the *Southern Review* Papers in the Beinecke Library at Yale, in the Allen Tate Collection at Princeton University, and in the Morton Dauwen

Zabel Papers and the Malcolm Cowley Papers at the Newberry Library in Chicago.

The *Partisan Review* Papers are held by the Rutgers University Library in New Brunswick, New Jersey. Because they would seem such an obvious source for this work, I am duty-bound to say that I was unable to make use of them. Despite repeated attempts over several years, to which a substantial file of correspondence can attest, I could not persuade William Phillips to grant me access to the papers or to any of the specific items singled out by me at his request. Fortunately, as the index to the papers at Rutgers clearly shows, the collection there is very thin on the period of this study; and with perhaps a handful of exceptions, the items are apparently routine letters to and from contributors. Given what is in the Macdonald Papers, this is not surprising.

Of several unpublished dissertations on *Partisan Review* or closely related topics read for this study, two proved most valuable. Andrew James Dvosin, "Literature in a Political World: The Career and Writings of Philip Rahv" (New York University, 1977), contains information on Rahv's background not available elsewhere. Stephen A. Longstaff, "The New York Intellectuals: A Study of Particularism and Universalism in American High Culture" (University of California, Berkeley, 1978), addresses at length the question of identity among the New York Intellectuals and argues for the influence of World War II in altering their course.

Index

335

Proletarian literature: and Mike
Gold, 33–34; *Partisan Review*
version, 71–72, 77; decline, 81;
Partisan Review's departure
from, 89; mentioned, 78, 84, 90
Proletariat: doubts about politics
of, 178
Proust, Marcel, 159

Radicalism: as cultural expression,
31; and Jews, 31–32; native
American, 32; of literary tradition, 32, 153; as excitement, 43–
44; and bohemianism, 45; and
belonging, 46–47; and opportunity, 47–48; and utopianism,
62–63; and mature American
culture, 69; undermined, 136–
37; promise of, 164; weakening
in 1940s, 174, 179, 188, 212;
mentioned *passim*
Rahv, Philip: discovery of Western
literature, 15; and founding of
Partisan Review, 38–39; background, 40–41, 284n; and modernism, 41, 54, 87; radical fervor, 41; literary sensitivity, 41–
42; on radical opportunity for
writers, 47; on Soviet success,
51; literary outlook, 51, 53, 55,
56, 61–62, 73, 78, 89–94, 164,
196, 197–99, 216–17, 317n; on
Marxism, 54–55, 178–79, 308n;
attitudes toward past, 60–62;
rejection of perfectionism, 63;
and Sidney Hook, 64–65; concern for balance, 72; on T. S.
Eliot, 74–75, 88–89; attack on
"leftism," 76–78; on committee
of League of American Writers,
81–82; on Stephen Spender and
modernism, 87; positive vision
of, 92–94; and Moscow Trials,
97, 136–39; moving away from
Stalinism, 98–100; and Second
Writers' Congress, 104–6; conflict with party, 112–13, 123;
construction of *Partisan*'s history, 113–14; attacked by Hicks,
116; characterized, 118–19, 184;

on publishing Gide, 122; on
Trotsky, 127, 128, 137; reply to
Trotsky, 130–32, 164–65; on
Stalinists as anti-cosmopolitan,
135–36; on intellectual integrity, 135–36, 137; sued by
League of American Writers,
139; on Ignazio Silone, 148–49;
on Dostoevsky, 152–53; on
Hemingway, 153; marriage and
time in Chicago, 186; shift to
support for war, 187–88; split
with Macdonald, 190–92; on religion and science, 194; on intellectuals as a special grouping,
198–99, 200; and Allen Tate,
209; on American literature,
212–14; on Kafka and Tolstoy,
215–16; on Henry Miller, 216;
demand for discipline in art,
216–17; on Arthur Koestler,
222–23; on strife in *Partisan*
circle, 245; on secularization
and Jews, 245–46; expectations
of younger writers, 249; and
status, 254; and cultural bolshevism, 265; arrogance concerning *Partisan Review*, 266–67;
on embourgeoisement of intellectuals, 270; on postwar anti-
Stalinism, 271, 329n; and
Biblical references, 301n; on
value of Brooks's analysis, 317n;
and Trilling, 319n; on cosmopolitanism and tradition, 324–
25n; mentioned *passim*
Rationality: defense of, 155; as
basic value of New York Intellectuals, 243; mentioned, 192,
194, 215, 216, 219, 220, 267
Reaction (reactionary): in T. S.
Eliot, 74, 75; Stalinism as, 138–
39; mentioned, 79, 88, 92, 134,
143, 153, 194, 198, 208, 215,
244, 258, 265, 267
Reed, John, 19, 20
Regionalism, 89–90, 165, 203
Religion: as negative reference,
72, 74, 75, 90, 94, 135, 143,
149, 150, 160, 165, 175, 192,

DESIGNED BY CAMERON POULTER
COMPOSED BY METRICOMP, GRUNDY CENTER, IOWA
MANUFACTURED BY BOOKCRAFTERS, CHELSEA, MICHIGAN
TEXT AND DISPLAY LINES ARE SET IN TRUMP MEDIEVAL

Library of Congress Cataloging-in-Publication Data
Cooney, Terry A.
The rise of the New York Intellectuals.
(History of American thought and culture)
Bibliography: pp. 331–333.
Includes index.
1. Communism—New York (N.Y.)—History—20th
century. 2. Intellectuals—New York (N.Y.)—History—
20th century. 3. Partisan review (New York, N.Y. : 1934)
—History. I. Title. II. Series.
HX92.N5C64 1986   335'.005   86-40049
ISBN 0-299-10710-8